Human Sexuality

IN FOUR PERSPECTIVES

OTHER WORKS BY FRANK A. BEACH

Sex and Behavior
Patterns of Sexual Behavior
Hormones and Behavior

Human Sexuality
IN FOUR PERSPECTIVES

FRANK A. BEACH
EDITOR
MILTON DIAMOND • JOHN MONEY
JEROME KAGAN • WILLIAM H. DAVENPORT
MARTIN HOFFMAN • ROBERT J. STOLLER
RICHARD E. WHALEN • FREDERICK T. MELGES
DAVID A. HAMBURG

The Johns Hopkins University Press
BALTIMORE AND LONDON

Manufactured in the United States of America
The Johns Hopkins University Press, Baltimore, Maryland
21218
The Johns Hopkins Press, Ltd., London

Chapter 11, in slightly modified form, has appeared as an
article in the *Archives of Sexual Behavior,* Volume 5, Number
5, 1976.

Library of Congress Cataloging in Publication Data
Main entry under title:

Human sexuality in four perspectives.

Includes index.
1. Sex—Addresses, essays, lectures. I. Diamond, Milton, 1934–
II. Beach, Frank Ambrose, 1911–

    HQ21.H74   612.6   76-17235   ISBN 0-8018-1845-1

CONTENTS

1

HUMAN SEXUALITY
IN FOUR PERSPECTIVES

Frank A. Beach

Introduction

When it is viewed in its entirety, this book will be seen to incorporate several different perspectives on human sexuality. This is not apparent if the chapters are examined individually, for each one has been contributed by a specialist writing about a subject concerning which he is an authority. It is the task of the editor to put together the individual contributions so as to achieve a synthesis which, it is hoped, will reveal general trends or principles that will help us to understand human sexuality, as we know it from personal experience, and as a subject of broad scientific and social significance.

Some readers may be primarily interested in understanding their own sexual feelings or actions, and those of their closest associates. Others may be more academically concerned with the scientific, sociological, political or moral aspects of human sexuality. Whichever the case, it is unlikely that a narrow focus upon problems of immediate interest will yield satisfactory solutions. Answers to specific questions often are elusive until the questions themselves are seen in a broader context; and in the case of our subject, this may best be achieved by adopting two complementary angles of attack which can be termed the cross-sectional and trans-temporal approaches. Both are employed to varying degrees by the authors of the chapters that follow, and both are represented among the four perspectives that will be developed in this chapter.

The cross-sectional approach is essentially ahistorical, which is to say it involves asking questions about currently observable sexual phenomena. A classic example is the research of Alfred Kinsey and his coworkers, who wanted to know all that was knowable about the sexual behavior of American males and females. As Kinsey, Pomeroy, and Martin soon discovered, simple questions concerning frequency of masturbation, or age at first intercourse elicited dissimilar answers from males and females; and among males answers from college graduates were different from those of grade school dropouts. To arrive at answers applicable to Americans as a group, it was necessary to make a cross-sectional analysis, taking into consideration not only national averages or trends, but also wide differences between the sexes, between socio-economic levels, between blacks and whites, and between Protestants, Catholics, Jews, and others.

If the "Kinsey Report" impressed its readers with the diversity of sexual behavior in contemporary America, readers of this book will find Chapter 5 positively overwhelming. Its author presents a cross-sectional analysis based upon not one but scores of societies which vary more widely from one another than any two of the most divergent groups described by Kinsey.

Casting a still wider net, Chapter 11, on sexual behavior in animals, samples cross sections of the zoological kingdom, discovering evidence of several significant continuities and equally important discontinuities between the sexual life of man and those of his closest living relatives.

The trans-temporal approach represents a necessary complement to cross-sectional analysis. Instead of concentrating on the current characteristics of sexual behavior, this method is to pose questions about how behavior developed its present form. It is worth restating that both cross-sectional and trans-temporal analyses are essential. To understand why a particular pattern of behavior exists, we must know "how it got that way" in the first place.

It is sometimes implicitly assumed that trans-temporal analysis is necessary only in the case of so-called "deviant" sexual patterns and, as a result, books have been written about the causes and childhood origins of homosexuality. In fact, the same approach must be followed in studying "normal" behavior, and as yet the "etiology" of exclusive hetero-sexuality is far from perfectly understood.

The ways in which different contributors to this book have combined cross-sectional and trans-temporal treatment of their special topics combine to yield four different perspectives on the structure and functions of human sexuality.

In the remainder of this chapter we shall consider each perspective in turn with two objectives in mind. The first is to emphasize key issues, crucial evidence or seminal concepts brought out in individual chapters. The second is to discover any general principles, unifying concepts or integrating theories that may emerge from comparing, contrasting and integrating the separate chapters.

DEVELOPMENTAL PERSPECTIVE

Success in achieving a developmental perspective on human sexuality depends on our ability to retrace the individual's life history from its beginnings and, in doing so, to answer two kinds of questions. How have the sexual characteristics of adult men and women developed from infancy or even from the prenatal beginnings, and what factors have determined the direction of this development? A reader may wonder why such questions are worth asking and why it is not much more important to begin immediately with the pressing task of analyzing and explaining the fully-formed sexual patterns of mature human beings. The answer is experience has taught us that this approach does not work. Long ago, Sigmund Freud recognized that the roots of sexual dysfunction can lie in early childhood experience, but what is immeasurably more important is that the foundations for a normal and healthy sexual life are laid down over a period of many years, extending from early infancy up to puberty.

It is impossible to read a single chapter in this book without discovering some reference to the ontogeny of sexual attitudes or behavioral patterns, but there are three chapters in particular which deal specifically with this trans-temporal approach to sexuality. They are Chapter 2, "Human Sexual Development," Chapter 3, "Human Hermaphroditism," and Chapter 4, "The Psychology of Sex Differences." The first two, by Milton Diamond and John Money, respectively, start literally from the beginning, and trace the process of differentiation between the sexes from the moment of fertilization to birth, into early infancy, childhood, and adolescence. Chapter 4, by Jerome Kagan, concentrates primarily upon the appearance of psychological differences between male and female infants in the pre-speech period and seeks to explain how these relatively simple distinctions give rise to more complex and broader sex differences in later years.

If these summary sentences give an impression that the developmental perspective centers upon the origins and ontogeny of differences between the sexes, the impression is correct, and the reasons are not far to seek. A moment's thought will prove that any concept of sexuality would be impossible without the accompanying concepts of male and female. Ever since life on this planet began, organisms have produced descendants by one means or another, but the relatively advanced method of sexual reproduction necessitates the union of two types of cells, which in all higher plants and animals come from two types of individuals—males and females. Viewed in the broadest possible perspective, i.e., that of evolution, sex is first and foremost a mechanism by means of which species reproduce themselves.

There can, of course, be reproduction without sex, as in the case of living forms which multiply by simple division; and there can also be sex without sexuality, as in the case of plants and some lower animals;

but there cannot be sexuality without sex. This is the principle reason
for beginning our examination of the development of sexuality by studying how males and females become differentiated in the first place. We
cannot understand sexuality until we understand sex. We must comprehend differences between male and female before we can grasp differences between masculine and feminine.

Several basic problems and principles concerning sexual differentiation
and development are illuminated in the three chapters which deal with
this subject.

Continuities and discontinuities in sexual development. The general
picture of sexual differentiation provided by these chapters is one of
emergent ontogenesis—of a continuous process in which new stages
evolve out of preceding ones, and then in turn give rise to still newer
stages, each succeeding stage involving increasingly complex levels of
organization. In this case, our concept of continuity must include recognition of discontinuous or qualitative changes as essential to the general
process.

Hand in hand with the shift from one level to the next goes evidence
indicating sequential changes in the sources of control over sexual development. In Chapter 3, Money uses the metaphor of a relay race in
which the first runner passes the baton to the second, who in turn passes
it to the third, and so on. The first runner symbolizes the chromosomal
determinants of biological sex; the second is the fetal sex-hormonal determinant, and so forth, until eventually society assigns each newborn
infant to one sex or the other and thus imposes a specific program of
discriminatory training and conditioning pointed toward development of
a feminine or masculine gender identity.

As we consider successively the embryological and fetal development
of the gonads, then the internal sex accessories, and then the external
gentalia, we seem to be viewing a progressive reduction of options or
narrowing of alternatives for subsequent sexual differentiation. As a
first step, either the cortex or the medulla of the gonad can develop, but
once a testis has differentiated the option for ovarian differentiation is
lost. Next, either the Mullerian or the Wolffian ducts may be stimulated,
but if oviducts and uteri develop the option for a vas and epididymis is
foreclosed. Urogenital sinus anlagen have the initial potency for producing male or female external genitalia, but development of a penis
precludes the differentiation of a vagina and clitoris.

Differences in brain development. An extremely important question
relating to the same prenatal periods and stages of development has to
do with possible sex differences in differentiation of the brain. Evidence
surveyed in Chapters 2 and 3, and other facts brought out by Richard
Whalen in Chapter 8, are consonant with the hypothesis that there are

differences between the brains of newborn males and females. It appears, however, that very few such differences are mutually exclusive in the same sense that a penis and a vagina are mutually exclusive end products of genital differentiation.

What seems more probable is that in animals and humans alike both the brain mechanisms responsible for male and those responsible for female behavior differentiate and are retained throughout life; but one system or the other tends to be functionally dominant in every individual. Furthermore, in the human species behavioral manifestations of these two systems depend heavily upon events occurring during postnatal development, which includes much learning, conditioning and social channelization. According to this view, it is reasonable to conceive of congenital sex differences in brain function not as out-and-out "determinants" of subsequent behavioral differences, but as sources of bias, or of predispositions to respond differentially to sexually divergent programs of social training. Conversely, females and males might very well react in different ways to identical treatment, which means that some sex differences would exist even if boys and girls were given the same training, an outcome predicted by Diamond and also by Kagan on the basis of his psychological studies of children in different countries.

One implication of this viewpoint is that, by and large, females and males might most readily and successfully learn different kinds of sexual roles, and this in turn is relevant to a hypothesis to be developed later in this chapter, when we consider the evolution of sexuality. The hypothesis is that major features of feminine and masculine roles may have been selected and standardized over thousands of years of human evolution. It is further postulated that a congruence between adaptively discriminable sex roles, and congenital sex differences in the predisposition to learn and perform these roles, accounts in part for the existence of those male-female differences which are observable today in most, if not all, human societies.

Endogenous and exogenous controls. At any point in ontogeny it is theoretically possible to differentiate between the internal and external factors influencing the functioning of a living system. At a later stage, previously external factors may have become internalized or original internal influences may have ceased to operate. Therefore, the distinction between endogenous and exogenous causal agents is time-limited but, nevertheless, often is useful.

With respect to sexual differentiation, it is clear that both exogenous and endogenous factors are constantly operative, although the identity of these factors and the nature of their effects may change from one stage to the next. Most important of all is the generalization that the final product of development is determined jointly by the impact of external stimulation and the endogenously controlled reactive potential of the system upon which such stimulation impinges.

In normal prenatal development of males, hormones secreted by the fetal testis act upon tissues derived from the urogenital sinus to induce differentiation of a penis and scrotum. In the case of females, where testosterone is lacking, the same primordia give rise to the external vagina, labia and clitoris. The importance of androgen as an exogenous agent is revealed by the fact that males whose testes fail to produce testosterone develop female genitalia, and that females who are prenatally exposed to androgenic stimulation may be born with a phallus resembling the male penis, rather than a normal vagina and clitoris.

At the same time, there are clear-cut endogenous sex differences in the capacity to respond to male hormone; for masculinized females very rarely develop a fully normal penis, regardless of how much androgenic stimulation they may have received. Before it begins its development, the genital tubercle appears identical in males and females, but it is not actually the same because its sensitivity or potential responsiveness to androgenic stimulation is much greater in males than in females.

A broad concept of endogenous sex differences in responsiveness to similar as well as to different kinds of exogenous stimulation is, as we shall see, generalizable to the phenomenon of postnatal psychosexual differentiation.

Progressive divergence between the sexes. At the time of conception, the only observable difference between the male and female zygote or fertilized egg is in the sex chromosomes. During the following embryonic period, development of gonads into ovaries or testes adds a new distinction; and then, under the influence of testicular secretions or in their absence, the Mullerian system either is inhibited or allowed later to develop into oviducts, uterus and upper vagina, while the Wolffian system either regresses or gives rise to the vas, epididymis and seminal vesicle. Males and females are thus becoming more and more different from one another; and then, in the fetal period, one more dissimilarity is added when the external sex organs differentiate into either a penis or a vagina.

The consequence is that when they are born, human males and females differ in many ways, but only one of these differences is clear cut and immediately obvious. All human societies seize upon the difference between male and female external sex organs, and, on the basis of this single criterion, assign the newborn individual to one or another of two mutually exclusive social categories. To a certain degree this procedure is at variance with the biological nature of sex differences because, whereas differences in reproductive anatomy are, perforce, dichotomous and mutually exclusive, the vast majority of congenital sex differences are continuous or quantitative rather than qualitative and discontinuous.

The fact remains that every society treats its newborn members collectively, as if they were drawn from one of two distinct populations rather than two statistically separable subgroups. Through a complex and extremely protracted process of conditioning, society, in effect, drives a wedge between the two subgroups, forcing them farther and farther apart along many dimensions and often creating dichotomies and discontinuities where there originally existed no differences at all, or at most differences only in degree. As expressed by Kagan, in Chapter 4, "sex differences arise, in part, because . . . different patterns of experience gently but firmly push boys and girls in different psychological directions."

SOCIOLOGICAL PERSPECTIVE

A sociological perspective on human sexuality is achieved through several variants of the cross-sectional approach. One is to compare and contrast the sexual aspects of different human societies, and another is to study differences in the sexual characteristics of members of the same society. The first of these methods has been very effectively exploited by William Davenport in his chapter, "Sex in Cross-Cultural Perspective." The second is exemplified in Chapters 6 and 7 by Martin Hoffman and Robert Stoller, respectively, which deal with homosexuality and with sexual deviation in American society.

Almost any discussion of sex and its manifestations in societies other than one's own is intrinsically interesting, as Davenport's chapter amply demonstrates; but descriptions of how people behave sexually are the least important parts of what he has written. The most significant passages in Chapter 5 are those which explain the ways in which each society structures male and female sexuality, and clarify the significance of sex with respect to the total fabric of a society's organization. In order to develop these seminal notions, we must begin with some basic definitions.

A *society* is an enduring, cooperating, self-reproducing group of individuals with organized patterns of interrelationships. Societies are dynamic, open, functional systems whose organization is determined by endogenous rather than exogenous factors. From the evolutionary point of view, to be described later in this chapter, the primary functions of a society are protection of its members and perpetuation of itself.

Culture refers to a society's shared patterns of belief, thought, speech and action. A culture is a body of customary beliefs, social forms and material traits characterizing a society or a subdivision thereof. Cultures are the tools with which societies achieve their functions. The same culture may be shared in whole or in part by different societies, and several subcultures may exist within the same society.

Although a society is composed of individuals, it represents a new, supra-individual level of organization, and its activities possess emergent properties not predictable from the behavior of its separate members.

Societies are not designed; they evolve, which is to repeat that they are endogenously rather than exogenously organized. Like any product of evolution, a society survives as long as it can meet the test of natural selection, and to do this a society must fulfill the primary functions already mentioned. For any society, implicit recognition of these functions is reflected in the shared value systems of the population, and in a general consensus as to proper and effective ways of achieving them. Rules, traditions, jural systems and the like constitute empirically-derived mechanisms for preserving a society's functional integrity, and they comprise its culture. It is self-evident that, if a society is to survive, the influential majority of its members must agree upon the nature of its detailed functions and upon the most appropriate ways of achieving them.

The internal logic and consistency of societies. As emphasized by Davenport, if a society is to "work," i.e., to survive for a significant duration of time, it must develop and maintain its own "internal logic and consistency." He also stresses the important conclusion that the sexual culture of a society is an essential part of the total culture and must always be both "shaped and constrained" by the latter.

These two conclusions have far-reaching and fundamental implications for the interpretation and comparison of sexual behavior in different societies. What they imply, as Davenport points out, is that for sexual, as for all types of behavior, *"the salience and meaning of any and all acts can be fully grasped only with complete knowledge of the cultural context in which they occur"* (italics added).

Without such knowledge, it is sometimes impossible to know even what is and what is not "sexual." For example, in some tribal societies, brothers and sisters never eat in each other's company, because to do so would constitute an exceedingly embarrassing breech of sexual rules, somewhat like a man's passionately kissing his sister in our society. In these societies, food sharing is a private component in the marital relationship, and food consumption in general has sexual connotations. In the East Bay society, studied by Davenport, a very intimate act between a man and a woman is sharing certain ingredients of betel, which is chewed as an immediate intoxicant. The three constituents are a nut, pepper and lime. The lime is a nonsexual, impersonal item which is shared freely with male or female friends; but to offer the nut and pepper to a member of the opposite sex is an act of sexual intimacy. To choose a different example, there are many societies in which men always dance with other men, but in our society such behavior is seen as involving sexual overtones.

To examine the way in which sexual behavior is interrelated with other aspects in a society's structure, it will be instructive to consider different ways of dealing with three types of sexual activity generally disapproved of in the United States.

The case of incest. It is generally believed that, no matter how widely they may differ in other respects, all societies prohibit incestuous sexual relationships. This is true in the abstract, but in actual practice the generalization tells us very little of value about human sexuality because definitions of incest are almost infinitely variable. For some societies, the incest taboo operates against every one of an individual's identifiable relatives, however distant, and this may include half or more of the available population. Some peoples who trace descent unilineally prohibit sexual relations between all individuals of the same clan, regardless of the genealogical separation between them. If this were the practice in the United States, and if unilineal descent were the rule, any man and woman with the same family name, e.g., Smith, could not have relations without committing incest.

Incest, for some societies, includes all relations between both first and second cousins. In other cases, relations between the offspring of two sisters (parallel cousins) are strictly forbidden, but children of a brother and sister (cross cousins) not only are free to marry but may actually be socially favored partners. For some peoples, intercourse between a mother and son is the worst form of incest imaginable, whereas for others sexual relations between a man and his sister's daughter constitutes an even more serious crime.

Although their array is formidable, these intersocial differences are not fortuitous. When viewed in the context of the total culture, the rules governing incestuous relations are found to bear a meaningful relationship to other, often nonsexual, rules which serve important functions in preserving the society's integrity. The related rules may deal with laws of inheritance, with the legal rights of the uninvolved spouse, with the economic responsibilities of a woman's male relatives, her husband, and so on. Whatever the precise nature of their immediate and ostensible rationale, the point is that sexual rules and customs are inextricably interrelated with the rest of a society's "internal logic" and can only be comprehended within this total context.

The case of premarital relations. For most Americans, even today, premarital sexual intercourse is socially disapproved of, despite the fact that it has always occurred, probably is occurring more frequently at the present time, and currently meets with less severe criticism than it did one or two generations ago.

In contrast, there are many societies which tolerate, and some which actively encourage, sexual intercourse between unmarried young people. Some societies regard sexual practice as essential to successful marital relations later on; and both males and females are expected to begin experimenting as soon as they are ten or eleven years old, or at the latest as soon as the girls have reached menarche. One rule of primary importance is always enforced, and this is the prohibition against indiscriminate sexual promiscuity. Even when premarital relations are considered highly desirable, the resulting behavior is regulated and channelized by society so that it does not lead to results which would disrupt or counteract other important regulations maintaining the essential fabric of the social structure.

Youngsters may be allowed to have relations only with partners belonging to the same class from which a spouse will later be selected. In contrast, precisely the opposite rule can obtain, so that premarital relations, while generally approved of, must never involve a potential marital partner such as one bethrothed in childhood. Some societies consent to premarital sex only when it involves cross-cousins, or even only a cross-cousin on the mother's side. Any form of sexual contact between young unmarried people may be totally forbidden, and at the same time every adolescent may be expected to receive initiation into intercourse by an older relative of the opposite sex.

In our own and other societies which punish or merely disapprove of premarital intercourse, moralistic rationalizations constitute a screen for a legitimate social concern: the problem of how the society will accommodate and assimilate any offspring which may result from such a union. Many societies simply have no sociological machinery to deal with such problems, with the result that the rights and responsibilities of bastards are undetermined and therefore constitute a source of difficulty for the society as a whole.

It is significant to note that for societies which encourage premarital intercourse the social legitimacy of an infant is not determined by the circumstances of its birth. A child born to an unmarried woman is accorded full sociological status when she marries. The concept of illegitimacy simply does not exist. In some societies, even children born to married couples do not gain full sociological status until reaching puberty. The general rule is articulated by Davenport in the following quotation:

> . . . societies that permit or encourage premarital sex freedom are organized so that all children born outside of marriage are fully provided for and in no way suffer social disabilities or stigma.

The case of homosexual behavior. Two chapters in this book deal with sexual behavior which many members of our society regard as immoral, undesirable, abnormal or indicative of mental illness. Hoffman discusses facts and theories about male homosexuality, and Stoller deals with other types of "deviant" sexual behavior. Material covered in both chapters takes on new meaning when viewed in sociological and cultural perspective.

On a strictly phenomenological level the cross-cultural literature demonstrates conclusively that homosexuality is regarded in very different ways by different societies, some being even more hostile and punitive than our own, and others being almost totally permissive or even approving. Contemplation of such variety is in itself illuminating, but more instructive results accrue when the attitudes and rules pertaining to homosexual behavior are viewed in relation to regulations affecting other sexual and nonsexual aspects of the society's total structure, i.e., to its "internal logic and consistency."

In Davenport's account of East Bay society, he describes an institutionalized form of masculine bisexuality, in which nearly every male engages in homosexual relations during certain periods of his life. Premarital intercourse is strongly disapproved of, and boys are encouraged to masturbate until they reach marriageable age, but after this time the same behavior is ridiculed as a sign of immaturity, sexual inadequacy, or both. To avoid the stigma of childish behavior, males in late adolescence shift from mutual masturbation to anal intercourse. Passive and active roles are played alternately by both participants. This behavior occurs between friends and is taken as an accommodative gesture of comradship with no special emotional bonds or love relationship implied.

Homosexual anal relations are viewed as a mature, temporary substitute for heterosexual intercourse. Until recently, East Bay society prohibited marital coitus for many months after the birth of a child. The culture is monogamous, but concubinage was formerly approved of and provided a legitimate sexual outlet for husbands whose wives were temporarily taboo. However, concubines were expensive, and many married men whose wives were nursing took young boys as sexual partners, a practice which was socially condoned as long as a boy's father gave his formal approval and the lad himself received small presents. Arrangements of this type were seen as secondary, and anal intercourse with boys was classed as an acceptable and necessary substitutive form of sexual behavior while a wife was unavailable. At the present time, single men often leave the community for extended periods to work for pay on other islands. Until they return with enough money to marry, they are expected to find sexual satisfaction in homosexual intercourse with friends.

In East Bay there is simply no recognition of, nor any cultural category for, exclusive male homosexuality. Unmarried males whose sexual relations are confined to masculine partners are classified, not as individuals who prefer homosexual to heterosexual activity, but as men too parsimonious to marry or too unattractive to find a woman who will accept them.

There are other societies whose cultures embody some form of institutionalized male bisexuality. In accordance with what, according to Davenport, "can be regarded as a general principle of social integration," these are, at the same time, cultures in which for one reason or another, men and women are physically or socially separated for long periods of time.

In view of the cross-cultural evidence, one is inclined to agree with Davenport's conclusion that *preferential* or *exclusive* homosexuality is a "fundamentally different phenomenon from bisexuality." So, also, is the much less common, but well-known, occurrence of institutionalized male transvestism, which can occur in conjunction with either exclusive homo- or heterosexual object choice. In either case, it involves publicly acknowledged assumption of most of the aspects of a feminine gender role, usually without stigma.

PHYSIOLOGICAL PERSPECTIVE

A physiological perspective on behavior is achieved by analyzing the ways in which separate parts of the organism, i.e., the nervous, muscular, endocrine and other systems, contribute to the integrated, adaptive responses of the individual to his physical and social environment. We have already examined the role of hormones in sexual differentiation before birth, but here we are concerned with what might be termed "systems analysis" from a broader point of view.

Chapters most relevant to the physiological perspective are those by Whalen on brain mechanisms, by Beach on hormonal mechanisms in general, and by Frederick Melges and David Hamburg on hormones and psychological responsiveness in women. Before considering details of the physiological method, it will be advisable to discuss briefly the general relationship between physiological and psychological approaches to behavior.

In essence, the difference is one of levels. At the physiological level we study the organization and interrelations of organs and organ systems; at the psychological level we concentrate upon functions of the total individual as he relates to his physical and social environment. Comparison between physiological and psychological dimensions is a special case of the broader concept of a hierarchy of levels in Nature, as described in the following quotation.

New levels of complexity are superimposed on the original units by the organization and integration of these units into a single system. What were wholes on one level become parts on a higher one. Each level of organization possesses unique properties of structure and behavior which, though dependent on the properties of the constituent elements, appear only when those elements are combined into a new system. (Novikoff, 1945, p. 209).

As applied to interpretation of behavior, this method of analysis by levels is a safeguard against the confusion produced by dualistic formulations which imply a mind-body dichotomy. Physiology and psychology relate to different levels of organization and not to different kinds of causal agents. Behavior of the total organism is an emergent product of the functioning of its component physiological systems. Organismic behavior is termed "emergent" because it is more than a simple, summed product of the separate functions of the different systems, just as, at a different level of organization, the functional characteristics of the endocrine system have emergent properties, which could not be predicted from separate analyses of the individual glands of which it is comprised.

Psychological processes, or phenomena, such as learning, feeling, remembering and the like, are *sui generis,* but they cannot be divorced, nor exist separately, from their physiological underpinnings, which include activity of the central nervous system. Ideas and emotions are accompaniments of brain activity, just as learning is the psychological manifestation of enduring changes in the brain consequent to previous stimulation or "experience."

Relationship of the brain to sexual feelings and behavior. One virtue of the physiological approach is that it forces us to view behavior in terms of the *stimulus-response paradigm,* which in turn focuses enquiry on the variables that elicit behavior and the particulate units of which behavior is composed. Contrary to a popular superstition, stimulus-response formulations do not symbolically transform the individual into a flesh-and-blood reflex machine, whose every act or impulse represents an automatic, stereotyped reaction to changes in the external environment.

All behavior consists of responses to stimulation, but the term "stimulus" encompasses a complex variety of changes, some of which take place in the external, and some in the internal, environment. A stimulus may be a glance from a friend, a blow from an enemy or a conversation overheard. It may be change in blood chemistry caused by secretion of adrenalin, or injection of heroin. It can even arise as neural activity within the brain itself, in which case we may speak of being stimulated by an idea.

The same stimulus gives rise to different psychological or behavioral responses at different times, because the brain's reactive state may change from moment to moment. The brain is not a complex telephone switchboard that simply relays messages from peripheral receptors to the effector machinery and thus produces automatic behavioral responses. It is a dynamic organ, characterized on the one hand by extreme sensitivity to stimulation from without, and on the other by its own endogenous patterns of internally organized activity. Not only does each individual brain change through time, but no two brains are identical, even from the moment of birth; and for this reason the same stimulus never evokes precisely the same behavior on the part of different individuals.

As far as human beings are concerned, the most important single source of postnatal modification in brain function is learning or experience. When we speak of the effects of social conditioning upon sexual attitudes and behavior, we are talking about psychological manifestations of changes produced in the brain as a result of individual experience. The importance of learning in shaping human behavior is so obvious and profound that many students of human sexuality are inclined to emphasize experience as the only cause for similarities and differences in sexual behavior. What this point of view overlooks is that experience never writes on a blank slate, for even at birth the brain is not equally responsive to every new message from the environment, or equally affected by all types of experience.

Especially relevant to theories about human sexuality is evidence reviewed earlier which suggests the existence of sex differences in the brains of newborn infants. If indeed such differences exist, as Diamond insists and Kagan at least suspects, they could interact with differential methods of sexual training in important ways. It is conceivable that males on the average would more quickly and effortlessly learn one set of behavior patterns, while girls would be congenitally prepared to acquire more readily and easily a different set of patterns.

Hormone-behavior relationships. Chapters 8, 9 and 10 present evidence which leaves little doubt that hormones can and do influence sexual feelings and overt behavior. In fact, the impact of hormonal control on sexual characteristics is evident long before we are born, as Diamond and Money have amply demonstrated. No one doubts that hormones can *indirectly* affect an individual's psychological attitudes, by causing the development of secondary sex characters or by regulating the events of menstruation, pregnancy, lactation, et cetera. There is no argument that establishment of a firm gender identity usually is facilitated by possession of a normal masculine or feminine anatomy, but there is less certainty in some quarters with respect to the ability of hormones to influence psychological characteristics.

The discrepancy arises from the fact that anatomical and physiological indicators of sex show less individual variability than behavioral tendencies; and, in addition, behavior is subject to control through temporary or long-term modification by brain differences, referred to above. In the absence of gross abnormality, the uterine endometrium of any woman will react in predictable fashion to an increase in estrogen or the withdrawal of progesterone, but the psychological effects of the same hormonal changes will depend upon the reactive state of brain mechanisms which also are affected by unique experiences in the woman's past history, as well as by a multitude of contemporaneous non-hormonal stimuli. Finally, as noted in the editorial preface to Chapter 10, in humans as in animals, hormones play a permissive role vis-à-vis behavior. They can increase the probability that certain types of behavior will occur, but they cannot make behavior happen.

EVOLUTIONARY PERSPECTIVE

Explicit or implicit references to the evolutionary origins of human sexuality appear in more than half of the chapters of this book. Money notes that some aspects of psychosexual differentiation depend on, "phyletically written parts of the program." Davenport opines that sexual behavior is one of the few universal categories in human culture, "because the bases are to be found in the physiological inheritance of every individual." Diamond states that cross-cultural continuity of some sex-related behaviors are "what would be anticipated from evolutionary considerations," and then adds the hypothesis that "these patterns have persisted among such widespread cultures most probably because they are adaptive."

Basic concepts pertaining to evolution and behavior. An important feature of Darwin's evolutionary theory was the proposal that natural selection not only affects the physical characteristics of every species, but also influences species-specific behavior. This suggestion has been examined, tested and refined, until today it is considered axiomatic that many behavior patterns not only are end products of variation and natural selection, but, in addition, are themselves mechanisms capable of influencing the evolutionary process. In describing the modern "synthetic" theory of evolution, George Simpson writes as follows:

> It not only points the way to evolutionary, historical explanations of existing behavior patterns but also involves behavior as one of the factors that produce or guide evolution. Some phases of selection, as in zygote and embryo, are not directly behavioral, but aspects of breeding, care of young, and subsequent survival are pre-eminently so and are obviously crucial elements in selection. (Roe, A. R., and Simpson, G. G., *Behavior and Evolution*, 1958).

It is fundamentally important to realize that classifying some behavior as a product of evolution does not imply that it is totally or irrevocably controlled by the genes and therefore immune to modification by experience. Quite to the contrary, learning and practice may be absolutely essential for the functional organization of patterns necessary to survival of the individual, and even more so for those involved in perpetuation of the species. Experiments and observations discussed in Chapter 11 show that for various nonhuman primates experience acquired by the individual while growing up in the normal "sociosexual matrix" is indispensable to successful mating and rearing of young. Two important corollaries are (1) that opportunities for, and conditions conducive to, the essential learning experience are basic and ubiquitous features of the physical and social environment in which every species member develops, and (2) that the species' heredity provides both the potential for the special types of learning that must occur, and the inclination or motivational basis which makes such learning rewarding or autonomously reinforcing for the individual.

Successive stages in human evolution. Man's origins have been traced back approximately 2,000,000 years to an ancestral form of bipedal primate which was, or closely resembled, *Australopithecus,* whose fossil remains suggest an ape-sized brain of about 500 cc. combined with an upright posture and consequent freedom of the hands for more efficient manipulation and transportation of objects. Indications are that these "apemen" manufactured very crude stone tools which were used in hunting, killing and dismembering small- to medium-sized animals. Campsites have been identified and estimates are that *Australopithecus* probably lived in small, nomadic groups consisting of no more than 20 to 50 individuals. Important features of behavior are reflected in the following quotation.

> In the little australopithecine bands the ape way of life changed into a new human way. Membership in the group directly influenced survival and reproduction. The group offered protection against predators, helped in finding food and water, and a way to cope with injury and illness. It also facilitated the production of young and their care and training. It was . . . the male who went hunting. The female australopithecines became gatherers. They apparently picked fruits and roots and brought them back to the camp or cave for the others to share. The new hunting was a set of ways of life. It involved a division of labor between male and female, sharing according to custom, cooperation among males, planning, knowledge of many species and large areas, and technical skill. (Washburn & Moore, 1974, pp. 132, 135.)

Six hundred thousand years ago, if not earlier, a different type of primate appeared, with physical characters sufficiently like ours to place him in the same genus. *Homo erectus* possessed a brain twice the size of *Australopithecus* but considerably smaller than that of modern man. He had mastered the use of fire, and his stone tools, while still relatively crude, represented a distinct improvement upon those made by *Australopithecus*. Like the latter, *Homo erectus* depended on hunting and gathering for his livelihood.

The fossil and archeological record indicates no major physical change in man's forerunners for the next half million years, but approximately 40,000 years ago there are signs of an entirely new type with a brain of 1,250-1,500 cc. and a complex array of stone and bone implements specialized for hunting, skinning, scraping, pounding, fishing, sewing, etcetera. *Homo sapiens* had arrived and created a culture marked by local diversity of artifacts, exchange between geographic regions, art expression in cave paintings and decorative carving, and so on. His society must have been tremendously more complex than that of *Homo erectus,* but one aspect remained unchanged. He was still a hunter and gatherer, for domestication of animals for food had not yet begun and agriculture was still to be invented.

It was in fact only 10,000 years ago that man first developed the techniques of planting and harvesting crops and thus laid the foundation for an entirely new way of life that would permit permanent residence in one area, provide sustenance for larger and larger social groups, allow the growth of villages, then towns, then cities, and, in sum, would pave the way for what we call civilization.

As far as this book is concerned, the most important implications of the foregoing evolutionary synopsis can be derived from the following quotation.

> The common factors that dominated human evolution and produced *Homo sapiens* were preagricultural. Agricultural ways of life have dominated less than 1 percent of human history, and there is no evidence of major biological changes during that period of time. The kind of minor biological changes that occurred and which are used to characterize modern races were not common to *Homo sapiens.* The origin of all common characteristics must be sought in preagricultural times. Probably all experts would agree that hunting was a part of the social adaptation of all populations of the genus *Homo,* and many would regard *Australopithecus* as a still earlier hominid who was already a hunter. . . . If this is true, and if the Pleistocene period had a duration of three million years, then pre-*Homo erectus* human tool using and hunting lasted for at least four times as long as the duration of the genus *Homo.* . . . It is for this reason that the consideration of hunting is so important for the understanding of human evolution. (Washburn & Lancaster, 1968.)

Implications for human sexuality. The evolution of every new species depends upon constant screening of the genotype by natural selection which preserves genetic combinations that favor survival and perpetuation of the interbreeding population while eliminating those which are counteradaptive. If we accept the conclusions of Washburn and Lancaster, one implication is that twentieth-century man possesses a species genotype shaped during hundreds of thousands of years of natural selection in response to the adaptive demands of a hunting and gathering way of life.

Among such demands was the imperative need for dichotomous specialization of sex roles, not only with respect to reproductive functions as in all other mammals, but also in connection with the life-preserving economy of the social group. It was essential that, in addition to bearing and caring for children, women also make various nonreproductive contributions to group survival, such as gathering plant foods, collecting fuel, and tending fires. Men's nonreproductive roles included procurement of meat by hunting, trapping and fishing, performing domestic tasks beyond the strength of women, protecting the group against dangers of attack by animal predators and conspecific enemies.

It is conceivable that, as human evolution proceeded, natural selection operated to produce or widen genetic differences between males and females, which slowly but progressively improved the capacities of the two sexes to perform their separate roles, and thus increased the effectiveness of the social group as a survival mechanism. Potentially adaptive sex differences could have involved both emotional and intellectual traits, but the most significant variables might well have been sex-related differences in certain motivational characteristics and special types of learning ability.

The suggestion is not that evolution provided human males and females with ready-made, instinctively organized behavior patterns for hunting, in one case, and child rearing, in the other. It is that as mankind evolved, the male and female genotypes differentiated along lines which provided males with a higher potential for acquiring patterns consonant with the total masculine role, and females with a more marked propensity for developing patterns fitted to the entire feminine role. Sex differences in such "potentials" or "propensities" would be relative rather than absolute. They would be manifest in more rapid and efficient learning of masculine patterns by males and feminine patterns by females. In addition, females would generally be more inclined to, and endogenously rewarded for, the mastery and practice of the feminine role, whereas males would have comparable reactions to the masculine role. Of course, such sex-related genetic differences, if they existed, could only become manifest in a social environment which stimulated and reinforced their actualization; but this is precisely what every hunting and gathering society did do. The hypothesis is that, over hundreds of millennia, social and genetic forces conspired to encourage the elaboration of primitive mammalian differences in reproductive responsibility into much broader sex differences involving intellectual and emotional traits and capacities quite unrelated to species reproduction.

Social evolution and sexuality. Human sexuality has been influenced not only by biological but also by social evolution, in which transmission of behavior patterns from one generation to the next is achieved by instruction and imitative learning. Genetic and social inheritance worked together to facilitate emergence of the uniquely human phenomenon termed "culture," which is defined and discussed in Chapter 5 and the editorial preface thereto.

Processes basic to social inheritance and enculturization of behavior were not originated by *Homo sapiens,* but undoubtedly they were tremendously accelerated and expanded, as development of language provided a mechanism for the systematization, preservation and transmission of the rules and traditions that eventually become sexual culture, which is analyzed by Davenport. It is here suggested that as human culture grew more and more complex, operation of these processes led to two results, namely the *socialization of sex* and the *sexualization of society.*

In a sense, these concepts are complementary and represent opposite sides of the same coin. Socialization of sex has already been alluded to; it stands for changes in which primary male-female differences essential to reproduction serve as a central core from which more and more differences between the sexes are derived. The most enduring and ubiquitous of such secondary differences are those related to division of various sex-related economic functions essential to group survival; but third-order differences arose to separate the sexes on the basis of still other types of behavior, important to the internal logic and consistency of the culture, though not immediately relevant to the vital functions of survival and reproduction.

Sexualization of society refers to the consequence of the foregoing process which is to lend sexual color or significance to many aspects of social behavior having no obvious or obligatory connection with biological differences between males and females. Those aspects of sex which are socialized are more or less the same in all societies, but the kinds of behavior which are sexualized may vary markedly from one society to the next, as cross-cultural comparisons in Chapter 5 amply demonstrate.

Social evolution has accelerated at an ever-increasing pace since the spread of agriculture, and especially since the industrialization and urbanization of large parts of the world's population. Man's relationship to his environment has been modified so drastically that many behavior patterns which evolved to meet the demands and exploit the opportunities of a hunting and gathering existence no longer are functional, and may in fact be maladaptive. In his essay "Emotions in the Perspective of Human Evolution," David Hamburg makes several observations of immediate relevance to the evolution of sexuality.

> Any mechanism—structure, function, or behavior—that is adaptive *on the average* for populations *over long time spans* . . . may become largely maladaptive when there are radical changes in environmental conditions. When we consider the profound changes in human environmental conditions within *very recent* evolutionary times, it becomes entirely conceivable that some of the mechanisms which evolved over the millions of years of mammalian, primate, and human evolution may now be less useful than they once were. Since cultural change has moved much more rapidly than genetic change, the *emotional response tendencies* that have been built into us through their suitability for a long succession of past environments may be less suitable for the very different *present* environment. In this sense, there may be some respects in which modern man is obsolete. (In Washburn & Jay, 1968.)

Conclusions. This evolutionary perspective on contemporary sexuality is certainly not a theory, or even a working hypothesis, subject to empirical test and validation. It is an assemblage of some facts, and more speculations, which suggest one way of looking at the sexual characteristics of modern man. It may help us to understand certain cultural universals including some that seem to have no rational basis and even appear counteradaptive in present-day society. It provides a foundation for consideration of such widespread phenomena as sexual jealousy, desire for children, certain sex differences in emotional and intellectual traits, to name a few, that undoubtedly depend upon learning but are difficult to explain on these grounds alone. Finally, it can help us to understand many of the similarities as well as the vast differences between man's sexuality and the sex-related behavior of his mammalian and primate relatives.

SUMMARY STATEMENT

This chapter has presented four different but interrelated perspectives or vantage points from which human sexuality can be examined. Each of them is employed to varying degrees by other contributors to this book. Some may prove more fruitful than others; some certainly are more congenial than others to contemporary intellectual and sociopolitical fashions; but each has its own virtues and heuristic value. They are reviewed in this introductory chapter because of the writer's conviction that the possibilities for progress toward an intellectually satisfying and practically effective interpretation of our subject are maximized if it is viewed in macroscopic and microscopic dimensions simultaneously.

REFERENCES

Beach, F. A. 1947. Evolutionary changes in the physiological control of mating behavior in mammals. *Psychol. Review* 54 (6): 279-315.

————. 1974. Human sexuality and evolution. In *Reproductive Behavior*. Edited by W. Montagna and W. A. Sadler. New York: Plenum Press. pp. 333-65.

DeVore, I., ed. 1965. *Primate Behavior: Field Studies of Monkeys and Apes*. New York, Holt, Rinehart & Winston.

Ford, C. S., and Beach, F. A. 1951. *Patterns of Sexual Behavior*. New York: Harper & Hoeber.

Hamburg, D. A. 1968. Emotions in the perspective of human evolution. In *Perspectives on Human Evolution. I*. Edited by S. L. Washburn and P. C. Jay. New York: Holt, Rinehart & Winston.

Kinsey, A. C.; Pomeroy, W. B.; and Martin, C. E. 1948. *Sexual Behavior in the Human Male*. Philadelphia: Saunders.

Novikoff, A. B. 1945. The concept of integrative levels and biology. *Science* 101:209-15.

Roe, A. R., and Simpson, G. G. 1958. *Behavior and Evolution*. New Haven: Yale University Press.

Simpson, G., 1951. *The Meaning of Evolution*. New Haven: Mentor (paperback abridged).

Washburn, S. L., and Lancaster, C. S. 1968. The evolution of hunting. In *Perspectives on Human Evolution. I*. Edited by S. L. Washburn and P. C. Jay. New York: Holt, Rinehart & Winston.

Washburn, S. L., and Moore, R. 1974. *Ape into Man: A Study of Human Evolution*. Boston: Little, Brown.

2

HUMAN SEXUAL DEVELOPMENT: BIOLOGICAL FOUNDATIONS FOR SOCIAL DEVELOPMENT

Milton Diamond

EDITORIAL PREFACE

This chapter and the two that follow employ the trans-temporal approach to adult sexuality, as defined in Chapter 1, by tracing the way in which males and females differentiate from the beginning of embryonic development to birth, and then during infancy and childhood.

Because this same method is used, a certain degree of redundancy is inevitable. Chapters 2 and 3 run about the same course as long as they are dealing with the facts of prenatal sexual differentiation, and some question may arise as to why both authors have dealt with the same evidence. However, closer analysis reveals differences in interpretation which presage even wider theoretical differences to come.

Milton Diamond's interpretive bias is heavily physiological, placing very strong emphasis on prenatally organized sex differences in the brain as determinants of behavioral differences throughout life. John Money's formulation also strongly implicates biological control of sex differentiation during very early development, but he lays primary responsibility for the final determination of psychosexual differences upon social conditioning from infancy onward. It has been judged desirable to provide a forum for both points of view, since many of the unsolved issues demand as catholic an approach as can be presented.

According to Diamond's hypothesis, sex differences in the brain are established very early, under the influence of genetic and hormonal factors, so that within 4 to 5 weeks after conception "crude neural programs are organized which eventually will mediate the individual's reproductive and sexual patterns." Diamond is quite explicit in defining just what these "patterns" may be, and in fact structures his entire theory in terms of them. A person's *sexual patterns* are his or her ways of behaving which reveal maleness (aggressiveness, assertiveness, et cetera) or femaleness (subtlety, passivity, dependency, et cetera). *Sexual identity* refers to each individual's self-perception as a male or a female. *Sexual object choice* is the sex of persons preferred as "erotically interacting partners," and *sexual mechanisms* are the physiological responses involved in performance of the male or female role during physical sex acts. Each of the foregoing patterns depends upon separate brain circuits or "neural programs." Male and female programs are laid down in both sexes; but masculine mechanisms are more strongly developed in genetic males and feminine mechanisms supervene in genetic females. Because of these inborn differences in reactive capacity, very young boys and girls are likely to show different responses to the same treatment. This prediction is in accord with some of the observations made by Jerome Kagan in Chapter 4. The concept of a basic but unbalanced bisexuality in the brain is set forth also in Money's discussion of human hermaphroditism and in my own chapter on animal sexual behavior.

In Chapter 5, William Davenport stresses those sex differences in behavior which seem to occur in most, if not all, human societies; and Diamond asserts that in all cultures there are sex differences throughout childhood that "reflect a basic sexual organization which is constitutionally based." At this level of generality, there might be appreciable agreement among authorities, but Diamond's views grow more controversial as he becomes more specific, in statements such as the following:

The effects [of hormonally induced brain organization] on sexual behavior . . . [are] believed to [include] erotic response levels, arousability, genital mechanisms, sexual identity, and sex-related biases in the spontaneous initiation or acceptance of various activities, as well as choice of sexual objects.

A few other points concerning Diamond's theoretical point of view should be mentioned. Although there are frequent references to the importance of environmental determinants of sexuality, their principal role appears to be seen as one of evoking the expression of behavioral characteristics which were "biologically programmed" earlier in development.

In addition to the chapters by Money and by Kagan, there are others which deal with determinants of sex differences and which can profitably be compared with Diamond's treatment. In particular, Chapter 9 points up the difference between masculinization and defeminization in females, and between feminization and demasculinization in males. Chapter 11 further develops the concept of bisexuality in brain organization and relates it to the occurrence of homosexual behavior in nonhuman species.

Introduction

We must bear in mind that some day all our provisional formulations in psychology will have to be based on an organic foundation. It will then probably be seen that it is special chemical substances and processes which achieve the effects of sexuality and the perpetuation of individual life in the life of the species.

Sigmund Freud, as translated
by Sandor Rado

The obvious and manifest differences in physical appearance and behavior of the typical adult human male and female prompt inquiry concerning the factors which produce these differences. Some argue that physical differences are brought about primarily by biological factors, whereas learning and cultural conditions and forces are responsible for behavioral differences. On the other hand, there are others who attribute all differences to biological causes. The facts seem to indicate that both biology and environment are intimately involved in producing both the morphological and behavior characteristics. The present chapter will deal primarily with the biological factors which contribute to the differences or similarities in sexuality between human males and females. Of primary concern will be those periods of development during which primary sexual differentiation occurs and then becomes manifest.

At the outset, it should be made clear how biology, environment and culture must all be considered in the overall picture of human sexual differentiation and development. Firstly, biology acts to set potentials, limits and response biases in each individual. These establish the parameters within which culture and environment can exert their influence. From the moment of fertilization, the individual has a sex genotype bias which is constitutional and which operates to modify the responsiveness of all tissue to subsequent influences. It is the basic premise of this chapter that early biological influences affect subsequent behavioral development. For example, while steroids can affect all developing individuals, much lower doses of a male hormone are needed to induce growth of male structures and development of male behavior patterns in males than in females. Similarly, development of masculine body structures and behaviors is more sensitive to the lack of androgen in males than is the case in females. Thus, in considering behavior, two individuals of different sex with equally high motivation to be good swimmers, musicians, or lovers might differ greatly in their inherent abilities, even though they both practice equally hard and long.[1] The constitutional makeup which they bring to the swimming pool, concert hall, or bedroom is different. Furthermore, interaction between the individual and the environment is two-way. Not only does the environment work on the individual to mold and shape his or her physical and behavioral character, but the individual, biased organically, works on the social and physical environment in a mutual exchange of effect. Two individuals of different size or behavorial attitude will be treated differ-

---

[1]The recent prominence of East Germany in sports has been ascribed to that country's policy of first selecting for training those individuals whose physiques are considered best for each competition. Indoctrination with regard to motivation is considered secondary.

ently in the same situation by the same people. All that is said in the rest of this chapter should be appreciated within the context of these reciprocal interactions.

In any discussion of sexuality, it is extremely important to realize that definitions of male or female (even for the description of traits) are often affected by retrospective judgments involved in establishing the original categories. For example, the conclusion that roundness or softness are feminine traits, whereas angularity and hardness are masculine, is a judgment based on the findings that most males have physical features which can be categorized as hard and angular and related to muscular activity, and, in contrast, most females have characteristics classifiable as soft and round and which can be related to childbearing and nurturance.

While these generalizations hold true for most populations, the criteria may not apply to any specific individual. The generality is valid, nevertheless. Another example would be the decision as to whether mounting behavior or aggressive sexuality should be considered masculine, while being mounted or being sexually submissive should be regarded as feminine. We certainly can choose items that will reflect such sex differences, but the items of choice, while they may be reality-oriented, are idiosyncratic and may be subject to contrary opinion. Finally, we can consider subtle observer bias in the definition of male versus female behavioral characteristics. Masculinity or femininity of an individual may be considered reflected in the choice of an out-of-the-home career or preference for a domestic role. Choice of a career might be considered an indication of masculinity. In addition, the desire to have, or spend time with, children might be considered an index of femininity. These, however, are observer-determined retrospective categories of choice, based upon what our culture usually regards as the end product of typical male or female development. One must always be mindful of the fact that it is the culmination of all interacting forces to which we attend. Therefore, attributing a particular facet of behavior or morphology to biological innateness or environmental determinism, while it may be true in fact, can be difficult to document. As a generality, without other data, it is probably best to consider traits as inherently male or female in humans if they follow logically from what we can expect, on an evolutionary continuum, as revealed in the behavior of males and females of many other mammalian and primate species. To this, we of course add the flexibility and adaptability which are highly developed human characteristics. When humans are considered to deviate from what we might consider normal in evolution, we should be skeptical.

DIFFERENTIATION

The complexity of the variables involved in human development allow for an infinite variety of inputs into any individual. Starting from the genetic inheritance involved when sperm and egg meet at zygote formation, a progression is seen between simultaneous and sequential influences. Initially these are mainly genetic and endocrine forces which affect the development of the gonads, the external and internal morphology, and the nervous system. These will be seen to be related to sex assignment, sex rearing, psychological bias, gender roles, behavioral patterns, sexual identity, sex object choice, sexual mechanism, and other concerns during childhood, puberty and adulthood.

Genetic and endocrine factors, while always affecting the individual, may be considered to exert their primary influence during three biological periods: predifferentiation, differentiation and development. The first period biases the outcome of the second and the second influences the third. These periods differ in duration and significance. The particular influential features within each period can be categorized as follows:

Predifferentiation
  Genetics
  Gonads
  Endocrines
Differentiation
  Endocrines
  Internal morphology
  External morphology
  Nervous system
Development
  Internal morphology
  External morphology
  Nervous system
Sex assignment and rearing
Psychological sex (sexual patterns and mechanisms, sexual self identity, sex object choice)
Puberty
Adulthood

The predifferentiation stage is the initial period of ontogeny which precedes the appearances of visible differences between the sexes. During this early embryonic period (the first 7 weeks in human beings), the individual might be considered to be in a sexually indifferent stage (Fig. 2.1). The lack of visible distinction between the sexes leads to the common application of such terms as "neuter" or "indifferent" to these stages, or to the organs and systems under discussion. It should be understood that this refers only to appearances (phenotype)—the potential *competence* of the tissues differs markedly between the sexes and also among individuals. *Competence* is the ability of a tissue to react to a particular developmental stimulus. At this point in ontogeny, the genital primordia maintain a bisexual potential to develop along either male or female lines. *This bisexual potential does not necessarily involve an equal capability to be male or female* in every individual, nor are the tissues equally competent to be masculine or feminine. From the time of zygote formation, genetic differences among individuals impose upon each person certain limitations with respect to masculine or feminine development. These limits can be approached under the influence of suitable stimuli, but in normal humans cannot be transcended by subsequent biological or environmental factors.

The second period of interest is that of sexual differentiation, which occurs during the 4- to 5-week period following predifferentiation. During this interval, the individual loses a great deal of his or her relative pansexual potentiality and progresses definitively toward a predominantly male or female existence. At the end of this stage, the individual might accurately be described as a "primitive" male or "primitive" female (Figs. 2.2 and 2.3). The internal reproductive organs are concordant with the genetic sex of the individual and the external sexual organs are appropriate to his or her genetic and endocrine nature. In addition, crude neural programs that eventually will mediate the individual's reproductive and sexual patterns are organized.

Subsequent to the period of sexual differentiation occurs the much longer and diversely influenced phase which goes by the all-inclusive term of *development*. Due to its complexity, the protracted time span involved in development can be subdivided into post-differentiation gestational, prepubertal, pubertal and postpubertal, and mature intervals. It is during the post-gestational periods that the individual matures biologically (Figs. 2.4 and 2.5) and psychologically. It is also during this period that the person is most influenced by environmental forces, although strong biological factors remain nevertheless crucial. This chapter will concentrate on those periods preceding puberty.

Predifferentiation

From the time of fertilization, the genetic stamp of the individual is established. As cell division progresses, this mark is transferred to every cell of the body. Typically, the mark reflects either a female XX constitution or a male XY constitution. In human embryos, the effect of this heritage usually does not become manifest until the sixth or seventh week in utero. Prior to this time, the human fetus can be regarded as appearing neuter or indifferent. It is indifferent in internal and external

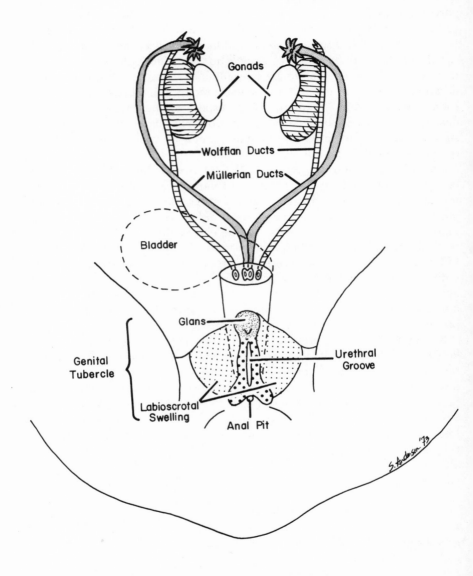

Fig. 2.1. Predifferentiated genitalia. Refers to phenotype, which is similar in males and females; the tissues are already genetically competent towards male or female.

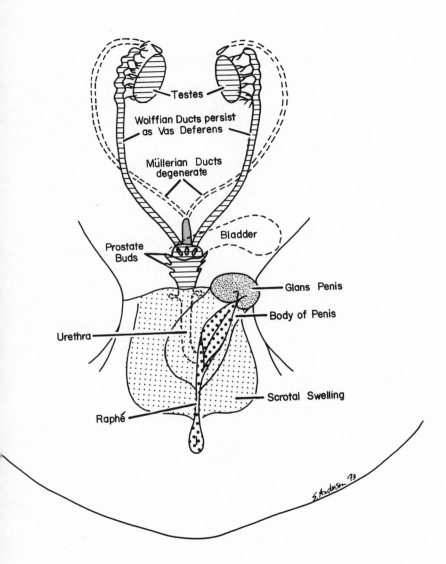

Fig. 2.2. Primitive male. Male form clearly distinguished; female potential lost.

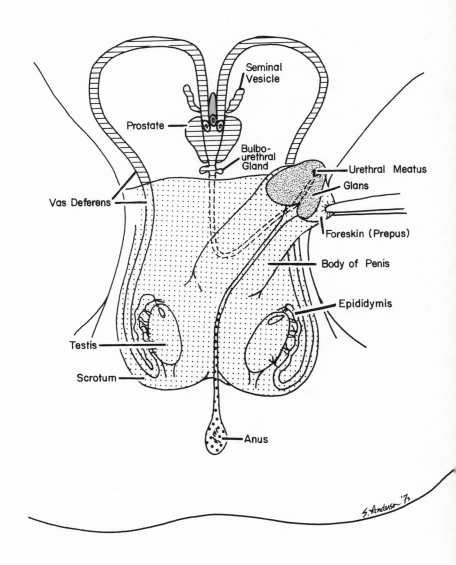

Fig. 2.3. Definitive male. Male differentiation completed.

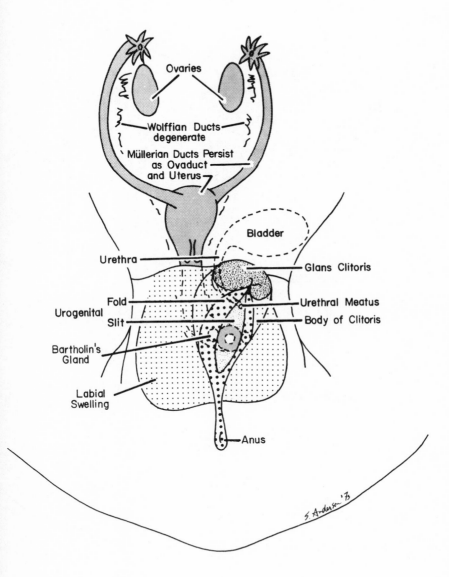

Fig. 2.4. Primitive female. Female form internally clearly distinguished; externally less so.

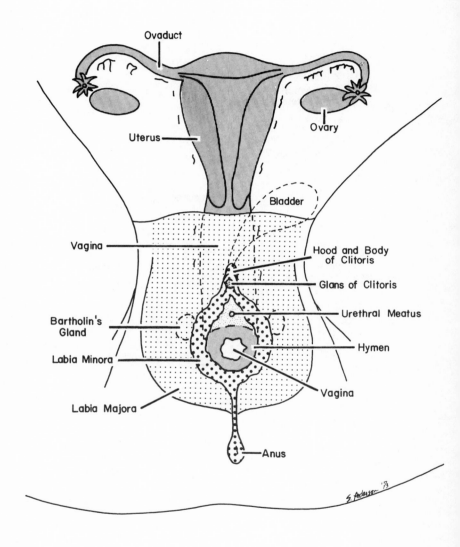

Fig. 2.5. Definitive female. Female differentiation completed.

appearance (phenotype), containing neither testes nor ovaries, but only undeveloped gonads located near the kidneys.

At this stage of development, two systems of primitive ducts exist in the fetus: One is the Mullerian duct system with the potential to give rise to oviducts, uterus, and upper vagina; the other is the Wolffian duct system, which can give rise to the male epididymides, vas deferens, and seminal vesicles. Despite the simultaneous existence of both duct systems and the apparently indifferent gonads, the genotype has pre-established inherent male and female potentialities in these embryonic structures. The inductive nature of the genotype is such that the indifferent gonads will develop into ovaries in individuals containing two X chromosomes, whereas the gonads will normally develop into testes in individuals bearing a Y chromosome. In the human male and female, chromosomes are not balanced biologically, as they are in several other species, nor is there, at this stage, an overriding male differentiating influence from the autosomes. If a single X chromosome is present, gonadal agenesis or dysgenesis will result. If an individual's genetic constitution includes any combination of more than two sex chromosomes, the presence of a single Y chromosome will insure the development of testes, regardless of the number of X chromosomes present. The presence of more than two sex chromosomes does not impart any sexual advantage to an individual; in fact, the opposite is more likely to occur. Most such individuals are sterile and, regardless of their upbringing, display low libidinal levels. It is instructive to note that individuals with genetic constitutions other than XX or XY are not uncommon in human beings, occurring in as many as one in 100 or 200 persons.

The manner in which chromosomal factors influence the direction of development of the gonad is not yet clear, but it seems apparent that the male and female potentialities in the gonad are pre-established in the medullary and cortical gonadal components at a very early stage. This seems obvious, since differentiation of the gonad into an ovary or testis involves the gradual predominance of either the medullary or cortical component over the other, rather than the transformation of one sex element into the other.

In an individual with a Y chromosome, the medulla develops so that it envelops developing germ cells, which will become the future spermatogonia. In the individual containing two X chromosomes, the medulla forms in a circular pattern, excluding the germ cells from their midst and pushing them to the periphery. These germ cells will give rise to the ova. Thus the relative distribution of cortex and medulla develops, with the allocation of germ cells establishing the prototype for the future ovary or testis. The sex genotype is considered to act primarily in initiating sexual differentiation by determining the developmental pattern to structure the gonad. It is appropriate here to define *differentiation*. This refers to the developmental process responsible for instrinsic and irreversible differences in form and function among tissues. Differentiation, in this sense, is common during embryonic and fetal growth, and is uncommon in the adult. Differentiation must be contrasted with *modulation,* which is more common in the adult. Modulation refers to temporary and often reversible changes which occur in response to different stimuli and different environmental conditions.

Considering this histological differentiation of the gonad, we may say that, after genetic sex determination at fertilization, the differentiation of the gonad is the most basic event in sexual development. The type of gonad—ovary or testis—possessed by an individual is defined as his or her *primary sex characteristic.*

Sexual Differentiation

Sexual differentiation occurs in analogous ways in the genitalia and in the nervous system.

Genitalia. Once a definite male or female gonad differentiates, it, in turn, gives direction to the development of the two coexisting pairs of genital duct structures. If the gonad differentiates as a testis, it produces an as yet unidentified hormonal substance which has the capability of simultaneously inducing masculine development of the Wolffian duct system and inhibiting development of the Mullerian duct system (Fig. 2.1). This formative influence exerted by one tissue (or substance) on a neighboring tissue is called *induction,* and it results simultaneously in two types of determination. Induction insures the continued or developed presence of a particular tissue (*evocation* determination), and at the same time it determines the characteristics possessed by that tissue (*individuation* determination). The significance of specifying the dual nature of this determination will be enlarged upon below.

Since the biochemical nature of the inductor substance is unknown, I have for convenience termed it "fetal morphogenic testicular substance" (FMTS). The name serves to define the period of activity and the source and primary level of action of the hormone or hormones involved. If the gonad differentiates as an ovary, no substance corresponding to FMTS (i.e., acting to induce development of the Mullerian duct system and regression of the Wolffian duct system) appears.[2] In crucial distinction from the case in the male, where the presence of FMTS is required for normal differentiation, in the female, it is the *absence* of

[2]FMTS, as far as is presently known is not testosterone, androstenedione, estrogen, progesterone or other common adult steroid.

Some investigators refer to this substance as Mullerian Inhibiting Substance (MIS). In the present context, the name is conceptually limiting.

FMTS that results in preservation of the Mullerian duct system and regression of the Wolffian ducts (Fig. 2.3). This finding is corroborated by results of animal experiments and by clinical experiences, which show that fetal castration, gonadal destruction, or absence of gonads prior to differentiation invariably result in sexual development along female lines. The Wolffian ducts regress and the Mullerian duct derivatives become dominant. If differentiation occurs along male lines, the major portion of the Wolffian duct system gives rise to the vas deferens and also portions of the epididymis, common ejaculatory duct, seminal vesicle and trigone of the bladder. If differentiation proceeds along female lines, the Mullerian ducts persist as the oviducts, uterus and upper vagina.

Simultaneously with differentiation of these genital reproductive structures, sexual differentiation of other common urogenital structures takes place. For example, the common urethral glands, and glands of the urogenital sinus seen in the indifferent stage, give rise to the prostate gland in the male and urethral and Skene's glands in the female.

The significance of the *evocation*-determining properties of an inducing substance like FMTS is thus apparent; a structure is physically maintained and its *existence*, or that of its derivatives, is assured. Those tissues that are not evoked, regress. The significance of *individuation* determination is that a tissue is given a certain *sexual bias*, so that it maintains permanently a *modified responsiveness* to future stimuli. For example, Wolffian duct derivatives such as the vas deferens are more responsive to androgens than to other steroids, whereas Mullerian duct derivatives such as the uterus are always more responsive to estrogens.

Following differentiation of the internal genitalia, analogous processes come into play, promoting sexual differentiation of the external genitalia. Prior to sexual differentiation, a seemingly indifferent genital tubercle and pair of genital swellings exist (Fig. 2.1). In human embryos, these genital structures remain phenotypically undifferentiated until approximately the end of the third month of fetal life. This long interval prior to differentiation of the external genitalia, in comparison with the earlier development of the internal genitalia, is believed to be an important factor accounting for the frequency and wide variety of genital incongruities seen in human. Whereas differentiation of the internal genitalia along male or female lines is dependent upon FMTS, this substance is not crucial for differentiation of the external genitalia. Instead, sexual development of the external genital structures is mainly dependent upon the presence or absence of testicular androgens, such as testosterone. The tubercle, genital swellings and associated structures differentiate as female genitalia in the absence of male hormones. While usually in the testes, the origin of the androgens to which the external genitalia can respond is immaterial; testicular, adrenal, maternal or exogenous androgens all are effective. This is a crucial point, since there are many clinical conditions in which the presence of nontesticular androgenic substances induce masculinization of a female. For example, an overactive fetal or maternal adrenal may produce androgens at an appropriate time in development, and under such conditions that the female fetus will develop virilized genitalia (adrenogenital syndrome). Aberrantly functioning tumors of the maternal ovary also can masculinize the female fetus (arhenoblastoma). Still another cause of such masculinization is seen when pregnant women take, or are given, androgenic substances (drug-induced masculinization).

Normally the newly developed testes produce the androgens necessary for male development. In the male (or female) with androgens, the genital tubercle elongates and incorporates the urethral groove so that an imbedded, tubular penile urethra develops within a cylindrical phallus—the penis. The genital swellings enlarge to form the scrotal pouch, which eventually will contain the testes, when they descend from their position near the kidneys (Fig. 2.4). During the predifferentiation phase, conditions and appearances of the external genitalia of the female are essentially like those of the male except that the urethral groove is shorter. In the absence of androgens, the urethral folds flanking the urethral groove do not fuse, but persist as the labia minora, flanking the urogenital vestibule. Instead of pouching, the genital swellings grow together between the anus and the urogenital vestibule. Their point of fusion becomes the posterior commissure and the lateral portions grow as labial swellings to persist as labia majora. The lower vagina develops concomitantly with formation of the urogenital vestibule. Estrogens are not crucial for differentiation of the external genitalia of either sex (Fig. 2.5).

While necessary for differentiation of masculine genitalia, the presence of circulating androgens is not by itself sufficient for masculinization. The capability for the appropriate end organ response of the pertinent tissues is required. By virtue of his genetic inheritance, the male with a normal XY genetic component typically has tissues which are more responsive to androgen than does the female with her normal XX genetic makeup. However, various specific genetic conditions can preclude or alter this natural responsiveness to androgens. An extreme example is seen in some males who, despite an XY chromosomal complement, and despite the presence of testes and normal levels of androgen production, have the appearance of females. An inherited inability of their tissues to respond at all to these androgens causes these males to develop phenotypically as females, and they are called "testicular females" or "androgen-insensitive males." Since differentiation of the internal genitalia depends upon FMTS, and not upon androgen, these individuals have internal genitalia which are typically male. This would be a case of the internal genitalia having been evocated as a normal male *without* normal male *individuation determination* of external or other tissues. This example illustrates a crucial point. An individual's genetic heritage remains crucial throughout life for psychosexual and morphosexual development.

In the 1940s and 1950s, human sexual differentiation was conceptualized as depending upon both male and female *evocator* substances. Male differentiation was thought to be dependent upon androgens and female differentiation upon estrogens. For the human, this theoretical framework has been supplanted by the present concept of only FMTS and androgens being necessary for development along male lines. The absence of FMTS and androgens is necessary for development along female lines. The magnitude of effect of FMTS and androgens is dependent upon genetic heritage.

Period of maximal sensitivity (critical periods). Heretofore, we considered various inducer substances and their effects on various tissues. It must be emphasized that the ability of tissues to respond varies with time. This responsiveness is dependent upon the time of onset, duration and magnitude of exposure to the inducing substance. The critical nature of these time relations is known best from experimental studies, but some clinical data are also available. In general, for humans, it seems that the timing involved with the many facets of sexual differentiation and development are only slightly known. For morphological characteristics, however, most organization occurs between the 7th and 12th week of the gestation.[3]

Sexual differentiation of the neural tissues. In addition to genital tissues, sexual differentiation of a different type is also directly related to our interest. This involves primarily sexual differentiation of the neural tissues and the neural-endocrine axis associated with reproduction and sexual behavior. Present evidence indicates that processes somewhat analogous to the hormonal mechanisms involved in genital differentiation are also active in differentiation of the behavior-mediating and reproduction-mediating neural tissues. But, in terms of time, these neural tissues are the last to differentiate, the process probably continuing until after birth. Sexual differentiation of the internal and external genitalia is apparent prenatally; sexual differentiation of neural tissues in general is initiated prenatally, but is not apparent until after birth and is especially vivid afther puberty. The concept of neural tissues being programmed

---

[3]The specificity in time may be quite short-lived, i.e., limited to days, if these tissues respond toward teratogens such as thalidomide as do limb tissues. The intake of thalidomide between the 27th and 30th day, for example, will affect only arm development, whereas intake between the 30th and 35th day will affect mainly the legs.

prenatally for later manifestations recalls the genital tissue response of individuation to evoking substances. Emphasis is focused on neural development, since all behavior is invariably a neural function.

In the adult individual, this neural organization will affect reproduction mainly via gonadal, and, in the female, genital tract cyclicity. In the human male, cyclic activity is not seen and spermatogenesis is the reproductive process affected.[4] The effect on sexual behavior is on a broad plain and believed to influence: erotic response levels, arousability, genital mechanisms, sexual identity, and sex-related biases in the spontaneous initiation or acceptance of various activities, as well as choice of sexual objects. The analogy between differentiation of the genitalia and neural tissues must be employed with caution and therefore will be discussed in detail.

The development of the neural tissues is much more complicated than that of the internal and external genitalia. The genitalia are usually considered functional or appropriate in simple, male-female categories, without conflict. Differentiation of the genitalia is relatively obvious and once it has occurred, future development involves little more than growth and functional activation. For the neural tissues, whose capability and functioning are revealed only after birth, and in some cases only after puberty, a comparable, stable male-female dichotomy is observable, mainly for purely reproductive functions such as gamete production, the menstrual cycle, pregnancy and lactation. An individual may be stimulated by hypothalamic-pituitary influences to show either cyclic ovulation and menstruation, or tonic spermatogenesis, but not both simultaneously. For differentiation of the genital tissues along male or female lines, fairly unidimensional processes are involved. A genital tubercle will develop as a penis or a clitoris, but never both simultaneously. Similarly, the Mullerian duct system will either survive or regress reciprocally with the Wolffian duct system. In the mature individual, both do not usually coexist. Thus, the functioning of the internal genital tissues is like that of the neural tissues for the reproductive obligations; the individual is either male or female.

In the case of behavior-mediating neural tissues, the male or female dichotomy is not clearly distinguishable. Stereotypes of male and female behavior exist, but the observable points to be considered are multiple and their definitions often superficial. Also, sexual behavior is modifiable postnatally while gonadal and genital functions typically are not. Indeed, facets of sexual behavior are only finally differentiated during the processes of maturation. When behavior-mediating neural tissues are considered, behavior patterns considered male and female may exist simul-

---

[4]In many nonhuman species, even primates, seasonal cyclicity in breeding activities is indeed seen; however, no evidence exists for this type of cyclicity in the human.

taneously in the same individual and may be manifest at various times to a greater or lesser degree. This notwithstanding, development of the genital tracts and external genitalia does have its counterpart in endocrine effects upon development of the behavior-mediating neural tissues. In males, the presence of androgens is crucial for development of normal male sexual behavior patterns and mechanisms. The absence of androgens seems to impede or completely prevent such development and simultaneously to facilitate the emergence of feminine patterns and mechanisms—this, despite the style of male upbringing. In females, androgens present during the period of differentiation to some degree foster the development of masculine behavior and simultaneously inhibit behaviors more typically female—this, also, despite female upbringing. The magnitude of the effect produced by the presence or absence of sexually differentiating hormones is dependent upon the time of onset, duration and degree of endocrine exposure on the one hand, and the responsiveness of the androgen labile tissues on the other hand. There can be no doubt, however, that males are usually more responsive to androgens than females at any time of development, and similarly females are more responsive than males to the absence of androgens in their development. With this caution, we thus should not anticipate androgenized females to be comparable to males or androgen-deficient males to be comparable to normal females.

This distinction between the factors determining sexual differentiation of the external and internal genital tissues and those affecting differentiation and organization of the behavioral mediating neural tissues is significant. In the case of the external genitalia, it is legitimate to regard male and female as representing ends of a continuum, where the development of the genital tubercle toward the phenotype of one sex precludes simultaneous development toward the other sex. This can be called *mutually exclusive differentiation.* An example is seen in the case of phallus length. An individual cannot simultaneously have a large penis and a small clitoris. Similarly, when one of the two sets of internal genital duct systems differentiates, one becomes dominant and the other regresses; usually to vestigial status. This can be termed *simultaneously exclusive differentiation.* For the neural tissues mediating reproduction and sexual behavior, we have at present no way of knowing whether one or two, or more sets of tissues must differentiate. Experimental and clinical data, however, lead to the belief that the neural tissues differentiate in yet a third manner, with characteristics of both internal and external genitalia. It is probable that differentiation of the neural tissues involved in procreational processes, like the external genitalia, is mutually exclusive in character. The individual can show hypothalamic-pituitary-gonadal processes which are either tonic or cyclic, but not both. In the presence of androgens, the neural tissues involved in procreation are organized along male lines, i.e., a tonic, non-cyclic, hypothalamic-pituitary relation will obtain. In the absence of androgens, a female, cyclic type of control will develop.

Human reproductive capacity is characterized by its cyclic nature in females and its tonic nature in males. For example, the cyclic process of ovulation, uterus preparation and menstruation, requires a complexity of neuro-endocrine coordination which is provided only by a female hypothalamic (nervous system) differentiation. Transplants of ovaries and uteri to a male do not show cyclic activity despite adequate vascular and histo-immunological acceptance by the host tissues. Spermatogenesis in the male, while a cyclic process in itself, is dependent upon relatively tonic hypothalamic-gonadotropic stimuli.

The neural tissues involved in sexual behavior, like those of the external genitalia, respond to testoids. In contrast with those involved in procreation, however, they differentiate somewhat like the internal genitalia, but in a manner of differentiation that might be considered *simultaneous but not exclusive*. Behavior patterns, biases and mechanisms of one sex will be dominant, but those of the other sex may regress only slightly and remain subordinant or latent (subdominant). The determination of which are dominant behaviors and which subordinant depends upon threshold levels of response or response probabilities (biases) for the behaviors, and must be considered in terms of evoking or suppressing stimuli. Behavioral tissues thus form a unique category, since male and female patterns and biases may coexist and, depending upon how they are evaluated, appear equally well developed simultaneously. The mode of differentiation, initiated now, will only become apparent much after birth. For example, one individual may show a good deal of sexual aggressiveness and promiscuity in initiating sexual contact (considered a male trait), and at the same time exhibit a great deal of passivity or submissiveness when engaging in coitus (considered a female trait). Without clearly defining the actual behavioral traits affected by genetic and endocrine factors, it can be said that they probably are invested with limits and biases influencing the direction and emphasis that will be mediated by crucial neural tissues and later may be affected by culture. These limits need not lie upon a simple male-female continuum. The behavioral repertoires of males and females can be considered parallel and discontinuous rather than continuous, and thus they should not be subject to the same evaluation criteria as applied to morphology. An additional, complicating, factor is that behavioral sexual differentiation and development most profitably must be evaluated on at least four levels. Usually these are in concert, but their development need not be.

Differentiation along four levels of behavioral sexuality. The four levels of sexuality under consideration will be presented here in their adult mode to enable the reader to follow their trend of development. It is assumed that the neural tissues involved are individuated pre- and neonatally in development. With varying degrees of modifiability, they will continue to develop throughout life. In addition to these levels, others may be distinguished, but these basic four are considered a minimum to provide a sexual profile for an individual.[5]

The first manifestation of sexual behavior can be assessed by *sexual patterns,* e.g., for maleness: direct aggressivity, assertiveness, large muscle motor activity; and for femaleness: subtlety, passivity and dependency, nurturance, small muscle motor activity. Patterns are largely susceptible to cultural and learning factors. The second manifestation of behavior is *sexual identity,* i.e., the sex to which an individual ascribes: male or female. This feeling of identity is typically reinforced by society, but can exist independently of society's inputs. The third is *sexual object choice,* i.e., the sex of the individual chosen as an erotically interacting partner, usually a male for a female, and vice versa. This, too, is typically reinforced by society, but can exist independently of its support. The fourth assessment of sexual behavior involves *sexual mechanisms,* e.g., those features of sexual expression over which the individual has little conscious control: the ability of a male to get and maintain an erection, have an orgasm and/or ejaculate; the ability of a female's vagina to lubricate and for her to be orgastic.

In most individuals, these four characteristics will be in concert among themselves and with other criteria of sex. This is to say that normal genetic males or females will develop the appropriate sexual anatomy, will see themselves as males or females, and will eventually act erotically and characteristically with an opposite-sexed partner. It is hypothesized that closely related and interacting, but different, sets of neural tissues are involved in pattern, identity, object choice and mechanism functioning, as there is a separate set for reproduction. While there is as yet little anatomical evidence that separate neural tissues exist for each of these components of sexual behavior, clinical considerations will be presented below to indicate that indeed quite distinct tissues might develop and exist. I believe most difficulties in ·interpreting or discussing either developing or existing adult sexuality and gender characteristics, similarities as well as differences, is that these different levels of behavior are often mistakenly discussed along one male-female continuum despite the disparate nature of the traits under consideration.

Each set of tissues theoretically should have its own critical period for differentiation, and should develop in its own mode. Due to various

[5]A fifth area of sexuality would be the primary biological one of reproduction itself. This area will not be elaborated upon here.

situations, a distortion of normal, unified development may occur. An immediate clinical example of two seemingly divergent levels coexisting in the same individuals is the female who identifies herself as a female, and is so identified by others, but who simultaneously has erotic preferences for other females (i.e., a lesbian). Clinically, this concept of different sets of neural tissues provides a framework, a method of conceptualization, within which the most vexing etiological problems of sexuality could readily be interpreted, e.g., how can individuals become homosexual, heterosexual, bisexual, transsexual, etcetera. An individual would thus be biased toward transsexuality when the tissues associated with morphology and those associated with identity differentiate out of phase with each other, so they come under different influences, one under male stimulation, the other not. An individual would be biased toward homosexuality by the neural tissues for gender identity and object choice developing out of phase with each other. Since the factors of tissue competence, developmental timing and hormone secretion dosage could vary, all grades of heterosexuality, homosexuality or transsexuality could be induced (evoked and individuated) to interact with future environmental influences.[6]

The effects of considering the differentiation of the neural tissues as extensively as presented here, and contrasting such differentiation with the development of the morphological tissues, allow us to entertain different expectations for the separate tissues involved. An apparently well-developed and masculine-appearing penis normally is anticipated to function as one. In contrast, there are no comparable landmarks for the behavioral mediating neural tissues. However, it is conceivable that since both the penis and neural tissues are dependent upon the presence or absence of androgen for normal development, growth of the penis might serve as a bioassay for the capacity or potential of the nervous system. In other words, an individual showing a good-sized and adequately functioning penis might be accepted as having been primed along masculine lines in regard to sexual behavior. It has been argued that deficiencies in copulatory performance due to lack of androgen during development actually reflect underdevelopment of copulatory organs. To this argument it should be added that underdevelopment of the phallus may be accompanied by underdevelopment of central neural

---

[6]Ounsted and Taylor (1972) have recently presented a theory wherein the Y chromosome acts as a pace regulator for the various processes and characteristics associated with sex and gender. The pace of development in the male is thus very different from that seen in the female. Since all the Y chromosome does, according to this theory, is regulate pace and not supply characteristics of its own, and since every individual otherwise has autosomes and at least one X chromosome, it is unlikely that males have basic genetic information which females cannot have. Thus basic differences between the sexes are brought about by developmental timing differences.

tissues mediating masculine behavioral patterns. A different order of behavior would therefore be inevitable. The cause and effect relationship involved is still under investigation, and it cannot be gainsaid that an individual with a small penis may have sexual drives and performance levels considered normal, whereas other individuals with quite adequate genitalia may be unable or unwilling to do much sexually. These discrepancies may be due to varying rates of development between the tissues involved and their individual ability to change in response to evoking substances or modifying circumstances. This can obviously lead to "anomalous" disparities between genital structures and indices of sexual behavior, since the genitalia differentiate much earlier than the neural tissues but the various behaviors themselves may be dichotomized. It is likely that, starting from this stage of differentiation, different neural tissues develop separately for basic sexual patterns, sexual identity, bias toward sexual objects, and genital mechanisms.[7]

DEVELOPMENT

Subsequent to the period of sexual differentiation, the individual passes into a phase of growth. Phenotypically, this phase is noted mainly for quantitative changes and restructure. With some exceptions, this remains generally true for all sex-related structures and reproductive neural functions until puberty. In regard to sexual behavior, neural development, in contrast, continues to undergo significant qualitative changes. The entire span of development can best be described in terms of three main subperiods: a) differentiation until birth, b) birth until puberty, and c) puberty and maturity.

Development from Differentiation until Birth

After sexual differentiation, the internal and external genitalia continue to gro win size proportionate to their neighboring organs. The gonads, however, in late fetal life begin to migrate to positions other than those they occupied in the embryo. Migration of the gonads is termed *descent* and may be considered in two stages. The first stage, in which the gonad moves inferiorly from its position of origin toward its eventual adult location, is common to both the testis and ovary. The second stage, peculiar to the testes, involves movement to an extra-abdominal position in most mammals. This is not only functional in pro-

---

[7]A reminder: all behavior, psychic phenomena, feelings, emotions, et cetera, must be localized within the nervous system. It remains a value judgment as to whether or not it is constructive to pursue or not pursue this reductionist approach to understand sexual behavior. I definitely feel the effort of value, since it provides a realistic basis upon which predictions can be made.

viding a thermal environment suitable for spermatogenesis, but the scrotal bulge may provide added erotic visual stimulation to the female and allow for added tactile stimulation for the male.

Passage of the testes from the abdominal cavity to the scrotum usually occurs during the seventh or eighth fetal month. At the time of birth, however, approximately 2 to 5 percent of human males still retain undescended or abdominal testes (cryptorchism). In the female, the ovaries, attached above the suspensory ligaments which persist, are prevented from descending out of the abdominal cavity as do the testes. The ovaries come in proximity with the superior fimbriated ends of the oviducts. Thereafter, they remain in this relative position which eventually will be crucial for capture and migration of the ovulated eggs.

In other regards, general body morphology seems not to be distinguished by sexually dichotomous characteristics. At the time of birth, individual males and females cannot be separated by somatotype without recourse to genital inspection; but that the sexes are constitutionally different during gestation cannot be denied. One indication of a major sex difference is differential fetal mortality. It is estimated by some researchers that at the time of fertilization 3 males are conceived for every 2 females. However, by the end of gestation, there remain only about 110 males for 100 females. The factors involved in these fetal deaths are unknown.

During this period of development, the external genitalia are no longer subject to the hormonal forces affecting sexual differentiation, but the penis and clitoris are modifiable to a marked degree. For example, virilization of females may occur due to late-developing adrenogenital problems. The neural tissues modifying sexual behavior also are still labile to steroidal influences and this lability probably is maintained for some time after birth.

Development from Birth until Puberty

At birth, although there is no positive gross visual method of distinguishing the sexes, aside from the genital differences, the sexes develop with different physiological capabilities and reactive potentials to environmental stimuli. It is obvious that from the moment of birth human males and females may be treated differently, either consciously or unconsciously. This differential treatment usually begins at the time of sex assignment which typically is made at birth and depends upon the appearance of the neonate's external genitalia. Sex assignment biases the way in which society in general will interact with the individual and will anticipate his or her responses. However, the individual who is subjected to these sex-related differences in rearing policies and practices is not a blank slate to be written upon. As explained previously, he or she comes to the world with constitutional, genetic and hormonally mediated, diasthetic behavioral biases and innate patterning related to all the different basic levels sexuality. These induced influences orient the way the individual will act and in turn be treated; i.e., the individual can evoke or can be responsive only to specific types of stimuli from the environment.[8]

Sex-related mechanisms. Aside from morphological differences, there are inherent constitutional differences of appreciable magnitude. Within the first 28 days after birth, as a national average, about 25 percent more males than females die. This differences is even greater if we do not consider infants born below 1000 gms where any individual is at a disadvantage. The ratio of male to female deaths continues throughout life. The factors involved in these different mortality figures are yet unknown, but they obviously reflect inherent physiological sex differences. Considering that mortality is an extreme index, it is reasonable to assume that the morbidity differences between the sexes are similar, if not actually larger. These conditions of illness most probably evoke more attention given to males by mothers or other adults. In general, significant sex differences continue throughout life for the time of onset and severity of most diseases and, as is well known, for mortality.[9]

At birth, male and female populations may show significant physiological differences. Boys generally are 5 percent heavier and 1 to 2 percent taller than girls. These differences persist until ages 10 through 13, when the girls catch up with the boys and even pass them slightly. This change reflects the earlier prepubertal and pubertal growth characteristic of females.

The years between birth and puberty are often considered relatively noneventful in terms of physiological sexual development. This unfortunate misconception arises mainly for two reasons: 1) the pace of what is happening is slow; and 2) concentration is often focused only on reproductive functions and genital development.

[8]The reader is referred to the large volume of work being produced by behavioral geneticists who show how definite and precisely worked out these interactions between biology and environment can be. Most important is the concept, as clearly enumerated by Ginsburg (1969), that more labile behaviors are no less biologically based for being less stereotyped, and "genes can pre-programme the possibilities for labile interaction with the environment as well as restrict the degree of freedom of behavioral capacities." See also Hirsch (1962) who shows how individual behavioral differences have a genetic basis. There is an abundance of papers reporting the genetic input to homosexuality and other sexual behaviors (e.g. Kallmann, 1952; and Imperato-McGinley, et al., 1974).

[9]Ounsted and Taylor (1972) have compiled a significant publication enumerating the myriad sex differences of medical and developmental importance. This volume in itself should go far in documenting the basic constitutional differences between the sexes.

Starting in late childhood, general body structure morphologically and functionally develops quite differently in the two sexes. Boys grow faster than girls for the first 6 months of life. The differences attained persist for approximately the first 4 years. At 6 years of age boys are assuming the general somatotype appropriate to adult men, with shoulders broader than hips and long, muscular chests. Their vital capacity (measure of the sustained energy output possible for an individual) is 7 percent greater than girl's and their muscular capacity is 10 percent greater. This difference in muscular capacity exists even though the general muscle mass is similar in both sexes. From between 7 and 9 years of age, differences in muscular abilities and vital capacity between the sexes increase markedly and the boys rapidly increase their lead, even prior to puberty.

From the age of 1 year, there are significant sex differences in growth and deposition of skin and subcutaneous fat tissue. The skin and fat layer in girls is approximately 50 percent thicker than it is in boys. At the age of 7, girls begin showing signs of feminoid distribution of this fat deposition, mostly around the hips and buttocks. These differences continue to increase until puberty when they are markedly accelerated. From the age of 6, boys have bigger chests than girls the same age and from this age onward, girls have relatively broader hips than their cohorts.

Children destined to early puberty tend to be tall and to have an advanced bone age. Those children who reach puberty later tend to be short and to show retarded epiphyseal closure. However, epiphyseal development of girls is consistently advanced in comparison with that of boys, throughout childhood. Following the pubertal growth spurt, the child whose puberty is delayed will become a bigger adult than one in whom puberty occurs earlier. Thus girls most often end up significantly shorter than boys, and their pubertal growth usually occurs earlier than that of boys and is of relatively short duration.

Prenatal growth is extremely rapid. However, for the first two years after birth, a deceleration in skeletal growth and weight gain is noted. Subsequently, a steady decrease in growth is seen. A rapid acceleration in growth and weight in both boys and girls indicates the onset of pubertal changes.

Much of the physical development of the infant and child interrelates and correlates with psychological development. The infant discriminates self from non-self and knowledge and mastery of the environment come with increasing muscular coordination and sharpening of the sensory systems.

The more frequent and rapid gross body movement of boys correlates with their superior three-dimensional and abstract visual abilities and with their usual superiority over girls in meeting novel tasks and new situations. Boys seem better able to replace an old "set" with a new one for problem solving. The more sedentary activity of girls corresponds with their greater visual field dependency, better ability at rapid repetitive tasks and small motor movements. These constitutional differences in muscular ability and size are reflected in differences of behavior patterns.

Sex-related patterns. Allowing for individual differences with wide ranges, boys more often, without encouragement, choose those activities which require muscularity and stamina, e.g., running, climbing, wrestling. Girls more often select relatively less strenuous and conservative activities, e.g., hopping, jumping, playing house and mothering dolls. Boys generally choose to be more gregarious than girls and play in larger groups. They are more competitive but also better able to cooperate among themselves. Consider, for example, in no culture have girls' games or activities evolved such as baseball (9 on a side), rugby, football, or soccer (10-12 on a side). Rather than role-modeling behavior, dependent upon social conditioning, these general behavior patterns are believed to be innate since they are consistently seen despite extreme differences in culture and environment. The culture will determine which games are played and by what rules. The general male patterns, however, dictate that physically aggressive, competitive games will be played.

From the phylogenetic point of view, it is instructive to note that comparable sexually dichotomous behavior patterns are seen in both free-ranging and laboratory housed nonhuman primates. Prepubertal rhesus males run and chase, wrestle, and climb more than prepubertal females; the females stay close to their mothers and play with babies more than do males. Male juveniles play in larger groups. The behavioral sex differences seen in humans represent consistent evolutionary trends.[10]

Practically all cultures do show these sex-associated patterns, yet different cultures do not have to show such similarities for the findings still to be significant. An anthropologically distinct culture may be considered to possess a relatively large genetic pool which is significantly different from othere gene pools. Morphological traits, such as body and hair pigment are genetically transmitted yet can vary between groups; so can behavioral traits and predispositions. Sexual behaviors, then, as other genetic characters and differences between cultures, can be accepted without being considered as inconsistent with a theory of genetic involvement in behavior. Several cultures thus need not manifest specific or similar sex differences any more than they need show similar skin color or hair type (both very obvious genetic traits). The fact is, however, that the overwhelming majority of independent cultures do show certain

[10]See Tiger (1969) for a full treatment of this theme.

consistent sex-related behaviors; e.g., male physical aggression, leadership and dominance, and female nurturance and subtleness (see Ford & Beach, 1951). This is what would be anticipated from evolutionary considerations. These patterns have persisted as such among widespread cultures, most probably because they are adaptive.[11]

The mediating biophysical forces involved in demonstrated behavior differences between the sexes may include direct or indirect neural influences. Sex differences in neural functions and sexual mechanisms are apparent quite early. Girls 3 to 6 days of age, for example, have a skin conductance—used as a measure of autonomic activity—significantly higher than males. As neonates, girls never remain in regular deep sleep without occasional short, irregular startle movements. Neonatal boys, on the other hand, show comparatively long periods of restful sleep and periods of repeated rhythmic startle movements. The rapid body movements seen more often prenatally in boys than in girls persist into the neonatal period.

The cerebellum, responsible for muscle coordination and balance, develops differently in boys and girls. In girls, during the first five postnatal months, the cerebellum increases in size and weight about 100 percent, whereas during the same period the increase is only about 60 percent in boys. The differences between the sexes begin to level off after the first year. While the total brain weight is greater in boys, the cerebellum of girls remains relatively larger. This relative size has been related to greater coordination, grace and delicacy in feminine motility.

An extensive series of studies which, due to their clarity and implications will probably become classic, are appropriately reported here. Freedman and Freedman (1974) observed Chinese-American (C-A) and European-American (E-A) infants while in a Hawaiian hospital nursery. The babies were observed for many categories of behavior: temperament, sensory development, autonomic and central nervous system maturity, motor development, social interest and response. A multivariate analysis of variance indicated that, while there was considerable overlap in range on all scales between the C-A and E-A infants, the two groups were decidedly and significantly different (p=.008). To cite two examples: (1) the typical supine E-A infant immediately struggled to remove a cloth placed firmly over his face; to the same stimulus, the C-A infant typically lay impassively; and (2) when placed in a prone position, the C-A infant lay as placed with face flat against the bedding whereas the E-A infant vigorously turned his face or lifted his head (there was no difference in *ability* to move the head between the groups). These measures indicate inherent (genetic) differences between the groups.

[11]This is not to say that this must similarly hold true for the future; only that this has been so for the past and forms a basis for predictions.

These investigators summarized their work by concluding that the two groups generally differed at birth in items which might be considered in the category of temperament. "The Chinese-American [infants] tended to be less changeable, less perturbable, tended to habituate more readily, and tended to calm themselves or to be consoled more readily when upset." Other studies show these differences seem to characterize the groups at all later ages as well.

One might consider that these differences are due to other than genetic causes, e.g., nutrition or maternal temperament during gestation (embryonic environment). This is an unlikely explanation, however. On the one hand, all babies were selected from middle or higher socioeconomic class mothers with good diets. On the other hand, Navajo neonates in Arizona, studied by these same investigators, have essentially the same basic genetic stock as the Cantonese Chinese and show the same behavioral contrast with E-A infants. These behavioral dispositions at birth seem to persist throughout life and set the biases with which the individual will interact with his world.

Sexually dichotomous behaviors in all cultures become increasingly apparent throughout childhood so that between birth and puberty qualitative as well as quantitative pattern differences begin to manifest themselves. These reflect a basic sexual organization which is constitutionally biased. For example, the typical sex-related behaviors mentioned above hold for normal children, but girls subjected to androgenic influences during gestation, either from a malfunctioning adrenal or due to iatrogenic involvement, in comparison with normally developing girls and despite typical female unbringing, routinely show "tomboy" behavior in gross motor and muscular activity, and demonstrate choice preference for boys' toys and games, together with a lack of interest in typically feminine pursuits such as infant care, playing house and being a homemaker in adulthood. On the other hand, males or females who are deprived of androgenic stimulation or exposed to excessive estrogens during gestation or whose tissues cannot respond to androgens, develop with feminoid behavioral traits regardless of how they are reared.

An extreme example in the other direction is seen with XY individuals who, due to a genetic trait, cannot respond to testosterone, crucial for normal male differentiation and development. These so-called "testicular females" or "androgen-insensitive" males display behavior traits which might be considered "hyper-female" despite typical female upbringing. These females almost invariably want children, a home life rather than careers, and when adopting children lavish them with attention and "mothering." Without the ability to react to androgens they seem to have significantly few so-called male traits. Hermaphroditic and pseudo-hermaphroditic individuals whose rearing may be either male or female due to ambiguous genitalia and who adjust to the sex of assignment do so because associated with the condition is an accompanying biological flexibility unavailable to normal individuals (Diamond, 1968).

These social findings are predictable due to the biological inheritance of these individuals. In the normal population, of course, females with a typical upbringing may develop as "tomboys" and males may develop in a very passive effeminate mode; however, these occurrences are not abnormal and would not necessarily be predictable. The upbringing would be strongly effective in molding behavior in those children individuated to the respective patterns. That biology is crucially involved is apparent from the findings that, despite the aberrant hormone intervention, an androgenized female never is as fully masculinized as a male can be. Both genes and endocrines are mutually and interactionally involved with the environment, but the environment must work within the confines of biology.

While constitutional diasthetic biases exist, an individual's behavior is modifiable by experience and environment. In a crude analogy: biology sets the sails and rudder, experience determines the direction and strength of the wind and tides. In normal development, positive reinforcement (reward) is evoked in the culture by the display of behaviors which are sex- (genital) appropriate, whereas those that are inappropriate either are not rewarded or are negatively reinforced. In all individuals, this conditioning process helps modify and shape behavior and, in complicated patterns such as the establishment and maintenance of social dominance or coitus, may even be necessary. There is no evidence, however, that such conditioning can completely structure behaviors such as are here discussed. In fact, by definition, learning is a modification of behavior rather than an initiation of original patterns. On the other hand, there are many clinical cases in which individuals are reared in a sex counter to their composite biology and yet, despite the social situation, the child strongly manifests his or her biological sex (Diamond, 1965). The conditioning processes hypothetically can be considered as evoking the neural circuitry related to the basic male and female patterns. The reward value of different reinforcements may, in its own way, be diasthetically organized by prior induction. For example, conditioning can strongly influence preferred games and activities, erotic situations, and partner types, but the greater male tendency and response to be aggressive and exploratory and the female tendency and preference to play in small groups, be nonaggressive and stay close to home is evolutionarily consistent. The environmental influences and upbringing must contend with these facts but can modify these patterns.

This does not mean that males and females cannot biologically be disposed other than as typically presented. It does mean, however, that when gender atypical behavior is seen, it might represent either an atypical biological development or a significantly strong experiential influence. Within certain constitutional diasthetic limits, individuals can be conditioned in any direction, but there may be a price to be paid if these limits are approached in a heterotypic direction. The price may be in a personal individual doubt of self-correctness (in performance, identity and choice of sexual partners). There is a growing body of data that show differential growth and development between boys and girls, and it is probable that the rate and extent of the neuro-physiological—including learning potential—, as well as general somatic developmental processes, underlying sex identification and object choice also differ between the sexes and thus mold sex-related behaviors.

Consider these signs of innate neural differences associated with learning and pattern acquisition that are manifest between birth and puberty. All such neural differences could influence perception and response capabilities. Neonatally, girls and boys visually fixate differentially to different targets. At 10 to 14 weeks of age, girls learn visual responses significantly better than boys when reinforcement is auditory and not visual. On the other hand, boys learn better when given visual reinforcement. Neonatal boys and girls differ in the amount of time they will visually fixate on a target object. Innate differences in response to, and use of, various sense modalities persist, as indicated by the well-known superiority of boys and adult males in visual-spatial skills. Males are significantly better than girls in adapting to glare and light stress. Girls, on the other hand, seem to have the advantage over boys in verbal and linguistic skills.

Many studies correlate well here. Two (Kimura, 1967; Taylor, 1969) have shown that the cerebral hemispheres of boys and girls develop differently with linguistic and auditory consequences. The right hemisphere develops earlier in females and this is supposedly the hemisphere more responsible for processing language; the left hemisphere is more crucial for speech detection. Lansdell (1962), by testing adults before and after brain surgery, has shown that males and females process visual and verbal material differently and in different hemispheres. He concludes that the physiological mechanisms underlying verbal ability and artistic judgment seem to overlap in the female but reside in opposite hemispheres in the male. Related to this are psychometric findings that girls show positive correlations between their level of artistic interest and their competence on verbal tests, while boys do not. Lansdell also, as others, noted sex differences related to short-term stress after which women are more relaxed than men, and men more vigilant.

The hemispheric myelination process itself appears to differ in boys and girls. This could no doubt account for some of the functional differences seen between the sexes. In the brains of 8 4-year-old children studied, myelination was greater in girls in the left-hand area of the motor cortex than in the motor cortex on the right. The reverse was true for boys.

Boys and girls show striking developmental differences in tactile thresholds in relation to dominant and nondominant hemispheres. Girls show significantly greater sensitivity on the dominant hand at age 5, with sensitivity changing to the nondominant hand, the adult pattern, at age 6. The boys show no significant difference in tactile sensitivity between their hands until age 11 when the nondominant hand becomes tactilely more sensitive.

Other neural differences between the sexes are manifest during infancy and childhood. Neonatal girls are more sensitive to general tactile stimuli, blanket removal, and airdraft stimulation than boys (they cry more quickly to these stimuli). The sexes, even cross-culturally, regularly differ in the age at onset of smile response.

In studies of 6-month-old children, girls, significantly more often than boys, showed visual interest fixation to pictures of human faces. Girls begin to smile before boys, and they are consistently easier to provoke to smile. As they develop they show greater interest in personal contact and a greater need for approval than do boys. These traits are believed to influence as well as be molded by culture. (Girls, by their smiles, may attract more attention or vice versa.)

As adults, more men than women report erotic arousal (reinforcement?) by visual stimuli. The auditory acuity of women is significantly greater than that of men, and women, more than men, seem to be aroused by "sweet talk" and reading (talking to the eye). To paraphase an old saying, this may indicate that "the best way to a woman's heart is through her ears." (Interestingly, babies of both sexes respond preferentially to female voices—the higher pitches—than to male voices.)

Manifestation of cognitive and conative differences between boys and girls are seen in sexually different perceptual responses to Rorschach forms throughout the first 10 years of life, starting with codable verbal responses at 3½ years of age. Boys give more responses in every category, see more movement, and make more mention of urogenital structures. Their comments tend to be more complicated, detailed, involved and rambling than those of girls, who respond more concretely and concisely with global responses.

As early as 7 months of age, boys show more anger, aggression and hostility than do girls. The development of fear reactions appears to be sex-linked. Males showing an early onset of fear during the first year of life show a significantly heightened fear reaction during their second year. This relationship does not exist for girls. Girls show more affection and friendliness than do boys. These differences persist to adulthood and are generally seen cross-culturally. These different social patterns also are seen consistently among many nonhuman species, thus following an evolutionary trend.

Sexual identity and object choice. From birth, with the assignment of a name and myriad other influences, individuals are subjected to environmental-social forces conducive to a specific sexual identity and choice of objects with which to interact. Since these will generally reinforce inherent tendencies, no difficulty will normally ensue. Typically, a boy will view himself as a boy, preferentially model after a male, and choose other boys as companions; vice versa for a girl. Society will encourage this. In some individuals, however, conflict (even where it is not yet recognized as such by the individual) may start prepubertally. In such children, discomfort in the assigned sex or toward certain objects or persons will be seen. For example, a child mistakenly brought up in a malassigned sex, or the one he or she prefers less, will often begin to expose this feeling of doubt or discomfort. The biological (neuroendocrine) forces attendent to identity and object choice for such individuals may not be fully active prepubertally, however, so the strength of conviction and ambivalence will not necessarily lead to socially unacceptable levels of demonstration.

Sexual identity, as the term is used here, refers to the individual's personal and private assessment of his or her gender. Object choice, too, has a private and personal dimension. Sexual gender identity and object choice, publicly expressed in word or behavior by an individual, is comparable to his *gender role*. The gender role is stipulated by society, the identity is what the individual accepts for him or herself. In retrospect, despite the public gender role, many homosexuals and transsexuals (individuals in which sexual identity and object choices are called into question) report feelings of conflict occurring as early as 6 to 10 years of age. Among these groups will be many who, during these early years, displayed patterns more typical of members of the opposite sex than of their own. This public display is significant but not essential as a prognosticator of personal ambivalance.

Particularly revealing here are studies of female children who, during their prenatal and early postnatal life, were subject to abnormal amounts of androgenic hormones (those with the adrenogenital syndrome). These girls, significantly more often than normal girls, prefer to play with boys' toys, have an aversion to, or are indifferent to, the care of babies, engage more often in intense outdoor activities, and are ambivalent toward being a girl or expressly desire to be a boy. These girls express less interest in future marriage and more interest in a career than do normal girls (Ehrhardt, Epstein, and Money, 1968).

To be sure, in the period between birth and puberty, the environment strongly affects the sexual development of the individual. Environmental influences serve, and in fact are needed, to elicit those behavioral characters programmed and allowable biologically. For example, a potential swimmer, musician, or copulator must have the opportunity to develop his or her ability and learn ways to maximize her or his potential. The extent to which the development or learning will occur will depend on the innate capacity of the individual to perform the particular behaviors at issue, as well as the ability of the individual to learn and practice. The flexibility of the dominant and subdominant sets of neural structures, and their sexual orientation, will determine how nurture and nature interact to influence human sexuality. It is likely that individuals with various types of biological anomalies of sexual development, e.g., pseudohermaphrodites, gain from the anomaly a flexibility and range of sexual dispositions much greater than found in normal persons. This flexibility would allow for a great deal of conditionability so that, regardless of conflicts between basic genetic sex and upbringing, the individual could accept his sex of rearing. This is possibly because prenatally the genetic-endocrine influences from one sex alone do not dominate. Simultaneously, this flexibility increases the extent to which an individual, in our gender oriented society, can gain from a strong, unisexual, unambiguous heritage.

Starting early in life, certainly much before the onset of puberty, a normal individual, to a limited degree, manifests levels of behavioral sexuality appropriate and specific for a male or female. Sexual patterns, a sense of sexual identity and bias toward certain sexual object choices, and genital mechanisms gradually develop and compose what passes for the individual's *personality* and *temperament*. If these personality facets are manifest in a cultural manner appropriate to the morphological sex, all will go well. If, on the other hand, discrepancies exist the "environment" (e.g., parents or society) may become hostile, concerned or solicitous to the child and further complicate the developing process. In a hostile environment, the individual, too, may react in unpredictable ways.[12] Despite a great deal of environmental input, the sexual personality of most individuals remains fairly stable from childhood to adulthood. Allowed to develop without undue restraint, no sudden changes in personality really occur. It might be good to repeat that generalities are being discussed. A great deal of individual variation exists.

[12]Consider this example of how complicated it is to dissociate cause and effect in environmental effects on sexuality. A boy's effeminate gross body motions may be thought due to: genetic or endocrine factors, an affinity to emulate the mother, response to rejection by the father, rejection of the father by the boy, a bid for more attention from the parents or a response to over-solicitation by the father. At the same time, despite the effeminate mannerisms, the boy may develop to be quite typical in his heterosexual genital contacts and object choices and see himself as a "good" male.

Any complete discussion of sexual development should cover puberty and continue the theme through adulthood, maturity and into senescence. Sexual development is a continual process and predictable changes are seen to accompany all stages. For the present discussion, however, we will stop here, having shown how the prenatal processes are continued postnatally in a natural sequence, the early influences of induction affecting subsequent behavioral development.

As a last consideration, the following types of clinical findings are believed significant in exemplifying the power of inductive biological forces in organizing sexual identity and object choice in the face of conflicting environmental forces. Imperato-McGinley et al. (1974) report that in a small community in the Dominican Republic, due to a familial genetic-endocrine problem a large number of males were born which, at birth, appeared to be females. These males had bilateral testes as inguinal or labial masses, a labia-like scrotum, a urogenital sinus with a blind vaginal pouch, and a clitoris-like phallus. These males were raised as girls, yet:

> Psychosexual orientation (post-pubertal) is male, and this is of considerable interest, since the sex of rearing in 18 of the affected males was female. Despite the sex of rearing, the affected were able to change gender identity at the time of puberty. They consider themselves as males and have a libido directed toward the opposite sex. Thus, male sex drive appears to be endocrine related, and the sex of rearing as female appears to have a lesser role in the presence of two masculinizing events, testosterone exposure in utero and again at puberty with the development of a male phenotype.

These individuals had obviously been so induced and organized biologically as males that their rearing, from birth to puberty as females, was not able to modify their gender identity nor object choice.

Transsexuals are individuals that as a group demonstrate a similar phenomenon. Although raised in one sex, these persons feel a "mistake in nature has been made" and request surgical alterations of their body to change to the opposite sex (see Benjamin, 1966). There is usually no evidence of an aberrant upbringing in the history of these individuals to account for this conflict between assigned sex and personal gender identity. In a similar vein, most homosexuals and heterosexuals seem to have been offered similar developmental environments and opportunities but develop differently in their object choice.

Lastly, in addition to those mentioned earlier, several groups of medically recognized individuals exist that are notable because their sexual behavior is incongruous with their upbringing but in keeping with their genetic-endocrine heritage. Such categories include: XXY (Kleinfelter's syndrome) individuals who are phenotypic males, raised as males but usually show feminoid traits and atypically low libido; XO (Turner's syndrome) individuals who are phenotypic females, raised as females and also showing atypically low libido; and boys born to mothers who received high doses of estrogen during pregnancy which induced extreme feminine behavior patterns despite normal upbringing as boys (Yalom, Green, and Fisk, 1973).

It is postulated that all types of heterosexual, homosexual and transsexual individuals are induced and biased by such biological forces. The environment in which an individual finds himself or herself will provide exposure to ways of modifying the *sexual patterns* or *gender roles* which he or she displays so as to feel most comfortable; it will do relatively less to the biases involved in *gender identity* and *object choice*. Each individual has an innate "feel" for what is right or comfortable sexually. The experiences of rearing are believed to provide enough different ways of achieving comfort within societally acceptable bounds. Nevertheless, enough data exist to indicate that even when society does not approve of certain sexual behaviors they will be manifest. The most rigid innate biases in this regard are believed to be in the area of gender identity and object choice. Clinical attempts in the use of psychoanalytic or aversion therapy to change extreme identity (e.g., transsexualism) and object choice (e.g., homosexuality) preferences have been routinely unsuccessful.[13]

Maccoby and Jacklin (1974) provide a great service by reviewing much of the literature relative to psychosexual and sociosexual development. They ask some highly significant questions and draw important conclusions:

> Our analysis of the arguments concerning the role of modeling in sex-typing and our review of the research on selective imitation has led us to a conclusion that is very difficult to accept, namely that modeling plays a minor role in the development of sex-typed behavior. This conclusion seems to fly in the face of common sense and to conflict with many striking observations of sex-typed role playing on the part of children (p. 300).
>
> In any case, existing evidence has not revealed any consistent process of "shaping" boys and girls toward a number of behaviors that are a normal part of our sex stereotypes (p. 348.)
>
> It is reasonable then to talk about the process of sex-typed behavior—the *learning* of sex-typed behavior as a process built upon biological foundations that are sex-differentiated to some degree (p. 364.)

To interpret the findings of sexual development, they, as do others, consider the process of cognitive development as most explicitly formu-

---

[13]It would prove considerably difficult to change a normal heterosexual into anything else (e.g., a transsexual or exclusive homosexual) just by upbringing. No account of such having been done is available.

lated by Kohlberg (1966). This orientation postulates the child as organizing his or her life to conform to "cognitive organization of social-role concepts around universal physical dimensions which accounts for the existence of universals in sex-role attitudes. [The] theory then is cognitive in that it stresses the active nature of the child's thought as he organizes his role perceptions and role learnings around his basic conceptions of his body and his world (Kohlberg, 1966, pp. 82-83)." To Kohlberg's ideas, Maccoby and Jacklin add importance to direct reinforcement and imitation. I would simply say that it is likely that the genetic and endocrine forces to which this chapter points are involved in the organization of cognitive development processes, reinforcement qualities and predispositions to imitate.[14]

SUMMARY

In this chapter, I have tried to trace the early development of sexual behavior capacity during the life span of an individual. The development of biological and behavioral potentials is seen to be related and thus have ramifications strongly affecting theories which relate to childrearing and adult sexuality.

In this discussion I have introduced three concepts which I believe will prove fruitful in dealing with some of the most mystifying anomalies of development, such as the way in which individuals can apparently be inconsistent or discordant in their expression of sexuality across various parameters of consideration. The first concept emphasizes a parallel between the simultaneous development of different structures and physiological mechanisms used in sexual and reproductive activities, and different behavioral patterns which would be associated with these same processes.

Second, I consider that a single continuum does not provide an adequate model of masculine or feminine sex behavior development. In many ways both sexes develop or could develop similarity. To distinguish the sexes, however, one must consider separate criteria for male and female, and masculinity or feminity, not put them as poles on one continuum. Further, these dichotomous comparisons must be considered for reproductive functions and a minimum of four behavioral areas which comprise a basic sexual behavior profile for an individual: patterns, mechanisms, identity and object choice. The combinations and permutations of these parameters of sexuality are numerous enough to provide a broad spectrum of sexuality, especially when learning effects

[14]With further extrapolation, the genetic-endocrine bias can be considered to affect those behaviors chosen for "scripting" as the term is used by Gagnon and Simon (1973).

are added. Seemingly, this reflects an unfathomable admixture. Actually, these should be seen as indicating the extreme flexibility inherent in human sexual behavior.

Third, I have presented a concept of differing rates or susceptibilities of development among neural tissues mediating these behavioral areas and morphology, to provide a framework within which the etiology of transsexualism, homosexualism and heterosexualism can be equally considered.

Our culture now is involved with a strong concern with the societal stereotypes of gender roles and their inflexibility. The generalities of behavior and its biological basis presented in this chapter must be considered with the constant memory that the variability for each category is large, and each individual always must be judged in his or her own right. A goal for our culture might be to recognize and accept that generalities can exist simultaneously with allowable deviation from the typical. This allowance would permit each individual sufficient freedom to develop and express his or her potential in any direction, on all levels of sexuality, without attaching a negative value to any variation just because it is different. We can, however, continue to explore what factors produce these differences.

REFERENCES

*Benjamin, J. 1966. *The Transsexual Phenomenon.* New York: Julian Press.

   A classic comprehensive book which details the magnitude of the dichotomy that can exist between an individual's upbringing and his or her personal self concept. The book contains much good and practical clinical data.

Burns, R. K. 1961. Role of hormones in the differentiation of sex. In *Sex and Internal Secretions.* Edited by W. C. Young. Baltimore: Williams & Wilkins. Pp. 76-158.

   This is a very basic chapter which covers a broad range of embryonic processes in various species of animals. Recommended for those with an interest in comparative development.

Campbell, B., ed. 1972. *Sexual Selection and the Descent of Man.* Chicago: Aldine.

   Cogently expands on many themes relating sexual selection as a vital, though less often considered, factor in natural selection.

*Diamond, M. 1965. A critical evaluation of the ontogeny of human sexual behavior. *Quart. Rev. Biol.* 40:147-75.

   The first modern paper seriously to challenge and force a reversal on the strict environmentalist and learning approach to the development of human sexual behavior. This paper presents clinical and nonclinical evidence supporting a biological disposition to sexuality and counters evidence used to support the thesis that sexuality is a function primarily of upbringing.

————. 1968. Genetic-endocrine interactions and human psychosexuality. Pp. 417-43. In *Perspectives in Reproduction and Sexual Behavior*. Edited by M. Diamond.

This paper discusses human sexual development while tracing the most common clinical conditions which link biological development with sexual behavior.

°Ehrhardt, A. A.; Epstein, R.; and Money, J. 1968. Fetal androgens and female gender identity in the early-treated adrenogenital syndrome. *Johns Hopkins Med. J.* 122:160-67.

Exposure of females to androgens prenatally shown correlated with "masculine" behavior. Classic study.

°Ford, C. S., and Beach, F. A., 1951. *Patterns of Sexual Behavior*. New York: Harper & Row.

A classic for its basic information. The similarities among cultures are as fascinating as the differences.

°Freedman, D. G. 1974 *Human Infancy: An evolutionary perspective*. New York: Wiley.

A comprehensive compilation of data related to the development of the child from birth to puberty. Cross-cultural studies are presented in detail.

Gagnon, J., and Simon, W. 1973. *Sexual Conduct: The Social Sources of Human Sexuality*. Chicago: Aldine.

Reflects many popular views for the development of sex differences.

Ginsburg, B. E. 1969. Genotypic variables affecting responses to postnatal stimulation. In *Stimulation in Early Infancy*. Edited by A. Ambrose. New York: Academic Press. Pp. 73-96.

Good discussion of how the genic effects actually interact with the environment.

Hamilton, W. J.; Boyd, J. D.; and Mossman, H. W. 1945. *Human Embryology*. Cambridge, England: W. Heffer and Sons.

This is an excellent general embryology text. Particularly pertinent are the sections on determination, differentiation and organization: pp. 121-24; and the development of the urogenital system and hermaphroditism: pp. 235-60.

Heston, L. L., and Shields, J. 1968. Homosexuality in twins. *Arch. Gen. Psychiat.* 18:149-60.

Particularly good data. The discussion of the interaction of genes and environment in homosexuality is incongruous, however.

Hirsch, J. 1962. Individual differences in behavior and their genetic basis. In *Roots of Behavior: Genetics, Instinct, and Socialization in Animal Behavior*. Edited by E. L. Bliss. New York: Hoeber. Pp. 3-23.

Discusses the genetic basis for individual differences.

°Imperato-McGinley, J.; Guerrero, L.; Gautier, T.; and Peterson, R. E. 1974. Steroid 5 α-reductase deficiency in man: an inherited form of male pseudohermaphroditism. *Science* 186: 1213-15.

An extremely significant report, since the methodology and findings are presented clearly and unambiguously with implications for the present chapter.

Kallmann, F. J. 1952. Comparative twin study on the genetic aspects of male homosexuality. *J. Nerv. Ment. Dis.* 115:283-98.

Excellent classical study showing high concordance of homosexuality among monozygotic twins; low concordance among dizygotic twins. This study has engendered much controversy but no study has appeared to refute or challenge the basic findings.

Kimura, D. 1967. Functional asymmetry of the brain in dichotic listening. *Cortex* 3:163-78.

Kohlberg, L. 1966. A cognitive development analysis of children's sex role concepts and attitudes. In *The Development of Sex Differences*. Edited by E. Maccoby. Stanford University Press.

A workable hypothesis on how sex differences develop. Fills in well with a theory of neural bias.

Lansdell, H. 1962. A sex difference in effect of temporal-lobe neurosurgery on design preference. *Nature* 194:852-54.

*Maccoby, E. E., and Jacklin C. M. 1974. *The Psychology of Sex Differences*. Stanford: Stanford University Press.

A compendium of most of the research studies on psychological sex differences. Must reading.

Ounsted, C., and Taylor, D. C. 1972. The Y Chromosome Message: a point of view. In *Gender Differences: Their Ontogeny and Significance*. Edited by C. Ounsted, and D. C. Taylor. Baltimore: Williams & Wilkins. Pp. 241-62.

Presents the Y chromosome as the regulating agent for developmental processes associated with the X chromosome and other sex-linked characteristics. The book is a broad review of up-to-date findings and analysis covering the range of sexual differences found in medical data which are too often ignored in practice.

*Phoenix, C. H.; Goy, R. W.; and Resko, J. A. 1968. Psychosexual differentiation as a function of androgenic stimulation. In *Perspectives in Reproduction and Sexual Behavior*. Edited by M. Diamond. Bloomington: Indiana University Press. Pp. 33-49.

A significant paper in that it documents how prepubertal behavior patterns of sexually dichotomous non-erotic characters are influenced by prenatal endocrine effects.

Taylor, D. C. 1969. Differential rates of cerebral maturation between sexes and between hemispheres: evidence from epilepsy. *Lancet* 2:140-42.

Tiger, L. 1969. *Men in Groups*. New York: Vintage.

A comprehensive, well written review of sex differences in behavior as seen from a social evolutionary perspective.

Yalom, I. D.; Green, R.; and Fisk, N. 1973. Prenatal exposure to female hormones: Effect on psychosexual development in boys. *Arch. Gen. Psychiat.* 28:554-61.

Exposure to estrogens prenatally shown correlated with effeminate behavior.

*Young, W. C. 1965. The organization of sexual behavior by hormonal action during the prenatal and larval periods in vertebrates. In *Sex and Behavior*. Edited by F. A. Beach. New York: Wiley. Pp. 89-107.

A comprehensive initial paper presenting the wide range of evidence that in animal species, including primates, the prenatal endocrine environment is crucial for behavioral development.

*Highly recommended source

The preparation of this chapter was made possible by support from Public Health Service, National Institutes of Health grants NICHHD 05179 and NICHHD 05853, and the Ford Foundation. Mrs. Susie Anderson of the Health Instructional Resources Unit, College of Health Sciences and Social Welfare, University of Hawaii, prepared the figures.

Part of this chapter was revised while the author was Visiting Professor at the Human Development Research Unit, Park Hospital for Children, Oxford, England.

3

HUMAN HERMAPHRODITISM

JOHN MONEY

EDITORIAL PREFACE

John Money's chapter on human hermaphroditism summarizes his theory of psychosexual differentiation which stresses interaction of genetics and environment, and places strong emphasis on experience in early childhood. His general thesis is represented in the following quotation.

> Interaction, as applied to the differentiation of gender identity, can best be expressed by using the concept of a program. . . . Phyletically written parts of the program . . . exert their determining influence particularly before birth, and leave a permanent imprimatur. Even at the early stage of life, however, the phyletic program may be altered by idiosyncrasies of personal history [toxins, excess hormones etc.]. . . . Postnatally, the programing . . . becomes, by phyletic decree, a function of biographical history, especially social biography. . . . The social-biography program . . . leaves its imprimatur as surely as does the phyletic. The longterm effects of the two are equally fixed and enduring, and their different origins are not easily recognized. Aspects of human psychosexual differentiation attributable to the social-biography program are often mistakenly attributed to the phyletic program.

Here, it seems to me, is clear evidence of Money's conviction that, although hormones and other biological determinants play a major role, particularly during early stages of differentiation, psychosocial forces usually have, so to speak, the last word.

The relative importance of biological and social determinants differs in different species, so that for animals 'lower in the phyletic scale" prenatally determined behavior is relatively uninfluenced by later history, whereas the higher primates and man, especially, are more subject to postnatal biographical history. For this reason, two humans having the same hermaphroditic characteristics can differentiate opposite-sexed gender identities if they are oppositely reared from infancy, "although they share common traits of temperament or personality, presumably in consequence of their similar prenatal hormonal environment."

To expand briefly on the last point, Money's own research on girls who have been prenatally exposed to androgenic stimulation indicates that during childhood they are likely to display attitudes and actions typically called "tomboyish." However, these characteristics do not prevent differentiation of a normal feminine gender identity provided the appropriate sociosexual learning has taken place, i.e., provided the affected individual has been unequivocally assigned and reared as a girl. In fact, psychosexual feminization is possible even if the androgen stimulation continues after birth and produces outright signs of virilism. In such cases, according to Money, "the variable that holds the balance of power would seem to be the consistency of the experiences of being reared as feminine, especially in the early years."

In his discussion of changes associated with puberty, Money brings in the important, but often neglected, experience of falling in love. Evidence relating to cases of precocious puberty suggests that "the biological clocks for hormonal puberty and for falling in love are, apparently, differently set." Other sorts of prepubertal determination underlie the development of the various paraphilias discussed at length by Robert Stoller in Chapter 7. In fact, it is Money's working hypothesis that bases for behavioral normalcy, anomaly, ambiguity or incongruity of gender identity are laid down long before puberty, and that pubertal hormones "regulate the strength of libido, but not the stimulus to which libido responds." This point of view is echoed in that part of Chapter 9 which deals with the "concurrent" effects of sex hormones.

Reaching, as it does, from the phenomena of hermaphroditism in earthworms and bisexualism in fishes and birds, to transvestism and transexualism in humans, this treatment is very comprehensive on the phyletic continuum. It gains breadth in another dimension by virtue of the author's extensive firsthand experience with clinical material as well as his personal study of different human cultures.

This chapter should be compared not only with Chapters 2 and 4, but also with those dealing with homosexuality and with sexual deviations. A somewhat different, but complementary, interpretation of animal experiments on effects of prenatal hormone treatment upon adult sex behavior is given in Chapter 9.

INTRODUCTION

Hermaphroditism can be induced at will in experimental animals for the purpose of investigating the effects of genetic, hormonal and morphologic sexual dimorphism on sexual behavior. Ethical rights forbid parallel experiments in human beings. Therefore, the spontaneous occurrence of human hermaphroditism is of special value for psychologists who study sexual behavior, as also for those interested in the special human variable, verbal report.

TERMINOLOGY AND NATURE OF HERMAPHRODITISM

Nonhuman Species

Among creatures as low in the phyletic scale as the garden worm, hermaphroditism represents a condition of simultaneous bisexuality. A worm produces both eggs and sperms. However, it provides its own eggs with new genetic material by fertilizing them with sperms from another member of the species, while transferring its own sperms to fertilize the eggs of the partner. Higher in the phyletic scale, among certain fishes, hermaphroditism represents a condition of sequential bisexuality. This condition is characteristic of various species of serranids, sparids, maenids, and monopteri, and in one member of the family, poeciliidae, well-known as the Mexican swordtail (Xiphophorus helleri). Such a hermaphroditic fish spends part of its life as a female, producing eggs, and the other part as a sperm-producing male.

Still higher in the phyletic scale, among birds, bisexuality of breeding capacity does not normally occur, though occasionally the adult gonads may change their secretions, as is the case when a hen takes on the plumage and some of the behavioral traits of a cock.

At the highest level of the phyletic scale, among primates, there is neither simultaneous nor sequential hermaphroditism of reproductive capacity. The reproductive system of primates and other mammals is incapable of postnatal sex reversal of anatomy or fertility; and postnatal reversals of hormonal function are pathological and rare.

Human Beings

As ordinarily defined, hermaphroditism, or intersexuality, in human beings is a condition of prenatal origin in which embryonic and/or fetal differentiation of the reproductive system fails to reach completion as either entirely female or entirely male. In the very strictest sense, one could speak of chromosomal hermaphroditism, as in individuals with a 47,XXY chromosome count (Klinefelter's syndrome), or one of its variants, such as 48,XXXY. In such individuals, the reproductive system passes as male, except for infertility of the testes. In ordinary usage these individuals are not classified as hermaphrodites. The same is true of rare cases of chromosomal mosaicism in which the pattern is 46,XX/46,XY, and the gonads are dysgenetic—provided the external genitals are not ambiguously formed, which they may be.

Hermaphroditism means, therefore, that a baby is born with the sexual anatomy improperly differentiated. In other words, the infant is sexually unfinished. If the external genitals are involved, they look ambiguous, for an incompletely differentiated penis may be indistinguishable from an incompletely differentiated clitoris, irrespective of the baby's genetic and gonadal sex. Moreover, a genetic female may be prenatally androgenized to such a degree that the newborn girl looks like a boy with undescended testes. Conversely, a genetic male may be born with a genital appearance indistinguishable from that of a normal female.

Today the terms *hermaphroditism* and *intersexuality* are properly used interchangeably, even though some earlier writers tended to apply hermaphroditism to cases of known hormonal etiology, whether genetic or otherwise, and used intersexuality to refer to cases of unknown, but ostensible, genetic etiology. These authors contrasted "true hermaphroditism" with "pseudohermaphroditism," in the mistaken belief that only the gonads revealed the truth. Thus, a true hermaphrodite was defined as an individual possessing both ovarian and testicular tissue, either separately or in the form of ovotestis. A pseudohermaphrodite, in contrast, was defined as one having only ovarian or testicular tissue. Both true hermaphrodites and pseudohermaphrodites were thought of as showing ambiguity of the internal and/or external reproductive structures. There was no place in this scheme for the hermaphrodite with gonadal tissue that was incompletely differentiated as either male or female. In current usage, a male or a female pseudohermaphrodite is the same as, respectively, a male or a female hermaphrodite, the shorter term being preferable. Hermaphrodites with vestigial or undifferentiated ovaries or testes are said to be "gonadally dysgenetic."

CHROMOSOMAL AND GONADAL SEX

In normal differentiation of sexual morphology in the embryo and fetus, one expects that the dimorphism of the sex chromosomes will determine dimorphism of the gonads. This expectancy is reasonably fulfilled in hermaphroditism. One does not find bilateral ovaries combined with a 46,XY (i.e., male) chromosomal pattern, nor bilateral testes with a 46,XX (i.e., female) chromosomal pattern, except in controversial cases.

Female hermaphrodites characteristically possess ovaries, along with the 46,XX chromosomal pattern of the normal female. The 46,XX pattern does not, however, guarantee that two ovaries will differentiate. Thus the 46,XX pattern is the one most commonly found in true hermaphrodites who possess one or two ovotestes, or one ovary and one testis. It is also found in very rare cases with two ovaries and two testes. The same chromosomal pattern may also exist in individuals possessing dysgenetic gonads, neither gonad being clearly ovarian nor clearly testicular.

Possession of bilateral testes is not necessarily characteristic of male hermaphrodites. One of the pair may be either missing, vestigial or dysgenetic. The chromosomal pattern is usually 46,XY, as expected in a male, but chromosomal mosaicism, such as 45,X/46,XY, or some other chromosomal anomaly is sometimes found. The same anomalies of the sex chromosomes may be associated with the gonadal anomalies of true hermaphroditism and also when both gonads are dysgenetic.

GONADAL, HORMONAL AND MORPHOLOGIC SEX

In normal fetal development, sexual dimorphism of the gonads and of the sexual anatomy are parallel, i.e., both masculine or both feminine. This is not the case in hermaphroditism. The reason is that gonads do not directly dictate the developmental fate of the anlagen of the genital structures, but do so by way of the hormones they release. Errors, excesses or deficiencies of these hormones, even if they are of extragonadal origin, are critical in hermaphroditism, and are responsible for the anatomical incongruencies that constitute the hermaphroditic condition.

In normal embryonic development, the primordial gonad begins its differentiation as a testis, if that is to be its fate, after the sixth week of gestation, which is about six weeks ahead of the timing of ovarian differentiation, according to Jost. This priority of the appearance of typical testicular tissue is perhaps related to another embryologic fact, namely, that if both embryonic gonads are removed prior to the critical period when the other sexual anatomy is formed, then the embryo will proceed to differentiate as a morphologic female, regardless of genetic sex. Nature's rule, it would appear, is that if masculinization is to occur, something must be added. There are two additive principles. Both are governed by the developing testes. One is known only inferentially and is called the Mullerian-inhibiting substance, by reason of its capacity to suppress all further development of the primitive Mullerian ducts, which in the female form the uterus, fallopian tubes and upper segment of the vagina. If this substance fails in a genetic male embryo, a boy is born, with a uterus and fallopian tubes in addition to normal male internal organs. The external organs may be normally male, except for cryptorchidism.

The second additive principle is a testicular androgen, presumably testosterone, the male sex hormone. In early embryonic life, testosterone released by the testes initially has a localized influence. It promotes bilateral proliferation of the Wolffian ducts to form the internal male reproductive structures. Subsequently, testosterone influences more distant structures. Circulating in the bloodstream, it reaches the anlagen of the external sexual organs and dictates their developmental program. As a result, the genital tubercle becomes a penis rather than a clitoris. The folds of skin on either side of the genital slit wrap around the penis and fuse in the midline, forming the urethral tube and foreskin. In the female the same anlagen give rise to the bilateral minor labia and the clitoral hood. In the male, the outer swellings, on either side of the genital slit, fuse in the midline to form the scrotum, which later will receive the testes, instead of remaining in place as the bilateral labia majora of the female.

If testosterone is added to the bloodstream of a genetic female fetus during a critical period in development, the girl will be born with either a grossly enlarged clitoris or, in rare instances, with a normal-looking penis and empty scrotum. In human beings, such masculinization may occur as one aspect of the adrenogenital syndrome of female hermaphroditism, in which the source of excess androgen is the fetus's own abnormally functioning adrenocortical glands. It may occur also if the mother has a male-hormone-producing tumor while pregnant, or if she should be given a now-obsolete, synthetic, pregnancy-saving hormone that in some rare instances masculinized the daughter fetus (progestin-induced hermaphroditism).

The obverse of masculinization of the external genitalia in the genetic female is failure of masculinization of the genetic male. Such failure has been known to occur in human beings as the result of a genetically induced metabolic error (17α-hydroxylase deficiency) which prohibits the normal synthesis of hormonal steroids, in particular androgen, by the testes or adrenal cortices. Affected babies rarely survive. External demasculinization of the genitalia is total also in the testicular feminizing syndrome of androgen insensitivity. Here, the fault lies not in the testes, but in a genetically transmitted defect that prohibits the uptake of androgen by target organs at the cellular level. Affected males are born looking like females.

The androgen-insensitivity syndrome may occur in partial form, so that a genetic male baby is born with external genitalia incompletely masculinzed and ambiguous in appearance. It is more common, however, that such ambiguity, whereby the phallus cannot be distinguished upon inspection as either an enlarged clitoris or an imperfectly formed penis lacking fusion of the urethral tube, is the end result not of androgen insensitivity, but of failure of the fetal testes to produce sufficient androgen at the critical period of external genital differentiation.

The ambiguity of the external genital appearance, which is the rule in true hermaphroditism, may represent the end product of rivalry between masculinizing and feminizing tendencies, i.e., too much androgen to permit perfect feminization, but not enough to induce perfect masculinization.

Fetal Hormonal Sex, the Nervous System and Behavior

Normal differentiation of genital morphology entails a dimorphic sex difference in the arrangement of the peripheral nerves of sex which, in turn, entails some degree of dimorphism in the representation of the periphery in the structures and pathways of the brain.

The concept of sexual dimorphism in the central nervous system was neglected until it was brought into focus by the contemporary surge of research on the influence of prenatal hormones, by way of the brain, on subsequent dimorphism of sexual behavior in laboratory animals. This surge of research was initated largely by Young, partly in response to early clinical studies on human hermaphroditism. These studies had shown that individuals of the same hermaphroditic diagnosis would, if reared oppositely, differentiate a gender identity in agreement with their rearing irrespective of chromosomal, gonadal, or hormonal sex, and even perhaps, of uncorrected morphologic appearance.

Investigation of human hermaphroditism has, meanwhile, benefited from new experimental findings on animals, which suggest that, during a critical few days of brain development, the prenatal hormonal environment does exercise a determining influence on neural pathways that subsequently will mediate sexually dimorphic behavior. In human beings, the pathways have not yet been anatomically identified. The lower an animal is in the phyletic scale, the more likely is its prenatally determined behavior to be stereotyped and uninfluenced by later history. The higher primates, and man especially, are more subject to the influence of postnatal biographical history. Hence, humans of the same hermaphroditic diagnosis who have been oppositely reared, differentiate opposite-sexed gender identities postnatally, although they share common traits of temperament or personality, presumably in consequence of their similar prenatal hormonal environment. These shared traits are generally classified as sexually dimorphic. They are not, however, exclusively the property of either sex. They may be incorporated into either a male or a female gender identity pattern, if not in conformity with the cultural norm, then as a culturally acceptable variant of it.

Illustrations of the general principle can be found in both male and female hermaphroditism. In the case of female hermaphroditism, one assumes that the excess of male hormone which brings about masculinization of the external genitals will be present in sufficient quantity at the critical developmental period to influence the brain. To establish a relationship between prenatal hormonal masculinizing influence and subsequent behavioral traits, the preferred cases are those in which hormonal masculinization ceases at birth. This condition is met in progestin-induced hermaphroditism, since the masculinizing agent was synthetic progestin administered to the mother. It also is met in adrenogenital hermaphroditism, provided that from birth onward the excess of adrenocortical androgen is kept suppressed by cortisone therapy.

In either syndrome, it is more likely that the baby will be assigned and reared as a girl than as a boy, though the opposite case does sometimes occur. Those reared as girls are more instructive for present purposes, since the possible sequelae of prenatal hormonal masculinization on behavior are not confounded with the effects of social masculinization.

It is a handicap in the study of sexually dimorphic behavior that, for all the millennia that men and women have existed, no one yet has an exhaustive and definitive list of what kinds of behavior should be included. Today's information is not, therefore, final or absolute. With the safeguard of the proviso, one may sum up current findings by saying that genetic females masculinized in utero and reared as girls have a high chance of being tomboys in their behavior. The elements of tomboyism are as follows.

(1) The ratio of athletic to sedentary energy expenditure is weighted in favor of vigorous activity, especially outdoors. Tomboyish girls like to join with boys in outdoor sports, specifically in ball games. Groups of girls do not offer equivalent alternatives, nor do their toys. Tomboyish girls prefer the toys that boys usually play with.

(2) Self-assertiveness in competition for position in the dominance hierarchy of childhood is strong enough to permit successful rivalry with boys. Tomboyish girls do not, however, usually compete for top-echelon dominance among boys, possibly because their acceptance among boys is conditional on their not doing so. Rivalry for dominance may require fighting, but aggressiveness is not a primary trait of tomboyism. In fact, aggressiveness per se is probably not a primary trait of boyishness either, except as a shibboleth of shoddy popular psychology and the news media. Tomboyish girls are relatively indifferent to establishing a dominance position in the hierarchy of girlhood, possibly because they are not sufficiently interested in all the activities of other girls. They are more likely to establish a position of leadership among younger children who follow them as hero worshippers.

(3) Self-adornment is spurned in favor of functionalism and utility in clothing, hairstyle, jewelry and cosmetics. Tomboyish girls generally prefer slacks and shorts to frills and furbelows, though they do not have an aversion to dressing up for special occasions. Their preferred cosmetic is perfume.

(4) Rehearsal of maternalism in the form of childhood dollplay is negligible. Dolls get relegated to permanent storage. Later in childhood, there is no great enthusiasm for babysitting or any caretaker activities with small children. The prospect of motherhood is not ruled out, but is viewed in a perfunctory way as something to be postponed rather than hastened. The preference, in anticipation, is for one or two children, not a large family.

(5) Romance and marriage are given second place to achievement and career. Priority of career over marriage, preferably combining both, is already evident in the fantasies and expectancies of childhood. The tomboyish girl reaches the boyfriend stage in adolescence later than most of her compeers. Priority assigned to career is typically based on high achievement in school and on high IQ. There is some unconfirmed evidence to suggest that an abnormally elevated prenatal androgen level, whether in genetic male or females, enhances IQ. Once sexual life begins,

there is no evidence of lack of erotic response—rather, it is the other way around. There is no special likelihood of lesbianism, though bisexualism is a possibility.

(6) In adulthood, according to preliminary evidence, responsiveness to the visual (or narrative) erotic image may resemble that of men rather than women. That is to say, the viewer objectifies the opposite-sexed figure in the picture as a sexual partner, as men typically do. Men objectify the female figure. Tomboyish women objectify the male figure. Ordinary women less often objectify. They project themselves into the figure of the stimulus woman and fantasize themselves in a parallel situation, but with the romantic partner of their own desire.

Further evidence is needed to know whether the tomboyish response to erotic imagery is contingent on elevated androgen levels in adulthood, or only on a delayed prenatal androgen effect.

The same traits that make for tomboyishness in a prenatally androgenized chromosomal and gonadal female assigned and reared as a girl, will be readily assimilated into a purely boyish gender identity differentiation if the baby is assigned and reared as a boy. In the latter case, there may be special problems of adjustment for the growing child to solve with respect to phallic repair, implantation of prosthetic testes, and eventually fatherhood by means either of the sperm bank or adoption. But these problems are no different from those encountered in the genetic male hermaphrodite with a hypospadiac phallus and dystrophic, undescended gonads. The genetic male may actually be confronted with a more distressing problem if he happens to be afflicted with androgen insensitivity, a condition which does not occur in the genetic female.

For chromosomal hermaphrodites with the complete and totally feminizing form of the androgen-insensitivity syndrome, the behavioral findings are the obverse of tomboyism in chromosomal females. In such chromosomal males, however, the prenatal hormonal effect cannot be distinguished from the postnatal cultural effect, since the baby is born with female morphology and is assigned and reared as a girl. The more pertinent cases are those of a forme fruste of the androgen-insensitivity syndrome, that is, partial prenatal androgen failure with ambiguous genitals at birth, and rearing as a boy. Such cases are rare, and sufficient data have yet to be collected, but present impressions fit in well enough with the thesis that they represent the obverse of tomboyism. There is no name for the opposite of tomboyism. It is not sissyness, as ordinarily defined and understood.

EXTERNAL MORPHOLOGIC SEX AND ASSIGNED SEX

Like a runner in a relay race, the fetal sex-hormonal determinant, or precursor of gender-identity differentiation, passes on the developmental program that was handed to it successively by way of the gonads from the sex chromosomes. The new program-bearer is the morphology of the external genitals, which exercise their initial influence by way of the responses of the parent to the child.

Parents wait for nine months to see whether the mother gives birth to a boy or a girl. They feel themselves so incapable of influencing what nature ordains that it simply never occurs to them that they are also waiting for the first cue as to how to behave toward the new baby. Yet, as soon as the shape of the external genitals is perceived, it sets in motion a chain of communication: It's a daughter! It's a son! This communication itself activates a chain of sexually dimorphic responses, beginning with pink and blue, pronomial use and name choice, that will be transmitted from person to person to encompass all persons the baby ever encounters, day by day, year in and year out, from birth to death. Dimorphism of response to the new child on the basis of the shape of its sex organs is one of the most universal and pervasive aspects of human social interaction. It is so ingrained and habitual in most people, that they lose awareness of themselves as shapers of a child's gender-dimorphic behavior, and take for granted their own behavior as a no-option reaction to the signals of their child's behavior, which they assume some eternal verity has preordained to be gender-dimorphic.

Some parents are so culturally imbued with parental ideals of juridical fair play that they have a blind spot even for the fact that their behavior toward a daughter is, by certain criteria, different from that toward a son. They insist that they treat all siblings alike, and mean, by implication, that they are impartial in the distribution of rewards and punishments. A videotape would rapidly show, however, that these same parents do indeed have a dimorphism of expectancy built into their interactions with daughters as compared with sons. For other parents, a videotape is not necessary. They are more articulate observers of their own behavior, and can report ways in which they differentially treat sons and daughters.

No parents encounter a more dramatic illustration of the dimorphism of their own behavior towards sons and daughters than do parents of a hermaphroditic child whose announced sex is reassigned after the period of earliest infancy. Ideally, the clinical evaluation of a hermaphroditic baby should be exhaustive and complete at the time of birth, so that the criteria governing the sex of assignment can be properly weighted and the announcement made unequivocally once and forever.

However, this ideal is not always met, because few people are prepared ahead of time to know how to react when a baby is delivered and found to have ambiguous genitals.

All too often, a decision as to the sex of announcement is improvised. Subsequently, after a detailed evaluation, a revision of the announcement may be decided upon. If the revision is made neonatally, one speaks simply of a sex reannouncement. Later, after the baby has begun to absorb the gender dimorphism of the language unto the development of his or her sense of gender identity, one speaks not of a reannouncement, but a reassignment of sex. A reannouncement requires changes only in the behavior of other people. Reassignment requires a change in responses made by the baby. It is ill-advised to impose a sex reassignment on a child in contradiction to a gender identity already well advanced in its differentiation—which means that the age ceiling for an imposed reassignment is, in the majority of cases, around eighteen months.

For a sex reassignment, the age of eighteen months, or the few months preceding it, is quite late enough to make parents overtly cognizant of the gender difference in their behavior when they take a son to the hospital and bring home a daughter, or vice versa. This can be illustrated by one father's story of his romper-room activities with his two young children when he arrived home from work in the evenings. The younger child, a genetic male hermaphrodite with a phallus the size of a clitoris and otherwise ambiguous genitals, had been reassigned as a girl at age 15 months. The older sibling, a boy, liked a rather rowdy kind of rock-and-roll type solo dancing. The younger child liked to follow suit, but the father's impulse was to bring her close to himself, to dance as a couple. Though initially she preferred to copy her big brother, the girl soon learned to enjoy her privileged daughter role with her father.

This anecdote illustrates very well the principle of complementation in the experiences of rearing, which shape the differentiation of gender role and gender identity.[1] Traditionally, this principle has passed unrecognized in psychology, especially social psychology, and attention has been directed exclusively to the principle of identification. The fact is that children differentiate a gender and identity by way of complementation to members of the opposite sex, as well as by identification with members of the same sex.

It is prerequisite to the effective developmental manifestation of both complementation and identification that the sexes be distinguishable from one another. This is important, regardless of how great or small the amount of overlap in appearance and in behavior culturally pre-

---

[1]*Gender identity:* The sameness, unity and persistence of one's individuality as male or female (or ambivalent), in greater or lesser degree, especially as it is experienced in self-awareness and behavior; gender identity is the private experience of gender role, and gender role is the public expression of gender identity.

Gender role: Everything that a person says and does, to indicate to others or to self the degree that one is male or female or ambivalent; it includes, but is not restricted to, sexual arousal and response; gender role is the public expression of gender identity, and gender identity is the private experience of gender role.

scribed or permitted in any place or period of history. Nowadays it is a popular pastime to talk and write about the American male's loss of masculinity, thereby misinterpreting what should more accurately be interpreted simply as an accommodation of certain traditional facets of gender role, male and female, to changing times and circumstances. Nature herself supplies the basic, irreducible elements of sex difference which no culture can eradicate, at least not on a large scale. Women can menstruate, gestate and lactate, and men cannot. The secondary sexual characteristics of adulthood are reminders of this dichotomy, but the external sex organs are, of course, the primary visible evidence of the different reproductive roles of male and female.

Provided that a child grows up to know that sex differences are primarily defined by the reproductive capacity of the sex organs, and to have a positive feeling of pride in his or her own genitals and their ultimate reproductive use, then it does not much matter whether various child-care, domestic and vocational activities are or are not interchangeable between mother and father. It does not even matter if mother is a bus driver and daddy a cook. It does not even matter if the father (by adoption) is a female-to-male transexual, provided his hormonal and surgical masculinization have given him the outward appearance and voice of a man, and provided he relates to the child's mother as her lover and husband—irrespective of how they actually perform coitally.

What is difficult—and very difficult indeed—for a young child, is to have a father (or mother) who switches roles. Some cases have been recorded of a transexual father who naïvely believed that after his own reassignment he could return to his family, playing the role of aunt to his own children. In other cases, the transexual father knows that it is in his young children's best interest if he separates from them and does not burden them with his gender problem.

The parents most likely to burden their children with blurring of gender differences are transvestite fathers. Their compulsion to impersonate a woman may be so overpowering that they fail to hide it from their children. In some cases, the children may be obliged to play elaborate deceits, addressing their father in public as a woman. His impersonation may be so effective that a younger child will have no way of ascribing male sexual status to his father, in female dress, unless he realizes that the penis, though covered by the clothing, is still the final arbiter.

For all their rarity, and indeed because of it, parental transexualism and transvestism draw attention to the child's recognition of comparative sexual anatomy as a basis for the secure differentiation of his or her own gender identity. Simply seeing the nudity of his own agemates, without being aware of the changes of pubescence and the appearance of adulthood, may not be enough. There are, indeed, some inventive young children who come up with the idea that, just as breasts and pubic hair grow later, so also may a penis grow out on a girl, or drop off from a boy. Children who hold to such theories are likely to be the ones whose sense of gender identity differentiates insecurely.

Valuable as it is, knowledge of visible sexual anatomy is not sufficient. The ideal is for children to be reared to know also the reproductive roles of the sex organs, and to be able to look forward with approval to the proper use of their own, when the time is right. They then are secure in being able to distinguish between the imperative and the optional elements of gender-dimorphic behavior. Their own gender identity then becomes more securely differentiated.

The significance of a style of rearing that allows ordinary boys and girls to become acquainted, unostentatiously, with the facts of nudity and reproduction is made even more evident by its absence in the rare case of an hermaphroditic child raised in secrecy, prudery and without early corrective surgery. When physicians fail to schedule first-stage corrective genital surgery for an hermaphroditic infant, this usually signifies covert postponement of a fixed commitment to the sex of rearing because they do not feel secure in committing themselves to one decision or the other. The experts' uncertainty is rapidly conveyed to the parents, whose own equivocation is in turn covertly transmitted to the child, as contagiously as though it were rubella. Small wonder, then, that the child may reach the stage of wondering whether older people are all knaves and fools. By the laws of binary arithmetic, if one claim is wrong, then perhaps the other is correct. The dilemma of uncertainty may thus lead to a child's growing conviction that this uncertainty can be resolved only by changing to live as a member of the other sex. A child so affected may become a good candidate for sex reassignment, whether or not chromosomal and gonadal sex agree with the reassigned sex.

Other hermaphrodites whose sex assignment and anatomical status are left ambiguous, and whose ultimate surgical prognosis is not disclosed to them, may adapt to the sex of ostensible assignment and still be handicapped by a sense of shame and mortification. The only other option for the child is to swing on a boy-girl pendulum, alternating the one role with the other. This is only a theoretical option, fraught with too much cognitive dissonance to be found in the histories of hermaphrodites, except the very rare history of an hermaphrodite who qualifies secondarily as a transvestite. Most human beings cannot tolerate such a biographical inconsistency.

DIFFERENTIATION OF GENDER IDENTITY

Assignment of sex is not synonymous with the registration of sex on the birth certificate. Registration is a discrete act, whereas assignment becomes synonymous with rearing. In innumerable reaffirmations of assignment a child is daily confronted with his boyhood, or her girlhood, including the gender forms of personal reference embedded in the nouns and the pronouns of the language he or she responds to and speaks.

Gender identity does not always differentiate in conformity with registered sex. A self-evident example is that of an hermaphroditic child whose name is first registered as that of a boy and then changed to that of a girl without change of the birth certificate. If the parents are consistently unequivocal in rearing their child as a girl, then the chances are high that the child will differentiate a girl's gender identity. However, parents who neglect to change a birth certificate are thereby indicating the likelihood that they have no conviction that their child is a son instead of a daughter (especially if masculinized external genitals remain surgically uncorrected). Consequently, such parents are likely to be ambiguous in the gender-dimorphic signals and expectancies that they signal to the child. For example, if the child should show a tomboyish level of athletic energy expenditure, the parents might respond as though such behavior is an expected (and maybe dreaded) confirmation of masculinity, instead of behaving as though it is an acceptable variant of a female personality.

When a hermaphroditic child with uncorrected genital ambiguity manifests early in life the signs of differentiating an ambiguous gender identity, or one contradictory to the assigned sex, then it is probably that the child has been responding developmentally to the evidence of the ambiguous and uncorrected sex organs. The evidence of the body may be even more ambiguous in the special case of a genetic female with the surgically uncorrected and hormonally untreated adrenogenital syndrome, being raised ambiguously as a female. For this child, the body will be accelerated in pubertal development, as a male, beginning as early as the age of three. Such early virilization is due to the fact that the same excess of prenatal adrenal androgens that created the hermaphroditic sex organs continues, unchecked by cortisone therapy.

Yet, even such a premature excess of body masculinization does not inexorably preordain that a hermaphroditic child living as a girl will differentiate either an ambivalent or a masculine gender identity. The variable that holds the balance of power would seem to be the consistency of the experience of being reared as feminine, especially in the early years. The noteworthy years are those beginning with the onset of language acquisition, at around eighteen months, until between the ages of three and four. As a rule, a child upon whom is imposed a sex reassignment during this formative period does not fare well in psychosexual differentiation. Such a child may, in fact, never differentiate the appropriate new gender identity so as eventually to fall in love appropriately in it. If a change of sex is forced at a still later age, without consideration of gender-identity status, iatrogenic psychopathology is likely to result.

Further testimony to the importance of the early years in gender-identity differentiation may be found in records of young children of normal genital anatomy who manifest behavior and express desires appropriate to the opposite sex. In some, though not all, such cases, one can identify insidious ambiguity in the gender-appropriate signals transmitted from the parents to the child. The diversity of parent-child interaction in such cases, together with the fact that other siblings differ from the index case, requires one to consider the possibility that the boy who becomes an extreme sissy, or the girl who becomes an extreme Amazon do, in fact, get born into the family with some degree of prenatally determined disposition to be easily vulnerable to postnatal disorders of gender-identity differentiation.

In support of this thesis, one may take the case of boys with the XXY (Klinefelter's) syndrome. They constitute a high-risk group for psychopathology in general, including psychosexual pathology which itself includes bisexuality. By contrast, girls with 45,X (Turner's syndrome) constitute a low-risk group for homosexuality or bisexuality. The same is true of either boys or girls with physical sexual precocity.

Genetic females with a prenatal hermaphroditic history of exposure to androgens differentiate psychosexually as boys if they are assigned and reared as boys and if given congruent surgical and hormonal therapy, as indicated. However, if the same individuals were assigned as girls, but raised ambivalently, they might easily differentiate a gender identity as lesbians—more easily than girls not known to be subject to intrauterine androgens.

No one knows how many genetic females born with normal female genitals may, in fact, have been subject to prenatal androgen excess too weak to influence the external anatomy, though perhaps sufficient to influence the brain. A hitherto unsuspected example of such a prenatal influence in rats was recently reported by Lynwood G. Clemens (1974). He found that the larger the number of brothers in a litter, the greater the likelihood that the sisters would display masculine mounting behavior when hormonally primed with androgen in adulthood.

The converse of the prenatally androgenized genetic female with normal genital anatomy would be the genetic male with normal genitals but a prenatal history of androgen deficit. There is another recent discovery, by Ingeborg Ward (1972), that points in the direction of an androgen-deficit effect on the brain of genitally normal males. She exposed pregnant rats to the extreme stress of constraint under glaring light in order to test the effect on the offspring of the mother's hormonal response to stress. The result was that the male offspring grew up to have lessened testicular weight and penis length. When tested in adulthood with receptive females, they were deficient in male mating behavior. If castrated and treated with estrogen and progesterone they more readily displayed the lordosis response, typical of the female. These findings inevitably raise unanswered questions about the origins of masculine failure in some effeminate, homosexual men.

It has proved possible in animal experiments to counteract the normal influence of androgen on the fetus. Experiments by Kobayashi and Gorski at the University of California at Los Angeles demonstrated that if a pregnant animal is injected with androgen in order to have her give birth to daughters with a penis, and at the same time is injected with sleeping-pill medication (phenobarbitol or pentobarbitol), then the masculinizing influence of the exogenous androgen will be cancelled. The same cancellation effect can be achieved wtih injections of the experimental antibiotics, puromycin and actinomycin-D. In the male fetus, the influence of its own testicular androgen can be suppressed by injections of antiandrogen, e.g., cyproterone acetate, into the pregnant mother.

As far as human beings are concerned, no one yet knows the possible effects of potential prenatal influences upon the central nervous system of the fetus and the subsequent gender-dimorphic behavior of the child, boy or girl. Such influences might conceivably include food or drugs during pregnancy, the mother's own, perhaps anomalous, placental hormones, or anomalous hormones or hormone deficiency from another maternal source. These are only possibilities and, therefore, this paragraph has to be left incomplete, except by way of warning. It is premature to attribute all aspects of gender-identity to the postnatal period of gender-identity differentiation.

Nonetheless, the evidence of human hermaphroditism makes it abundantly clear that nature has ordained a major part of human gender-identity differentiation to be accomplished in the postnatal period. It takes place, as does the development of native language, when a prenatally programed disposition comes in contact with postnatal, socially programed signals. The test cases are matched pairs of hermaphrodites. These are individuals who are chromosomally, gonadally and otherwise diagnostically the same, but antithetical in sex assignment, biographical history, and gender identity. The contrast between two such young adults with respect to gender role and gender identity is complete, and the ordinary person meeting them socially or vocationally has no clues as to the remarkable contents of their medical histories.

A similar extraordinary contrast was observed when a child born as a normal male was surgically reassigned as a female, following an accidental burn in circumcision by cautery. The burn totally ablated the penis. The child is not yet postpubertal and erotically mature, so that the final word remains to be written. Meanwhile, in gender behavior, she is quite gender-different from her identical twin brother.

Gender-identity differentiation bears an instructive resemblance to the differentiation of bilingualism in the child who has two native languages.

Bilingualism is confusing for an infant if both languages are spoken to him interchangeably by all people in his linguistic environment. If this occurs, he is likely to be slower than unilingual children in mastering either language. By contrast, the child's bilingual learning is unconfused if it is clearly delineated according to the principle of one person one language, and always the same language, exclusively. Thus, a child may delineate Chinese as the language of exclusive communication with the persons at home, and English as the language of persons in the neighborhood and school. Under such conditions, the complete separateness of the persons who talk and understand only one language from those who talk and understand only the other, allows the demarcation of boundaries around what would otherwise be a chaotic confusion of sound waves. The separateness of the language models defines the separateness of the languages.

The same principle applies to the models of gender from whom a child establishes his or her own gender-identity differentiation. It is preferable if the irreducible elements of the male gender role are exhibited exclusively by males, and those of the female gender role by females. Then children learn by identification with persons of the same sex, and by complementation to persons of the opposite sex. Confusion arises when an important person, like a parent, of either sex, gives equivocal or negative signals, either of identification or of complementation, regarding the irreducible elements of either gender role. Such signals would be covert, i.e., from a mother that she despises her son's father's penis, and, therefore, her son's also; or her own capacity for pregnancy, and, therefore, her daughter's prospects of pregnancy also. Parallel messages may be transmitted covertly by a father.

Clear demarcation of the boundaries of the masculine and the feminine gender roles, as indicated above, is important to the child differentiating a gender identity, because he or she actually learns and must learn both. The parallel with bilingualism can be closer than it seems if one thinks of those bilingual children who despise the outmoded language of their immigrant elders in favor of the prestige language of their new community. These children may learn to understand the language they hear at home, but may utter never a word of it, if the parents understand what they say in the new language. The child is ashamed of the old peoples' language, and subjects it to a heavy veto of inhibition. In the brain, the parents' language is coded with a negative sign, meaning unfit for use.

For the ordinary little boy growing up, everything pertaining to the female gender role is brain-coded as negative and unfit for use. The opposite holds for little girls. In neither instance is the negatively coded system a void. It serves as a template, so to speak, of what not to do, and also as a guide of what to expect in the behavior of the opposite sex, when one's own behavior must be complemental.

The positively coded system is the one in which the individual becomes truly proficient in all minor details. The negatively coded system may never manifest itself, throughout an entire lifetime. There is always a possibility, however, that in senility, when inhibitions weaken, the old man or woman may show some traits, even erotic traits, of opposite-sexed gender identity, unthinkable in earlier years. The key in the lock of inhibition may also be turned by a brain lesion, as in the rare case of a temporal lobe epileptic focus that induces not only seizures but compulsive transvestism. Both have been known to disappear when successful temporal lobe surgery metaphorically turned the lock of inhibition into position again.

There are some children who do not differentiate the initial dualistic potential of gender identity into an exclusively monistic realization of gender identity. In rare instances, a child may have a genital deformity, hermaphroditic or otherwise, which in adulthood prevents effective copulation in agreement with the sex of ostensible assignment. Such a child may leave the door ajar, metaphorically speaking, especially in imagination, as though to guarantee an exit into a sex reassignment, should the original assignment prove utterly untenable. In a hormonal male, after puberty, the imagery of sex reassignment, either way, may appear vividly in masturbation fantasies. The hormonal female is less likely to masturbate or have erotic orgasm-dreams.

Another type of retained dualism of gender identity is that found in the adult transvestite, especially the genetic male transvestite. It is characteristic of this condition that, in the dissociative manner of Dr. Jekyll and Mr. Hyde, the two gender identities may be expressed alternately. Each of the transvestite's two personalities has its own name and its own wardrobe, male or female. The degree to which each personality will appear publicly convincing will depend, for the most part, on the extent of its experience in eliciting gender-appropriate reactions from other people, until its own responses, in turn, become habitual and artless. Of course, this usually means that the male transvestite first becomes publicly convincing as a male since this usually is the way he is required to dress. He may, nevertheless, practice cross-dressing from early boyhood, and in consequence become able, by the time of adolescence, to present himself very convincingly in the female role. It is possible for impersonation to be so effective that one is hard pressed to believe that the person to whom men feel erotically attracted in the role of "Brenda," is the same person whom women fall for as "Bob."

A full-time cross dresser may eventually achieve the goal of his lifetime's longing and cease changing back to his masculine clothes and role. Some such people have for so long felt so utterly out of place in the role congruent with their external genitals that they demand the body, as well as the clothing, of the other sex. Properly speaking, such individuals are not transvestites but transexuals. Their compelling desire is for hormonal and surgical sex reassignment so that they can live full time in the gender role for which they feel themselves always to have had the matching gender identity.

One does not as yet understand the etiology of the unresolved dualism of transvestism, or of the paradoxical resolution of transvestic dualism into transexualism. There may well be an as yet undiscovered fetal metabolic or hormonal component which induces a predisposition to ambiguity or incongruity of postnatal gender-identity differentiation. There may be a special disposition in the organization of the brain toward the acquisition of roles and their dissociation in the manner of multiple personality or fugue state. In either case, a prenatal disposition is probably in itself an insufficient cause, which needs to be augmented by postnatal social experience. In studying some, but by no means all, families, it is relatively easy to implicate familial interaction as a component factor in gender-identity maldifferentiation in one of the offspring. This same statement applies to obligative (as contrasted with facultative) homosexuality, and also to transvestism, transexualism and related psychosexual malfunctions.

GENDER IDENTITY AND PUBERTAL HORMONES

The fact that the early postnatal years are the critical ones for the establishment of gender identity is clearly revealed by the postnatal phenomena of hermaphroditic gender-identity differentiation, with and without sex reannouncement or reassignment. They are critical for the establishment of gender identity as male, female, ambiguous or incongruous. The same applies to children, particularly boys, of normal sexual anatomy in whom the beginning signs of incongruous gender identity have been observed as early as the third or fourth year.

It is highly probable that these early years are a critical time for laying down the precursors of the paraphilias, though hermaphroditism, per se, does not help shed light on this particular proposition. It still is not possible to be explicit and definite as to the long-term effect on ultimate psychosexual and erotic function of erotic and erotically related experiences during the middle and later years of childhood. Clinical data can be marshaled to suit both sides of the argument. Thus, children on whom a sexual experience is imposed by an older playmate or adult may not manifest deleterious long-term effects, especially if the aftermath of the experience is wisely managed by adults. By contrast, teenagers and young adults often enough trace an aberration of their own psychosexual expression to earlier childhood exposure. An example is that of a teenaged boy who had a recurrent, obsessive fantasy of rediscovering in actual experience what had happened to him at age ten, when he was awakened by his teenaged male baby-sitter, a frotteur, rubbing his penis on the patient.

The theory of a period of complete psychosexual latency in the middle to prepubertal years of childhood is now outmoded. Given the necessary privacy, children of this age do play normally at copulation and other sexual activities, rehearsing in play what will become serious business later. At the same time, the sexes tend to segregate for most of their play, as if to keep themselves away from the contamination of the gender role of the opposite sex while consolidating their own. This is also the age for spontaneously establishing and consolidating the concepts and practices of modesty, privacy, and selective inhibition, in relationship to love and sex.

Love, in the sense of falling in love or having a love affair, typically does not occur until after the onset of hormonal puberty, though the correlation between the two is not perfect. Children whose hormonal puberty is precocious, perhaps as early as at the age of three, do not fall in love at the same early age. The earliest ages yet observed are ten for a girl and twelve for a boy. The biological clocks for hormonal puberty and for falling in love are, apparently, differently set. The difference is apparent not only in hormonal pubertal precocity, but also in its delay. In some cases of delayed hormonal puberty, falling in love can precede the onset of hormonal puberty.

Isolated precocity or delay in falling in love, relative to normal onset of hormonal puberty, is a phenomenon that needs further study. There is some preliminary evidence to suggest that an abnormally early, and perhaps intense, prepubertal love affair is a precursor or augury of adolescent psychosexual malfunction, though the age and sex of the partner may be the crucial factors.

All things considered, it seems feasible, as a working hypothesis, to say that the anlagen of behavioral normalcy, anomaly, ambiguity or incongruity of gender identity are laid down long before hormonal puberty. The same probably applies to the anlagen of partial or complete adjunctive paraphiliac complications, for example, sado-masochism or exhibitionism-voyeurism. The change that comes about with the advent of hormonal puberty is not one that determines the relationship between erotic image and erotic arousal. It determines only the degree of arousal to an image already predetermined to have some degree of arousal power. In other words, the pubertal hormones regulate the strength of libido, but not the stimulus to which libido responds.

Knowledge regarding hermaphroditism is of particular pertinence in relation to pubertal hormones and the stimulus to erotic response. Studies have been made of matched pairs of hermaphrodites, concordant for diagnosis and pubertal hormonal output, but discordant for sex of rearing. Such pairs typically are discordant for sex of erotic-stimulus arousal. Their love affairs and erotic responsiveness may emerge as concordant with the sex of rearing, even if the hormonal sex and body development of puberty have not been therapeutically corrected to agree with the sex of rearing.

This finding of compatibility between sex of rearing and postpubertal erotic stimulus image, even when pubertal hormonal sex is discordant, is all the more surprising in that estrogen given to a genetic and hormonal male has a functional castrating and antiandrogenizing effect. By contrast, androgen given to a genetic and hormonal female has a libido-enhancing effect. A likely resolution of this seeming contradiction lies in the hypothesis that androgen is the libido hormone for both men and women. It has long been known that both sexes produce both estrogen and androgen, though in different proportions. Hormonal sex differences are a matter of ratios, not absolutes. Clinical evidence of iatrogenic changes in the androgen/estrogen ratio of human males and females, as reflected in behavior, has long been familiar. Quantitative experimental evidence has recently been reported for the rhesus monkey by Herbert (1967; 1970) and Everitt and Herbert (1969; 1970). Their experiments revealed that, without ovaries and without androgen from the adrenal cortex, the rhesus female lost sexual interest in the male. At the same time, her nonodiferous vagina failed to attract his interest. Michael, with Keverne and Bonsall (1971) showed that the sexually stimulating odiferous substance is constituted of short-chain aliphatic acids.

By the time of puberty, most hermaphroditic and nonhermaphroditic humans have a gender identity, plus or minus paraphiliac complications, so firmly set that it cannot be changed. In consequence, one cannot force or dictate any adolescent hermaphrodite into a successful sex reassignment, even if such reassignment carries a guarantee of fertility. Only a hermaprodite with an ambivalent gender identity will be able to negotiate the change. By the same token, one cannot expect every individual of normal anatomy and discordant gender identity, to be susceptible to psychotherapeutic change of gender identity. If their gender identity is not ambivalent, but clearly incongruously monosexual, such persons are best helped by being rehabilitated according to the sex of their gender identity. Individuals most likely to respond to psychotherapy are those with an ambiguity problem—for example, bisexuals as compared with exclusive monosexuals (homosexual or heterosexual).

Hermaphroditic children who reach puberty and then are confronted with an incongruous hormonal sex relative to their gender identity can, in the majority of cases, be helped with hormonal therapy. In some instances gonadectomy may also be necessary. The only cases for which no successful hormonal therapy has yet been devised are those cases of genetic males who are unresponsive to androgen and are living as men. There are two types, both rare. One is a variant of the adrenogenital syndrome with 17-α hydroxylase deficiency that blocks the synthesis of steroids, including androgen. The other is the incomplete form of the testicular-feminizing, androgen-insensitivity syndrome. This involves blockage of androgen uptake at the cellular level, a defect of hereditary origin, but as yet biochemically undeciphered. If they are reared as males, affected individuals are able to maintain a masculine gender identity despite total lack of secondary sexual masculinization and defective erectile capacity of the incompletely-formed, hypospadiac micropenis. Life is not easy for them, however, as one can well imagine. It would have been their great good luck had they originally been assigned as females.

In developmental psychosexual theory, it is no longer satisfactory to utilize only the concept of psychosexual development. The preferential concept is psychosexual, or gender-identity differentiation, because the psychodevelopment of sex is a continuation of the embryodevelopment of sex. Alone among the divers functional systems of embryonic development, the reproductive system is sexually dimorphic. So, also, in subsequent behavioral and psychic development, there is sexual dimorphism.

The theory of psychosexual differentiation does not juxtapose nature versus nurture, the genetic versus the environmental, the innate versus the acquired, the biological versus the psychological, or the instinctive versus the learned. Modern genetic theory avoids these antiquated dichotomies, and postulates a genetic norm of reaction which, for its proper expression, requires phyletically prescribed environmental boundaries. If these boundaries are either too constricted or too diffuse, then the environment is lethal, and the genetic code cannot express itself, for the cells carrying it are nonviable.

The basic proposition should be not a dichotomization of genetics and environment, but their interaction. Interaction, as applied to the differentiation of gender identity, can best be expressed by using the concept of a program. There are phyletically-written parts of the program. They exert their determining influence particularly before birth, and leave a permanent imprimatur. Even at the early stage of life, however, the phyletic program may be altered by idiosyncrasies of personal history, such as the loss or gain of a chromosome during cell division, a deficiency or excess of maternal hormone, viral invasion, intrauterine trauma, nutritional deficiency or toxicity, and so forth. Other idiosyncratic modifications may be added by the biographical events of birth. All may impose their own imprimatur on the genetic program of sexual dimorphism that is normally expected on the basis of XX or XY chromosomal dimorphism.

Postnatally, the programing of psychosexual differentiation becomes, by phyletic decree, a function of biographical history, especially social biography. There is a close parallel here with the programing of language development. The social-biography program is not written independently of the phyletic program, but in conjunction with it, though on occasions there may be disjunction between the two. Once written, the social-biography program leaves its imprimatur as surely as does the phyletic. The long-term effects of the two are equally fixed and enduring, and their different origins are not easily recognized. Aspects of human psychosexual differentiation attributable to the social-biography program are often mistakenly attributed to the phyletic program.

In the history of the egg from fertilization to birth, the sequence of developmental events can be likened to a relay race. The program of sexual dimorphism is carried first by either the X or the Y sex chromosome, supplied by the male parent to pair with the X chromosome from the female parent. The XX or XY chromosomal combination will pass the program to the undifferentiated gonad, to determine its destiny as testis or ovary. Thereafter, the sex chromosomes will have no known direct influence on subsequent sexual and psychosexual differentiation.

The undifferentiated gonad differentiates and passes the program to the hormonal secretions of its own cells. More accurately, the program is passed to the secretions of the testis. In the total absence of fetal gonadal hormones, the fetus always continues to differentiate the reproductive anatomy of a female. According to present evidence, ovarian hormones are irrelevant at this early stage. Testicular hormones are imperative for the continuing differentiation of the reproductive structures of a male.

Testicular secretions, their presence or absence, or their intrusion from exogenous sources, account not only for the shape of the external genitals, but also for certain patterns of organization in the brain, especially, by inference, in the hypothalamic pathways, that will subsequently influence certain aspects of sexual behavior. Thus, the testis hormones pass on the program, dividing it between two carriers, namely, the genital morphology and that peripheral and intracranial part of the central nervous system which serves the genital morphology.

Genital morphology completes its program-bearing work by passing the program on, first to those responsible for sex assignment and raising the child as a boy or girl, and later to the child in person as he or she perceives the genital organs.

The central nervous system, insofar as prenatal hormonal factors made it sexually dimorphic, passes on its program in the form of behavioral traits which influence other people, and which traditionally and culturally are classified as predominantly boyish or girlish. Although these traits do not automatically determine the dimorphism of gender identity, they exert some influence on the ultimate pattern of gender identity, for instance in tomboyish feminine identity in girls, and its opposite in boys.

The predominant part of gender-identity differentiation receives its program by way of socal transmission from those responsible for the reconfirmation of the sex of assignment in the daily practices of rearing. Once differentiated, gender identity receives further confirmation from the hormonal changes of puberty, or, in instances of incongruous identity, lack of confirmation.

With the initiation of parenthood, the whole program is set in motion yet once again, as a new generation comes into being.

REFERENCES

Bartolos, M., and Baramke, T. A. 1967. *Medical Cytogenetics.* Baltimore: Williams & Wilkins.

Chan, S. T. T. 1970. Natural sex reversal in vertebrates. *Phil. Trans. Royal Soc. Lond.* 13, 259:59-71.

Clemens, L. G. 1974. Neurohormonal control of male sexual behavior. In *Reproductive Behavior.* Edited by W. Montagna and W. A. Sadler. New York: Plenum.

Everitt, B. J., and Herbert, J. 1969. Adrenal glands and sexual receptivity of female rhesus monkeys. *J. Endocr.* 51:575-88.

————. 1970. The maintenance of sexual receptivity by adrenal androgens in female rhesus monkeys. *J. Endrocr.* 48:xxxviii.

Federman, D. D. 1967. *Abnormal Sexual Development. A Genetic and Endocrine Approach to Differential Diagnosis.* Philadelphia: Saunders.

Gardner, L. I., ed. 1969. *Endocrine and Genetic Diseases of Childhood.* Philadelphia: Saunders.

Gorski, R. A. 1971. Gonadal hormones and the perinatal development of neuroendocrine function. In *Frontiers in Neuroendocrinology.* Edited by L. Martini and W. F. Ganong. New York: Oxford University Press.

Green, R., and Money, J., eds. 1969. *Transsexualism and Sex Reassignment.* Baltimore: Johns Hopkins University Press.

Herbert, J. 1967. The social modification of sexual and other behaviour in the rhesus monkey. In *Progress in Primatology.* Edited by D. Starck; R. Schneider; and H. J. Kuhn. Stuttgart: Gustav Fischer.

————. 1970. Hormones and reproductive behaviour in rhesus and talapoin monkeys. *J. Reprod. Fertil.* (Supplement) 11:119-40.

Jones, H. W., Jr., and Scott, W. W. 1958. *Hermaphroditism, Genital Anomalies and Related Endocrine Disorders.* Baltimore: Williams & Wilkins.

Jost, A. 1972. A new look at the mechanisms controlling sex differentiation in mammals. *Johns Hopkins Med. J.* 130:38-53.

Kobayashi, F., and Gorski, R. A. 1970. Effects of antibiotics on androgenization of the neonatal female rat. *Endrocrinology* 86:285-89.

Michael, R. P.; Keverne, E. B.; and Bonsall, R. W. 1971. Pheromones: isolation of a male sex attractant from a female primate. *Science* 172:964-66.

Money, J. 1968. *Sex Errors of the Body: Dilemmas, Education and Counseling.* Baltimore: Johns Hopkins University Press.

Money, J., and Ehrhardt, A. A. 1972. *Man and Woman, Boy and Girl: Differentiation and Dimorphism of Gender Identity from Conception to Maturity.* Baltimore: Johns Hopkins University Press.

Nielsen, J.; Sorensen, A.; Theilgaard, A.; Froland, A.; and Johnsen, S. G. 1969. A psychiatric-psychological study of 50 severely hypogonadal male patients, including 34 with Klinefelter's syndrome, 47,XXY. *Acta Jutlandica* 41, No. 3. Copenhagen, Munksgaard: Publications of the University of Aarhus.

Overzier, C., ed. 1963. *Intersexuality.* New York: Academic Press.

Ward, I. 1972. Prenatal stress feminizes and demasculinizes the behavior of males. *Science* 175:82-84.

Wilkins, L. 1965. *The Diagnosis and Treatment of Endocrine Disorders in Childhood and Adolescence.* 3d ed. Springfield, Ill.: Charles C. Thomas.

Young, W. C. ed. 1961. *Sex and Internal Secretions.* 2 vols. Baltimore: Williams & Wilkins.

4

PSYCHOLOGY OF SEX DIFFERENCES

Jerome Kagan

EDITORIAL PREFACE

Jerome Kagan's treatment of the development of psychological sex differences in infancy and childhood is especially valuable because it combines the results of many experiments with a genuinely cross-cultural point of view. Other chapters with which this one is most closely connected are Chapters 2 and 3 on sexual differentiation and Chapter 5, by William Davenport, which deals with sexuality in different human societies.

In concert with other authors, Kagan stresses the importance of interaction between biology and experience in the production of differences between men and women in all societies. Some of these differences, such as aggressiveness in males and nurturance in females, are present in so many societies as to resemble universal human traits. The existence of analogous differences in some nonhuman primates is remarked by Kagan as it has been by Milton Diamond and by John Money, and cross-species comparisons of this sort are relevant to the evolutionary perspective on human sexuality discussed in Chapter 1.

A different sort of cross-cultural comparison is revealed as Kagan calls attention to evidence suggesting a surprising degree of commonality in the "connotative understanding of *male* and *female* across the world." Even though details of male and female gender roles vary from one society to the next, the "symbolic dimensions of masculinity and femininity" may turn out to be relatively constant. As one possible explanation, Kagan suggests that the connotative resemblances may derive from similar reactions to basic biological differences between the sexes.

> The cross-cultural uniformity on these symbolic dimensions of masculinity-femininity has important implications. All individuals possess a set of basic assumptions about the essence of maleness and femaleness. Even if we could change the familial treatments to which children are exposed and could arrange the social environment so that all adults treated boys and girls equivalently, we might not totally eliminate sex differences because of the symbolic interpretations of masculinity and femininity derived from irrevocable differences in size, strength, differential anatomy, and life functions. . . . Psychological differences between the sexes are, in large measure, the result of differential socialization; nevertheless, the general agreement on the content of sex role standards across many cultures suggests that

different societies are responding in the same way to biological differences in size, bodily proportion and normal life functions. As a result, they are constructing similar sets of psychologically limiting sex role standards.

This passage is reminiscent of Diamond's suggestion that identical treatment can produce different results in different sexes, and also relates to Davenport's search for "cultural universals."

In his discussion of the effects of parental treatment on psychosexual differentiation, Kagan agrees closely with Money. Both authors stress the fact that parental attitudes are powerfully influenced by the infant's sex of assignment and by the parent's concept of gender role behavior appropriate to the assigned sex. He also presents evidence that the type of sex-related behavior which is encouraged within the family tends to generalize to other situations, so that boys assigned feminine duties at home are apt to exhibit feminine attitudes in their outside activities.

In his analysis of gender role development, Kagan employs the notion of "cognitive schema," i.e., the individual's symbolic representation of proper attributes of male and female. The schema are built up slowly, beginning at a very early age.

Each child, therefore, unconsciously but continuously looks to his culture— his parents, his siblings, his friends, his teachers and the mass media—to discover the psychological definitions of male and female.

At every step in development the child or adolescent repeatedly compares his self-image with the model he has learned, and the closer the fit the firmer and more confident is the sense of gender identity.

Success in performing the role which is perceived as appropriate is reinforcing, while failure is not. For instance, the adolescent male who successfully establishes heterosexual social relations is reinforced in his masculinity. Another male who fails to do so is not reinforced and, as a solution, he may be inclined to choose less masculine ways of behaving in various kinds of sexual or nonsexual situations.

Of special importance to our understanding of human sexuality, is Kagan's perceptive combination of observational, experimental, physiological and cross-cultural evidence pertaining to sex differences in cognitive functions. For example, the relative precocity of language development in females is considered in connection with brain maturation and with other sex differences in intellectual functions during childhood. The fact that males are more variable than females is seen as a possible explanation of the "more lawful relation between environmental experiences and psychological development" in females. Conceivably, this in turn could influence stability of sexual patterns and bear a meaningful relation to the fact that all kinds of deviation, as described by Robert Stoller in Chapter 7, are much more common in men than in women.

INTRODUCTION

An analysis of the psychology of sex differences proceeds from two simple facts. The first is that in every known society males and females differ, not only in genes, physiology, and growth patterns, but also in profile of behaviors and organization of beliefs. The second, which is less well documented, is that boys and girls are treated differently from infancy through adulthood. This information suggests two questions.

The first of these can be disposed of quickly, for it asks whether biological differences between the sexes necessarily imply different roles in Western society. On the basis of current knowledge, there is no good reason for arguing that the anatomical and physiological differences between human males and females, which are summarized in other chapters, place serious constraints on the successful assumption of the total variety of vocational and social roles available in our society. Even if we acknowledge that a small proportion of vocations—probably less than one percent—are biologically better suited to one sex (a male hod carrier is more efficient because of his heavier musculature), most jobs in Western society probably can be filled satisfactorily by adults of either sex. Hence, the ideas presented in this chapter do not have strong sociopolitical implications. Instead, the following discussion is purely an intellectual adventure.

The second, and more profound, question inquires into the nature of the interaction between biology and experience that will explain the differential psychology which has characterized men and women throughout history, and continues to do so across the contemporary cultures of the world. It is *interaction*, rather than the relative contribution of biology or experience, which is the primary issue. An analogy to the weather may be heuristic. Meteorologists want to understand how temperature and humidity interact to produce snow. They do not conceptualize their task as one in which they must determine the degree to which snow is produced by a cold temperature or high humidity. Analogously, psychological differences between the sexes are products of an intimate interaction between life events and physiology. This chapter summarizes current progress toward understanding that enigmatic process. As one tries to weave the pattern of facts into a coherent theme, it is important to remerber that interpretation of the significance of a particular pattern of behavior or a belief in one sex is completely dependent on the corresponding value for the other sex. For example, American men, in general, are sexually more aggressive than American women. At the same time, American women are more aggressive sexually than Japanese or Mexican women. Thus, when we speak of sex differences in aggression, dominance, sexuality, passivity, or dependence, we are not talking about absolute values or intensities. We are referring to the differences in that dimension for males and females in particular culture.

PSYCHOLOGICAL DIFFERENCES BETWEEN THE SEXES

Patterns of Interpersonal Behavior

In most cultures of the world, boys and men are more aggressive, engage in more dominant and power-maintaining actions, are less nurturant, and are more active initiators of sexual contact than are girls and women in the same society. Of course, there are exceptions at the individual and societal levels, but in general it remains true that females are more co-operative, more passive, socially more responsible, and more conforming to the rules of the group than are males.

A recent study of children in 6 widely different societies illustrates the cross-cultural generality of these statements. Children between 3 and 11 years of age were observed in and around their homes in one of the following 6 settings: (1) a small village in northeastern Okinawa, (2) a village of 5,000 in north central India, (3) a town in Oaxaca, Mexico, (4) hamlets in northern Luzon in the Philippines, (5) villages on the rolling hills of the western provinces of Kenya, and (6) a small town in New England. In 5 of the 6 cultures, girls helped adults and other children more often than did boys, and in all 6 groups girls offered psychological support more frequently than did boys. By contrast, the boys, in the majority of cultural settings, more often sought attention from adults and attempted to dominate other children (Whiting and Whiting, 1975).

Sex differences in cooperation and aggression are evident in very young children. In one study, 2-year-olds who were strangers to each other were brought, in same sex pairs, to a room in an apartment located in the building complex where the children resided. After both children had become adapted to the setting an attractive toy was placed between them, and the observer withdrew to see what would happen. Girls were much more trusting of each other than boys. A girl without the toy would approach her temporary playmate, and the latter usually permitted the first child to play cooperatively. The first girl reacted as if she expected that the one who possessed the prize would be gracious.

Boys were more suspicious and sometimes more aggressive. Typically, one boy would pick up the toy, while the other would stare at his face and inspect his posture, as if trying to determine if he would be permitted cooperative access to the toy. If the second boy attempted to play with the object, a fight occasionally erupted (Shapiro, 1969, unpublished). Such mutual suspicion and easy disposition to aggression in the service of protecting possessions occurred less frequently among the girls.

Such differences among children of varied ages and varied residential settings resemble the behavior of nonhuman primates. Female baboons, chimpanzees, and langurs are more likely to groom other members of the species; males are more likely to challenge other males in attempts to gain a higher position in the dominance hierarchy (Crook, 1970; Devore & Hall, 1965; Poirier, 1970). Even among some species of birds, the male is less tolerant of incursions into his behavioral space, for a male chaffinch will not tolerate another male to come within 25 centimeters of his location, while a female will tolerate an approach as close as 7 centimeters (Marler, 1956).

Dreams, Beliefs, and Attitudes

The dreams of males and females vary in ways that are consonant with the differences in behavior (Brenneis, 1970). The dreams of American college women, as contrasted with those of men, contain more familiar settings and people, more parent figures, and are generally more pleasant. The dreams of men contain more action, are less realistic, often bordering on the improbable, and portray the hero as active rather than passive. The following dream of a college-educated, politically liberal woman who favors egalitarianism among the sexes is a good example of dreams of adult women in our society (Auchincloss, 1971) for it captures the passive orientation still present in the pyschological posture of women vis-à-vis men.

> I and several other people were taking a walk through a city which was in Europe. We passed a strange antique shop, a restaurant with sheep in the window. Finally, we started up a long passage in the rocks and near a wall by the sea which became vertical and narrow and had to be climbed by hauling oneself up small, metal rings. *The men were ahead—out of sight—when I got to the top there was a sheer drop into the sea around three-fourths of the exit. The men were there to help, but there was nothing too secure to hold on to in making the last move to safety. I am terrified of heights. I felt I couldn't do it. I forced myself to wake up.* (Italics supplied.)

Sex differences in dream themes are in accord with the stereotypes of Western men and women and strengthen the assumption that behavioral differences noted in the laboratory or in the natural environment are not a thin or misleading veneer, but a reflection of profound psychological factors. The presence of more familiar people and scenes in women's dreams is usually interpreted to mean greater fear of the strange.

Female primates of some nonhuman species tend to be more fearful and less adventuresome than males. For example, in the langur of South India, females are more reluctant than males to leave familiar surroundings (Poirier, 1970); and infant female rhesus monkeys are less likely to leave the safety of proximity to their mothers than males (Jensen, Bobbitt & Gordon, 1967).

There are more subtle sex differences among children that may be limited to only a few cultures. For example, both in the United States and among rural Guatemalan Indian children there is a higher positive correlation for girls than for boys between the family's social class and the child's IQ. Similarly, duration of attention to interesting pictures—which is an index of cognitive development among 1- and 2-year-old children— is more closely related to the family's social class for girls than for boys (Kagan, 1971). Finally, quality or level of intellectual performance is more stable across time for girls than for boys. For example, if 1-year-old boys and girls are given a test for measuring IQ in infants, the correlation with a second intelligence test given when the same children have reached school age will be much higher for girls than for boys. This finding is consonant with the girls' more impressive continuity for physical growth.

The Basis for Sex Differences

How can we explain these provocative observations? Most developmental and social psychologists assume that the behavioral differences between men and women are largely the result of different standards surrounding the socially approved psychological profile for their sex. A person's belief about the culturally appropriate response for his sex is called the *sex role standard,* and it defines the physical attributes, overt behaviors, and attitudes most appropriate for each sex. The sex role standards are conveyed to the child through a process called *sex typing.*

A standard is a cognitive belief about the appropriateness of a characteristic, whether it be an attitude, an emotion, or an overt action. Children and adults try to maintain continued congruence between what they do and think, and what they believe is correct. They renounce and avoid actions and attitudes incompatible with the standard for their sex, and strive to adopt and maintain those that are compatible.

The discrimination of people into distinct conceptual categories based on sex is facilitated by the presence of a variety of clearly discriminable cues, including dress, genital anatomy, bodily form and proportion, distribution of hair, depth of voice, posture during urination, and interactive style with other people. Observation of other individuals, complemented by patterns of reward and punishment, give the child the information he requires to construct the symbolic dimensions that define the sex roles.

Among American children, boys regard height, large muscle mass, and facial and bodily hair as desirable physical characteristics, whereas girls wish to be less muscular, smaller and pretty. Physical aggression and dominance over others have been, and continue to be, primary sex-typed behaviors. This standard requires inhibition of extreme forms of physical and verbal aggression among girls and women, but grants boys and men license and, occasionally, encouragement to strike another when attacked, threatened, or dominated. The same standard influences the fantasies of children as well as the child's perception of adults.

Young boys and girls agree that the father is more aggressive, punitive, and dangerous than the mother; and this characterization of the parents is maintained, even when aggressive and nonaggressive animals are used symbolically to represent the sexes. If a 6-year-old is shown pictures of a rabbit and a tiger, he will say that the tiger is more like his father, the rabbit more like his mother (Kagan, Hosken & Watson, 1961). Nurturance, dependency, conformity, and passivity are essential elements of the female sex role standard in many societies, and females are allowed more freedom than boys and men to express these behaviors.

Mexican society is even more extreme than our own. Octavio Paz describes his conception of women in contemporary Mexico:

> The Mexican woman, quite simply, has no will of her own. Her body is asleep and only comes really alive when someone awakens her. She is an answer rather than a question, a vibrant and easily worked material that is shaped by the imagination and sensuality of the male. In other countries, women are active, attempting to attract men through the agility of their minds or the seductivity of their bodies, but the Mexican woman has a sort of hieratic calm, a tranquillity made up of both hope and contempt. . . . Instincts themselves are not dangerous; the danger lies in any personal, individual expression of them. And this brings us back to the idea of passivity: woman is never herself, whether lying stretched out or standing up straight, whether naked or fully clothed. She is an undifferentiated manifestation of life, a channel for the universal appetite. In this sense she has no desires of her own. (P. 37.)

As the foregoing quotation implies, attitudes and beliefs are part of the sex role standard. The feminine standard in our culture announces that a woman should be able to elicit sexual arousal in the male and to gratify him. The desire to be a wife and mother, and the correlated desires to give nurturance to children, affection to a love object, and the capacity for emotions, have been more clearly feminine than masculine. Bardwick (1970) has described the difference in the following words.

> Whereas masculinity is at least partially defined by success in marketplace achievements, femininity is largely defined by success in establishing and maintaining love relationships and by maternity. A woman's attractiveness is clearly instrumental in attracting men and her self-evaluation as a woman will largely depend on her sexual and maternal success. (P. 3.)

Bardwick suggests that women perceive the world in interpersonal terms and regard themselves positively to the degree that they are esteemed by those they love. Hence, women seem, at present, to be more dependent than men upon the affectionate reaction of their lovers, husbands and children.

The primary covert attributes in the sex role standards for men include a pragmatic attitude, sexual prowess and capacity, and the ability to control expression of strong emotions that signify weakness, especially fear, sorrow, and loneliness. Whether it be ancient Mesopotamia and Sumeria (Kirk, 1970), or contemporary Mexico, "manliness is judged according to one's invulnerability to enemy arms or the impacts of the outside world" (Paz, 1961, p. 31).

Group Differences in Polarization of the Sexes

Since male dominance and female passivity are central sex role standards in many societies, it is reasonable to expect that these polarized attitudes might influence other psychological processes, besides preferred posture vis-à-vis other individuals. For example, a person who believed it was improper to be assertive, inquiring or exploring might perform poorly on difficult intellectual tasks because of an ingrained passive attitude which could lead to inhibition of persistent effort and weakening of any tendency to search for novel solution strategies. Passivity breeds caution, inhibition, and defensiveness—attitudes that constrain creative intellectual work. Hence, we would expect that the magnitude of sex differences on tests requiring intellectual analysis should covary with the degree to which the culture imposes a sharp psychological distinction between the sexes.

The Temne of Sierra Leone rigidly promote a passive attitude among the females, and in that society boys and men perform better than girls and women on tests of spatial reasoning. Among the Eskimo, however, who do not enforce feminine passivity as severely as the Temne, there are no sex differences in performance on the same tests (Berry, 1966).

Similarly, Mexican society stresses passivity as an essential feminine trait much more emphatically than American society, and sex differences in performance on arithmetic and spatial tests are more striking in children living in Mexico City than in those living in Austin, Texas(Díaz-Guerrero, 1967).

Comparable differences exist in our own culture. Children of working-class parents are exposed to more polarized attitudes toward sex role standards than are middle-class children, and sex differences in behavior and intellectual performance are greater for working-class boys and girls than for those reared by middle-class parents. In general, the higher the educational level of a girl's family, the greater her involvement in what our culture regards as "masculine activities."

This liberation of the middle-class female from the dominant sex role standard of the culture affects the quality of her sexuality, for it is claimed that the women who have attended graduate school, "tend to be the most successful sexually—at least if one is willing to accept as a measure of success the relatively crude indicator of the proportion of sexual acts that culminate in orgasm. . . . In a society which still strongly encourages women to form primary allegiances to roles as wives and mothers the decision to go on to graduate school represents something of a deviant adaptation. This adaptation represents, in turn, a failure or alienation from modal female socialization pressures" (Simon & Gagnon, 1969; p. 747).

Because the early acquisition and continued operation of sex role standards are the primary mechanisms responsible for differences in the behavior and attitudes of men and women, it is important to understand *how* these standards become so strong and remain so resistant to change. We shall, therefore, examine three sets of explanatory factors that contribute to the psychological differences between the sexes. They include direct familial treatment of children, symbolic creation and assumption of sex roles, and biological factors that appear during infancy.

Differential Treatment in the Family

From the moment the infant is born its biological sex influences how it will be treated by its parents. In Western culture mothers engage in more muscular rough-and-tumble play with their sons than with their daughters. The mother tickles them, throws them in the air, rubs their tummies, and stresses their musculature with greater vigor than she does her daughter's (Moss, 1967). Mothers of daughters enter into more quiet play and engage in more face-to-face talking and imitation than mothers of sons. If a 4-month-old girl smiles or babbles the American mother is more likely to bend toward the infant and respond in the same mode than if her son should display the same action (Moss, 1967). However, comparable observations of mother-infant interaction in poor, rural Indian villages in eastern Guatemala reveal that, unlike the situation in the United States, boys receive slightly more vocal interaction from mothers than girls. Furthermore, Indian male infants are fed more than females because it is important that sons grow strong enough to make a contribution to the family economy.

Although in most cultures mothers assign the chores of cooking, feeding younger children, and gardening to girls rather than to boys, there are always differences within a culture and, occasionally, a boy in a particular family is given these feminine assignments. Ember (1970) observed children 7½ to 16 years old in a Luo community in Kenya. The boys who had been assigned feminine work in the home were less masculine in their social behavior outside the home. They were less dominant, less likely to seek attention and recognition, and more likely to nurture others in a responsible manner. Thus, even within a culture with sharp sex role differentiation, familial experiences that promote feminine behavior in the home can generalize and influence behavior outside the home. This result clearly establishes an important effect of individual experience on sex role behavior.

The American mother tends to be more concerned with potential physical harm to her daughter than to her son. If a 2-year-old girl wanders near the partly open door to the cellar, the mother is likely to warn her about the possible danger; she is less likely to warn her son in the same situation (Minton, Kagan and Levine, 1971). Similar warnings occur in different settings several times a day, seven days a week, month after month, and must have a strong influence on the child's tendencies toward fearfulness and inhibition. Moreover, the middle-class American mother is most critical of her first-born daughter, setting higher standards for her, criticizing her for a less than perfect performance, and pressuring her for success (Rothbart, 1971). As the drama of socialization unfolds, this consistent socialization pressure is accompanied by a more harmoniously orchestrated relationship between mother and first-born daughter than between mother and eldest son. If the mother makes a request, the girl usually obeys it. The boy is usually more resistant, and the relation with the mother less harmonious (Minton, Kagan, and Levine, 1970).

Differences in parental behavior toward sons and daughters are partly determined by different reactive styles displayed by the infant. For example, an active child invites more vigorous reciprocal play, whereas a quiet infant provokes gentler handling. Since infant boys generally are more active than girls, we should not expect to see identical parental practices toward young children of different sexes. Nevertheless, a more important determinant of differential treatment derives from the parent's representation of the ideal boy or girl. Each parent possesses an idea of one perfect set of traits for males and another for females. These ideals are, of course, influenced by the values of the culture. The parents' actions usually are attempts to mold the child in accord with the cultural standards.

In one investigation, mothers of children 3 or 4 year olds listened to a taped voice of a child, and some mothers were led to believe the voice was that of a boy, whereas others believed it was the voice of a girl. The parents heard the taped voice make various statements involving disobedience and requests for help, and then wrote down how they would respond to that statement if the child were their own. The mothers composed more permissive replies to what they thought were boys than to girls; fathers were more permissive with daughters than with sons (Rothbart and Maccoby, 1966).

It is likely that comparable parental practices interact either with biological traits of the child or with parental style to produce different effects in the two sexes, because boys and girls do not develop similar behaviors when treated similarly on a particular dimension.

The behavior of a large group of preschool middle-class children was observed over a 5-month period in a nursery school setting. (In general, boys were more hostile, resistant and dominant than girls.) The parents of the children were observed and interviewed at home. Following analyses of these data, the investigator assigned the parents to various "personality" types on the basis of their interaction with their children. Sons of parents rated as being highly authoritative were less hostile than sons of less authoritative parents, but the same relationship did not hold in the case of girls. In contrast, authoritativeness produced independence in girls and not in boys. But if, in addition to being authoritative, the parents were also nonconforming, then authoritativeness toward sons produced independence (Baumrind, 1971).

This finding illustrates an instance in which similar parental practices produced dissimilar effects in boys and girls. Let us now consider a different situation in which a certain type of mother reacts differently toward her infant, depending upon its sex. During their first pregnancy, mothers were interviewed and rated for degree of excitement and enthusiasm detectable in their speech—a variable reflecting emotional expressiveness. Following the birth of the baby, the mother-child interaction was observed on three separate occasions during the first three months of life. The prenatally expressive mothers who had given birth to sons were physically affectionate with them, kissing and holding them frequently. Emotionally expressive mothers of daughters tended to provide the infant with visual and auditory stimulation, as if they were trying to accelerate its intellectual development (Moss, Robson, and Pedersen, 1969).

Even this brief review of existing knowledge is persuasive of the conclusion that parents impose different patterns of treatment on sons and daughters from the very first weeks of the infant's life. It is probably impossible to find groups of boys and girls, especially in Western culture, who receive similar patterns of handling. It is not clear whether this is due solely to differential ego ideals parents hold for their children, or whether biological differences between boys and girls prevent parents from displaying identical treatment strategies toward their children. It is possible, finally, that even if we found boys and girls who received identical familial handling, the sexes would still differ because boys and girls react differently to the same experience, as a result of biological factors.

In sum, sex differences arise, in part, because each parent holds a representation of what the ideal boy or girl should be like as a young adult, and, in part as a result or the parents' theory of how to guide the child through infancy and childhood to adulthood. Since the ideals are different for the sexes, familial treatment will not be the same. Different patterns of experience gently but firmly push boys and girls in different psychological directions.

Symbolic Conceptualization of Sex Roles

Another basis for sex differences derives from the fact that man is a "symbolic" creature who continually evaluates the congruence between his profile of attributes and his understanding of the concept male and female or masculine and feminine. Certain human dimensions are so salient that they force every child to symbolize them. Two of these dimensions are age and sex. It is impossible for a culture to avoid inventing the opposing categories young versus old, male versus female, and every child knows that he or she is a member of these categories. A 6-year-old boy knows that certain beliefs, wishes, and actions are most appropriate for the category young male, or more simply, *boy*. He has no choice but to tailor his psychology to the ideal definition of that category. Humans behave as if "what is, ought to be." Each child, therefore, unconsciously but continuously looks to his culture—his parents, his siblings, his friends, his teachers and the mass media—to discover the psychological definitions of male and female.

Western society is presently changing those definitions at a rapid rate, and it is more difficult now than it was a decade earlier to formulate unambiguous psychological definitions for the sexes. The differences were clearer a decade or two ago, when a male was supposed to be able to defend himself physically, be competent at athletics, independent and autonomous, able to inhibit emotions like fear, sadness, and loneliness, and be heterosexually successful. Females were supposed to be socially skilled, noncompetitive, sexually attractive, and passive with males. Each child and young adult elaborated the definition which was presented to him and continually reinforced by his culture, his friends and parents, and by the fictional heroes promoted by schools and the media.

It is important to note that despite societal differences in standards, there is some minimal cross-cultural uniformity to the connotative understanding of *male* and *female* across the world.

In one cross-cultural study, various pairs of designs were shown to adults in 6 different cultural settings, and each individual was asked to decide which design best represented males and which females. Large objects were designated as male, small objects as female; dark colored objects were male; light colored objects were female; pointed objects were male; rounded objects were female (Osgood, 1960). In a different investigation, young American children, 5 and 6 years of age, were found to make the same set of symbolic associations (Kagan, Hosken and Watson, 1961). Moreover, femininity is more closely linked to the symbolic dimension of naturalness than is masculinity.

Why is there this mysterious agreement on the symbolic dimensions of the concepts male and female? The association of maleness with size is a natural consequence of the fact that boys and men are almost always larger than girls or women. The association of masculinity with aggression probably derives from the fact that in most cultures males are more aggressive, either in the service of soldiering, hunting, fighting, or in rough-and-tumble play during childhood. The symbols of aggression, be they harm, fear, or terror are also preferentially linked to masculinity. Hence, darkness or pointedness is usually classified as masculine, and young children who select a pointed design as "more like their father than their mother" often explain their choice by saying "That can hurt you." The preferential link between femaleness and naturalness is understandable, because birth and nursing are quintessential nautral functions, and it is easy for a child to come to the unconscious conclusion that to be female is to be closer to the experiences that nature intended.

The cross-cultural uniformity on these symbolic dimensions of masculinity-femininity has important implications. All individuals possess a set of basic assumptions about the essence of maleness and femaleness. Even if we could change the familial treatments to which children are exposed and could arrange the social environment so that all adults treated boys and girls equivalently, we might not totally eliminate sex differences, because of the symbolic interpretations of masculinity and femininity derived from irrevocable differences in size, strength, differential anatomy, and life functions.

Earlier in this chapter it was asserted that psychological differences between the sexes are, in large measure, the result of differential socialization; nevertheless, the general agreement on the content of sex role standards across many cultures suggests that different societies are responding in the same way to differences in physical qualities and normal life functions. As a result, they are constructing similar sets of sex role standards.

Sex Role Identity and Conflict

The symbolic dimensions associated with concepts of male and female lead directly to the meaning of the phrase *sex role identity*. Sex role identity is a belief concerning the degree to which a person's own biological and psychological characteristics are congruent with his or her idealized view of the concept male or female. The definition of the ideal is always influenced by the culture. A Japanese girl concludes that gentleness is an essential feminine quality; an American girl believes that physical beauty is a critical feminine trait. Once the boy's or girl's sex role identity emerges the child is vulnerable to conflict, for he or she wants to avoid the display of behaviors or acknowledge the occurrence of thoughts and feelings that are incompatible with the idealized sex role standard. Each violation weakens the integrity of the sex role identity. As indicated earlier, aggressive and independent behaviors are sex-typed in our culture and, hence, there is greater conflict over hostile feelings and aggressive behavior among women, greater conflict over passive and dependent behavior and thoughts among men.

In one study, middle-class American men and women were shown a series of black-white pictures at extremely fast but varying speeds which ranged from .01 to 1.0 seconds. Each picture showed one adult acting either aggressively or dependently toward another. The subject described what he or she saw on each of seven exposures of the pictures. The women required longer exposure times to identify the aggressive scenes and describe them accurately. The men, on the other hand, required longer exposure times before they could describe the pictures illustrating dependent behavior. Each sex had greatest difficulty interpreting action that violated its own sex role standards (Kagan and Moss, 1962).

Although quality of intellectual performance is not as clearly a sex-typed attribute as are aggression or passivity, exceptional intellectual talent in science and mathematics is regarded as more appropriate for men and is, in fact, more common among males than females. One reason for this division is that today academic excellence at these skills facilitates vocational success and is, therefore, a more essential component of a male's sex role identity. Moreover, adolescent girls are more anxious over excessive competitiveness than boys, and many females view intellectual striving as a form of hostility. Since hostility, competition and aggression violate traditional sex role standards for females, some young women inhibit intense intellectual effort in academic settings.

Horner (1968) asked college men and women to write a story in response to the following first sentence: "After first term finals, (Ann) or (John) finds himself/herself at the top of his/her medical school class." Women were much more likely than men to tell a story in which success seemed to produce anxiety. The stories contained indications that the girl was afraid of social rejection or deviation from the normal expected role for women. The following story is exemplary:

> Ann has planned for a long time to be a doctor. She has worked hard in her school work to enable her to learn better how to fulfill her dream. Now the hard work has paid off. Unfortunately, Ann suddenly no longer feels so certain that she really wants to be a doctor. She wonders if perhaps this isn't normal. . . . Ann decides not to continue with her medical work, but to continue with courses that she never allowed herself to take before, but

that have a deeper personal meaning for her.

While they are in college, many capable, professionally oriented young women change their plans, shifting to less ambitious, more traditionally feminine roles (Tangri, 1969), in order to preserve the integrity of their sex role identity. A Wellesley co-ed protested plans to admit undergraduate male students:

> How can a girl maintain her role as a woman, when she is in intense academic competition with men, especially if she is excelling? Many capable girls have faced the frustration of accusations of aggressiveness, lack of femininity and the desire to beat the boys, when they were in high school and college. (*Harvard Crimson*, 1969).

It is interesting to note that in the primary grades girls in general are much more persistent and obtain better grades than boys in all subjects, including arithmetic. In the United States, the ratio of boys to girls with reading problems ranges from 3 to 1, to 6 to 1. It seems likely that the relative superiority of girls to boys in the primary grades derives from the fact that the average American 6-year-old male perceives school as a feminine place. His introduction to the academic community is monitored by women. It is women who initiate the activities of painting and singing, and place a premium on obedience and suppression of restlessness and playful aggression. These are feminine values and the young children of both sexes see the school as a feminine environment.

This conclusion is supported by results of the following experiment. Second-grade children were taught to assign one of three different nonsense syllables to pictures illustrating masculine objects, feminine objects, and farm-related objects. After the child had learned to do this well (about 5 minutes), he or she was shown pictures of objects found in classrooms, such as a blackboard or a page of arithmetic, and asked to assign one of the nonsense words to these pictures. Both boys and girls were most likely to associate the school pictures with the nonsense word they had assigned earlier to the feminine objects (Kagan, 1964). If young boys perceive the mission of the school as feminine, they will resist complete involvement in classroom activity and, of course, will fall behind girls in academic progress. As boys approach adolescence, they begin to view acquisition of knowledge as appropriate to their sex because masculine vocational fields require intellectual skills taught by the school.

Firmness of Sex Role Identity

Real objects in the world are most often defined by their physical appearance, their functions, and the conceptual categories to which they belong. For example, a lemon is a small round citrus fruit used for flavoring. Objective definitions of the human male and female emphasize a small set of biological, and psychological characteristics, ranging from genetic constitution to hobbies. But man, unlike the lemon, defines himself to himself, and this view is not identical with the definition found in the dictionary. All men who are 5 feet 11 inches tall, have X and Y chromosomes and male genital anatomy, should, on the basis of sheer logic, regard themselves as equally masculine. However, the mind in its perversity does not trust these concrete, physical signs and insists on including psychological evidence in its final judgment. Therefore, a sex role identity as a personal belief about one's own maleness or femaleness is not any simple derivative of how masculine or feminine his or her public appearance may be.

As a child matures, he comes to recognize the sex role standards promoted by his reference group and he senses the degree to which his characteristics match those standards. If the match is close, and he desires it to be, his sex role identity will be firm. If the match is distant and he does not possess the sex role characteristics he desires, his sexual identity will be fragile.

Differences among children in firmness of sex role identity arise from several sources. First, most children believe they are more like their same sex parent than any other adult, and tend, preferentially, to imitate that parent, especially if he or she possesses desirable traits. Galen of Pergamon was acutely aware of this process.

> I cannot say how I got my nature. It was however my great fortune to have as my father a most good tempered, just, efficient, and benevolent man. My mother on the other hand was so irascible that she would sometimes bite her serving maids and she was constantly shouting at my father and quarrelling with him, worse than Xantippe with Socrates. When I saw, then, the nobility of my father's conduct side by side with the shameful passions of my mother, I made up my mind to live and cleave to the former behavior and to hate and flee from the latter. And besides this enormous difference between my parents, I observed that he was never depressed over any affliction while my mother became annoyed at the merest bagatelle. You yourself doubtless know that boys imitate what they are fond of and avoid what they do not like to see. (Brock, 1929, p. 171).

The boy whose father is skilled at tennis or golf is more likely to believe he has athletic talent than a boy whose father does not play any sports. Children are also strongly influenced by the definition of sex role identity shared by their peer group. The boy who is clumsy on the baseball field is more likely to question his sex role identity if his friends regard aptitide for baseball as an important masculine trait than if they value skill at chess.

Finally, the integrity of the sex role identity is dependent on the quality of sexual interactions in adolescence. If the adolescent is unable to establish successful heterosexual relationships he will begin to question his sex role identity. The potential for attracting the affection of a member of the opposite sex and building a satisfactory sexual union is the quintessence of the sex role standard for the adult. Each person tries to match his attributes to his notion of the ideal. If he believes he is close to his standards, his spirits are buoyed and he makes further attempts to come even closer. If he feels his behavior is far from the standard, he may turn away from it and begin to accept the role of a feminine man or a masculine woman. Movement toward homosexuality, though laden with apprehension, often frees the person from the awesome responsibilities of heterosexuality. Acceptance of a culturally inappropriate sex role reduces the anxiety that comes from recognition of serious deviation from an ideal that cannot be attained. The only possible solution is to redefine the ideal in terms of what can be mastered.

SEX DIFFERENCES IN EARLY INFANCY

Other chapters in this book deal directly with biological differences between the sexes. We shall not summarize these here but, instead, will adopt a strategy that allows us to concentrate on infancy. Let us assume that the earlier a particular profile of sex differences occurs in ontogeny, the more likely it is to be heavily influenced by biological factors. If newborn infants differ in vigor of their reflexes, we are tempted to conclude that this variation is biological in origin, either genetic or the result of pre- or perinatal conditions. We shall use this strategy in examining early sex differences. The young infant has not been influenced by symbolic conceptualization of his role; and differences in parental treatment, although present, are less extreme during the first year than later. Rather than list in almanac style all of the known sex differences, we shall organize them around a few theoretical ideas.

Susceptibility to Fear

It appears that the infant female is more prone than the male to the distress state normally called fear. If a mother and her 6- to 12-month-old infant are taken to a strange room, a girl stays near or in contact with her mother for a longer period of time than does a boy. Mitchell (1968b) studied rhesus monkeys under similar circumstances and found that infant females stayed closer to their mothers than did males during the first 90 days of life. However, the rhesus mother tended to push her son away, while restraining her daughter, and hence the sex difference in behavior of infants does not derive solely from the fact that males are more likely to wander.

Human females show distress and upset to novel stimuli at an earlier age than males, for the young female infant under 6 months is more likely than the male to cry in a strange laboratory or unusual setting (Kagan, 1971). Around 3 to 4 months of age, girls begin to inhibit active motoric responses in a strange situation; hence, if a toy is placed behind a barrier, the girl is less likely than the boy to reach for it. In one study, a mother and infant were situated behind a wire barrier and, on a signal, the mother put the infant on the opposite side. Many 1-year-old girls "froze" and began to cry. Boys were more likely to initiate some action. The boy might see a piece of lint on the floor and pick it up and examine it, or note the latch at the end of the barrier and explore it. Each of these responses diverted the boy from the source of the frustration or uncertainty. It is suggested that the action aborted his fear and prevented subsequent crying. As long as the child was involved in some action, or attending to some event, fear seemed to be held at bay (Kagan, 1971).

If boys have a natural disposition to action in situations of uncertainty, even though the action may be task-irrelevant, the activity may protect them from overwhelming fear. The female's earlier display of fear, motor inhibition, and preference to stay close to the mother is not easily interpreted as a result of differential treatment by parents, and is certainly not a product of symbolic conceptualization of one's sex role.

One possible explanation for earlier display of fear in the female begins with the fact that the female is biologically precocious to the male. Growth of bone and of myelin sheath surrounding the nerves proceeds precociously, and the infant female seems to be a physically more mature organism. If this biological precocity contributed to or was accompanied by advanced psychological functioning, a set of important corollaries would follow.

Cognitive Schemata

The first class of cognitive structures the infant develops are called *schemata*. A schema is an abstract cognitive representation of experience that allows the child to recognize past events. Before the end of the second month, the infant has already developed many schemata for objects in his life-space. If females developed these schemata sooner than males, females would possess, at an earlier age, a better delineated representation of their world. An important principle of psychological dynamics states that a discrepant stimulus (that is, an event that is slightly different from the original that produced the schema) alerts the infant and provokes him to attempt to assimilate the unfamiliar event, to resolve the uncertainty it generates.

For example, a 4-month-old baby who has schemata for his crib and room at home is brought to a different crib and room in the laboratory.

The discrepancy alerts the infant, and one of two things can happen. The infant can either assimilate the discrepancy or deal with it by withdrawal. If either of these reactions occurs, he is able to cope successfully with the unusual stimulus and the infant will relax, and may even smile. But if he cannot cope with the discrepancy, he will become afraid.

The early signs of fear displayed by the female infant in discrepant situations may reflect the fact that she has developed better delineated schemata for her life-space than the boy, and is, therefore, more likely to be alerted by new situations. The boy, who possesses less articulated schemata, may not note the discrepancy. However, the girl may be immature in her "coping mechanisms," and have no way to deal with the primitive realization that she is not in a familiar context. Hence, she begins to cry. This argument is supported by the finding that girls who were most frightened in a laboratory setting when they were 4 months old played the most creatively with toys when they were 1 year old. This predictive continuity did not emerge among the boys (Kagan, 1971).

It is possible that the infant female may pay for her early physical precocity with more frequent bouts of fear during the first year. In most young mammals, a prepotent reaction to fear is withdrawal. If the infant and child habitually withdraw in response to fear during the first year of life, a strong disposition to display withdrawal can be established. If this line of reasoning has merit, it would help explain the more frequent cautiousness and withdrawal of older females in situations that are threatening.

On the other hand, the higher frequency of female withdrawal may result from innate response tendencies favoring passive retreat under conditions of fear arousal. If rhesus males and females are raised individually in isolated chambers and later brought together, the females withdraw and show more fear, while the males are more likely to attack (Mitchell, 1968a). The actions are not the result of differential precocity of schemata, for both males and females were sub-adults at the time of testing. Hence, it is possible that the infant female is simply more strongly disposed to withdraw in response to threat. At the moment there is insufficient evidence to allow us to choose one of these hypotheses in preference to the other.

Cognitive Functions

There is a second set of potential implications that follows from the fact that females are developmentally precocious to males. With growth, the paired cerebral hemispheres become increasingly asymmetric with respect to relative dominance. Gazzaniga (1970) suggests that the newborn is like a "split-brain" animal with equal hemispheric dominance, the left hemisphere gradually gaining dominance over the right with age.

For most people, the left hemisphere is the major site of language functions. Some capacity for language comprehension is contained in the right hemisphere, but, if the left hemisphere is removed or damaged, expressive language is destroyed in a more serious way than if the right hemisphere is impaired. If the female is precocious, she might attain left-hemisphere dominance ahead of the boy due, in part, to precocious myelination of the corpus callosum and the medial surface of the temporal lobe (Gazzaniga, 1970; Lancaster, 1968). As a result, the important speech functions of the left hemisphere might develop at a faster rate among girls. This fact might explain why girls begin to speak earlier than boys.

It is, of course, possible that sex differences in neural structures *qua* neural structures mediate sex differences in early language skill. However, it is more likely to be the result of differential precocity in the attainment of left-hemisphere dominance, for the boy eventually develops a language as complex and rich as that of the girl. At 18 years of age, there are minimal sex differences in language ability. If the language functions of the left hemisphere are developing at a more rapid rate in the female, language functions should acquire preference in the processing of experience. Kimura (1967) administered dichotic listening tests to young boys and girls, in which the child simultaneously heard a different consonant or a different digit in each ear; the right ear may have heard the number 7 while the left heard the number 3. The child reported which number he heard. Because the contralateral auditory fibers are more elaborated than the ipsilateral ones, if the child reports the information fed to the right ear, we infer that the left hemisphere was more involved in its processing. At 5 years of age, girls tended to be slightly more left-hemisphere-dominant than boys. Boys caught up quickly, for by 7 years of age there were no sex differences on this test. These results support the idea that girls may acquire left-hemisphere dominance at an earlier age than boys.

An extensive longitudinal study of Caucasian children (4 to 27 months age) suggested that, during the first year, non-meaningful vocalizations —called babbling—were a better index of the state of excitability created by encounter with an interesting event among girls than boys (Kagan, 1971). To illustrate, girls were more likely to vocalize differentially to stimuli of different interest potential. Further, when speech was played to 8-month-olds through a speaker baffle, the girls, who were more attentive during the stimulus presentation (as indexed by depth of heart deceleration), were more likely to vocalize for a few seconds when the speech terminated. This relation was absent for boys. Moreover, the girl's parental social class was an excellent predictor of the amount of increase in vocalization to interesting events during the last half of the first year. The boys' social class was unrelated to changes in vocalization over the same period.

In general, the infant girls who vocalized a lot during the last half of the first year were, at 2 years of age, more active, more excitable, and more impulsive than quiet female infants. However, there was no comparable relation among the boys. In still another study, 4-month-old infants were shown an unusual 3-dimensional stimulus in the laboratory. These infants were then exposed to different versions of the original stimulus at home for a period of 3 weeks. All infants returned to the laboratory after 3 weeks and were shown the original stimulus, which was now a little different from the one they viewed at home. The girls displayed increases in vocalization to this "interesting" event; the boys did not (Super, *et al.*, 1972).

These data suggest that vocalization in the girl is a more sensitive index of intellectual excitement than it is in the boy, and this inference is in accord with the fact that vocalization scores derived from infant intelligence tests during the first year are better predictors of future intellectual functioning among preschool girls than among boys (Cameron, Livson, and Bayley, 1967; Moore, 1967).

Finally, Lansdell (1964, 1968) found a group of adult epileptic patients who had an epileptic focus in the right or the left temporal lobe. As a result of surgery, some adult patients lost part of their left temporal lobe, others the right. Language and non-language tests were administered following surgery. When the left temporal lobe was lost, verbal functioning was more seriously impaired in the women than in the men. As hinted earlier, the right hemisphere seems to be preferentially competent at mediating nonverbal tasks, especially spatial problems. Removal of the right hemisphere impaired spatial performance more seriously for men than for women. This finding is consonant with the idea of sex differences in brain functioning.

Sex Differences in Variability

In addition to their precocious development as compared with boys, girls also show less variability for biological attributes. For example, there are more extreme instances on physical dimensions among males than females, i.e., more very tall and very short men than women, more very heavy and very light men than women. This greater variability among males also holds for intelligence. There are more men with very high and very low IQs than there are women. The greater male variability is accompanied by lower long-term predictability for psychological and physical variables. Height, weight, or number of ossification centers in the wrist show higher correlations from one age to a subsequent age among females than among males. Similarly, a child's relative rank for scores on vocabulary, IQ, and achievement tests is more stable over time for girls than for boys.

It is possible that the lower variability among females contributes to this firmer intraindividual stability of traits. Lyon (1962) has hypothesized that in the female there is buffering for the two X chromosomes. One of the female's X chromosomes is partially inactivated by the other X. That is to say, one of the X chromosomes is active, the other relatively inactive. However, chance determines whether the paternal or maternal X will be the less active one in any particular cell. Thus, if there is any allele on the X chromosome that contributes to an extreme psychological deviation, it will be buffered in the female but not in the male, since he possesses only one X chromosome. Some rare blood diseases carried on the X chromosome are fatal to males, but not to females. It is possible, therefore, that biological forces that produce extreme lethargy, activity, or irritability will be buffered in the female and lead to a more lawful relation between environmental experiences and psychological development. This hypothesis forms a nice bridge to the last theme.

Sex Differences in Relation to Social Class

Many independent studies of American infants have shown that there is closer covariation between indexes of cognitive development and social class for girls than for boys. It has generally been found that correlations between social class (as measured by education and occupation), on the one hand, and attentiveness in young infants or IQ scores in children of school age on the other, are higher for girls than for boys (Werner, 1969; Hindley, 1965; Kagan, 1971). This is as true of black families as it is of white ones (Hess, et al., 1968, 1969), and the same sex difference exists in rural Guatemalan Indians in Spanish-speaking agricultural villages. How can we interpret this interesting phenomenon?

The sex differences noted in children of school age can be interpreted by assuming a stronger adoption of the family's values by girls than by boys. Since there is a major difference between less well and well-educated parents with respect to concern with intellectual mastery, we would expect greater covariation between class and cognitive achievement for girls than for boys. Although this dynamic may be operating with school-age children, it is clearly not operating during the first year of life. At this early age, it is likely that there is greater variability across social class levels in maternal reactions to daughters than to sons.

Most mothers in American culture, whether they be high school dropouts or college graduates, believe their sons will have to develop independence, responsibility, and a vocational expertise. When lower-middle-class mothers of 4-year-olds were asked to teach their children a new task, they were more achievement-oriented and adopted a more businesslike attitude toward sons than toward daughters (Hess, Shipman, Brophy, and Bear, 1968, 1969). Lower-class mothers of daughters seem to project their greater sense of impotence and inadequacy onto them, and are less likely to stimulate, encourage, or reward their daughters' simple accomplishments. Observations of lower-middle-class mothers of infants during the first 2 years affirm this suggestion. Middle-class, in contrast to lower-middle-class, mothers spend more time talking to and entertaining their daughters and chide them more often for task incompetence (Rothbart, 1971; Minton, *et al.*, 1971).

One group of mothers, whose children were 27 months of age, were observed at home with the children, and the observer recorded descriptive statements related to all mother-child interactions. For most of the variables there were no major class differences, but when a class difference in maternal behavior did emerge it was likely to involve daughters rather than sons. The most striking difference was that upper-middle-class mothers were more likely to note and criticize incompetent behavior in daughters than in sons (Minton, *et al.*, 1971). Well-educated mothers were 3 times more likely than poorly-educated ones to chide their daughters for failing to perform up to a standard held by the mother. There was no comparable class difference for sons. This class difference in treatment of boys and girls was specific to competence in performing specific tasks. Well-educated mothers were generally more tolerant than lower-class mothers toward other categories of misdemeanor in daughters.

A recent study of 5-year-olds from middle-class families that included no other children of the same sex yielded similar results (Rothbart, 1971). In contrast to younger sisters, first-born girls experienced the greatest pressure for competent performance on a series of problems. Their mothers most often reminded them of incompetent performance and were most intrusive while the child was working at the problems (Rothbart, 1971).

It is possible that mothers from a broad range of educational backgrounds are more divergent in their concern with proper behavior and intellectual development in daughters than in sons. This phenomenon would help to explain the closer relationship between maternal social class and aspects of cognitive development among the girls than among the boys.

A second factor, alluded to earlier, assumes that there is less variability in temperamental dispositions among girls than boys, and implies that there are more infant boys who are extremely irritable, alert, active, or lethargic than girls. Infants who, as a result of biological factors, are at either extreme of a particular psychological dimension, should be less influenced by specific caretaking experiences than those who are of a normative disposition. It is difficult to engage in long periods of reciprocal vocalization and joyful play with a highly mobile, extremely apathetic, or intensely irritable baby. Moreover, the mother who initiates these caretaking actions will influence the child less than one who initiates the same sequence with a less extreme child.

There is some empirical support for the notion that social experience affects girls' cognitive development in a more orderly fashion than it affects boys'. Observations of mothers and their 3-month-old infants were made in the home, and the amount of face-to-face contact between the mother and child was quantified. Soon after the home observations, the infants were brought to the laboratory and shown representations of faces and geometric stimuli and during presentation of these stimuli the infants' visual fixation time was coded. With respect to girls, there was a positive relation between the amount of face-to-face interaction with the mother at home and the infant's attentiveness to the faces among the girls, but no such relationship obtained for the boys (Moss, 1967). On the other hand, the tendency to remain quiet at one month of age and to show low irritability at 3 months correlated with attentiveness for the boys, but not for the girls. One interpretation is that specific interaction experiences with the mother exert a major influence on the attentiveness of the girl, while congenital temperament is more influential for boys (Moss and Robson, 1970). The effect of familial experience on attention is more faithfully reflected in the infant female than in the infant male. Perhaps the greater male variability in both maturational development and display of temperamental attributes is responsible for this difference.

SUMMARY

Differential physical precocity, decreased variability, symbolic representations of sex roles, different child-rearing practices, and patterns of reward offered by extrafamilial peers and adults—all of these factors interact in affecting the psychological product we see among school-age children and adults. It is neither possible nor appropriate to state how much of a girl's language precocity or non-aggressiveness is caused by biology and how much by experience.

The attractiveness of any specific question about the sexes depends upon the questioner's theoretical interest. The social psychologist asks whether the culture is strong enough to offset the influence of biological vectors and to attenuate those sex differences that normally are the partial product of the biology-experience interaction. The biologist wants to know more about the physiological mechanisms that are functionally different for the sexes and how they might lead to differential growth under identical environmental experiences. The psychiatrist wants to understand how the differing standards that comprise sex role identity make each sex selectively vulnerable to anxiety, and disposed to adopt particular defenses. The developmental psychologist is puzzled by the increasing differences between the sexes that accompany maturation, for males and females are more similar during the first week of life than they will ever be again.

Men and women in every society march to different pipers, are sensitized to different aspects of experience and gratified by different profiles of events. These differences do not preclude an egalitarian relation between the sexes and the benevolent change in Western man's prejudiced attitude toward women over the past half millenium is beautifully captured by two quotations written over four hundred years apart.

> What else is a woman but a foe to friendship, an unescapable punishment, a necessary evil, a natural temptation, a desirable calamity, a domestic danger, a delectable detriment, an evil of nature painted with fair colors. Therefore, if it be a sin to divorce her when she ought to be kept, it is indeed a necessary torture for either we commit adultery by divorcing her or we must endure daily strife. . . . The tears of a woman are a deception for they may spring from true grief or they may be a snare. When a woman thinks alone, she thinks evil. (*Malleus Maleficarum*)

Our progress is surely apparent in Goldmund's advice to Narcissus, as he lies dying in his friend's arms, "But how will you die when your time comes, Narcissus, since you have no mother? Without a mother one cannot love. Without a mother one cannot die." (Hesse, 1930.)

REFERENCES

Auchincloss, S. S. 1971. Dream content and the menstrual cycle. Honors Thesis. Harvard University.

Bardwick, J. M. 1971. *Psychology of Women*. New York: Harper & Row.

———. 1970. Psychological conflict and the reproductive system. In Bardwick, J. M.; Douvan, E.; Horner, M. S.; and Guttmann, D. *Feminine Personality and Conflict*. Belmont, California. Brooks-Cole. Pp. 3-28.

Baumrind, D. 1971. Current patterns of parental authority. *Developmental Psychology Monographs*, vol. 4, no. 1, part 2, pp. 1-103.

Berry, J. W. 1966. Temne and Eskimo perceptual skills. *Int. J. Psychol.* 1, No. 3, 207-29.

Brenneis, B. 1970. Male and female ego modalities in manifest dream content. *J. Abnormal. Psychol.* 76:434-42.

Brock, A. J. 1929. *Greek Medicine: Being Abstracts Illustrative of Medical Writers from Hippocrates to Galen*. London and Toronto. P. 171.

Cameron, J.; Livson, N.; and Bayley, M. 1967. Infant vocalizations and their relationship to mature intelligence. *Science* 157:331-33.

Crook, J. H. 1970. The sociology of primates. In *Social Behavior in Birds and Mammals*. Edited by J. H. Crook. New York: Academic Press. Pp. 103-66.

DeVore, I., and Hall, K. R. L. 1965. Baboon ecology. In *Primate Behavior*. Edited by I. DeVore. New York: Holt, Rinehart, & Winston. Pp. 20-62.

Díaz-Guerrero, R. 1967. Cross cultural studies of personality: cognitive and social class factors related to child development in Mexico and the U.S.A. Presented at the 10th Interamerican Congress of Psychology. Mexico City: F. Trillas.

Ember, C. R. 1970. Effects of feminine task assignment on the social behavior of boys. Unpublished manuscript. Harvard University.

Gazzaniga, M. S. 1970. *The Bisected Brain*. New York: Appleton-Century.

Harvard Crimson. "Must Wellesley go Co-ed to Survive?" December 16, 1969. P. 3.

Hess, R. D.; Shipman, V. C.; Brophy, J. E.; and Bear, R. M. 1968 and 1969. The cognitive environments of urban preschool children. Report to the Graduate School of Education, University of Chicago.

Hesse, H. 1930. *Narcissus and Goldmund*. New York: Farrar, Straus, & Giroux.

Hindley, C. B. 1965. Stability and change in abilities up to five years—group trends. *J. Child Psychol. Psychiatry.* 6:85-99.

Horner, M. 1968. Sex differences in achievement motivation and performance in competitive and non-competitive situations. Unpublished Ph.D. diss. University of Michigan.

Jensen, G. D.; Bobbitt, R. A.; and Gordon, B. N. 1967. The development of maternal independence in mother-infant pigtailed monkeys, *macaca nemestrina*. In *Social Communication Among Primates*. Pp. 43-53. Edited by S. A. Altmann. Chicago: University of Chicago Press.

Kagan, J. 1964. The child's sex role classification of school objects. *Child Develop.* 35:1051-56.

———. 1971. *Change and Continuity in Infancy*. New York: Wiley.

Kagan, J.; Hosken, B.; and Watson, S. 1961. The child's symbolic conceptualization of the parents. *Child Develop.* 32:265-36.

Kagan, J., and Moss, H. A. 1962. *Birth to Maturity*. New York. Wiley.

Kimura, D. 1967. Functional asymmetry of the brain in dichotic listening. *Cortex* 3:163-78.

Kirk, G. S. 1970. *Myth: Its Meaning and Functions in Ancient and Other Cultures*. Berkeley. University of California Press.

Knox, C., and Kimura, D. 1970. Cerebral processing of nonverbal sounds in boys and girls. *Neuropsychologia* 8:227-37.

Lancaster, J. B. 1968. Primate Communication Systems and the Emergence of Human Language. In *Primates*. Edited by P. C. Jay. New York: Holt, Rinehart, & Winston. Pp. 439-57.

Lansdell, H. 1964. Sex differences in hemispheric asymmetry of the human brain. *Nature* 203:550-51.

———. 1968. The use of factor scores from the Wechsler-Bellevue Scale of Intelligence in assessing patients with temporal lobe removal. *Cortex* 4:257-68.

Lucretius. *On the Nature of the Universe, Book IV, Sensation and Sex.* Translated by R. Latham. Baltimore: Penguin, 1951.

Lyon, M. F. 1962. Sex chromatin and gene action in the mammalian X-Chromosome. *Amer. J. Human Genet.* 14:135-48.

Malleus Maleficarum, translated and with an introduction, bibliography and notes by Montague Summers. London: Pushkin Press, 1951. In Veith, I. *Hysteria.* Chicago: University of Chicago Press, 1965. P. 63.

Marler, P. 1956. Studies of fighting in chaffinches (3), Proximity as a cause of aggression. *Brit. J. Animal Behav.* 4:23-30.

Minton, C. M.; Kagan, J.; and Levine, J. A. 1971. Maternal control and obedience in the two year old. *Child Development.* 42:1893-94.

Mitchell, G. 1968. Persistent behavior pathology in rhesus monkeys following early social isolation. *Folia Primat.* (a) 8:132-47.

Mitchell, G. D. 1968. Attachment differences in male and female infant monkeys. *Child Develop.* 39:611-20.

Moore, T. 1967. Language and intelligence—a longitudinal study of the first eight years. *Hum. Develop.* 10:88-106.

Moss, H. A. 1967. Sex, age and state as determinants of mother-infant interaction. *Merrill-Palmer Quarterly* 13:19-36.

Moss, H. A., and Robson, K. S. 1970. The relation between the amount of time infants spend at various states and the development of visual behavior. *Child Develop.* 41:509-17.

Moss, H. A.; Robson, K. S.; and Pedersen, F. 1969. Determinants of maternal stimulation to infant and consequences of treatment for later reactions to strangers. *Develop. Psychol.* 1:239-46.

Osgood, C. E. 1960. The cross cultural generality of visual-verbal synesthetic tendencies. *Behav. Sci.* 5:146-69.

Paz, O. 1961. *The Labyrinth of Solitude.* New York: Grove Press. Originally published by Fondo de Cultura Economica, Mexico City, 1959, under the title *El Laberinto de la Soledad.*

Poirier, F. E. 1970. The Nilgiri langur (*Presbytis johnii*) of South India. In *Primate Behavior, vol. I.* Edited by L. A. Rosenblum, New York: Academic Press. Pp. 251-383.

Robson, K. S.; Pedersen, F. A.; and Moss, H. A. 1969. Developmental observations of diadic gazing in relation to the fear of strangers and social approach behavior. *Child Develop.* 40:619-28.

Rothbart, M. K. 1971. Birth order and mother child interaction in an achievement situation. *Journal of Personality and Social Psychology.* 17:113-20.

Rothbart, M. K. and Maccoby, E. E. 1966. Parents' differential reactions to sons and daughters. *J. Personality Soc. Psychol.* 4:237-43.

Shapiro, L. 1969. A Study of Peer Group Interaction in 8 and 28 Month Old Children. Unpublished Ph.D. diss. Harvard University.

Silverman, S. 1970. *Psychological Cues in Forecasting Physical Illness.* New York: Appleton-Century.

Simon, W., and Gagnon, J. H. 1969. On psychosexual development. In *Handbook of Socialization Theory and Research.* Edited by Goslin, D.A. Pp. 733-52. Chicago: Rand McNally.

Super, C.; Kagan, J.; Morrison, F.; Haith, M.; and Weiffenbach, J. 1972. Discrepancy and attention in the five month old infant. *Genet. Psychol. Monogr.* 85:305-31.

Tangri, S. 1969. Role Innovation in Occupational Choice. Unpublished Ph.D.
    diss. University of Michigan.
Werner, E. E. 1969. Sex differences in correlations between children's IQs
    and measures of parental ability and environmental ratings. *Develop.
    Psychol.* 1:280-85.
Whiting, B. B., and Whiting, J. W. M. 1975. *Children of Six Cultures.* Cam-
    bridge, Mass.: Harvard University Press.

Preparation of this chapter was supported in part by research grant HD4299 from
NICHD, United States Public Health Service, and a grant from the Carnegie Cor-
poration of New York.

5

SEX IN CROSS-CULTURAL
PERSPECTIVE

WILLIAM H. DAVENPORT

EDITORIAL PREFACE

Instead of the trans-temporal approach used in the preceding three chapters
by Milton Diamond, John Money and Jerome Kagan, William Davenport's
method is that of cross-sectional analysis, as he compares human sexuality in
different societies around the world. A reader's first impression is one of tremendous variety, and this is desirable, because an appreciation of the differences between cultures is essential if we are to develop the perspective
necessary to understand sexuality in our own society. Eventually, of course,
we must seek evidence of uniformities and explanations for differences.

In this chapter, Davenport surveys a wealth of facts revealing intercultural
differences so numerous and broad as to make us ask if any constants lie
embedded within this confusing matrix of variety. They do exist, and Davenport provides a foundation for understanding them when he writes that in
every society the culture of sex is anchored in two directions.

> In one direction, it is moored to the potentialities and limitations of biolog-
> ical inheritance. In the other direction, it is tied to the internal logic and
> consistency of the total culture.

The potentialities and limitations of biological inheritance have been considered in earlier chapters on human development and also in the treatment
of human evolution in Chapter 1. The internal logic and consistency of human
cultures is a new concept, to be developed later in this chapter.

Before considering further the problem of intercultural constants, it will be
profitable to give closer attention to differences between cultures. Davenport
points out that the very meaning of "sexual" can vary so greatly that conduct
which is either lewd or highly erotic for one society may be totally unrelated
to sex for another. There are cultures, such as the Manus in Papua—New
Guinea and Inis Beag in rural Ireland, in which all aspects of sex are considered ugly and shameful; even marital intercourse is so degrading and sinful
that it is justifiable only in the service of procreation. At the opposite extreme,
there are other cultures in which sex and everything related to it is beautiful,
and beauty, in general, is erotically associated with sex.

The emotions usually associated with sexual arousal and gratification are not the same in all societies, and correlations that are considered aberrant in our culture may represent the norm for other peoples. For instance, among the Gusii of Kenya, sexual arousal occurs only in combination with hostility and antagonism. From girlhood, females are taught to encourage, and at the same time to frustrate, men, while boys are schooled to demand, and forcefully gain, sexual satisfaction. Normal intercourse has to take the form of ritualized rape if it is to provide mutual gratification.

Behavior patterns condemned and punished in one society are encouraged and rewarded in another. Premarital intercourse is virtually enforced by some peoples and heavily penalized by others. All adolescent males in one South Pacific society are urged to be exclusively homosexual before marriage, whereas such behavior is considered shameful and punished in other cultures.

Davenport cites many other examples of cultural diversity in sexual practices and beliefs, but he also notes that certain beliefs appear in all, or nearly all, societies, and that behavior in all cultures follows certain common patterns. Intersocietal similarities are of two kinds. First, there are formal similarities in attitudes or activities of individuals, and second, there are similarities in the relationship of sexuality to the structure and function of the society as a whole.

All peoples are convinced that sexual activity is necessary, although reasons for this conviction vary. It is also widely believed that a man's sexual needs exceed those of a woman, and this opinion persists even in cultures that grant equal sexual privilege to both sexes. All societies practice marriage in one form or another, and the institution always carries with it special sexual privileges and obligations. Marriage forms vary, but by far the most common one involves one man and one woman. Polyandry is extremely rare, and, although many societies approve of polygamy, very few men in any of these cultures actually have more than one wife. The reasons are partly social and partly economic; either a second partner is not available and willing, or the man cannot afford one.

There is one very obvious but very important generalization concerning human sexuality which applies without exception to all cultures. It has been mentioned in all preceding chapters and can be regarded as valid for the entire species. The general law states simply that every society shapes, structures and constrains the development and expression of sexuality in all of its members. This is universally achieved by social training from infancy and by constant social reward and punishment throughout life. There is not, and can never have been, a true society without sexual rules. One of the fundamental differences between sex and sexuality, as distinguished in Chapter 1, is that the latter is socially structured and regulated.

Davenport emphasizes a second basic principle which pertains to the nature and function of sociosexual controls: Rules for sexual conduct are not comprehensible in isolation. They became so only when we understand their relationship to other regulations that may have nothing to do with sex. To function successfully, a society must maintain a coherent structure and the social fabric consists of interrelated and interdependent rules governing all aspects of the behavior of its constituent members. Laws or customs concerning sexual activity are inescapably interconnected with rules dealing with marriage, with economy of the family, with inheritance, with social responsibility for minors, etcetera.

Lying behind all the rules, regulations, sanctions and taboos are the implicitly or explicitly shared value systems upon which a society must be founded, and which it must preserve or perish. These value systems and the cultural mechanisms related to them constitute what Davenport defines as a society's "internal logic and consistency." It is the relation of sexuality to this more general aspect of any society that we must seek to understand.

CULTURE AND SEX

Sexual behavior in human societies is embedded in a complex web of shared ideas, moral rules, jural regulations, obvious associations and obscure symbols. The image of a human society in which sexual behavior is (or was) completely free and unfettered by socially-determined controls is pure fantasy. Such a society does not exist, and, despite so-called scientific postulations of an earlier and totally promiscuous stage in human social evolution, it never did. The fundamental reasons for this are easy to find. Although human sexual behavior is directly based upon inherited biological factors, the biological bases are shaped and modified by learning in the inevitable process of maturation. Maturation is a social process as much as it is an individual learning experience. Inheritance equips the normal individual with the potentialities of adult sexual behavior but only through adequate socialization and maturation are the potentialities molded into behavior patterns that are uniform enough from individual to individual to permit sexual interaction.

There are not many categories of human culture that can be validly claimed to be universal—that is, a recognized category of human behavior that is valid for all human societies. However, sexual behavior is one of those few, and this is because the bases are to be found in the physiological inheritance of every individual. Nevertheless, there are significant and often broad differences between and among societies—even within them—as to the range and content of behaviors that are classed as "sexual." For example, in American society it is normal for a brother and sister to eat at the same table, with or without their parents. Indeed, the common meal is seen as a revered symbol of family cohesion and togetherness. Yet, in some tribal societies brothers and sisters who are sexually mature may never eat together. This is because a man and a woman sharing food or eating together is characteristic of the marital relationship; another important aspect of marriage is mutual sexual access. Therefore, according to this kind of cultural reasoning, food has a sexual connotation. A man and a woman eating together is seen as a mildly erotic act, which is quite appropriate for a husband and wife; but for a brother and sister to behave in this way is to commit a kind of alimentary incest.

It is the culture of a society that defines the boundaries between what is sexual and what is not sexual. It is the culture that determines what is appropriate and inappropriate sexual behavior in any given circumstance, and how such behavior is to be rewarded or punished. It is also the culture that governs in what ways each generation will learn the behavior, the lore and the ideational association of sex. While it is easy to see that human sexual behavior, whether viewed as patterned action of individuals or the collective actions of an entire society which shares the same culture, is always the product of inherited physiological potentialities and cultural learning, it is not at all possible to separate the biological from the cultural components. This is especially true when we observe intercultural differences, for cross-cultural differences also mean we are observing different societies (or the same society at different periods of time), and this raises the possibility of differing population genetics. Recently, for instance, tantalizing information about the sexual behavior of contemporary peasants of Abkhasia, an autonomous state of the U.S.S.R., suggests that there might be some quite basic genetic linkage between sexual-reproductive capacity and longevity. The Abkhasian peasants, a mountain people of the Caucasus region, enjoy a degree of longevity that is almost unknown among any other people. They also remain sexually active long after 70, and even after 100. Thirteen per cent of the women are reported to continue menstruation after the age of 55. For men, heterosexual behavior usually does not commence until marriage, which is after 30, and marital intercourse is regarded as a pleasure to be indulged in for as long as possible. Oldsters continue to work, enjoy their food and have heterosexual relations in diminishing amounts well beyond ages at which western Europeans and North Americans consider such activities to be almost impossible. While this suggests that there is a constitutional component that gives these Caucasian people their long lives and extended sexual vigor, there is also a cultural component that could make a contribution. The cultural ethic is one of continued activity, but with moderation. Persons of all ages are expected to do what they can; there is no retirement, and with advancing age individuals continue to do what they have always done, but in gradually diminishing amounts.

Whatever the possibilities of biological variation are (whether it is between individuals or genetically-defined populations), it is in what appears to be the purely cultural aspects of sex that we find the most apparent variations. In large, complex societies such as the United States, there is not a single culture of sex. Rather, there are many obvious subcultural differences that exert demonstrable effects on different segments of the society. The Kinsey studies took some of these, such as religious affiliation and amount of higher education, into account and revealed the effects they had on verbal reports of respondents about their sexual behavior. Other less extensive studies have shown significant differences in the sexual beliefs, attitudes and behavior of such diverse segments of the society as racial minorities, small religious communities, male prisoners, to name only a few. These and other studies in contemporary industrialized societies show clearly how profoundly social norms about sexual behavior are influenced both by early socialization and later changes in social circumstances or shifts in ideology. And to draw attention to the fact that cultural orientations toward sexual behavior can change very rapidly, we only need to point out the recent changes in these respects that have been central to so-called youth culture, the "counter-culture," gay liberation and women's liberation.

Even in so-called primitive or tribal societies, which are smaller and more homogeneous than modern industrial states, the culture of sex may not be uniform throughout. In the Hawaiian Islands, prior to the arrival of American Congregational missionaries in 1820, the sexual conduct of the hereditary aristocrats, who lived in or close to the political centers, was noticeably different from that of the commoners who, as agriculturists, fishermen and artisans, resided and labored apart from the chiefly courts. By our standards, the entirety of Hawaiian society was sexually very permissive, but at the courts erotic pastimes figured prominently in the lives of the leisured nobles. Sexual liaisons, both heterosexual and homosexual, were freely formed and just as freely broken off. It was not necessary to marry and form economically productive households. Highly born aristocrats of both sexes even had some sexual privileges over persons of lower social ranks. However, sexual relations with the lowest social order, who were, in effect, slaves, was absolutely proscribed on religious grounds. Infanticide among the aristocrats was common, both because the care of infants was considered by some women as irksome, because stable households were not inevitably formed out of even lengthy affairs, and because, for religious and political reasons, some hereditary lines had to be kept pure through specially arranged matings. So concerned were the ruling aristocrats about keeping genealogical purity they even occasionally mated full siblings, but more commonly half siblings; uncles and aunts mated with nieces and nephews, in order to produce "purebred" offspring. Even though commoners shared in the strong positive orientation toward the expression of sexuality, marriage and domesticity still prevailed. Children were adored, and if an infant could not be reared in a parental household, there were always willing foster parents. Marriage and a stable household were important to commoners, because the domestic unit was the productive economic group from whose toil the aristocrats also derived their living. Often how an aristocrat could or did behave sexually was explicitly denied the commoner under the threat of strong sanctions. Thus, different rules for sexual behavior were among the subcultural markers that defined hereditary differences in social position.

In some tribal societies that are stratified by neither hereditary social classes nor large economic differences, individual differences in social position or prestige may be accompanied by different rules of sexual conduct. This is the case in some of the contemporary societies of the eastern Solomon Islands of the southwest Pacific. Generally, in these societies adultery and forcible rape are very serious offenses which provoke strong, even violent, legal redress. Nevertheless, a few men in these communities, who by their special abilities and notable actions have achieved social renown and political influence, are less constrained by the explicit laws that regulate adultery and rape than are men with ordinary social standing. It is not that these important men are immune to these laws; rather, it is that they often use adultery and rape as a means of testing the powers inherent in their high social position. A man of low station would not be able to mobilize the legal machinery necessary to apply sanctions against an important man who had taken his wife or raped his daughter. In this case, the deviant behavior of the important man is not exactly condoned as being his privilege or right; however, it is expected that an important man demonstrate from time to time the potency of his influence, and the way he is expected to do this is by violating one of the laws governing sexual behavior. Here we have an instance where one aspect of sexual behavior is intricately bound to matters of power and authority in a nonstratified society that at the local level has no formal governmental structure.

The two examples just given reveal that sexual behavior often becomes loaded with special cultural meanings and relevancies that have no direct relationships to either the gratification of desire or its function in the reproductive cycle. In point of fact, the cross-cultural study of sex shows that seldom, if ever, are all forms of sexual behavior in a given culture regarded in only these two obvious psychological and biological dimensions. Each culture envelops sex with a different environment of ideas, beliefs, values and regulations, and no two are identical. In no way is sex unique in these respects. Hunger, eating and food, which is similar to sexual behavior in that it has clear biological foundations, is the same way. However, leaving the biological aspects aside, it is the cultural matrix in which sexual behavior is embedded, and the degree to which individuals have internalized this matrix, that determines and regulates sexual behavior to such a large degree. Human sexual behavior is not unlike human speech. Both have psycho-biological foundations that require lengthy social learning and reveal maturational changes; both are made up of many behavioral components which by implicit rules are combined into acceptable (or unacceptable) patterns of action; in both, the salience and meaning of any and all acts can be fully grasped only with complete knowledge of the cultural context in which they occur.

There was a time when moral philosophers and philosophical sociologists of Europe and the United States were certain that stages in human social evolution were marked by characteristic sexual practices. In the last century and the early part of this century, intellectuals thus persuaded firmly believed that human society commenced in a state of indiscriminate sexual promiscuity. Gradually, so the argument ran, mankind developed more enduring and more exclusive patterns of mating and marriage. These evolutionary changes brought about corresponding changes in the forms of the domestic unit. The culmination of this compelling yet hypothetical argument was the permanent and monogamous union, and the small nuclear family domestic group that was recognized as predominant in modern industrialized Europe and America. Ideally, all sexual behavior should be confined to this form of marriage and domestic arrangement. Premarital and extramarital heterosexual relationships were frowned upon; infantile and juvenile manifestations of eroticism were to be suppressed; all sexual acts save coitus between husband and wife were viewed as deviant, immoral or less evolved. The fact that contemporary European society never completely conformed to the ideal pattern was not overlooked. Nevertheless, faithful and stable monogamy was viewed as the stage of social and moral evolution toward which mankind was moving.

The scholars who were interested in proving such evolutionary trends —and there were several important theoretical schools of them—were the first to assemble the available data on relevant aspects of sex and marriage from non-European and primitive societies. The data were poor, the interests of the investigators were narrow, and the scholarly results failed to sustain the evolutionary schemes that had prompted the studies. Yet, this was the beginning of cross-cultural studies of sexual behavior—rather, some aspects of sexual behavior—and the studies did reveal that in all human societies a large sector of culture was focused on sexual mattters. In no society, is or was sexual behavior regarded as an inevitable and automatic response, like breathing or sweating.

As ethnographic field work became more professionalized, notably in the second decade of this century, better data on exotic peoples became available. Seldom, however, are descriptive ethnographies of unfamiliar cultures as rich in sexual data as they are in many other aspects of culture—in technology, social organization and religion, for example. Part of this is due to the fact that most ethnographers are from European or European-derived societies, where sexual matters are largely private matters. Hence, there was a reticence to pursue these lines of observation. Partly, too, the relative paucity of sexual data from other cultures is due to the fact that sex is often largely or partially private behavior and access to it is difficult. Moreover, since most, but far from all, ethnographers are men, the reliable data that are available on sexual behavior is subject to a clear masculine bias, both as to subjects and outlook of the observer. Thus, the cross-cultural study of sexual behavior is still in a formative stage. While some favorite assumptions and dated theories can now be shown to be either misconceptions or ethnocentric generalizations from our own culture, virtually no non-obvious and significant theoretical generalizations can yet be made. We are just beginning to sense the extent and limits of cultural variation. We do not know how and why these variations occur.

SEXUALITY

In most cultures, there seems to be either well-defined, explicit, or clearly derivable, views about the nature of human sexuality. In one of the subcultures of our own society, for example, all human sexuality is first regarded as evil, and since evil is to be avoided, sex should be avoided. Still, the society must be perpetuated, therefore sexual behavior, except for procreational goals, is to be either avoided or kept to a minimum. Carried to its extreme, in this instance, the persons seeking ultimate moral heights must adopt total celibacy. Doubtless, it is this evaluation of sexuality as sin that leads to the suppression of juvenile sexuality in socialization, and the consequence of the latency period, during which in young males little or severely diminished heterosexual interest is overtly shown. Sigmund Freud made a great deal of the latency period in his earlier writings, but he also noted in later work that it was not universal, even in the European society in which he worked; therefore, it was due to a subcultural pattern. Some extreme Protestant sects have carried the Christian doctrine of sex and sin so far as to attempt to avoid heterosexual relations altogether. The Shakers of New England are the notable example, and since they also attempted to found a separatist society, they were forced to recruit new members, not by reproduction in marriage but by adoption.

In this Christian tradition of sexual suppression, recent studies in a community in rural Ireland reveal a pattern of denial of sexuality that is notable for its severity. In Inis Beag (a pseudonym for a rural community of 350 persons) sex is ideally confined to marital intercourse.

There is no courtship. Marriages are contracted by elders with little concern for the personal preferences of either bride or groom. Marriage comes relatively late at mean ages of 36 for men and 25 for women. Men and women are highly segregated in public and women socialize with other women far less than men socialize with other men. There is a strong avoidance of discussion of any matters classified as sexual; hence, knowledge of sexual matters is extremely limited. In the Inis Beag theory of sexuality, desire in women is considered to be either less strong or more subservient to conscious control than it is in men. Even the ability of women to experience orgasm is either denied or, if admitted, it is considered to be deviant. Husbands are expected to initiate sex, because they have less ability to control their desires; wives are expected to comply willingly but passively. Sexual humor is almost absent, body modesty is extreme, recreation never involves both sexes. It is an ethos which negates sexuality, and as a result of this, all forms of sexual behavior are apparently infrequent.

The Christian tradition, with its theological identification of sex with evil, is not alone in its negative valuation of sexuality. In one small but notable tribal tradition on Yap Island, in the United States Trust Territory of the Pacific, there evolved a strong negative attitude toward sexuality; however, the cultural ideas upon which this negativism is based are different. In Yapese culture, sexual behavior and the state of health are linked. For men, sexual release through intercourse is believed to cause weakness and susceptibility to certain diseases. For similar reasons, women are strongly enjoined to avoid intercourse during pregnancy and for several years following the birth of a child. All evidence suggests that the Yapese did successfully suppress sexuality for these reasons. Early in this century, when the Yapese were beginning to have frequent contacts with Europeans, they contracted gonorrhea, along with a host of other foreign diseases. This caused a high rate of female sterility as well as a decline in the general state of health. One response to this deterioration in their health was to be more and more concerned with sexual continence. Not only did the mortality rates go up, but, because of the practice of sexual continence on therapeutic grounds, the birth rate declined. The population came perilously close to extinction before scientific medical treatment and education were introduced following World War II.

Another tribal tradition in which intercourse at least is regarded negatively is that of the pre-World War II Manus who lived in Papua-New Guinea. Intercourse between husband and wife was considered to be sinful or degrading, and was undertaken only in strict secrecy. Women considered coitus to be an abomination which they had to endure, even painfully, until they produced a child. The easily aroused sexuality of men was regarded as brutish. Intercourse outside of marriage was a crime which, because it offended the sensibilities of watchful spirits, brought on supernaturally ordained punishments. As with the Inis Beag, sexually tainted talk was not heard. Women were totally secretive about menstruation, and so effective was their concealment that Manus men even denied that their women experienced monthly cycles.

Turning away from cultures in which negation of sexuality is characteristic, the Polynesian cultures of the central Pacific have long been famous for almost the opposite orientation toward the expression of sexuality. Before some of this exuberance was blunted by the adoption of Christianity, in Tahiti, for example, there was a virtual worship of both masculine and feminine beauty, and beauty was erotically associated with sex. Infantile and juvenile expressions of aroused sexuality were considered to be normal and healthy. Youth of both sexes were encouraged to indulge in self-masturbation, and premarital intercourse was, with few restrictions, generally accepted. Marital and extramarital intercourse were openly discussed and practiced. Eroticism dominated the two important modes of aesthetic expression: song and the dance. Even a vagabond religious cult, the Arioi Society, in which extreme sexual license was permitted (but marriage and raising children was prohibited) carried exhibitionistically erotic theatrical presentations from island to island. In sum, in the pre-Christian Tahitian culture, the expression of sexuality was not just tolerated, it was a positive value that permeated many aspects of life.

Some of the erotic tradition of old Polynesia persists in contemporary Polynesian societies. In Mangaia, one of the Cook Islands, adult premarital intercourse is still strongly encouraged for both sexes. Men are expected to express their virility to the limit. Even though sexuality is assumed to be stronger in men than in women, still women are expected to be eager and active partners. From the masculine point of view, the object of the game of sex is to display, through intercourse, the limits of virility, and provide female partners with as much gratification as possible. Gratification for both sexes is equated with orgasm, and the strength of virility is measured by the number of successive orgasms a male can experience. Romantic love is not always a part of youthful heterosexual relationships. Affection is considered to develop out of satisfactory sexual relations; love develops later, in marriage, as the sexual appetites begin to decline. Implicitly at least, in the Mangaian theory of sexuality, sexual desire is expected to decline rapidly with age and after marriage, and there is the suggestion that during youth the maximum expression of sexuality can be achieved only when stimulated by beauty and other erotic stimuli, as well as by a variety of attractive partners.

Few societies seem to regard sexuality and its expression in heterosexual intercourse in such a simple and direct manner as do the Tahitians and Mangaians. Often a culture links sexual arousal with other emotional states in a variety of complex affective states. Ample evidence of this, as related to individuals, has been produced in the vast psychiatric literature on sexual deviations in our own society. Now we are beginning to see this phenomenon in cross-cultural perspective. The disgust with which women imbue intercourse in Manus culture is a case in point. The Gusii of southwestern Kenya provide another instance in which sexuality is aroused only in combination with hostility and antagonism. Coitus, even between husband and wife, is thought of as an act in which the man must overcome the woman's natural resistance and also cause her some form of physical pain, and possibly some humiliation. Women are encouraged and expected to frustrate men with sexual taunts. Men admit to heightened sexual gratification when their partners protest and cry during intercourse. Moreover, there is continuity in this from early socialization to adult behavior.

During childhood and adolescence the overt expression of sexuality in girls is consistently punished. In boys the manifestations of aroused sexuality is both encouraged and punished. Much of the character of adult heterosexual relationships is ritualized earlier during a boy's initiation ceremony. While young adolescent boys are secluded following circumcision, adolescent girls are brought to the seclusion area, nude, to perform erotic dances. They make disparaging remarks about the boys' mutilated genitals. The erotic dances are supposed to arouse the boys so that they have erections, which, in their postoperative condition, is excruciatingly painful.

In maturity, men are expected to be much more virile and demanding of sexual gratification than women; hence, the demands of men on their lovers and wives are considered by the women to be excessive and gives them reason to resist men's advances. Men demand gratification and proceed to overcome the resistance. Normal intercourse is then a kind of ritualized rape, complete with some aspects of the affective components of rape.

Lovers and wives must be selected from different clans. The social relationships between different clans is perenially tinged with hostility. Thus, heterosexual relationships are also a manifestation of political relationships. While premarital sexual relationships are tolerated, extramarital sex is a heinous crime with powerful, supernaturally-induced sanctions. If a Gusii wife commits adultery and continues to have intercourse with her husband, it is believed to put her husband in mortal danger if he becomes ill or suffers even a minor injury. It is a polygynous society, which again is rationalized as being possible because men require more sexual gratification than women.

In several societies of highland Papua-New Guinea, because of incest restrictions, wives must be taken from other clans and, like the Gusii of Kenya, the political relationships between different clans is often so hostile as to be on the verge of warfare. Men abduct women from hostile clans and this brings about armed retaliation and counter-abductions, which produces further redressive acts in an endless cycle. Marriage in these societies, and the sexual relationships within marriage, are always fraught with fear, hostility and anger.

In another Papua-New Guinea society, that of Dobu which is located on a small island off the coast of the main island of New Guinea, husbands are continually in fear of sorcery from their wives. They are particularly vulnerable to sorcery during intercourse; hence, a man is continually weighing the gratification of sexual desires against the possibility of sorcery as a result of that gratification.

The cultures of Romonum Island, in the Truk Group of the U. S. Trust Territory of the Pacific, also places the experience of pain and frustration in association with sexual gratification. Unlike the Gusii, the Romonum Trukese regard the expression of sexuality as natural and highly gratifying for both sexes. Although sexual play among children is not encouraged, it is expected that premarital coitus will commence for boys and girls during early adolescence, even before menarche for the latter. Boys may be given their first sexual intercourse by older, experienced women. According to the Romonum theory of sexual maturation, intercourse is thought to cause breasts to develop and menstruation to commence. Lovers commonly inflict pain on each other in foreplay. Suffering pain inflicted by a sweetheart is regarded as both a test of strong affection and as sexually arousing. The most erotic form of coitus, called "striking," is clitoral, with insertion into the vagina just before orgasm and ejaculation.

On the other hand, marital relations must always be maintained with decorous restraint. There can be no overt expression of anger or hostility between a husband and wife, and this same decorum extends to the close in-laws of each spouse. Husband and wife cannot engage in the painful eroticism that lovers enjoy, for such pain-inducing acts are regarded in the marital relationship as hostile. Marital intercourse is regarded as less satisfying than intercourse between lovers, yet the culture places high value on maximum sexual gratification. As a result, adults maintain both marital and extramarital relations.

These few selected examples illustrate the point that sexuality is not purely a matter of physiology. We have long been aware of the fact that individuals in one society, and presumably sharing the same culture, may show marked variation in this respect. Cross-cultural comparisons reveal that entire cultures vary in many respects as to how sexuality is defined, the extent to which it is expected to be expressed through intercourse, and, to some degree, the variations in the affective components of sexual gratification. We turn next to an even more variable aspect of the culture of sex: cultural stimuli that are regarded as sexually arousing.

THE EROTIC CODE

For every culture there is an inventory of signs and acts which, in appropriate contexts, convey special erotic meanings that both arouse sexuality and enhance its expression. Some, such as the Trukese affection-pain and Tahitian erotic dancing, have already been mentioned in passing. Physical features that constitute erotic beauty are recognized everywhere, although the criteria are markedly different. In old Hawaii, among aristocrats, what we would class as extreme obesity in women and would think of as possibly negatively seductive was highly erotic. Everywhere, the sight of sexual organs is regarded as having the potential of arousing sexual desire, yet in some cultures full nakedness may be thought of as slightly repugnant as well as shame-evoking. Segments of our own society still look on nakedness in this way. Rules of sexual modesty are observed everywhere, yet the rules themselves are as variable from culture to culture as any other form of symbolic communication. Most cultures require that the sex organs of adults be fully or partially covered in all but the most intimate situations. The degree to which covering is required is not consistent between the sexes. In some Arab societies, women are required to cover their bodies completely with only a band of the face and the eyes exposed. This is an extreme, and in most of the tropical tribal world, where clothing is not necessary for protection against the elements, women's breasts are usually exposed. For men, however, breasts seem nearly always to be erotic organs, even where they are rarely covered. However, this is not quite a cultural universal, for in Mangaia, a Polynesian society notable for its expression of sexuality, female breasts are not considered to be sexually arousing and do not figure into heterosexual foreplay or erotic communication. Concealment of female genitals is much more widespread than covering of male genitals, yet in some societies this is not the case. On Aoriki, in the eastern Soloman Islands, girls and women go entirely naked until after marriage and until they gain a kind of matronly status by having children, while men after puberty take great pains to cover their genitals. Even after genital modesty is observed, women cover the pubic area with only a small patch of fringe, which can be seen through at close range. Males, however, are expected never to look directly at a woman's pubic area, and to do so is considered to be an extremely lewd gesture.

In many societies of Oceania it is the men who are required only to partially cover their genitals, while the women are invariably completely clothed from waist to mid-thigh. In the highland areas of Papua-New Guinea, adult men must cover only the prepuce. This is done by inserting the head of the penis in a covering made from a brightly colored gourd. The tapered end of the gourd is held in an upright position by strapping it to the waist, thus leaving part of the penis, scrotum and pubic hair exposed. On Malekula Island in the New Hebrides, also of the southwest Pacific, the penis is wrapped in a mat or cloth which, as above, carries the organ upright by being tied around the waist.

In only a few societies that we know about do men and women go entirely naked throughout their lives. Some of the most notable examples of these are the Aborigines of Australia. Still, Australian Aborigines have strict rules that forbid staring at genitals, and women, when seated, are expected to maintain a modest posture so as to hide the vaginal opening.

With some form of sexual modesty observed in all human societies, it seems to follow that modesty customs are also everywhere manipulated so as to convey sexual meanings. Often dress and other forms of personal adornment serve to reinforce or negate sexual modesty behavior. As in our society, dress and behavior for some occasions may be deliberately provocative. At East Bay, a Melanesian society of the southwest Pacific, women normally cover their shoulders and breasts with a shawl when going outside the house after dark. The cultural rationale for this is that evenings are a time of relaxation and during these times men's thoughts turn to sexual matters. At night, too, it is more possible for a man to accost a girl without being seen. Thus, women increase their modesty behavior at night, and not to do so is to communicate an invitation to be accosted. And young women do manipulate this pattern to flirt and signify sexual interest in men who interest them. Women of East Bay normally wear skirts that cover the thighs, because the inside of the thigh is considered to be a very erotic area. To increase the erotic nature of the inner thigh, some women have tattoos made there. To a man, the occasional glimpse of these thigh tattoos beneath the covering skirt is a very arousing stimulus. Women, of course, know this and use it to convey sexual communications. At formal dances, both men and women, but particularly young unmarried adults, dress and adorn themselves to the limit. Males, especially, pay attention to maximizing the sensuality of their bodies by oiling their skin and tucking certain scented leaves and branches in their arm bands and belts. The mixed aroma of fresh perspiration, body oil, scented leaves and, nowadays, perfumed body talcs and brilliantine, sensed in a milieu of emotional songs and vigorous movement, is regarded as almost irresistible to women. In fact, one of the unstated, yet perfectly obvious, purposes of such dance is to create a very erotic situation which stands in sharp contrast to the somewhat prudish atmosphere that normally prevails during East Bay social occasions.

Thus, the culture of every society seems to provide a variety of erotic actions, the purpose of which is to arouse and maintain sexual interest in the opposite sex, even if complete gratification through intercourse may not be the immediate goal. In some, as at East Bay, various odors are provocative. Mangaians, as well as other Polynesians, regard flower fragrances as especially erotic, while stale body odors are often regarded as repugnant, and great attention is paid, as in our own society, to bathing and obscuring these natural smells. But the subtleties are enormous. Throughout Oceania there is a relatively uniform mode of caressing, which is sometimes called the Oceanic kiss. This consists of gently touching cheek to cheek or nose to cheek and inhaling deeply so as to sense the other's odor. As with our mouth to mouth kissing, it is done with subtle variation in totally nonsexual contexts, as a show of parental and grandparental affection, for example, and it is also an invariable component of sexual embrace. In many of the societies that use the Oceanic kiss, the European form of kissing is disgusting.

As mentioned above, the sharing or offering of food in certain contexts can be an act charged with sexual meaning. At East Bay, where this is the case, one of the most intimate acts that men and women engage in is the offering or exchange of ingredients for the stimulant, betel. There are three ingredients to betel: a nut, pepper and lime. When chewed in the right sequence and in the proper proportions, it produces an immediate intoxicating effect. The nut and the pepper are personalized items, the lime is not. Offering a person nut and pepper is considered to be a gesture of friendship between persons of the same sex, and an act of sexual intimacy when between persons of opposite sex. Lovers at East Bay make a great deal of exchanging betel nuts and pepper, as if it were a show of their sexual relationship.

Sexually tinged speech, erotic songs and poetry, and sexual jokes, and the way these are regarded are very culturally specific. In the Irish community of Inis Beag, none are permitted. In many societies, one or more of these uses of language may be elaborated to an extraordinary degree (as with dirty jokes in our society). In old Hawaii, but even continuing to the present day among Hawaiian speakers, one of the marks of using the Hawaiian language well is the ability to make clever sexual allusions through metaphor, pun, and multiple meanings. Sacred, as well as secular, songs are burdened with serious and humorous sexual meanings. This tradition in language, of course, was another manifestation of the strong positive sexual orientation of old Hawaiian culture.

With the contemporary Iban of Sarawak on the island of Borneo, conversations of adult men and women, regardless of their social relationships, do not go far before they become infused with sexual banter. Compliments, scoldings, expressions of respect and insult all can be given a special poignancy if couched in erotic terms. The dirty joke is also a prominent feature of male conviviality. On the surface, Iban culture appears to be very erotically oriented. However, it is a different kind of eroticism from that seen in Polynesian cultures. Great value is placed upon the gratifications obtained in intercourse, but, at the same time, women grant their sexual favors to men, with parsimony and manipulative skill. Men taunt women with sexual advances; women flirt back but stop short of full cooperation. Romantic love and the joys of copulation are extolled in song and poetry. However, the underlying understanding is that women, even wives, grant sexual gratification to men in accordance with how well they fulfill their masculine roles. The traditional expression of this is contained in many heroic stories and songs in which the vigorous young man professes his love. The girl urges him to go out and demonstrate his courage and skill in fighting. He returns with trophies that prove his bravery, and she grants him his desire. The Iban are the famous headhunters of Borneo, but nowadays they do not take heads of enemies to prove their masculine worth. Instead, the men go out to work in distant places and return to their remote longhouse communities with material riches.

Brief, but special, mention must be made of the widespread practice of so-called love magic, a form of sexual communication or action which relies upon some supernatural assumption for it to work. Presumably in all societies, some individuals experience extreme sexual frustration, either because a desired partner is legally forbidden, inaccessible or is not equally interested. Usually, as with the comparative strengths of sexuality that are ascribed to the sexes, it is men who appear more frequently to be the sufferers in these dire situations. Many cultures provide a way to overcome these obstacles by resorting to supernatural means. Whether or not these extreme measures are socially accepted—that is, can be performed openly—usually, but not invariably, depends upon whether the desired partner is legally available. In any case, love magic is a coercive technique based upon the assumption that there is supernatural power which can bring about the desired result. At East Bay, love magic is common; however, it is always unacceptable, because in this society all heterosexual intercourse is, ideally at least, supposed to take place within marriage or with women who are concubines or prostitutes. Thus, East Bay love magic is clandestine and, if discovered, is punishable in the same way as sorcery (supernatural methods to cause bodily harm or property damage) and forcible rape, both of which are very serious crimes.

The most common form of love magic at East Bay is the invocation of the desired power from one's own supernatural guardian and the transmission of the power to a concealable substance which will eventually be ingested by the target person. Since most persons chew betel in this society, the power is located in betel lime. Lime is the agent, because, as already pointed out, it is among the three ingredients which can be shared. The performer of the love magic must ask of his supernatural guardian the power to bring about some specific event which will best serve his purpose. If, for instance, the man is never able to catch the girl alone, then this is the opportunity he will ask for. There are many others, more complicated than that, most of which reveal ingenious, and often devious, strategies. The lime, or whatever other agent may have been selected, then must be placed where, in due course, the target will get it. This, of course, requires stealth of some kind, and it is the step in the plan where the possibility of discovery is the greatest.

In the Trobriand Islands, another society of the southwest Pacific, which is located off the main island of New Guinea, love magic is both common and openly practiced. The society not only views the expression of sexuality with great favor; it is also highly tolerant of pre- and extramarital affairs. Here, the target of the love magic is the performer himself. The object of the performance is to make himself so irresistibly attractive that the desired partner will be unable to withstand his entreaties. Trobriand men are also earnest traders in a famous overseas exchange system known as *kula*. By altering the supernatural formulae of love magic only slightly, the Trobriand man can also make himself attractive to his trade partner and thereby insure greater success in trading. In the Trobriands, then, love magic and trading magic are virtually one and the same. Both forms are legitimate means to achieve highly desirable ends. At East Bay, however, business and trading magic is totally different from love magic. Love magic is virtually one and the same as sorcery, and both are regarded as felonies.

These examples are but a few that could have been given to illustrate the complexities and cultural arbitrariness of erotic codes. All societies have one; none has been more than partially described. The only common feature that these codes have is that they are composed of a multiplicity of kinds of signs and cultural assumptions. They convey not only intellectualized information, but also directly elicit emotional states. In form and function, human erotic codes are comparable to sexual communication codes used by other species. They are different, however, in that man's erotic codes are culturally specific rather than species specific.

Beliefs Concerning Conception, Pregnancy and Menstruation

Just as all cultures contain rather well-defined views about the nature of sexuality, so, too, all cultures seem to have theories about the human reproductive process and, not surprisingly, these folk theories of reproduction sometimes figure prominently in the mystical and theological definitions of the nature of man. At East Bay, the human is clearly contrasted with other animals by three features, two of which are sexual: humans do not copulate indiscriminately, humans observe modesty rules by wearing clothes, and humans cook their food. Animals (and certain other known peoples who are regarded as being animal-like) are believed to mate according to whim, go naked and show no shame, and devour their food without preparation. Some of the same and very similar distinctions occur repeatedly in culture after culture. Man seems to have discovered and rediscovered that his sexual nature and habits, because of his culture, do differ from those of the other animals.

East Bay also has an explicit theory about conception, but here the human theory is thought to be analogous to agriculture. Semen is equated with seed, the womb is likened to garden soil, and the bodily liquids that secrete into the womb (and which are regularly expelled as menstrual discharge) are the moisture and nutrients upon which the human fetus lives. Semen must be strong and concentrated in order to be viable; thus, conception is most likely to occur after a man has been continent for a period. Repeated intromissions of semen are thought to be the cause of multiple conceptions. Since multiple births are dreaded, men are supposed to avoid ejaculation within the vagina during pregnancy.

This is only part of the East Bay theorizing about conception, and other parts of the total theory will subsequently be outlined. Whether or not these speculations correspond to the scientific facts of human reproduction is not the main point; what is important is that by deducing from these assumptions, people in all cultures seek to exercise some control over reproductive capacities. Folk theories about reproduction are another significant source for the regulation of sexual behavior.

Some theories of reproduction are far more mystical and metaphorical than that espoused at East Bay. Traditionally, the Ashanti of Ghana would state that the human fetus is formed in the womb by the mingling of the woman's blood (accumulations which are discharged at menstruation) and man's ejaculate. The blood of the mother becomes the blood of the child; the semen from the father becomes the spirit and life force of the child. From this point, the theory goes sociological. Blood is identified with matrilineal descent and continuity of clans. The patrilineal life force is a complementary form of continuity through which every Ashanti also inherits important social statuses. Sociologically speaking, the complete Ashanti person must receive both clan status and patrilineal statuses, just as the biological individual must have both blood and vital spirit in order to be physiologically and psychologically complete.

The Ashanti theory does provide an accounting of the relationship between coitus and conception, from which some measure of birth control can be derived. There are few societies, however, who, in the past at least, do not seem to have fully noted the relationship of semen, or something contained in it, and conception. Since these societies are anomalies, a great deal has been written about this aspect of their culture.

On the continent of Australia, a large number of groups are reported once to have believed that there was no direct relationship between man's semen and conception. Pregnancy, it was said, occurred when an already-formed spirit child entered the womb, where it was nurtured until birth. It was men's psychic powers—their dreaming—that caused the fetal spirit to enter the body of the female, and, at most, intercourse only made it easier for the spirit to enter. Even though the details concerning the relevance of coitus to pregnancy and parturition varied greatly from one Aborigine group to another, the overall conclusion drawn is that such mystical theories did not suppress intercourse and probably acted to encourage it. Today, Aborigines are perfectly well-aware of the relationship between semen and conception, and there is some doubt as to whether the traditional ignorance of paternity which has been ascribed to them was anything more than an alternate way of expressing the mystical side of conception, in a similar way that we might say, in some contexts, that babies are brought by the stork or that children are manifestations of God's work.

In the Trobriand Islands, which were mentioned above, similar beliefs to those held by Australian Aborigines were expressed until one or two generations ago. Pregnancy commenced when a spirit invaded the body, through the head, of a sexually mature woman. The spirit fetus is the incarnation of a once-living person who, following death and a period of existence in the spirit domain, wishes to be reborn. After entering the body of its "mother," who must belong to the same matrilineal subclan as the deceased from whom the spirit fetus is derived, it is nurtured by the woman's blood, and this causes menstrual periods to cease. The Trobriand theory also points out that, while it is not impossible for a virgin to conceive (and instances of virgin conceptions are provided), it is very difficult for one to do so. The sexually mature woman should first be "opened up" by intercourse so that there will be space in the womb for the spirit fetus to grow.

Again, there is some doubt as to whether this theory of conception is to be taken literally. Trobrianders do not believe in the literal meaning today, because they have learned the scientific facts of reproduction theory. Moreover, before they were completely aware of scientific biological theory of human reproduction, they did exercise considerable control over the breeding of their pig herds by castrating the boars that they did not wish to impregnate sows. This suggests that they always possessed the expected knowledge about paternity and pregnancy, and that the mystical explanation, as with the Ashanti, was a metaphorical statement about the sociological continuity of the matrilineal subclan, which is an exceedingly important social group in Trobriand society.

The Mangaian folk theory holds that spreading semen among several women reduces the probability of conception. Intercourse during pregnancy is encouraged because it is thought to be more pleasurable then than before conception, and some Mangaians go so far as to state that continued intercourse during pregnancy makes for an easier birth.

In many societies, intercourse between husband and wife may be interdicted following childbirth. The period of avoidance can be relatively short—a few days, until the lochial flow ceases. It can be a few weeks, until the mother has fully regained her strength, or it can be relatively long—many months, until the child is weaned or is walking. It may even be several years—until the child is relatively independent of its mother. In some societies, with lengthy and strict postpartal restrictions on intercourse, the reason for prolonged avoidance is to protect the woman from too-frequent pregnancies, or to insure that the child will receive the undivided attention of its mother until it is past infancy, and hence past the period during which infants most frequently die. However, in most societies that have long postpartum taboos on intercourse, the reasons are mystical and are understandable only in terms of extraordinarily abstract mystical concepts.

Often, pregnancy and birth are surrounded by a plethora of mystical and religious beliefs. There is probably no human society that does not have magical ways of attempting to control the sex of the child and ritual acts that seek to avoid abnormal births. Some of these are based upon such obvious analogies that they are self-explanatory. Desiring male children, a woman, upon finding herself pregnant, may engage in some masculine activity. Seeking to avoid a difficult birth, a woman may avoid looped ropes or vines in fear of the umbilical cord becoming looped around the child's neck. Slimy and viscous foods may be prescribed to insure an easy birth. Countless situations may be avoided, such as looking into the faces of animals, in order to prevent ugliness or malformations. In all societies, it seems, there are practices that are based upon the assumption that the events acting upon the mother will affect the fetus she carries. These are not always believed in with great conviction, but the practices remain. Similarly, all societies have ways in which they attempt to cope with childlessness, usually diagnosed as barrenness of the woman, and to avoid unwanted births. In the latter case, none, save those that do violence to the fetus, are actually effective. Those that do cause abortion are so traumatic that they endanger the life of the woman as well.

Occasionally, there are cultural assumptions that directly link the father with the unborn child. On the basis of these, the father must avoid situations and events that, through him, will affect the fetus. One of the most well-known practices, based upon mystical connections between the father and both the child and its mother, is that known as the *couvade*. First recorded among the Basques, but also widespread among South American Indians and occasionally elsewhere as well, in the *couvade*, when the mother goes into labor, the father goes through a ritualized sympathetic form of labor. In South America, the father may also follow with a lying-in period and a lengthy time during which he severely restricts his activities. It is thought that the newborn infant is highly vulnerable to adverse experiences its father might encounter; hence, the father avoids the possibility of encountering such adversities by remaining housebound during the vulnerable period of his child.

While all societies seem to have noted the relationship of menstruation to pregnancy, the menstrual period may be regarded as something more than a calendric physiological phenomenon. Often menstrual discharge is regarded as disgusting and menstruating women may refrain from the preparation of food and indulging in intercourse. While just as often this is not the case, occasionally the menstrual discharge is regarded as polluting or exceptionally debilitating, even dangerous, to men. Under the urgency of such beliefs, men may avoid the dwelling where the menstruating woman lives, or, more commonly, the woman may segregate herself to a special isolation hut where she remains until her period is over.

Pre-Christian Hawaii is an example of a culture with a strong menstrual avoidance. The domestic arrangement for all Hawaiian households, regardless of social rank, included at least three areas: one exclusively for women and young children of both sexes, another for men and older boys, and a third where both sexes could congregate. During menstruation and childbirth, women were rigidly confined to their quarters, and because of this the female part of the dwelling, from a masculine point of view, was considered to be always polluted. Men never entered the women's quarters. During certain religious periods, men were considered sacred, and they were confined to their quarters; therefore, women never entered the men's living areas. For a man to be contaminated by contact with anything associated with menstruation or childbirth, placed him in a state of ritual pollution, and the pollution could only be removed by purification rituals. Certain foods that were considered sacred to the gods (and were eaten by males as well) were forbidden to women, because women were never completely free of menstrual pollution; anything associated with the high gods was never to be polluted.

In their most extreme forms, beliefs about menstrual pollution can become generalized into what amounts to a perpetual avoidance between men and women. Among the Enga-speaking people of highland Papua-New Guinea, it is firmly believed that men and women differ in many fundamental ways. Because of these fundamental differences, men can be contaminated by contact with menstrual discharge; contamination causes illness, debility, decline and eventual death. Even though men studiously avoid contact with women in order to avoid contamination, they realize that they cannot avoid all contamination. This leads to a highly segregated life for males and females. Still, sexuality is recognized as demanding some heterosexual outlet, and children must be begotten through marital coitus. As a result of this approach-avoidance conflict toward intercourse, single men almost never engage in heterosexual intercourse, married men sleep with their wives reluctantly and for begetting children only, and all men are deeply concerned with purification rituals to purge the contamination they receive from the women.

In another Papua-New Guinea society, Wogeo, not only are menstrual discharge and menstruating women themselves dangerous to men, but reciprocally men, when in a sacred state, are dangerous to women. However, the sacred state that makes men dangerous is ritually induced by them, and the ritual is an imitative menstruation. The ritual menstruation is achieved by scratching the penis deeply so that it bleeds freely. It is thought that periodic bleeding in this way rids the body of contaminations received from women, and this keeps the body healthy and vigorous. Contaminations that women receive from men are discharged automatically through the menses. Unlike the Enga, however, the Wogeo do not avoid intercourse in order to avoid pollution.

Often, folk theories of reproduction include ideas about the probability of conception in relation to menstruation. At East Bay, the period of greatest probability of conception is midway between menses. According to their theory, this is the time when enough nutrient fluids have accumulated to nurture the semen into a fetus; before this the womb is too dry; the nearer the menstrual time that impregnation of semen occurs, the greater the possibility that the semen will not take root and will be discharged when the time for the menstrual period arrives. With the Navajo and Havusupai Indian of the United States, it is thought that intercourse during menstruation brings immediate conception. The Masai of east Africa consider the period of four to five days following menstruation to be the most favorable for conception, and in north India it is believed that the most fertile period is five days before menstruation.

Often a folk theory of reproduction implicitly or explicitly associates failure of important undertakings, with intercourse, and success in such efforts with sexual continence or complete isolation of men and women. More frequently, these periods of continence and separation concern masculine activities such as hunting, fishing and religious ritual. Less frequently, they concern such work of women as a crucial phase in the agricultural cycle and highly skilled crafts. On Aoriki Island, men leave their dwellings and sleep in the sacred canoe house when continence is required of them or of their wives. Men must never have intercourse just before or during the time they are involved in fishing for the seasonal schools of bonito and tuna. The rationale for this is that intercourse leaves an odor on a man that the tuna and bonito can sense and will avoid. Fishing for these species, which are considered to be one manifestation of protective deities, is both an important economic and ritual activity, for success not only brings highly valued food, but also indicates that the deities are looking with favor on the community. Similarly, women must avoid intercourse and contact with masculine activities before performing their garden magic, and there is crucial magic to be performed at the commencement of every critical phase of the gardening routine. If continence is not observed, there is a possibility that the garden magic will work in a negative rather than a positive manner.

When comparing and analyzing nonscientific theories, it is not always possible to distinguish between those folk beliefs about sexuality (cited earlier) and those folk beliefs that concern human reproduction. The distinction between the two, as presented here, is probably not a valid one for all cultures. Nevertheles, by viewing folk theories about sex in this way it is possible to gain some insight into the ways that cultures differently affect sexual behavior. Some cultures seem to exert regulatory pressures on sexual motivation by being concerned with the nature of sexuality; others center on the reproductive aspects of sexual behavior. Some cultures class sexual matters as natural biological phenomena; others imbue some aspects of sex with mysticism and supernaturalism. In all societies, however, the ideas, beliefs and moral associations that the culture attaches to sexual behavior constitute powerful regulators of that behavior.

SOCIOLOGICAL ASPECTS OF SEXUAL BEHAVIOR

Let us adopt a more sociological stance and consider some of the ways that culture, as manifested in social institutions and social organizational forms, has an effect upon sexual behavior. In all societies, an important sector of the jural system is concerned with sexual behavior and its reproductive consequences. The jural approach involves such matters as how sexual rights and obligations are defined by a society, how they are discriminated from other rights over persons, in what ways and by what authorities sexual rights are allocated and reallocated during the life history of an individual, and under what conditions various kinds of sexual unions may be established, as well as the legal nature of different kinds of unions.

Since some form of permanent heterosexual union is to be found in all but a few societies, let us begin with a discussion of the sexual aspects of marriage. It is well known that all societies prohibit marriage and intercourse between certain categories of close relatives. This prohibition is called the incest taboo. While all societies have an incest taboo, the range of its extension and the categories of kin covered by it are extremely variable from one society to another, and even from one part of a society to another part. Some incest taboos include only brother-sister, parent-child and avuncular-nepotic kin relationships. However, as seen with the special sibling unions among ruling aristocrats of old Hawaii, the scope of the incest taboo under exceptional circumstances can be even more narrowly defined. Close unions contracted for reasons of political expedience, sometimes called dynastic incest, were also a feature of Inca society in pre-Spanish Peru and Ptolemaic Egypt. In some African societies, incestuous unions are deliberately arranged, on occasion, as a way of generating an emotionally charged mystical aura around the persons who committed the offense.

Many societies extend the incest taboo to cover first or second cousins. Sometimes it is extended to include all known or traceable relatives. Very often the incest taboo is extended asymmetrically. For example, cousins who are children of siblings of the same sex (parallel cousins) are forbidden as sexual partners while cousins who are children of siblings of opposite sex (cross-cousins) are permitted to become sexual partners, and in some cases may be regarded as the most favored partners. In many societies that recognize unilineal descent as an organizational principle, persons who belong to the same lineages or clans are categorically regarded as close kin, regardless of their genealogical distance from each other, and are placed under the prohibitions of the incest taboo. In such societies, each clan or lineage may be aligned with a species of animal or plant which is avoided or treated in some deferential way. Animals with these mystical bonds to social groups are called totems, and persons with the same totemic affiliation are prohibited from having any sexual relationship, even if no genealogical connection can be demonstrated. In other words, the incest taboo is not always a matter of known genealogical relationships. It is often based upon assumed or putative consanguinity.

The emotional intensity with which the incest taboo is imbued, and hence enforced, is quite variable. Some societies seem to be intensely concerned about the avoidance of incest and the supernatural sanctions that are believed to follow when incest does occur. Some aborigine groups of Australia are excessively preoccupied in this way, and regard the commission of incest as a serious crime that may have calamitous effects. Other societies only lightly acknowledge the incest taboo, and treat violations, except those involving parents, children and siblings, as minor offenses which can easily be rectified and forgotten. The degree of severity of incest offenses is often different from one society to another. In many societies, incest between parents and children, particularly between mother and son, is the worst form, but in many matrilineal societies incest between a maternal uncle and his sister's daughter is the capital offense. In order to understand these variations, which on the surface seem to be capricious, one must see how the incest taboo interrelates with other normative and prohibitive rules to form a coherent regulatory system for sexual behavior, procreation, marriage and the transmission of rights from one generation to the next.

All societies also look upon some unions not prohibited by the incest taboo with equal disdain. The only reason that can be given for this is that they violate conventions of propriety. In American society, many would regard the marriage of a man to his brother's former wife, although not incestuous, as improper. A sexual relationship between a stepfather and stepdaughter, or between step-siblings, while not technically incestuous, are acceptable in no quarters of our society. The culture of every society, then, has rules other than those governing incest that cover many social aspects of heterosexual unions, whether these be marriages or sexual affairs. Those most frequently encountered concern some aspects of kinship, race, ethnicity, religious affiliations, age and generation differences, discrepancies of social position and differences in wealth. Almost everything that has been said about restrictions and prohibitions, can be turned around and stated as preferential rules for selecting spouses and other sexual partners. In sum, the selection of spouses and sexual partners in all societies is subject to a complex mix of societal and cultural prohibitions and preferences which together we may call social rules, and an identical mix of these rules is probably never to be found in any two cultures. The best studied aspects of sex and culture are the rules governing the choice of sexual partners.

In each society, marriage, when viewed from a jural point of view, constitutes a diverse group of rights, privileges and obligations that cover a broad spectrum of social interests. So varied is the jural nature of marriage from one society to the next that there is not even a satisfactory legal or sociological definition of marriage that can be applied universally. Each society defines marriage, or its equivalent, in its own way. As with the incest taboo, the special configuration of rights and obligations that makes up marriage makes sense only when understood in context—in relation to other configurations and assignments of rights. However, in the configuration of rights that constitute marriage, and among those that concern rights of persons, there is always a set that covers sexual matters. Very often, too, a sharp distinction is made between sexual rights and reproductive rights. That is to say, the rights to sexual intercourse are distinguished from the reproductive issue of women. In every marriage there is a transfer of sexual and reproductive rights among concerned parties. Sometimes this transfer is accomplished with no tangible signs, but often it is acknowledged by some form of symbolic transaction. Many societies acknowledge the transfer of rights over the bride from her kin and guardians to the groom and his kin and guardians by a counter of wealth or suitable tokens. The most common form of this is called bride-price or bride-wealth. There are other transactions of this kind that symbolize the transfer of rights in the other direction, from the groom and his kin to the bride and her kin. Although often subject to intense negotiation, a bride-price is not the same as a purchase price for chattels. In the first place, economic profit is not the motive, and often a bride-price received for a daughter is automatically used to cover a bride-price paid for a son. Secondly, in the transfer of rights at marriage, some residual rights are retained by the original custodians. Such is not the case in most property transactions. As illustration, over large areas of Africa the bride-price, usually paid in valuable cattle, is transferred in two payments. The first is in return for sexual and other rights that go with residential cohabitation. With the first payment, the bride goes to live with her husband and the marriage is sexually consummated. However, not until the second payment is made, which may be much later, can the husband and his kin assume any rights over children that are born to the marriage. As long as the second payment remains unpaid, children remain under the sole authority of their mother and her kin. When the second payment is made, the husband and his kin assume what the society defines as paternal authority. However, paternal authority over children and the husband's authority over a wife are never total. Some residual rights over the children are retained by the mother and her kin, and rights over the wife are retained by her custodial relatives.

The example of African bride-price points up another universal phenomenon: the distinction between custodial rights and rights of exercise. In sexual matters, for instance, sexual rights over a woman may be held by her brother, father or maternal uncle, but none of the custodians can exercise these rights. When they are transferred at marriage to the husband and his kin, they are transferred to the former as rights to exercise his sexual claims but they are transferred as custodial rights only to his kin. Custodial rights become extremely important in tribal societies in the event of violations. Let us shift to East Bay in the southwest Pacific for an example. If a married man is prosecuted for adultery, he must pay compensation not only to his wife, whose sexual rights over him have been violated, he must also make redressive payments to his wife's brother who holds custodial sex rights over his sister and to whoever holds sexual rights over his partner in the adultery. If she is married (double adultery) he must pay her husband and her brother. If the partner is a single woman, for the offense of fornification he must pay her father, brother, maternal uncle and even more distant kin who jointly hold all of the girl's premarital sexual rights. If a child is born as a consequence of the offense, the biological father and his kin have no rights whatsoever over it. If the mother is married, then the child belongs to her and her husband, just as any of their own children would. If the mother is single, the child will eventually be considered the legitimate offspring of her parents, and, in effect, the child becomes the sociological sibling of its mother.

In our society, the distribution of sexual rights seems simpler than that encountered in tribal societies, but is it really? Instead of some custodial rights being distributed among a selected spread of kin, they are vested in the society as a whole or, as we say, in the law. If the person is a minor, then some are vested in parents or guardians. If the person has reached majority, then those formerly vested in parents and guardians are retained by the individual. Sexual violations are crimes, and redress is paid, in fines, to the court which represents society. If the offense is judged (by another judicial process) also to be civil, then redress must be made to all the aggrieved parties, that is, to those whose rights have been violated.

Custodial rights over sex and reproduction in women in some societies may be regarded as forms of capital assets which can be traded and accumulated. This is notably the case in some Australian Aborigine societies. The custodians are always men, and before marriage they are men of senior generations. Wealthy men are those who, in return for services performed, have received these rights from other men. Put simply, custodial rights over sex in women, in effect, mean the power to grant women in marriage, and in these societies which have very few forms of valuable capital, such rights constitute a source of power and influence. Furthermore, sexual rights in females not yet born are also recognized, and these, too, can be traded, accumulated and inherited. Thus, there is such a thing as sexual futures in these societies.

Many societies with regard to marriage, are polygynous. That is, it is possible and desirable for men to have more than one wife at one time. A very few societies are polyandrous, where a wife has more than one husband simultaneously. For obvious population reasons, the number of persons who can make and maintain plural marriages is limited, and so those who are engaged in them constitute a statistical minority. It must be stressed again that, while polygynous societies are very common,

polyandrous ones are very rare. The most well-known polyandrous societies are Tibet and some others of the Himalayan region. Polygyny
can be encountered in societies all over the world and appears in two
forms: sororal, where cowives are sisters, and general, where cowives
are of no particular relationship to each other and where marriage to
sisters may be explicitly forbidden or avoided. The few known instances
of polyandry seem to involve only husbands who are brothers in what
is called fraternal, sometimes adelphic, polyandry.

Cowives in polygynous marriages may not all have the same social
standing. In modern China before the socialist revolution, only the most
successful men could take secondary spouses, but the first wife was accorded a special status. In fact, it was customary to refer to the first
spouse as the wife and subsequent partners as concubines. The difference between wife and concubine was clearly defined. The wife was mis-
tress of the household; a concubine was a subordinate member of the
household. The wife was the legal mother of all children of her husband;
a concubine could not have full legal rights over her children. It was the
husband's privilege to direct his sexual attention where he wished, as
long as his wife had given birth to children. Indeed, one of the motiva-
tions for taking concubines was to gain young and attractive sex partners.

In Africa, where most societies are polygynous, wives may or may not
have different statuses, but husbands must pay equal attention to all.
Failure to do so constitutes grounds for divorce. In recognition of this
obligation, it is customary for a husband to spend his nights with his
wives in strict rotational order.

A few societies are simply not classifiable in terms of monogamy, polygyny and polyandry. Old Hawaii is one of these. Marriage there was flexible, and, while most marriages among commoners were monogamous,
polygynous unions were common (especially among the aristocrats) and
instances of polyandrous marriages could be found and were not regarded as deviant.

Polygyny is usually an indicator of superior status or wealth. However,
in some societies additional wives may be gained through the practices
of the levirate and wife inheritance. In the levirate, it is the duty of a
man to assume the marital responsibilities of his brother when the latter
dies. The levirate is primarily a way in which the domestic wellbeing of
a widow and her children is provided. It does not always mean that the
deceased husband's brother assumes the full marital role, including
sexual relations. Societies in which the levirate is customary vary in this
respect.

Wife inheritance differs from the levirate only in that it pertains to a
wife as part of the estate of a senior male relative. For instance, in some
societies it is customary for a man to be the principal heir of his mother's

brother, not of his father. The mother's brother's wife is part of the estate, but the inherited rights over the inherited wife may only be domestic, not sexual. The heir may inherit custodial rights insofar as sex and reproduction are concerned, but he may not exercise the sexual rights. There are a few societies in which an heir may inherit all of his father's wives except his own mother and he may exercise sexual rights over those who were formerly his stepmothers. There are many variations to these customs, and they illustrate, once again, how rights over sex and reproduction can be differently woven into the jural configurations of marriage.

Obviously, sexual intercourse is not confined to marriage alone in all societies. However, it is a convention to describe types of intercourse in terms of marriage and to classify nonmarital sex relations as either premarital or extramarital. In discussing both pre- and extramarital intercourse, it must be kept in mind that the moral and legal status of these forms varies from society to society. Each form, then, can and does occur in licit and illicit instances.

Few societies attempt to confine all coitus to legitimately married partners. Those that do, vary greatly in both the effectiveness with which all forms of nonmarital intercourse are prevented and the amount of social indignation displayed over violations. In sexual relations, there is always the distinction to be made between normative rules of behavior and statistical occurrences. The two rarely coincide, and to explain the discrepancies requires an examination of all the social factors that go into producing social conformity, adherence to moral and ethical ideals and cultural stability. Clearly this is too tall an order for this survey of sex across cultures. By and large we will confine ourselves to descriptions and comparisons that deal with normative aspects of sexual behavior rather than matters of conformity.

In some societies, there are designated categories of individuals, other than spouses, over whom sexual rights can be exercised. One of the most common instances of this is where a man has legitimate, but often limited, rights to intercourse with his wife's sister. Sometimes this is in anticipation of sororal polygyny, that is, the expectation that the wife's sister will become a secondary wife. However, the limited sex rights may be recognized even when the wife's sister marries someone else. Similar sharings of sexual rights occur between brothers, as when brothers have sexual rights to each others' wives, which can be seen as extension of the levirate custom.

Limited sharing of sex rights occurs sporadically in more situationally restricted forms, such as in ancient Rome where the father of a newly-married man had the right to initial intercourse with his son's wife. In a few tribal societies, a young man may be introduced to intercourse by an older, married, female kin, and the husband of the woman cannot object. This occurs in such scattered places as the Mota of the Banks Islands in the Pacific and the Pawnee Indians of North America. The Banaro of Papua-New Guinea allow ritual brothers (and every man has one ritual brother who is a sort of alter ego) mutual access to each other's wives. The Banaro also require that initial coitus with a bride be performed by her husband's father's ritual brother. As in polyandrous societies, where the identity of the biological father may not be certain, it is the sociological father, not the procreative father, who is important.

Another well-known instance of legitimized extramarital rights is that of some Eskimo groups in which a male visitor unaccompanied by a wife is offered his host's wife as part of hospitality. The difference between the examples just given and the current fad in the United States of wife-swapping is that the former are socially approved of and legally sanctioned, while the latter is neither approved of nor practiced by the majority of persons in the society and, in some states at least, may be classed as illegal.

Continuing extramarital affairs may be common in a society, even though the society makes a pretense of condemning them. Examples of this have already been mentioned in connection with the Gusii and Trukese. Countless more instances of this could be cited. It seems that systems of social control frequently fail to produce conformity in this area of sexual behavior, and the ethical norm is more frequently honored in the breach than in compliance. In most of these instances, the violations are overlooked as long as there is a pretense of keeping them secret. If, however, the affair is publicly flaunted, the forces of social control are brought into action.

The situation at East Bay is somewhat different. There, adultery (and fornication as well) is a very serious offense, and when discovered is always handled with severity. Nevertheless, most men and women at some time in their lives have engaged in illicit pre- or extramarital affairs. Because enforcement is a certainty, persons engaged in illicit relations go to elaborate precautions to keep them hidden, and most of them are revealed only years after they have lapsed. Discovery of adulterous affairs most frequently occurs when the woman, in a fit of pique at her lover, discloses it to punish him. Because the penalties for adultery are only mild for the woman, but extremely severe for the man, they are never revealed by the man, even when he is angry at his lover.

Then, there are societies that disapprove of extramarital sexual relationships, yet they class them as only minor offenses. Among contemporary Jamaicans of low socio-economic status, there are two jural forms of marital union: a consensual or common-law arrangement, for which there is no precise term, and a formally legitimized form called marriage.

Both are socially accepted, but there are distinctive jural differences between the two. The consensual form can be entered into and broken with no formal social observance, while marriage is legitimized by either the church or government and divorce is difficult to obtain. Children born in both forms are legitimate in most senses of the term, but children born of marriage may be given preference in inheritance. In both forms, however, sexual faithfulness of both spouses is an ideal expectancy. Extramarital affairs, however, are very common, and they are inevitably disclosed. When discovered they cause a great deal of acrimony, and frequently this may lead to the dissolution of a consensual union. In the case of legitimized marriage, the indignation is greater, but normally this does not precipitate a divorce. Rarely does adultery result in formal litigation and the application of legal sanctions. While adultery in Jamaica is considered a social irritation, it is not considered to be a crime.

Turning now to forms of premarital sexual relations, tolerance, even encouragement of intercourse before marriage is a feature of many societies. It is a mistake to think of this as promiscuity, as it is sometimes referred to in the literature, for premarital relations are subject to some form of control and regulation. As mentioned earlier, premarital intercourse is a notable feature of many Polynesian societies, both before and after the adoption of Christianity. It may even commence before a girl has experienced her first menstrual period, as with the Trobriands of Melanesia and the Bala of Africa, but this usually is not the case. Gaining sexual experience before marriage is considered to be a necessary part of maturational learning, and sexual affairs are thought to be an important aspect of courting. Some societies, such as the Trobriands and Managaia, stress only the rules against incestuous unions and age factors, which are the same as those governing the selection of a spouse. In some societies, however, the incest and other rules governing premarital affairs are more permissive than those governing marriage. It may be permissible for two first cousins to have a temporary premarital affair, but inconceivable for them to marry. The significance of this is that, even in societies that are permissive and supportive of premarital sexual affairs, there are limitations, and when these limitations are exceeded the affairs are considered to be illicit or illegal.

In a few societies that condone premarital sex relations, the choice of partners is narrowed to a single kinship category—a cross-cousin, perhaps, or even a cross-cousin on the mother's side only. This is almost always found in conjunction with a rule of marriage that designates this category of kin as the preferred spouse. As juveniles become interested in sex, they are directed to select partners from the preferred category from which a spouse will be selected. This does not eliminate all choices, for within the preferred category there may be several eligible individuals among whom choice can be exercised. Several individuals in the same preferred kin category are siblings or sibling equivalents, and premarital sexual privileges are continued on after marriage, which brings us back to the previous discussion about sexual sharing of spouses after marriage.

There are a few societies that operate in an almost opposite fashion. The designated categories from which spouses are to be selected, or specific individuals who have been selected as spouses by early betrothal, may be set apart by invoking a stringent avoidance. If the society is tolerant of premarital sex relations, then the premarital partners are those that can never become spouses. In such cases, there may be another designated category of persons with whom sex is permitted, such as the example given above of an older relative who initiates and trains a novice in intercourse.

In reviewing the variations among societies that are permissive toward premarital intercourse, questions arise about pregnancy and children born to unmarried persons. Two things are relevant to such questions: one is the sociological matter of legitimacy, the other is the physiological matter of adolescent sterility. In many societies, and particularly those that encourage premarital intercourse, the full social legitimacy is not fixed by the circumstances of birth. Legitimacy, or the ascription of all the statuses that comprise a social person, is conveyed later, often not fully until marriage. Often the status of a child born to an unmarried woman obtains its full sociological status when the woman marries. Often, too, the sociological statuses of all individuals, regardless of the marital circumstances of parents, are flexible until they reach the equivalent of an age of majority. Only a few societies deny full social status to children born outside marriage, and these are societies which, not unexpectedly, try to keep all intercourse confined to legitimate spouses. The answer, then, to the sociological side of the question is that societies that permit or encourage premarital sex freedom are organized so that all children born outside marriage are fully provided for and in no way suffer social disabilities or stigma.

On the physiological side, there is a period in every individual's life when he or she is capable of engaging in sexual intercourse, yet there is a very low probability of conception. Although variable from individual to individual, it usually occurs during adolescent years: hence, it is called adolescent sterility. Because of this, very few pregnancies occur during the premarital years of sexual experimentation. Therefore, no society that is permissive of premarital intercourse is plagued with children born before marriage occurs.

It is well to keep in mind, however, that marriage in all societies— those that permit or encourage, as well as those that do not allow, premarital intercourse—involves a reallocation of sexual rights, so that the rules governing sex behavior before marriage are always different from those that are in force after marriage.

The placement of high value upon female virginity at marriage does occur occasionally in cultures that are not in the Judaeo-Christian tradition. One of the most dramatic instances of this occurs, surprisingly, in one sector of some of the pre-Christian Polynesian societies. In Hawaii and Tahiti, over the entire society, a firstborn child outranked his or her younger siblings. In the case of the highest social ranks of the aristocratic class the firstborn child was the conveyor of special sacred prerogatives, and there were genealogical lines of firstborns to firstborns that received the highest respect. It was important, too, for the initial marital unions of sacred firstborn persons to be carefully arranged. For this reason, the sacred firstborn daughter was guarded against the possibility of intercourse before a suitable union could be arranged. The arranged unions were ritually consummated on a white sheet of bark cloth. Following the coitus, the cloth was publicly displayed. If it were bloodstained, there was supposed to be public acclaim; if not, there was supposed to be a public display of gloom or wrath. After the birth of the first child, however, these high-ranking female chiefs were free to philander in the accepted style of Hawaiian aristocrats.

In many subcastes of Hindu India, and in Ceylon as well, great emphasis is placed upon female virginity at marriage. In Hinduism, one aspect of maintaining religious purity is restricting all intercourse to marriage. While all societies that condemn premarital intercourse value female virginity at marriage, it takes on special significance when female chastity is identified with religious concepts of morality as it does in Hinduism and Christianity. Most societies that oppose premarital sex relations, look upon the matter more in terms of secular moral character than in terms of adherence to sacred law. East Bay provides an example. In this Melanesian society, all premarital intercourse is condemned as immoral and illegal. There is a kind of double standard in this which is the reverse of ours in that a male is held more responsible than a female and the sanctions applied against male offenders are much more severe than those applied to female offenders. Nearly all marriages are arranged by parents, but with consultation with the prospective bride and groom. Rarely is a young man or woman forced to marry someone he or she does not like. Children trust their parents' experience and wisdom in selecting a spouse. One of the most serious evaluations of a potential bride is that of her sexual morality. After a marriage is consummated, everyone concerned is very pleased if it turns out that a bride had an intact hymen. However, the proof of virginity is not found only in an unperforated hymen, and everyone is perfectly willing to assume a girl has been chaste if her reputation is good, even though she does not bleed after her initial marital coitus.

Even though some societies strongly disapprove of most nonmarital intercourse and levy heavy sanctions against these offenses, still not all pre- and extramarital intercourse is classed as fornication and adultery. At one time, American society was this way in some respects. For men, at least, pre- and extramarital intercourse with prostitutes was only a minor and excusable moral lapse, but pre- and extramarital affairs with women of good reputation was quite another matter.

Formerly, at East Bay, groups of wealthy men purchased girls from less well-off communities on neighboring islands to serve them as concubines. The purchase of a concubine was not the same as the bride-price transaction of a marriage. The concubines were entirely severed from their kind and had the status of a kind of domestic slave. They were not allowed to make gardens, and they were denied the sociological status of mother of the children they might bear. A concubine could be sold to other groups of men, she could be hired out as a prostitute and the fees collected went to her owners, and she could be given to the sons and nephews of her owners when it was felt that they needed some sexual outlet. A concubine was a source of sexual gratification, a mark of prestige, and she could prove to be a sound financial investment if her fees and resale to another group turned a profit. A concubine was a recognized exception to the laws of fornication and adultery.

When East Bay came under colonial authority, the practice of holding concubines was abolished. Yet the social need for legitimate female sex partners continued. In due course, there evolved an informal institution of prostitution, which was kept hidden from the colonial authorities and at the same time provided an opportunity for pre- and extramarital intercourse that was exempted from the laws of fornication and adultery. In general, the entire community approves of this new arrangement, for the availability of prostitutes is thought to reduce the commission of sexual offenses, which are extremely disruptive to this society. This same reasoning is often given to support legalized prostitution in our own society.

SEXUAL INTERCOURSE

The act of coitus reflects cultural and situational conditioning. The preferred coital position and attitude toward experimentation with novel positions varies from one culture to another. In the Trobriand Islands, intercourse usually commences with the man squatting before his partner, hands on the ground. He draws the woman toward him and brings her legs around his hips, and, as she moves closer, the man holds her thighs under his arms, but sometimes the woman will clasp the man outside his arms as she braces her back with her elbows. A less favored alternative position is with the woman supine, her legs spread and knees up. Some Australian Aborigines favor a similar position, with the man kneeling and the woman clasping him around the hips with her thighs.

In most of the societies for which there are data, it is reported that men take the initiative and, without extended foreplay, proceed vigorously toward climax without much regard for achieving synchrony with the woman's orgasm. Again and again, there are reports that coitus is primarily completed in terms of the man's passions and pleasures, with scant attention paid to the woman's response. If women do experience orgasm, they do so passively. In the Ojibwa, a North American Indian group, it is reported that women are passive during intercourse and orgasm; however, they may take the lead in initiating coitus. In the Guinea survey of young single adults from several African ethnic groups, the women overwhelmingly reported passivity during coitus, embarrassment at expressing satisfaction during intercourse, distaste for caressing and many admitted an inability to achieve orgasm.

There are some exceptions to the trend that was stated above. Experienced partners at East Bay engage in extended foreplay that begins with caressing, advances to fondling and mouthing of breasts and body, and, as passion mounts, there is mutual masturbation. Insertion often occurs only just before orgasm, and synchronized orgasm is regarded as very desirable. East Bay women do not seem to have difficulty in achieving orgasm. The delayed insertion at East Bay is similar to the practice called striking on Truk.

At East Bay, however, coitus in illicit affairs can rarely be completed in the way just described, because there is always the fear of discovery, and intercourse is completed as quickly as possible. Instead of prolonged foreplay, couples proceed directly with insertion and a rapid completion. The normal coital position is woman supine, man superior, but again in clandestine and hurried situations, which are almost always in the forest rather than in a house, a variant position is adopted with entrance from behind while the woman is bent over a log or rock or sometimes even standing.

Most marital intercourse at East Bay occurs, not at night in the village dwelling, but during the day in the garden hut. It is only in the gardens that couples can be assured of privacy, because gardens are scattered and young children can be left in the village while husband and wife go off to work. This is strictly recognized by everyone; consequently, no one approaches another's garden without first calling out and making one's presence known. Still, intercourse does occur in the village dwelling at night in the company of children and others who may live in the house. There is only one room to the East Bay house, and it is small. If the couple does not wish to attract the attention of others, coitus can be accomplished while lying on their sides, a position that is used late in pregnancy (although intercourse during pregnancy is interdicted, for reasons already given). Married couples do not object if children and others in the house are aware of their sex behavior, but they do object to being watched closely. Overly curious children are severely reprimanded.

The desire for privacy during coitus is reported everywhere, but in most tribal and peasant societies complete privacy is difficult to achieve. Fortunately, privacy is a culturally-defined matter, and it can be achieved for intercourse, as with other private behavior, without being alone. Over and over again it is reported that curious children must be taught to overlook the sexual activities of their parents. Adults know how to pretend to overlook what they recognize as private behavior.

One of the few eyewitness accounts of coitus comes from an observation by Captain James Cook, the explorer and early visitor to Tahiti. He reported seeing coitus completed in public, even as spectators congregated around the copulating couple and urged them on. He considered this not to be particularly aberrant for Tahiti at this time, but the nature of the situation was not explained.

Newly married couples at East Bay have difficulty with coitus, partly because of early training against consorting with persons of the other sex and partly due to the lack of privacy. Immediately after marriage, the couple invariably resides in the house of the husband's parents. Not until the next agricultural year will they have a garden and garden hut of their own. Although parents encourage them to have intercourse, and often even stretch a curtain across part of the house so that they can have a shielded area, still the couple is ashamed and afraid to have coitus in the dwelling. Often they resort to having intercourse in the jungle during the day. Once the new wife becomes pregnant and the couple's gardens are established, they are urged to build a dwelling of their own.

In societies that encourage premarital intercourse, and for those few that report ages for its commencement, the age at which coitus starts seems to be about 10 or 11. This may have been preceded by masturbation, as on Mangaia, or by imitative copulation, as in the Trobriands. Mangaians' interest in intercourse begins to wane after marriage and there is a corresponding fall-off of coital frequency. Among the few other peoples for whom there is data on coital frequency after marriage (Bala, Bengali Hindus and Muslims, East Bay, Kgatala, Navajo), the expected trend is noticeable: during the early years of marriage and up to the age of about 30, the mean frequencies are four to five times per week, although there is great individual variation. After 30 there is a tapering off, but in some societies, such as the Bala, the decline is slower. Overlooking the unreliability of all figures for coital frequency in marriage, but keeping in mind such extreme cases of low frequency as the Yapese and some peoples of highland Papua-New Guinea, the relatively slower decline among the Bala and the extraordinarily prolonged sexual activity of the Abkhasians, it appears that we are just beginning to get an idea of the cross-cultural variability in this quantifiable variable of sex behavior.

BIRTH CONTROL

As mentioned earlier in this chapter, there is probably no society that does not attempt to interfere with the reproductive process under certain conditions. Most of the potions and practices used to affect the outcome of pregnancies or to avoid conception are symbolic, magical or both, and their effectiveness is questionable.

Abstinence from coitus, a widespread method of deliberately avoiding conception, has been mentioned already in another context. Even more widespread is the practice of coitus interruptus. It is not surprising that these two methods are commonly found, for either can be arrived at from the simple awareness that conception results from the injection of ejaculate, and, except for a few questionable instances, all societies possess this knowledge. At East Bay, abstinence from marital intercourse was once the preferred method of birth control and was widely practiced both to protect women against the dangers to life that childbirth entailed and to space children so that each could receive optimum care. For men who had access to concubines, marital abstinence did not mean that all coitus was avoided. In illicit affairs, coitus interruptus had to be used in order to avoid pregnancy and detection. When concubines were forbidden by colonial edict, coitus interruptus became the favored mode of birth control for husbands and wives. The ideal spacing between children was about three to four years. This gave each child enough time to become fully mobile, weaned, and not in need of constant maternal attention. In more recent times, with the greater availability of medical attention and noticeably declining maternal and infant mortality rates, many couples have given up all attempts to space their children. Such couples are criticized severely for this by traditionalists.

East Bay is not without its magical methods to prevent conception, but the use of them was confined to concubines. Even though they are not used today, openly at least, the faith in their efficacy is undiminished. The reason that they are not used now with wives and lovers is that they are believed to cause permanent barrenness in the female. This was desirable for concubines but is a disaster for wives. Furthermore, they are classed as antisocial, along with love magic and sorcery whose procedures they also resemble.

One of the ironies of the rapid modernization that is now occurring in all nonindustrialized societies is that with increased medical and governmental services, which always lower maternal and infant mortality rates, the desire to limit family size also declines. The social psychological dynamics of this are not understood, but the difficulties of introducing new and effective family planning schemes are well appreciated.

MASTURBATION

Most information about masturbation in non-European societies and cultures is either anecdotal or stereotypic, and that which appears to have reliability is chiefly concerned with males. There are cultures in which masturbation is considered to be undesirable behavior, but the justifications for this attitude are apt to be different in each culture. The Kgtala-Tswana of Bechuanaland strongly disapprove of masturbation for males of all ages, but they are more tolerant of masturbation by females, and even condone it for married women who are either neglected by or are separated from their husbands for long periods. East Indians do not approve of male masturbation because of their theory of illness, which attributes weakness and debility to loss of semen. In the most detailed survey done in Africa, it was found that in all the subcultures represented, respondents disapproved of masturbation, and again it was widely held that masturbation caused weakness of spirit and body and increased proneness to personal disaster. In spite of these cultural attitudes, 40 percent of the single males reported having practiced masturbation one time, and 20 percent reported continued indulgence in it. Christians reported its occurrence more frequently than did Muslims, and Muslims more often than did those young men who had not been converted to these world religions. Young men and boys from rural backgrounds were more prone to this practice than were males from urban backgrounds. Very few girls in the sample admitted to masturbation, but the few who did reported both clitoral and vaginal types.

The Bala of the Democratic Republic of the Congo are tolerant of both male and female masturbation, and mutual masturbation among boys is reported to occur regularly. Young Mangaian boys and girls are expected to masturbate up to about the age of 10 years. At this age, boys undergo a genital operation, and the practice is discouraged, while at the same time both sexes are urged to have intercourse. Perpetuation of masturbation is considered to be the continuation of juvenile habits. The attitude toward it at East Bay is similar in some respects to that of the Mangaians. Masturbation among young boys is considered to be normal and is encouraged. It is tolerated, but considered to be slightly juvenile, for adolescents, and when continued after marriage is disparaged as the

continuation of a childish habit. Not much is said at East Bay about female masturbation. It is merely asumed that women are not as needful
of this kind of outlet as men are; therefore, they do not practice it much.

There is not sufficient information on alternate forms of sexual outlet
other than masturbation, such as nocturnal emissions and animal intercourse, to make comparisons. The existing data on masturbation suggests
that it is more generally considered to be a masculine habit than a feminine one, which is consistent with the widespread beliefs that women
manifest less sexuality, are less demonstrative during coitus and are less
prone to achieving orgasm than men. Yet, there are striking exceptions
to this general trend. The apparent female trend is suspiciously similar
to the assumptions of the Anglo-American cultural tradition, and one
cannot help but wonder whether this has not biased at least some of
the observations of other cultures.

HOMOSEXUALITY AND TRANSVESTISM

The cross-cultural data on homosexuality (and almost all of it concerns
males alone) is also scarce, of dubious quality and sometimes difficult
to interpret. There are, of course, the famous instances of widespread
male homosexual practices, but the data are often less than the fame.
Classical Greece and some Arab societies are cases of this sort, and one
is forced to consider the possibility that these examples have as much to
do with cultural stereotyping as with a genuine cultural pattern. An instance of cultural sterotyping is reported in Guinea. Guineans claim
that male homosexuality is rare amongst themselves but very common
among the Senegalese. Actually, the Guinea survey revealed that about
6 percent of the males admitted to having had homosexual contacts, but
there is no comparable data from Senegal. There is no hard data to support the assertion about institutionalized male homosexuality in some
Arab societies, and, in fact, Islamic law regards male homosexuality as a
heinous crime. On the other hand, the Guinea survey revealed that Muslims outnumbered Christians and others in reporting homosexual contacts; but it is doubtful that this difference is significant, for the number of respondents is very small.

In making cross-cultural comparisons of homosexuality, some distinctions of descriptive terms must be made. One is that between exclusive
homosexuality and bisexuality. The other is between exclusive homosexuality and bisexuality on the one hand, and transvestism on the other.
These semantic distinctions have been arrived at chiefly from behavior
in European cultures, and there is the very real question of whether they
are cross-culturally valid. Let us look at some of the data with this question in mind.

In old Hawaii, male homosexual practices are reported to have been common, especially among the aristocrats. It is not possible to determine what proportions of the individuals concerned were exclusively homosexual or bisexual. Some of these individuals also exhibited feminized behavior of specific sorts. The Hawaiian way of describing such behavior lumps all of it into one category. In contemporary Tahiti, which is a Polynesian culture close to that of Hawaii, there are male homosexuals who are granted semi-institutionalized positions in their communities. They also seem to exhibit transvestite behavior and the evidence suggests they are exclusive homosexuals. Thus, there is an unmistakable cultural tradition in parts of Polynesia of tolerance, at least, toward a feminized type of male homosexual individual. The Hawaiian admiration of men who sing in falsetto voices may also be a generalization from this tradition.

Among the Bala of Africa there are semi-transvestite men and women who, though considered to be deviant, are granted a partially institutionalized position in their communities. The Bala transvestites do not appear to be as much oriented toward homosexuality as they are inclined toward self-deprecation (what Freud called feminine masochism).

In contemporary urban Philippine society, feminized males who are mostly homosexual are recognized as a common deviant type of person, and, as in the United States, they are considered to be abnormal and psychologically sick. The Philippine male homosexual has been the subject of a number of sociologically and psychologically oriented studies.

The most famous instances of institutionalized male transvestism occurred in some of the American Indian societies, mainly of the Great Plains. Persons occupying these social positions engaged in feminine activities and adopted feminized modes of behavior. The Plains Indian transvestite usually had a history of feminized behavior during maturation. He adopted the role as an adult, and his switch was justified as being in response to a religious experience. There is some evidence to suggest that these transvestites were also exclusively homosexual. It should be pointed out that these Indian societies placed high value on male achievement of bravery, tolerance of physical pain and disregard of danger in battle. A common psychological interpretation of the male transvestite is that he was a man who could not face up to the demands for masculine achievement and opted out by adopting a female social position.

There are instances in African societies of women who undergo marriage with another woman, but this custom need not concern us, because it involves neither homosexual nor transvestite behavior. It is an inversion of gender status, undertaken in special circumstances when a woman must substitute for a man.

Now, the few examples just cited seem to lend cross-cultural support to what we already know from our own culture and society: male homosexual preferences and feminized or transvestite social behavior are not inextricably bound together, although in some societies it may be assumed that they are.

Bisexual behavior without transvestism is socially acknowledged in several societies. We know this to be the case in some totally male associations in our own society, although the reality of this may not be accepted by the society as a whole. In some Arab societies, however, it is reported that homosexual relations among women is accepted among widows and among women in harems who have no access to normal heterosexual contacts.

Among Melanesian societies of Papua-New Guinea and other islands of the southwest Pacific, there are numerous examples of institutionalized male bisexualism. East Bay again provides an instance. Nearly all East Bay men have homosexual contacts at one time or another. However, male homosexual relations follow a pattern that is best seen along the life history of the individual. Recall that boys and young men are encouraged to masturbate, but masturbation is supposed to be set aside after the age of marriage is reached, and it is especially ridiculed after marriage. In other words, masturbation is phased out as the opportunities for heterosexual relations are phased in. As boys reach late adolescence, they may also engage in mutual masturbation, but in the switch away from masturbation they also may have anal intercourse with friends and trade off playing the active and passive roles. No love or strong emotional bonds are developed out of the sexual aspect of the relationship. It is considered to be part of the accommodations expected of friendship. Such homosexual relations are considered to be a substitute for heterosexual intercourse and a substitute that is more mature than masturbation. Recall, too, that under the old regime married men were expected to stay away from their wives for extended periods, following the birth of a child. However, the husbands were not expected to remain sexually continent. Concubines were the favored object of gratification, but not all men had direct or easy access to them. Another substitute for older men was young boys, and they did take boys as passive partners for anal intercourse. Before a boy could be induced into such a partnership, permission had to be obtained from his father. A boy complied with the arrangements out of deference to parental and adult authority, although it was expected that he would be rewarded with small presents from time to time.

As East Bay men see it, anal intercourse is only a substitute for heterosexual intercourse. There is no culture category, therefore no recognition of the exclusively homosexual man who prefers relations with males to intercourse with females. Likewise, oral-genital practices, both homo- and heterosexual, are either unknown or considered to be a foreign aberration. There are some men who have never been married and whose sexual careers are assumed to be mostly homosexual, but their failure to marry is attributed to meanness with money or some other unpleasant character trait that makes them unacceptable to women.

At this time, the cross-cultural data on exclusive homosexuality, bisexuality and transvestism throws no new light on the genesis of these statistically infrequent sexual and gender inversions. Cross-cultural comparisons do suggest, however (as do studies of monosexual communities in American society), that bisexuality can, and frequently does, occur in social circumstances where partners of the opposite sex, though preferred, are not available and the social atmosphere is tolerant of such practices. In this connection, it should be noted that throughout Melanesian societies, where institutionalized forms of male bisexuality are most frequently encountered, there is also a widespread tradition of separating the men from the women. So pronounced is this nearly everywhere, it can be regarded as a basic principle of social organization. Men live in close association with one another and commonly have a communal house of some kind from which women are excluded. Women, on the other hand, stay close to the dwelling and the gardens. This creates an analogous situation to the monosexual communities in our society, such as prisons and the armed forces. One can entertain the hypothesis that in the strongly gender-segregated communities of Melanesia, when the cultural also imposes effective barriers to heterosexual intercourse, there is a likelihood that institutionalized male bisexual practices will result.

The cross-cultural data also tend to support the contention, which runs counter to psychoanalytic theory, that preferential or exclusive homosexuality is a fundamentally different phenomenon from bisexuality. In exclusive homosexuality, there seems to be an inversion of the individual's motivational and cognitive organization, which suggests that the origins are to be found in either biological inheritance, early socialization or, more likely, some combination of both. On the other hand, in bisexuality the organization of sexual motivation is directed toward persons of the opposite sex, but social barriers around the preferred objects of gratification increase the tendency to seek a substitute source of gratification.

Cross-cultural comparisons seem also to suggest that there are different kinds of transvestism. On the one hand, there is some evidence, but admittedly it is weak, that inversions of gender status-role occur without a corresponding inversion of gender preference for sex partner. On the other hand, there is ample cross-cultural data to confirm the appearance in other cultural milieu of the (male) homosexual transvestite.

If this distinction between two kinds of transvestism proves to be valid, we can then begin to search for their separate origins.

SEX IN RITUAL AND CULTURE METAPHOR

In very few cultures are sexual concerns confined solely to sexual behavior and related aspects of human reproduction. Inis Beag may be an instance where an ethos of sexual denial comes close to blotting out cultural ramifications of sexual themes. However, in most cultures sexual motifs and symbols occur in many contexts which are oriented in directions quite different from sexual behavior and reproduction. Hindu religious sculpture, for example, is filled with erotic elements that serve to enhance and embellish unrelated theological concepts. There are rituals which in their enactment dwell heavily upon spiritual and social matters, but into which may be introduced contrastive sexual themes lest anyone overlook the fact that the event being celebrated also has sexual significance. At some American weddings, the hazing of bride and groom after the religious ceremony, and often concerted attempts to destroy the privacy of the couple, stands in stark contrast to the lofty spirituality of the service, but, at the same time, this disruptive humor (which many consider to be in bad taste) introduces the sexual theme of the wedding night into the celebration.

Many societies mark maturational transitions with ceremonies that contain sexual themes. Aoriki, in the eastern Solomon Islands, is an example. All boys, usually when they are between the ages of 8 and 10 years, must undergo a ritual separation from the domestic environment, a lengthy separation from all females and a gala reintroduction into the social life of the community. Broadly stated, the purpose is to perform a spiritual transformation of the boys, who until this ritual are not socially distinguished from girls, into what is best described as immature men. The emphasis in the ritual separation is on bringing the boys into contact for the first time with sacred activities that are performed by men only. It is this initiation into the sacred realm that accomplishes the transformation. The subsequent isolation and reintroduction emphasize various aspects of the spiritual transformation.

The final act of the entire ceremony, which may have taken as long as a year to complete, is a ritual wedding for each initiate to a girl of his age. The wedding ceremony consists of a few brief acts that stand for some of the sexual aspects of marriage. The boys and girls are usually too young to understand fully the sexual meanings of what they are coached to do. Furthermore, there is no wedding ceremony in Aoriki marriage, and in no way is the ritual wedding considered to be a betrothal. Aorikians explain the wedding ritual in this way: originally the entire initiation was performed when the initiates were just approaching marital age. The wedding ritual signified their eligibility for marriage, and it could be used as a wedding to a girl they wished to marry. The wedding ritual is now somewhat of an anachronism because over the years the entire ceremony has been moved forward in the lives of the initiates.

Whether or not this historical explanation has anything to do with actual history is not important. As the entire ceremony stands, the meaning of the final wedding ritual seems to be this: now that a transformation in social gender has taken place, prepare yourself for the next transition in life which will be marriage. The actual transition into married status at Aoriki is a very gradual one. There are affairs which become more and more serious until the couple decides to start living together. There is no bride-price or ritual observance of any kind, the couple merely builds a house and cohabits. Even living together is not a full marriage commitment. When a child arrives, however, the union is regarded as a permanent arrangement.

For many years it has been noted that the isolation phase of initiations is marked either by some kind of ordeal, formalized teaching, or both. Of special interest here are those that include some kind of ordeal that is sexually meaningful. This usually means some form of genital surgery. The most common form is circumcision, which occurs in many societies other than those in the Judaic, Christian and Muslim traditions. It has already been mentioned, in passing, as occurring among the Gusii. In the Jewish and Islamic traditions the rituals around circumcision are not elaborate, but it is a mandatory operation for all males.

Almost all Australian Aborigine societies have an extensive circumcision ceremony. It is mandatory, and it clearly marks an important transition in life. Marriage, for instance, is not possible without circumcision, and women abhor the thought of intercourse with an uncircumcised man. Over a somewhat restricted area of Australia, there is a second ritual, never as extensive or as elaborate as that for circumcision but no less mandatory, during which a second operation is performed on the penis. This is subincision, which consists of splitting open part, or all, of the urethra along the under surface of the penis. Subincision is a necessary preparation for the ritual activities men perform during the rest of their lives, one of which is the circumcision ceremony for boys. During these rituals, a small quantity of one's own blood is required, and the ritual blood can only be drawn from the urethral surfaces laid open by subincision. The reasons for taking ritual blood in only this manner are derived from Aborigine theories about purity and the nature of mankind. Several attempts have been made to explain subincision in noncultural terms. One is that women derive more pleasure from coitus as a result of the broadening which subincision causes. Another is that it is a way of diverting semen away from the vaginal opening; thus, it is a crude attempt at birth control. Neither of these explanations is convincing. The obvious cultural meaning is that subincision represents, and is a necessary part of, a social status senior to that of ordinary circumcised males, and the deeper cultural meanings are to be found in the metaphysical concepts about human nature.

In Polynesia, a different penile operation is performed on all boys. It is called superincision and consists of making a slit through the upper portion of the foreskin. The foreskin is not removed as in circumcision; it is slit open only at the top, but in time the effect is to uncover the glans penis. Superincision is not now accompanied by an elaborate ceremonial observance, but it is, nonetheless, mandatory. In Mangaia it marks the point in social development when intercourse replaces masturbation. To women, the thought of intercourse with an unsuperincised man is disgusting. The usual explanations for superincision are given— cleanliness, more pleasure to the woman during coitus—but the important social point is that the operation marks an important transition into sexual maturity.

Among some groups of interior Borneo, young men undergo a painful transverse perforation of the glans penis. It is a voluntary operation, the purpose of which is to be able to insert into the perforation an object which is supposed to increase the pleasure experienced by one's partner during intercourse. Unfortunately, there is no confirmation from the women that this is the case. However, on the basis of superficial evidence, the practice seems also to concern the demonstration of fortitude during the operation. It is not a mark of social transition; rather, it seems more akin to forms of cosmetic operations such as tattooing, scarification, perforations of the nose septum and ear lobes. In this case, it is a kind of cosmetic operation which remains hidden, as with the thigh tattoos of East Bay women, but which, nevertheless, has great erotic significance.

Girls are also subjected to mandatory genital operations during transition ceremonies. The Sudanic region of Africa is particularly noted for these. The operations include scratching the walls of the vagina until bleeding occurs, surgical enlargement of the vaginal orifice, sewing up the vaginal orifice and later reopening it for marriage, ritual cutting of the hymen, and excision of part or all of the clitoris. As with the alteration of the penis, the significance is to be found in the nature of the social transition that it stands for, and often the cultural meaning is to be found in the metaphysical concepts that the culture has developed to explain the nature of mankind.

Sexual symbolism may also occur in rituals that mark, not the social transition of individuals, but a temporary state of transition for the entire society. For an example let us turn again to old Hawaii. When a paramount chief died, his political domain responded by a kind of emotional debauch, a bacchanalia. While some people exhibited exaggerated mourning, others gave vent to other passions that were normally kept in check. The idea was to show excess and lawlessness. Not unexpectedly, one of the main forms of behavior in which excess was shown was sexual. All restraints were cast aside, rules were broken, conventions were flouted, and for those who would normally be aggrieved by such violations, there was no legal redress. After some days of this excessive and promiscuous demonstration, a successor was installed and, as his first official act, he proclaimed the reinstitution of law and order, and the orgy ended.

The social meaning of this revolt against conventions is undisguised. It all signified the temporary absence of political authority during the interregnum. To Hawaiians, the temporary absence of an authority to enforce social regulations was especially conveyed by violating sexual conventions.

The sexual symbolism in some rituals can represent entire metaphysical theories as if the rituals were theatrical presentations rather than religious attempts to influence the natural course of events. On the south coast of Papua-New Guinea are the Kiwai who have a unified concept of vitality and reproduction which underlies an annual round of rituals aimed at revitalizing and renewing the fertility of all living things. The key species in this concept are man and the sago palm (*Metroxylon sp.*). The palm is an abundant source of carbohydrate which is stored in the form of starch in the trunk of the mature tree. At maturity the sago palm sends out a spectacular efflorescence, after which it withers, dies, falls and putrefies. Thus, in dying, the tree scatters the nuts that hang from the withered efflorescence until the tree falls. In human semen is a vital life-generating and life-sustaining substance. Female genitals possess a power to cause erections, which make coitus possible; coitus produces semen. Menstruation is equated with the death of the sago palm: bleeding leads to death and the smell of putrefaction. The starchy pith of the sago palm is equated with semen, the outer shell of the tree trunk with female genitals and the sago palm nuts with children.

With this inventory of concepts and equations, dozens of rituals are performed along the annual cycle aimed at invigorating different species, sociological groups and agricultural plantings. Each ritual uses a different combination of these symbolic elements, plus actual or imitative copulation. The most spectacular of these rituals is one in which the entire community participates. The object is to produce an exceptionally high-potency substance that everyone can use to increase fertility and vitality in any object. The ceremony also seems to have the purpose of infusing the entire community with the same vitality and reinvigorated fertility. The ceremony consists of several nights of erotic singing and sexual promiscuity. Many rules governing sexual behavior are suspended. All ejaculate is recovered from the women and collected in a single vessel where it is mixed with other ingredients with appropriate symbolic meanings. When sufficient ejaculate has been collected, it is shared out to all the participants, who use it to daub on anything they wish to infuse with vitality and fertility. During the ceremony an elderly couple acts as ritual leaders. The last ritual act in the extended rite is a mock mourning of the couple's death. The couple is treated as though they had given their lives so that out of their deaths new life and vitality could arise.

In some instances, the sexual allusions are purely metaphorical and without action. Their function is to explain natural phenomena in metaphoric images. The final example comes again from the cosmology of old Hawaii. In one long chant, the formation of the entire universe is depicted, in highly poetic form, as evolving from a beginning of undifferentiated darkness into its present complexity. The metaphor used throughout is sexual union and birth. From original darkness are born night and day, they copulate and produce offspring of sun and moon; they copulate and other celestial forms come into being, and so on to the birth of natural forces and geological forms. The phyla, then orders, then families of all living things are produced from the sexual unions of parental stocks. From the personifications of the awesome natural forces are born the gods, then demigods, then humans. By such an ordering, the universe exists in an understandable shape, with everything related to everything else by descent and consanguinity. The one force that is not accounted for is sexual reproduction. It alone exists as primal mystery and unchanging principle by which the Hawaiian is sustained.

CONCLUSION

Every society has a culture of sex, because the foundations of sex are part of the biological nature of man. Sex does not have to be discovered; its biological existence is pressed upon consciousness as an instinctive force. In man, however, the inherited aspects of sex seem to be nearly formless. Only by enculturation does sex assume form and meaning. Total cultures vary greatly from one society to the next, and they vary in the same society from one generation to the next. The sexual sector of culture varies in the same ways as the total culture of which it is a part.

The culture of sex is anchored in two directions. In one direction, it is moored to the potentialities and limitations of biological inheritance. In the other direction, it is tied to the internal logic and consistency of the total culture. As one sector of culture changes, all of the other sectors that articulate must undergo adjustments. However, there are limits to just how much change the culture of sex can tolerate, because inhertied biological limitations cannot be exceeded. Thus, in comparing cultures of sex, we can note that in some behavioral aspects there is not as much variability as in other aspects. Those aspects that are tied closely to biological foundations are conservative; those tied to the internal logic and consistency of the rest of culture are easier to alter. For this reason, it is readily apparent that the highly symbolic and intellectual aspects of sex are incredibly diverse, while aspects of sexual performance show less diversity. To understand one culture of sex, we need to know how sexual performance is conceptually joined to the total culture, which is the same as knowing how a participant in that society performs his sexual roles in accordance with the cognitive consistency of his culture. To have an analytic or theoretical framework for sexual behavior in all cultures, we must develop a single set of concepts and principles into which all cultures can be fitted without violating the uniqueness of each. The first we can do already, but we have only just commenced making headway on the second.

SUGGESTED READINGS

Danielsson, 1957. *Love in the South Seas.* (Original Swedish edition of 1954 translated by F. H. Lyon.) New York: Dell.

Davenport, W. 1965. Sexual Patterns and their regulation in a society of the Southwest Pacific. In *Sex and Behavior.* Edited by Frank A. Beach. New York: Wiley.

Ford, C. S. 1945. *A Comparative Study of Human Reproduction.* Yale University Publications in Anthropology, No. 32. New Haven. Yale University Press.

Ford, C. S., and Beach, F. A. 1951. *Patterns of Sexual Behavior.* New York: Harper & Row.

Hanry, P. 1970. *Érotisme Africain, le Comportement Sexual des Adolescents Guinéens.* Paris: Payot.

Hart, D. V., et al. 1965. *Southeast Asian Birth Customs: Three Studies in Human Reproduction.* New Haven: Human Relations Area Files Press.

LeVine, R. A. 1959. Gusii sex offenses: a study in social control. *Amer. Anthrop.* 61:965-90.

Malinowski, B. 1929. *The Sexual Life of Savages in North-Western Melanesia.* New York: Halcyon House.

Marshall, D. S., and Suggs, R. C. 1972. *Human Sexual Behavior, Variations in the Ethnographic Spectrum.* Englewood Cliffs, N.J.: Prentice-Hall.

Mead, M. 1949 *Male and Female.* New York: Morrow.

Nag, M. 1962. *Factors Affecting Human Fertility in Nonindustrial Societies: A Cross-Cultural Study.* Yale University Publications in Anthropology, No. 66. New Haven: Yale University Press.

Schapera, I. 1941. *Married Life in an African Tribe.* New York: Sheridan House.

6

HOMOSEXUALITY

Martin Hoffman

EDITORIAL PREFACE

This chapter deals exclusively with homosexuality in our own society, and the author treats the subject from two points of view. As a practicing therapist, Martin Hoffman is concerned with the special psychological problems often confronting homosexual individuals in the United States. Firmly opposed to the interpretation of homosexuality as a manifestation of mental illness, he nevertheless believes that society's treatment of homosexual individuals can, and often does, result in serious psychological malfunction. He sees the therapist's responsibility not as one of "curing" the troubled homosexual patient of his homosexuality but of helping to resolve basic conflicts—a process which *may*, in some instances, involve establishment of a heterosexual orientation, but in other cases may call for a nonconflictual adjustment to, or acceptance of, the homosexual pattern.

As a scientific investigator, Hoffman examines the sociological dimensions of the homosexual way of life in America today. His descriptions of the gay world, of the non-geographical homosexual ghetto, and of homosexuality as a minority group phenomenon are perceptive and illuminating.

Other chapters in this book contain ideas and evidence with immediate relevance to Hoffman's presentation. It is particularly instructive to compare parts of the present chapter with William Davenport's cross-cultural analysis of male and female homosexuality. Other cultures resemble our own, in that homosexual relations between women receive less attention, and probably are much less common, than similar behavior on the part of men. It also is clear that definitions of homosexuality as abnormal or as a manifestation of mental illness are culture-bound. In many societies, homosexual relations constitute an acceptable substitute when heterosexual behavior is prevented or contraindicated by temporary taboo or prohibition. Even exclusive male homosexuality may be sanctioned and ritualized.

In relation to Hoffman's theoretical position, it is particularly illuminating to discover that for other societies integrity of the masculine gender role is not imperiled by participation in homosexual activity. Furthermore, a satisfactory homosexual relationship between men need not, and in fact usually does not, involve any emotional bond, love relationship or dependency beyond those of common friendship. This cross-cultural finding is relevant to Hoffman's attempts to explain the transitory character of most homosexual alliances and the infrequency of long-term unions in American men. One is led to suspect that the psychodynamics of homosexual behavior tend to vary from one society to the next, and therefore its consequences for the individual in relation to his society will be equally diverse.

What has just been said should make it clear that we cannot seriously entertain the theory that exclusive heterosexuality represents the only "normal" or "healthy" form of sexual interaction for *Homo sapiens*. At the same time, it is impressive that, among all people, homosexual relations are classed as a *substitutive* form of sexual outlet as far as the majority of the adult population is concerned. Heterosexual behavior is always the norm, and the preferred pattern for most people most of the time. This observation is relevant to suggestions made in the discussion of evolution and sexuality in Chapter 1.

A clue to this apparent enigma may be found in Hoffman's discussion of bisexuality as represented by the following quotation.

A significant number of people . . . are sexually attracted to, and seek out, sexual partners of both sexes . . . [but] just because we say that a given individual is sexually attracted to both men and women does not imply that his or her feelings on seeing a man and his or her feelings on seeing a woman are the same. In both cases sexual arousal may occur, but the individual's entire perception of the situation may be quite different; and behavior with men, both in and out of bed, may be of an altogether different kind than behavior with women.

It is conceivable that potential bisexuality is much more common than this passage suggests, and, in fact, is the rule rather than the exception. An analysis of homosexual behavior in animals, described in Chapter 11, led me to propose a *principle of S-R complementarity*, which bears at least a formal resemblance to Hoffman's observations. Another possibly relevant concept incorporated in Chapter 11 is that of *sex-linked prepotency* of S-R patterns. If these hypothetical concepts are at all applicable to human sexuality, they would indicate several predictions. The first would be that individuals of either sex would be sexually attracted, and capable of erotic response, to both male and female partners. The second would be that in both males and females the nature of the response would differ according to the sex of the other individual; i.e., reactions to a like-sexed and to an opposite-sexed partner would not be the same. Furthermore, regardless of the genetic sex of responding individuals, stimuli normally associated with females would tend to arouse masculine sexual responses; whereas stimuli usually connected with males would tend to elicit predominantly feminine reactions. This reflects the complementarity principle, but is not consonant with Hoffman's assertion that homosexual men prefer masculine, rather than effeminate, men as sex partners.

The third prediction, based on the notion of sex-linked prepotency, would be that males would be more responsive than females to the female "stimulus pattern," whereas females would tend to respond more readily and intensely to the male "stimulus pattern." In other words, for both sexes, the probability for homologous responses to heterologous stimuli would exceed the probability for heterologous responses to homologous stimuli.

This final prediction is, of course, a restatement of what most people accept as the normal, or expected, set of relationships; but, as Hoffman cogently observes, the development of heterosexual patterns is just as much in need of explication as is the ontogenesis of homosexuality. Other authors have their own answers to this neglected problem of the "etiology of exclusive heterosexuality." Some, such as John Money and Robert Stoller, favor the view that individual experience and social conditioning provide the decisive controls, while others, as represented by Milton Diamond, believe that prenatally determined response biases in the nervous system play a major role.

Hoffman's position on this issue clearly rests upon a functional, rather than organic, interpretation, but his most general statement is, "*we do not know* the etiology of homosexuality." He is critical of traditional psychoanalytic explanations in general, while admitting that they "do apply in some cases." Although he does not attempt to explain its origins, Hoffman does interpret many of the undesirable consequences of homosexuality upon the homosexual as products of society's reactions to him. The chapter's closing section on the theory and practice of therapy is, therefore, appropriately oriented to assisting the homosexual who needs help (and there are many who do not) to function more successfully and less stressfully within his society, either by accepting and adjusting to his own homosexuality or by developing and strengthening alternative patterns of sexual expression.

INTRODUCTION

Homosexuality is a topic which is both complex and controversial, and these two attributes are interrelated because some of the controversy is engenderd by the multi-disciplinary nature of the subject matter. In some respects, the problem of homosexuality is analogous to the problem of the blind men and the elephant. Scholars from various disciplines look at homosexuality with their own disciplinary biases, so it is not surprising that they arrive at different, and often contradictory, conclusions. In this chapter, I shall attempt to present the findings from a number of disciplines and hope to achieve a fairly broad (multi-disciplinary) understanding of the subject, as well as an explication of some of the disputes.

Since homosexuality is defined by American society as deviant, since the practices it involves are illegal in most states, and since most participants in homosexual activity do not wish to discuss their experiences with others and often wish to conceal the meaning of their behavior from themselves, the student of homosexuality is faced with the "problem of sampling." This problem represents much more than a mere methodological quibble, since it implies that different investigators are studying different populations. Various investigators not only define "homosexual" or "homosexuality" differently; they bring different theoretical viewpoints to bear, and study different parts of the total homosexual population. Therefore, it is well for me to state very clearly at the outset that, although it is shared by other investigators, the viewpoint presented in this chapter is not universally held by students of the subject.

I will illustrate explicitly what I mean by the problem of sampling. Kinsey, who studied a cross section of the entire white American population, though it was neither a random nor representative sample from that population, could give us the kind of incidence figures which are usually asked for in any discussion of homosexuality. Clinicians, who often maintain that homosexuality is a mental illness or a symptom of such an illness, derive their impressions of homosexuality from patients in psychiatric treatment. Social scientists, who often disagree with psychiatrists about the "illness theory of homosexuality," typically derive their understanding of the subject from a study of homosexuals who are not in treatment but who are part of the larger "homosexual community." Although they are important, these sampling differences do not entirely account for the disagreement between the disputants. Much more fundamental theoretical assumptions underlie the arguments, and hence the differences are considerably more intractable than is implied by stating that they result *merely* from a difference in sampling technique.

It is probably well here to answer the inevitable first question, namely: "How common is homosexuality?" The 1948 Kinsey report on male sexual behavior tells us that 37 percent of the total white male population of the United States has had at least some overt homosexual experience to the point of orgasm between adolescence and old age. Twenty-five percent of the male population has had *more than incidental* homosexual experience or reactions for at least three years between the ages of 16 and 55. During their entire lifetime, 18 percent of American males have had at least as much homosexual as heterosexual experience for a period of at least three years. Ten percent of all men are *more or less exclusively homosexual* for at least three years between the ages of 16 and 55. Finally, Kinsey points out that 4 percent of the white males in his sample were exclusively, or nearly exclusively, homosexual throughout their entire lives.

It is difficult directly to compare Kinsey's 1953 data for women with the 1948 data for men, since for males it is possible to use erection as an easy index of sexual arousal, whereas a comparable index is not available for women. However, Kinsey does report the following figures: 28 percent of the women he interviewed had been conscious of erotic responses to other females. By age 40, 19 percent of the females in the total sample had experienced some sexual contact with other females. One-half to two-thirds of this 19 percent reached orgasm in at least some of these contacts. By age 35, there were 11 percent with orgastic experience as a result of homosexual interaction.

It should be stressed that these data were collected approximately three decades ago, and may not represent today's population. Furthermore, methodological objections have been raised to Kinsey's studies as a whole. Nevertheless, they constitute the only reliable approximation to a satisfactory statement of the frequency of homosexual response presently available.

It seems to me that the most interesting fact about the Kinsey data on homosexuality is not the exact figures themselves; it is the general finding that homosexuality is not a rare phenomenon, and that a tremendous amount of overt homosexual activity occurs in the United States. One of the most interesting findings is that 10 percent of American males are more or less exclusively homosexual for at least three years between the ages of 16 and 55. There are probably few people, including workers in the sciences, who are aware that homosexuality is this extensive. These figures make it safe to conclude that we are dealing with a phenomenon that involves literally millions of Americans.

DEFINITION OF HOMOSEXUALITY

I use the term "homosexual" to refer to those individuals who have a sexual attraction toward people of the same sex, for at least a few years of their lives. Obviously, this is not a definition which is universally agreed upon. Kinsey, for example, objects to using the terms "homosexual" or "heterosexual" as adjectives to describe persons. He prefers to reserve those words to describe the nature of the overt sexual relations, or of the stimuli to which the individual erotically responds. At the same time, Kinsey creates and uses a homosexual-heterosexual rating scale which includes both psychological reactions and overt experiences. So we see that Kinsey, himself, is forced into using the term as an adjective to describe persons. I think there is no way that we can discuss the subject in depth without speaking of individuals as homosexuals. To avoid doing so, would reduce any attempt at a common understanding ·of the subject to a quantified study of overt behavior. Even Kinsey, who was himself most sympathetic to a taxonomic approach to sexuality, does not quite do this. It would certainly behoove those of us who wish to arrive at a broad socio-psychological understanding of the phenomenon to adhere to the common-sense use of the terms, at least insofar as they can be made serviceable.

On the other hand, when I use the term "homosexual" to describe someone, I do not deny that he may *also* be heterosexual, for I think there is a significant number of people who are sexually attracted to, and seek out, sexual partners of both sexes. These people we could very conveniently call "bisexual," and I will do so; but, it is most important to realize that in such individuals the nature of the sexual attraction to men may not be the same as the sexual attraction to women. In other words, just because we say that a given individual is sexually attracted to both men and women does not imply that his or her feelings on seeing a man and his or her feelings on seeing a woman are the same. In both cases sexual arousal may occur, but the individual's entire perception of the situation may be quite different; and behavior with men, both in and out of bed, may be of an altogether different kind than behavior with women.

What kind of people are homosexuals? What do they look like and how do they act? To these questions, one can only give the most general (and unsatisfactory) answer, namely, that they run the entire gamut: from the individual who can be identified a block away (for example, the "swishy faggot"), to the husband, son or brother whom even fairly sophisticated observers would not suspect of harboring any homosexual interest. The "obvious" are a small minority of a homosexual population which includes people who are rich and poor, handsome and ugly, stupid and clever, and all combinations in between. Homosexuality penetrates every conceivable socio-economic, religious and geographical classification.

A great deal of nonsense has appeared in both the scientific and popular literature about "active" and "passive," "masculine" and "feminine" homosexuals. It is frequently implied that there is a sharp difference between these two kinds of individuals in both male and female homosexuality. It is certainly true that a minority of homosexual people can be classified, both on the basis of their own conscious definition of themselves as masculine or feminine, and as to what they will or will not do in bed. But this applies only to a minority. The truth is that most homosexuals cannot be so categorized, and, in fact, will generally take a variety of roles in sexual performance.

SEXUAL PERFORMANCE

Just exactly what do homosexuals do sexually? Most American investigators have found that there are four "classic" positions which a homosexual man may adopt when he is in bed with another male. These can be divided into oral and anal and then again into insertor and receptor roles. Thus, an individual may be an oral insertor, an anal insertor, an oral receptor, or an anal receptor. He can also participate in mutual fellatio and can engage in a great deal of alternation among these roles. In addition, there may be a considerable degree of change during an individual's sexual lifetime, so that he may start with a preference for one kind of activity (or perhaps no specific preference at all), and years later may have an equally strong preference for a different kind of activity (or perhaps for an expanded sexual repertoire).

The social psychologist Michael Schofield, who studied an English homosexual community, found that a large proportion of male homosexuals preferred to achieve ejaculation by "genital apposition" or very close body contact *without* penetration of a body orifice. In such behavior, the individual rubs his penis against his partner's body, e.g., against his belly or his leg. Schofield's finding is in sharp contrast to what all American investigators have found to be the sexual preference of their male subjects, who, by and large, think of "genital apposition" as rather adolescent and generally prefer one or more variations of either oral or anal insertion. Why this curious national contrast exists has never been explained, and as a matter of fact has not really even been noticed. It may or may not indicate something significant about sexual attitudes in the two countries. Self- and mutual masturbation play significant roles in homosexual practices, although male homosexuals also tend to regard this form of sexual expression as less than optimal.

With regard to female sexual practices, masturbatory contact is predominant until about age 40. After this age, masturbation and cunnilingus occur at approximately equal frequencies. Between 6 percent and 15 percent of the women studied in one survey used inanimate objects for sexual stimulation during a homosexual relationship. This technique was employed infrequently, occurring only once weekly for a period of several months. Inanimate objects were not used before the age of 15 nor after 39. A penis-shaped rubber object (dildo) was invariably used and the partners alternated using it on each other. Of those that used it, none stated that they recognized a symbolic significance. They never referred to it as a phallic symbol or as an assertion of masculine identification. They stated that they used it because it was physically pleasurable. As in the sexual relationships of homosexual men, the trend for women is for an interchange of "active" and "passive" roles.

DIFFERENCES BETWEEN MALE AND FEMALE HOMOSEXUALS

One of the most serious problems in studying homosexuality is the dearth of useful research on females. Almost all the material on homosexuality, and a disproportionately high percentage of that on human sexuality in general, is written about men. This may be explained by the fact that it is written *by* men. On the other hand, it may be a reflection of the second-class status of women in our society which considers feminine sexuality decidedly inferior to that of males. In spite of this research deficiency, it is still possible to make some interesting comparisons between the male and female homosexual worlds.

The key difference is the high degree of promiscuity and concomitant difficulty in establishing intimate relationships in the male homosexual world. This contrasts with the low degree of promiscuity and relative ease with which intimate relationships can be established between female homosexuals. Although they may agree about little else, most students of the subject agree upon this striking difference. Explaining it is not so easy. There are two general kinds of explanation, by no means mutually exclusive: the biological and the cultural.

It has been said that males are naturally promiscuous and females are naturally monogamous, and evidence from the study of homosexuality tends to confirm this statement. If a female homosexual tells someone knowledgeable about such matters that she has been with the same lover for nine years, the listener is not at all surprised. But, if a male says the same thing, a sophisticated listener is a little bit taken aback and may even congratulate the man on his good luck.

The cultural explanation for this difference follows. First, females, in general, are conditioned to develop a commitment to a close interpersonal relationship ("falling in love") *before* they become involved sexually, whereas the reverse is true for males. Second, repression of sexuality is an essential part of female socialization in Western culture.

However, regardless of the cultural determinants, a relationship involving sex between two males does not have the same character as one involving females, or one between a male and a female. In the Kinsey volume on women, the sixteenth chapter, "Psychologic Factors in Sexual Responses," contains many fascinating data which bear on this question.

> Among all peoples, everywhere in the world, it is understood that the male is more likely than the female to desire sexual relations with a variety of partners. It is pointed out that the female has a greater capacity for being faithful to a single partner, that she is more likely to consider that she has a greater responsibility than the male has in maintaining the home and in caring for the offspring of any sexual relationship, and that she is generally more inclined to consider the moral implications of her sexual behavior. But it seems probable that these characteristics depend upon the fact that the female is less often aroused, as the average male is aroused, by the idea of promiscuity.

In this chapter, Kinsey and his associates have assembled a great deal of evidence which indicates marked differences in the psychological responses of males and females to sexual stimuli. One of the central differences is that males are much more responsive to visual stimuli than are females. In other words, men tend to become sexually aroused *before* they make any physical contact with their potential partner, whereas women tend to become aroused only after this contact has been made. This fundamental difference, which appears to hold widely in animals as well as in human beings, gives great impetus to male promiscuity, for it means that for the male visual contact alone can provide the beginning of a sexual encounter, whereas a female will be relatively unaroused by such a stimulus.

As part of the evidence for this difference, it should be pointed out that commercialized "pornography" is an enterprise that functions almost exclusively for male customers. I speak here of visual pornography particularly. This is true, whether the material caters to a heterosexual or a homosexual audience, and for all combinations of actors in a pornographic plot. Women generally do not become erotically aroused by nude photographs of either men or women, regardless of their sexual orientation. The centerfold of *Playboy* is of frankly sexual interest to heterosexual men, not to homosexual women.

Males seem much more directly interested than females in the external sex organs. Men are more often sexually aroused by the sight of genitalia, either male or female, and much more frequently initiate a sexual relationship after some genital exposure or genital manipulation. Some of the focus on sexual organs which characterizes male homosexual relations must be attributed simply to the fact that two males are involved. Some of the criticisms that are made against homosexual men for focusing on the genitalia are very similar to complaints by heterosexual women that their husbands are excessively interested in genital contact and an immediate genital union.

It is important to ask to what extent these sex differences result from biological, and to what extent from cultural, factors. There is a good deal of evidence that these distinctions between males and females in American society are present in many cultures as well and may even be found in other species of mammals. Kinsey writes as follows:

> The males of practically all infra-human species may become aroused when they observe other animals in sexual activity. Of this fact, farmers, animal breeders, scientists experimenting with laboratory animals, and many persons who have kept household pets are abundantly aware. The females of the infra-human species less often show such sympathetic responses when they observe other animals in sexual activity. These data suggest that human females are more often inclined to accept the social proprieties because they are stimulated psychologically and respond sympathetically less often that do most males.

Kinsey's own data, especially when viewed in the context of studies of infra-human mammals, strongly suggest that the factors which account for these sex differences go beyond the cultural and involve some basic biologic differences.

It must be recognized that Kinsey's conclusions have been disputed, often by women who point out that either they themselves or female friends are sexually aroused by erotic visual materials. Furthermore, some recent psychological studies indicate this to be the case. It is certainly essential to keep the question open. Nevertheless, it would seem that even if all cultural restrictions on the expression of sexual interest by women were removed, there would still be significant differences in response between males and females, and the differences would be along the lines indicated above.

PUBLIC PLACES OF GAY LIFE

I have deferred a discussion of the public places of gay life in order to present the theoretical background for an explanation of the differential use of public places by male and female homosexuals. This seemed necessary in order to understand, among other things, the very great difference in the visibility and public awareness of the male and female homosexual communities. The fact that the male homosexual community is so much more visible than that of the female is probably one more reason why the former has been studied more extensively. For example, a list of public places where male homosexuals meet would include bars, public baths, restrooms and certain areas of particular streets and parks, but it is highly significant to note that only one of these—the bars—represent a public place which is of any interest to homosexual women. Furthermore, even bars are used quite differently by lesbians than they are by male homosexuals. There are many bars for homosexual men and very few for homosexual women, even in a city which supports a large homosexual population and many gay bars. The principal reason for this is that lesbians do not typically "cruise" (i.e., seek pickups) in the bars, as do homosexual men. Women tend to come to the bars with their lovers and to meet friends, so that for them the bars are primarily places for socializing. For homosexual men, on the other hand, although socializing certainly is an important feature of bar life, it is not the central feature. The salient fact about gay bars for men is that they are sexual marketplaces. This means that men go to these bars in the hope of meeting another person for an exchange of sexual services. The understanding is that the exchange will be made without obligation or commitment, i.e., without an obligation that further involvement will follow the sex act, although it sometimes does. The sexual interaction is an exchange which is made once (a "one-night stand") and typically does not go beyond this. Occasionally, however, such an exchange can lead to a relationship which lasts a number of years.

In attempting to explain the relative paucity of bars for homosexual women, it has been said that women in America do not feel it is proper to go to bars unescorted. This may be true, of course, but I think it is less true than it used to be, and I would offer as evidence the increasing number of heterosexual pickup bars. In my judgment, the reason for paucity of bars for lesbians is to be found in the analysis presented above, namely, that lesbians are not interested in cruising nor in one-night stands. The same point could be made in another way: people are men or women first and homosexuals second.

I do not intend, here, to describe in great detail the characteristics of the public places of gay life. I have done this, to some extent, in my book, *The Gay World: Male Homosexuality and the Social Creation of Evil.* Other sources are indicated in the bibliography. What characterizes all such places is the search for immediate sex, and the contractual relationship for sex without obligation or commitment. Again, I do not suggest that permanent relationships, or even temporary but very meaningful relationships, cannot be found in these locales; my point is simply that the contract between the parties does not include such relationship-formation.

With regard to the relative value of different sexual marketplaces to their users, I think the great divide is between the bar on the one hand, and the baths, streets, parks and restrooms on the other. The latter places are much more suitable for those whose immediate interest is focused upon genital contact and who will not go to the bars because they do not wish to stand around for several hours in the hope that they might possibly meet a sexual partner. They know that if they go to the baths, for example, they will almost certainly find one, if not many, partners. However, for such an individual the streets, parks and restrooms have two clear advantages over the baths. First, there is little immediate competition for the sexual partner. The homosexual who goes there generally runs into the other person alone, and thus the prospective partner will probably have to settle for him unless he wants to wait an undetermined amount of time for another person to come along. Second, there is an admission charge to the baths, whereas the parks, streets and restrooms are free (providing, of course, one does not get arrested, in which case the evening's diversion may be very expensive indeed). Furthermore, in none of the places, except the bar, are there the distractions of conversation, alcohol, music and sometimes dancing or entertainment.

The advantage of the bar, of course, is that it provides the chance for a conversation with a potential partner before the sexual contract is made. Individuals who are concerned about the psychological characteristics of their partners have opportunities to find out something about them. In addition, the environment of the bar lends an aura of respectability to the whole affair, whereas, in our society, meeting for a sexual encounter in a restroom is quite clearly defined as disreputable. There are, nevertheless, some individuals who do not want to engage in conversation with a potential partner before the sexual encounter occurs. The typical objection to preliminary conversation is that such social interaction will destroy the fantasy which makes the sexual experience desirable or even possible.

It is interesting that the specification of the sexual act(s) to occur is *not* part of the contract for a sexual encounter. In fact, men who meet in a bar or in a park and then adjourn to one of their apartments do not usually discuss what kind of sexual behavior is going to take place. Homosexuals are quite able to vary their sexual performance so as to find some satisfactory *modus operandi* in bed. While they might not find a partner who likes to do what they find most enjoyable sexually, the chances are very high that they will be able to find *some* kind of sexual behavior which is mutually satisfactory, at least to some extent.

Another aspect of such meetings is that it is not entirely predictable from the physical appearance and mannerisms of the potential partner just what he will or will not wish to do in bed. One can predict that a markedly effeminate man will take a receptor role with regard to his partner's penis; but aside from this, predictability is poor, and even in this instance it is not 100 percent. The only other exception is represented by the "straight" hustler (a male prostitute with homosexual customers) who classically only takes the insertor role, feeling that this is consistent with his image (to himself and/or his partner) of his "real" heterosexuality. However, this stereotype of the "straight" hustler is fading; there is much more prostitution by young homosexuals who are open about their homosexuality and will perform in the receptor as well as the insertor roles.

ORIGINS OF HOMOSEXUALITY

The simplest, and perhaps the most accurate, statement about the "etiology of homosexuality" would be: *we do not know* its etiology. While I am thoroughly sympathetic to such a statement, partly because it puts a lot of speculation—often presented as if it were fact—in its proper perspective, one cannot simply stop the discussion here. It is necesary to consider various theories which have been put forth to explain the origins of homosexuality. (Incidentally, the use of the term "etiology" implies that homosexuality is an illness, and, despite the fact that I do not subscribe to this view, I am willing to use the term as shorthand only if the reader understands that its use does not commit me to such a view.)

We should discuss first the biological factors which have been postulated as etiologic for homosexuality. There is no evidence at present that hormonal imbalance plays any role in determining a homosexual object-choice. At one time it was thought that if male hormone were given to a homosexual he would became heterosexual; such treatment does increase his sexual drive, but in the original direction, namely, a homosexual one. We *do* know that testosterone administered to pregnant animals during certain critical periods of gestation will produce profound changes in the female offspring. The changes involve both gender behavior (masculinity and femininity) and sexual behavior. While these experiments have been carried out in infra-human mammals, it may be that the results have some application to humans, although it is not clear what actual conclusions can be drawn. We are up against the very knotty problem of generalizing to human behavior results of experimentation with animals. When it comes to making such inferences about psychological matters, perhaps the most accurate thing to say would be: we know that such inferences can be made, but the criteria which govern their use in any given case are not necessarily clear and therefore the matter of making the inference is problematic. I think this is the situation with regard to the very important experiments which have been done in the administration of sexual hormones to pregnant members of infra-human species.

Kallmann's studies of human twins suggest that genetic factors may play a role in the etiology of homosexual object-choice. Kallmann investigated 85 predominantly or exclusively homosexual male twin index cases, the largest series of twins yet studied. All 40 monozygotic index pairs were concordant as to overt practice and, even more strikingly, were similar on a quantitative assessment of homosexual behavior, using the Kinsey scale. In the dizygotic group, more than half the co-twins of distinctively homosexual subjects yielded no evidence of overt homosexulity. These figures were only slightly in excess of Kinsey's ratings for the total male population. The differences between identical and fraternal twins is impressive, and, if even partly correct, would strongly indicate a genetic factor in the origin of homosexual object choice. However, a number of Kallmann's methods have come under severe criticism and therefore it is difficult to evaluate his findings. A replication of his work, using modern genetic techniques, is urgently needed. In the meantime, all that can be said is that genetic factors *may* play a role.

It is significant that although the question, "What is the cause of homosexuality?" is often asked, it rarely occurs to the questioner to raise the equally significant question, "What causes heterosexuality?" Failure to ask the second question is due to the fact that homosexuality is viewed as a problem and heterosexuality is not. Nevertheless, from a scientific point of view, the second question is just as legitimate and as important as the first. The question which really ought to be asked is, "What is the nature, and what are the determinants, of sexual object-choice?" If we knew the answer to this question, or series of questions, then we would know why homosexuality occurs and we would also know a great deal more about heterosexuality.

Those who inquire about origins of homosexuality, without recognizing that the existence of heterosexuality constitutes a scientific problem, assume, without any real evidence, that heterosexuality just "naturally occurs," and that there is no necessity to inquire into its origin. I would like to suggest that this is not a useful way of conceptualizing the problem of sexual orientation, nor even a useful point of view if one regards homosexuality as the main scientific dilemma. I feel that we are not really going to understand homosexual object-choice until we increase considerably our knowledge of the basic mechanisms of sexuality in general.

THE PSYCHOANALYTIC POINT OF VIEW

The most persuasive understanding of homosexual object-choice undoubtedly has been the one provided by psychoanalysis. It is not the most persuasive because it is supported by the best evidence. (As a matter of fact, the whole psychoanalytic explanation of homosexuality hinges upon the validity of psychoanalysis as a research tool, and this is seriously doubted by all except the faithful.) What is so convincing about psychoanalytic explanations is that they are concrete and understandable, and leave us with a feeling of surety not engendered by other kinds of explanation which are really only promissory notes for the fruitfulness of future research. In fact, I would go further and express the belief that the psychoanalytic explanations do apply in some cases.

The important point is that there probably are a number of kinds of "homosexuality," and that some of them can be explained by psychoanalytic theories while others cannot. The term "homosexuality" covers a number of different kinds of sexual response, and the principal error of the psychoanalysts is not that they have failed to uncover some important truths about homosexuality, but rather that they have overgeneralized their findings to a whole population of individuals, to some of whom their findings simply are not applicable.

One of the classic psychoanalytic explanations accounting for homosexual object-choice is "castration anxiety." This refers to the male homosexual's fear of the female genitalia. For example, Fenichel has stated that homosexual men are terrified by the sight of a partner who has no penis because of their own unconscious fear that they might be subject to castration. Castration anxiety is related to the well-known Oedipus

Complex, in which the boy is supposed to be frightened away from his incestuous feelings toward his mother by a feeling that the father will castrate him if he persists in his desire toward her. Fenichel writes as follows:

> The sight of female genitals may arouse anxiety in a boy in two ways: (1) The recognition of the fact that there are actually human beings without a penis leads to the conclusion that one might also become such a being; such an observation lends effectiveness to old threats of castration. Or (2) the female genitals, through the connection of castration anxiety with old oral anxieties, may be perceived as a castrating instrument capable of biting or tearing off the penis. Quite frequently a combination of both types of fear is encountered.

Note now the conclusions Fenichel draws from this formulation.

> Most homosexuals, however, cannot so easily free themselves of their normal biological longing for women. They continue to be attracted by women, but, not being able to endure the idea of beings without a penis, they long for phallic women, for hermaphrodites, so to speak. This acute longing for objects with a penis compels them to choose boys, but the boys must have a maximum of girlish and feminine traits. In the practices and fantasies of homosexuals, men in women's clothes as well as girls in men's clothes play a large part, and the homosexual ideal of the 'page boy' proves that they are actually looking for the 'girl with a penis.'

Actually, as a description of homosexual preference, the foregoing formulation is patently false. Male homosexuals are most attracted by masculine partners and not by effeminate ones. It is clear to any student of the homosexual world that effeminate men are held in much lower esteem than are the masculine-looking homosexuals, and it is masculinity rather than girlishness which is most desired in the sexual partners of most male homosexuals.

There is a dictum, common in contemporary philosophy of science, that when a theory leads to conclusions which are clearly falsified by the data, that theory should be discarded. According to this rule, the psychoanalytic theory of castration anxiety as an origin for homosexual object choice should be discarded, but psychoanalysts prefer to ignore the philosophy of science and I shall not belabor the point here.

According to psychoanalysis, the core of male homosexuality is identification with the mother. Fenichel says that after the decisive identification occurs, subsequent development may proceed in various directions. (1) There may be a narcissistic object choice. Having identified himself with his mother, the homosexual male behaves as he previously wanted his mother to behave toward him. Therefore, he chooses as sexual objects young men or boys whom he sees as similar to himself, or similar to what he would have been (or wanted to be) at a certain age.

He then loves and treats these sexual partners with a tenderness he had desired from his mother. This is considered to be a "narcissistic object choice" because the homosexual is emotionally centered in his love object, and in an unconscious sense is "loving himself." (2) Another example of psychoanalytic interpretation is represented by the male homosexual under the sway of an anal fixation. In this case, he chooses to enjoy sexual gratification in the same manner as his mother, thus developing a passive-receptive role in sexual encounters. (3) Still another psychoanalytic explanation for homosexual object choice is that it represents a means of dealing with a "reaction-formation" to hostility directed toward other males, such as siblings. In this case, the individual transforms his hostility into love, and chooses for his sexual object a person modeled after the individual or individuals he originally hated and/or feared.

Space does not permit a detailed description of all the possible psychodynamic combinations which have been cited as causes of homosexuality, but they are abundant in the psychoanalytic literature. I have indicated only a few of the major types to give the reader an idea of the kind of conceptualization that can be used in explaining a homosexual orientation. In making the criticisms which I have made above, I do not wish to imply that these explanations are of no value; on the contrary, I feel that they are very suggestive. My main objection to them is that they are generalized far beyond the data from which they arose. (This is a common criticism of psychoanalytic explanation and certainly is not limited to the study of homosexuality.)

A number of psychoanalysts, of whom Irving Bieber is probably the best-known, have emphasized a particular family constellation as etiologic for male homosexuality. The mother is pictured as overly close and overly intimate with her son. She is afraid of losing him, so she becomes possessive, and this results in a kind of "demasculinization" of the boy. She favors the pre-homosexual son over the other children and often over the father as well, thus fostering an alliance with him against the father. The son is thus discouraged from masculine identification and this failure is exacerbated by the passivity and detachment of the father, who makes no attempt to interfere with the mother-son alliance.

The difficulties with this explanation are twofold. First, many homosexual sons come from completely different kinds of households. Second, many heterosexual sons come from a family identical to that which has just been described. There is no predictive value to this "typical prehomosexual" family, i.e., if one were to establish that a child was growing up in such a family, one could not reliably predict that the boy would become homosexual. Nevertheless, it is well to keep this family constellation in mind, since it may interact with other factors to encourage a homosexual orientation in the young male.

THE ILLNESS THEORY OF HOMOSEXUALITY

The notion that homosexuality is an illness or a symptom of illness is very fashionable today, and is held by many psychiatrists as well as a substantial segment of the general population. Obviously, if one views homosexuality psychoanalytically (e.g., as a result of incapacitating fears of the female genitalia, leading to heterosexual incompetence and homosexual object-choice), then some variant of the illness theory logically follows. It is also quite possible to hold that homosexuality is genetically determined and that it is also an "abnormality."

My disagreement with the illness theory arises from several sources. In the first place, I do not subscribe to the theoretical assumptions of the psychoanalytic view, although I grant that it may describe certain cases. The psychoanalytic theory of homosexuality is based on the notion that homosexual object-choice results from fear of the opposite sex, whereas the data show very clearly that the majority of men with substantial sexual interest in other men and the majority of women with substantial sexual interest in other women have had extensive heterosexual involvement. In the second place, psychiatric advocates of the illness theory engage in a peculiarly naive version of the "problem of sampling." They begin with a clinical population, which has appeared in their consulting rooms because of psychiatric difficulties, and then conclude from this that all homosexuals are mentally ill. Third, in my judgment, one of the basic reasons for the illness theory is that it is, for our society, a way of dealing with a difficult and unwanted phenomenon without recourse to the theological idea of sin, which had previously been used to categorize it. In other words, I think that over and above their involvement with a skewed sampling of homosexuals, most psychiatrists are ready to accept the illness theory because they are so much a product of their own culture.

Advocates of the illness theory are generally unclear as to precisely what they mean by it, and a reader is very often confused or misled when he has finished reading what they have to say. They make two separate claims: (1) that homosexual behavior or preference is itself an illness; and (2) that homosexual behavior or preference is always associated with other clinical symptoms. The first claim is actually a matter of definition. It involves attaching a particular label (mental illness) to a particular kind of sexual object-choice (homosexual). For those who elect to attach this label, the sexual object-choice itself is sufficient ground for doing so, and no other evidence need be adduced. The second claim is capable of empirical test and has actually been empirically refuted.

The classic study which disproved this notion was conducted by research psychologist Evelyn Hooker and published in 1957. Hooker selected 30 homosexuals whom she felt were reasonably well adjusted and who were not in treatment. Next she chose 30 heterosexual men, matched with the homosexual subjects for age, education and IQ. Hooker then gave these 60 men a battery of psychological tests, including the Rorschach, the Thematic Apperception Test (TAT), and the Make-A-Picture-Story (MAPS), and also obtained considerable information on their life histories. She then submitted this material for analysis to several of her colleagues, who did not know which of the tests had been given to the homosexual men and which to the heterosexual. The clinicians who read the tests were unable to distinguish between the two groups, and there was no evidence that the homosexual group had a higher degree of pathology than the heterosexual group.

Hooker's general conclusion from the results of these analyses was that there is no inherent connection between homosexual orientation and clinical symptoms of mental illness. "Homosexuality as a clinical entity does not exist. Its forms are as varied as are those of heterosexuality. Homosexuality may be a deviation in sexual pattern which is in the normal range, psychologically."

If this evidence is not to be discounted, it is clear that the overtly homosexual male is not necessarily subject to clinical symptoms of illness or to neurotic or psychotic disturbance. There are, of course, a number of questions which remain unanswered. One of them is: If one could get a random sample of the homosexual population and a random sample of the heterosexual population, and one could compare these two groups, would there be any higher incidence of mental disturbance in the homosexual group? This is indeed a very interesting question, but there exists no answer because there is no feasible way of obtaining random samples of the hidden homosexual population. Even if one could get such a sample, one would run into extremely serious problems in the application of clinical criteria to such individuals. It would be incumbent upon those doing the research to do what Hooker did, namely, to keep from the clinicians knowledge of the sexual orientation of the individual whose clinical histories they were studying. Without this precaution, many judges would be immediately prejudiced by such knowledge.

Again, let me assert that although I find the illness theory of homosexuality wrong fundamentally, I do not find it without explanatory value. That is, I do think there are individuals whose homosexuality can be nicely explained by psychopathologic factors. It would seem as if they did indeed fit the psychoanalytic explanations. Nevertheless, their apparent concordance with these explanations is, in a way, still a matter for conjecture. For, even if they do appear to fit such explanations, this does *not* rule out the possibility that their homosexual orientation may be determined by genetic factors. It indeed is possible to find heterosexual individuals whose life histories include many of the psychodynamic constellations which are held responsible for the sexual orientation of known homosexuals. Perhaps the psychoanalytic explanations, which often seem to fit so beautifully, are just epiphenomena of a homosexuality determined by hereditary forces. The fact is we still do not know the origin of sexual object-choice in general, and homosexual object-choice in particular, and until we do know considerably more about these we will not really understand whether homosexuality can in some cases be appropriately considered a neurotic symptom.

HOMOSEXUALITY AS A MINORITY GROUP PHENOMENON

In spite of all that has been said above, there is a distinct impression on the part of many students of the homosexual community, including myself, that the rate of mental illness is definitely higher among homosexuals than among heterosexuals. Rather than explain this by the illness theory of homosexuality, I would prefer to interpret it as a reflection of the low social status which homosexuals have. The fact is that until very recently homosexuals as such had no status at all. It is only in the last several years that the subject of homosexuality has been a legitimate topic for portrayal or discussion in the popular media. Before that time, the subject was so taboo that an individual could actually be a homosexual and not know it. Individuals in mid-20th century urban America have been known to engage in homosexual sexual relations for a number of years without conceptualizing themselves as homosexual or without knowing of the eixstence of the gay world. This degree of alienation from one's own feelings and also from potential associates, may lead to very serious consequences for mental health.

Another factor which leads to mental illness, especially in the male homosexual population, is the fact that if a man is not young and attractive the gay world can be a very unhappy place for him indeed, for it has a very pervasive marketplace character. If one enters the market with very little to offer to the buyers to whom one desperately wishes to sell, then very serious personal troubles are likely to ensue, and one's self-esteem is constantly being deflated. Since large sections of the gay world view the homosexual as a commodity and judge him by his cosmetic qualities, he soon begins to develop that same view of himself. If he is viewed as a commodity of low value on the sexual market, he will begin to view himself as of little worth. For many homosexuals, this is the beginning of mental illness of the most serious kind. There is some evidence that the suicide rate among homosexual men is higher than that among heterosexuals. This is not difficult to understand in light of the analysis of the gay world as a sexual marketplace. Rejection by others produces a low assessment of one's own value. However, this is not the whole story.

Closely connected with this is the difficulty that homosexual men experience in establishing intimate, lasting relationships with each other. Especially as they become older, they find themselves increasingly less able to focus their lives around the seductive socializing that sustained them when they were younger. Sometimes they are able to establish a heterosexual marriage and rear a family. More often, they immerse themselves in their work and/or hobbies. If they can afford it, they may seek sex and a certain amount of (shallow) companionship from hustlers. This may be sexually satisfactory but it does little to shore up the homosexual's self-esteem, since he knows that without the cold cash he would be alone.

There is a "chicken and egg" paradox about the problem of promiscuity in the gay world. That world itself is a product of social repression, just as the existence of an ethnic ghetto is the product of an analogous kind of repression. And yet all inhabitants of our world are subject to its mores and customs. Consequently, pervasive promiscuity in the gay world arises partly from the guilt about homosexuality, and is itself reinforced by the gay community. One hears homosexuals talk about "gay marriages" as if they were desirable; and one knows that homosexual men are very often lonely and longing for some kind of permanence in their relationships with other males. Yet, at the same time, a premium is placed upon going to bed with a lot of attractive males, and upon the kind of carefree playing around that the gay world tends to promote.

Nevertheless, it cannot be denied that the most significant factor creating problems in relation to intimacy between homosexual men is the social prohibition against such intimacy which, in effect, is a prohibition against homosexuality. To put the matter in its most simple terms, the reason that males who are homosexually oriented cannot form stable relationships with each other is that society does not want them to do so.

The social prohibition operates as follows: Closeness between males is considered a sign that there is something wrong with the individuals involved. Unlike socially acceptable closeness between women, which casts no doubt upon their "femininity," closeness between two men is thought of as evidence against the masculinity of the two individuals. When such closeness is considered (at some level) by the individual himself, he immediately defines himself as sissy, faggot, degenerate, et cetera. The crucial fact about this kind of socially prohibited behavior is that the mechanism of repression depends upon the individual's incorporation into his own conscience of the prohibition against such a form of closeness. At this point the reader may ask: How is it possible, then, that such individuals can engage in sexual relations with other males? The answer to this seems to be that the effects of sexual arousal are potent enough to overcome the social prohibition against genital contact, but that the same degree of arousal is not sufficient to overcome the prohibition against intimacy. To supravene this second kind of condemnation would require a kind of freedom from social constraint that is not really to be expected, except in a few cases. This kind of freedom does occur from time to time, but what I want to point out is that the majority of homosexual men cannot overcome the social prohibition against intimacy.

Another way of making the point is to say that the same social forces which act to prevent most males from becoming homosexual also reach into the lives of those who do, and prevent them from developing closeness in a sexual relationship with another man. It seems reasonable to assume that the social counterforces do not simply stop having profound effects once an individual has developed a homosexual orientation. On the contrary, they affect the character of the individual's life in other ways. They give the individual a sense that his homosexual behavior is morally wrong, and that his partner also is bad. How, then, is he expected to develop a warm, intimate relationship with a partner whom he unconsciously devalues as a person for joining him in behavior which he defines as degraded?

The homosexual's own self-concept cannot easily commit him to being any more of a homosexual than is required by his sexual drive itself. To put the matter another way, it is one thing to cruise the park, pick up a guy, take him home, have sex, never see the partner again and forget the whole thing. It is another thing to commit one's self to a living relationship with another man in which, 24 hours a day, one is reminded of one's homosexuality by the presence of the other person. This requires a greater effort to overcome the social barriers toward homosexual feelings and many homosexuals are incapable of such an effort. The feelings of guilt—conscious or unconscious—produced by involvement in homosexual acts, serve to contaminate the relationship and to prevent the possibility of its developing into one of warm intimacy.

What is fundamentally wrong with the conventional disease theory of homosexuality is not that there is no connection between homosexuality and pathology, for there may indeed be such links. What is incorrect is that all the phenomena of gay life are analyzed in terms of individual pathology, as if there were no social forces acting upon the homosexual. The problem of paired intimacy, which in my judgment is the central problem of the male homosexual world, is a problem which cannot meaningfully be understood without considering the social context in which it occurs. It is this failure to understand the importance of the social milieu in which the gay world is situated, namely, the hostile character of the surrounding non-homosexual world, that accounts for the simplistic explanations in so much current discussion of the problem.

I will not discuss here the legal and social dangers of exposure of the homosexual. These include all kinds of sanctions, from less than honorable discharge from the military to denial of insurance coverage. However, a satisfactory analysis of a number of the apparently puzzling phenomena of gay life must take into account the relationship of the homosexual to the larger, hostile society. It is certainly very clear that one of the reasons for homosexual promiscuity is that it provides some degree of anonymity. When the partner is not known, then no follow-up of the relationship is possible. If a prominent individual has sex with another man in the park and no nonsexual contact is made, then there is less likelihood that he may be found out. In other words, the need to conceal information about one's activity leads to much of the anonymous promiscuity of the gay world. Thus, instability of relationships, which is frequently used as one ground for condemnation of homosexuals, is, in fact, the very product of this condemnation. There is, indeed, a strange irony in homosexuals being accused of not forming stable relationships, when it is social prohibitions by nonhomosexuals which largely prevent them from doing so.

Much of what goes on in the gay world can be understood if we understand that the homosexual community is a minority group subject to the same kinds of problems which other minority groups experience. Blacks are much more concerned with their skin color than are whites. The reason for this is obvious, namely, that their skin color has been defined as a problem by the larger society. In an analogous way, and for the same reason, homosexuals are much more concerned with their sexuality than are heterosexuals, because their sexual feelings have been defined as a problem by the "straight" world, and they have been subject to sanctions which are not altogether dissimilar from those confronting blacks because of their skin color.

The gay world may thus be seen as a kind of nongeographical ghetto. It is not located on the map in clearly marked-off areas as are ethnic ghettos (though sometimes high-density urban areas can be identified), but it is a ghetto, nevertheless, and its inhabitants are subject to many of the same kinds of problems that other minority groups face. As Hooker has pointed out, there is a striking parallel between certain characteristics of minority group members who have been victimized by the larger society and many of the phenomena seen in the gay world. Citing a number of "traits due to victimization" which are described by Gordon Allport in his book, *The Nature of Prejudice,* Hooker writes as follows.

It would be strange indeed if all the traits caused by victimization in minority groups were, in the homosexual, produced by inner dynamics of the personality, for he too is a member of an out-group subject to extreme penalties, involving, according to Kinsey, cruelties [which] have not often been matched, except in religious and racial persecutions.

Psychotherapy with Homosexuals

When confronted by a homosexual patient in a psychotherapeutic situation, many therapists ask themselves the following question: Can this patient be "cured" (of his homosexuality), i.e., can he be made heterosexual? In my view, to set the treatment in this frame of reference is to make a fundamental error.

In the foregoing argument against the idea that homosexuality is a mental illness, I have actually also stated the central argument against the related notion that even if it is not a disease, homosexuality is, nevertheless, a less desirable way of life in our present society. I grant that for very many homosexuals the gay world is indeed a sad and desperate place. It is hard to imagine how it could be otherwise given the state of affairs described above. Yet there are many homosexuals who find both social and psychological means to cope with these difficulties, and live as happily and productively as either they or we would wish. Perhaps the explanation is not so remote. We know that, in the socialization process, some parents give their children permission to "be what they are." With this buffering of a basic sense of self-esteem, self-acceptance as homosexuals may come without too much agony.

Let us assume, however, that the reader is a health professional with a homosexual patient who is frustrated with gay life and seems fed up with his homosexuality. He states that he has entered therapy for the express purpose of "curing" it. What is to be done?

First, the motivation for change must be assessed. It is very common for a patient to present himself in this way and yet not be genuinely motivated for any change in sexual preference. A breakup in a love relationship will typically produce such a situation. When the grief over the object-loss is dealt with, by time and therapy, the "wish for change" often evaporates with such rapidity that the therapist may be astonished at how soon the patient is out looking for more homosexual sex.

But, suppose the motivation for change is deeper than this. Then what? Here I come to my central point. The treatment of the homosexual who wishes to become heterosexual, and the treatment of the homosexual who wishes to remain so but who has problems adjusting to gay life *are the same*. In both cases, it is incumbent upon the therapist to aid the patient in accepting himself as he is, while simultaneously reminding him that such acceptance does not preclude, and may in fact enhance, the possibility of enrichment of his life style by new modes of adaptation, including heterosexuality. The homosexual patient is in therapy precisely because his parents did not provide a basis for the self-acceptance which his happier gay friends have been blessed with. The parents failed in this by neglecting to provide him with a basic sense of self-esteem. If he had been heterosexual, it is entirely possible that he would be in therapy because of other difficulties caused by this basic lack of a sense of self-value. Of course, as indicated above, the gay world itself very often tends to lower the individual's self-esteem. The therapist's task is clear. He must aid the patient to adjust to the difficulties of living in the homosexual community by developing modes of adaptation that serve to enhance rather than deplete his sense of self-value.

Therefore, the work of therapy must be to help the homosexual achieve a sense of his own value as a person. This is true, regardless of whether he says he wants to remain gay or go straight. It follows that it is inimical to such a therapeutic enterprise for the therapist to reinforce the patient's sense of worthlessness by telling him that a central part of himself, i.e., his sexual feelings, are "sick" and should be obliterated. This is why I cannot approve of "frontal attacks" on homosexuality by behavior therapists, whether they come in the direct form of electric aversion therapy or in the more subtle form of "desensitization." Desensitization appears to be based on the questionable premise that if only the presumed block to heterosexuality were removed, homosexuality would vanish. This premise has not been shown to be valid. Homosexuality and heterosexuality are not mutually exclusive forms of behavior, as any open-minded observer of human sexual activity soon discovers. The belief that if a man becomes heterosexually potent his homosexual feelings disappear has frequently been shown to be false.

If it is carried out according to the principle of analytical neutrality, classical psychoanalysis presumably is free of the disguised morality which is so denigrating to the patient. However, it is a sad fact that many therapists who say they do analysis, approach the homosexual patient with the illness theory of homosexuality in mind, and their claims to neutrality on this issue are patently false.

Furthermore, what are we to say to the psychotherapist who makes a strong plea for "curing homosexuality" and then tells us that, if his patients are exclusively homosexual, he can cure only 19 percent of them? (This is the statistic listed by one of the leading exponents of the illness theory, Irving Bieber.) What becomes of the other 81 percent? It would appear that they are left with a more difficult situation than they started with. They are still homosexual, but now, superimposed upon their initial shame and guilt, they are saddled with an added burden arising from their "unsuccessful cure." They have failed in their attempt at "cure" and have been, in the process, definitively labelled "sick" by their own therapist.

On the other hand, if we adopt a position of genuine neutrality with regard to the sexual orientation of our patients (at least insofar as our own counter-transference situation will allow), the matter is very different. We work with the patient in helping him to accept himself, a process which, however "corny" it may sound, must be the central task of the psychotherapeutic endeavor. Acceptance does not necessarily mean exclusive homosexuality forever. If the homosexual wants to add heterosexual sex to his life, we might think this is a feasible possibility. If not, we help him to adjust to a society which views homosexuality with disdain. I frankly do not see how we can do this if *we* view homosexuality with disdain.

REFERENCES

Bieber, I. et al. 1962. *Homosexuality: A Psychoanalytic Study*. New York: Basic Books.

Fenichel, O. 1945. *The Psychoanalytic Theory of Neurosis*. New York: Norton.

Heston, L. L., and Shields, J. 1968. Homosexuality in twins: A family study and a registry study. *Arch. Gen. Psychiat.* 18:149.

Hooker, E. 1957. The adjustment of the male overt homosexual. *J. Project. Techn.* 21:18. (Reprinted in: Ruitenbeek).

————. 1965. Male Homosexuals and Their Worlds. In *Sexual Inversion: The Multiple Roots of Homosexuality*. Edited by Judd Marmor. New York: Basic Books.

Kallmann, F. J. A. 1952. A comparative twin study on the genetic aspects of male homosexuality. *J. Nerv. Ment. Dis.* 115:283.

Kinsey, A. C.; Pomeroy, W.; and Martin, C. 1948. *Sexual Behavior in the Human Male*. Philadelphia: Saunders.

Kinsey, A. C.; Pomeroy, W.; Martin, C.; and Gebhard, P. 1953. *Sexual Behavior in the Human Female*. Philadelphia: Saunders.

Saghir, M. T., and Robins, E. 1969. Homosexuality: I. Sexual behavior of the female homosexual. *Arch. Gen. Psychiat.* 20:192.

Schofield, M. 1965. *Sociological Aspects of Homosexuality*. London: Longmans.

Simon, W., and Gagnon, J. H. 1967. Femininity in the lesbian community. *Social Problems* 15:212.

SUGGESTED READINGS

Baldwin, J. 1956. *Giovanni's Room*. New York: Dial Press.
    A fine novel, depicting the outcome of an attempt at homosexual love in our world.

Hoffman. M. 1968. *The Gay World: Male Homosexuality and the Social Creation of Evil.* New York: Basic Books.

A general survey of the subject, including more complete discussion of issues mentioned in this chapter, as well as aspects not covered (legal, philosophical, ethnographic). One defect, viewed a few years after the writing, is that it does not consider the possibility of biological factors in the origins of homosexual object-choice.

Hooker, E. 1968. Homosexuality. In *International Encyclopedia of the Social Sciences.* 14:222. Edited by David L. Sills. New York: Macmillan & Free Press.

An excellent survey of the research literature, written in 1966.

Humphreys, L. 1970. *Tearoom Trade: Impersonal Sex in Public Places.* Chicago: Aldine.

A fascinating and controversial study of male homosexual sex in park restrooms, including data on the lives of the participants in their nonsexual worlds.

Marmor, J., ed. 1965. *Sexual Inversion: The Multiple Roots of Homosexuality.* New York: Basic Books.

A collection of original papers, the best being the first five. "Introduction" (Judd Marmor), "Ambisexuality in Animals" (R. H. Denniston), "Hormones and Homosexuality" (William H. Perloff), "Etiology of Homosexuality: Genetic and Chromosomal Aspects" (C. M. B. Pare), and "Male Homosexuals and Their 'Worlds'" (Evelyn Hooker).

Rechy, J. 1963. *City of Night.* New York: Grove Press.

A very moving account of the homosexual world, seen through the eyes of a hustler. (For those who like this novel, I also recommend, by the same author and publisher: *Numbers* [1967], and *This Day's Death* [1969].)

Richmond, L., and Noguera, G., eds. 1973. *The Gay Liberation Book.* San Francisco: Ramparts Press.

A good collection of articles on gay (men's) liberation; gives the reader a sense of the movement and its more important themes.

Ruitenbeek, H. M., ed. 1963. *The Problem of Homosexuality in Modern Society.* New York: Dutton.

A collection of reprinted papers. In my view, the most interesting are by Freud, Lindner, Hooker, Devereux, Reiss, Raven, and van den Haag.

7

SEXUAL DEVIATIONS

Robert J. Stoller

EDITORIAL PREFACE

Robert Stoller's chapter is a cross-sectional analysis of selected types of sexual behavior which are classified as "deviant" in our society. The category is a traditional one, but its validity and explanatory value depend on the precision with which we are able to define a standard from which the so-called deviations can be measured. When it is used as a verb, *to deviate* means to turn or diverge from an established way. When employed as a noun, the same word identifies something which differs noticeably from the average or normal range of its kind. Sexual deviation should, therefore, be definable as behavior that departs from some generally agreed upon standard of normal conduct.

Anyone who has read Chapter 5 will appreciate the difficulty of establishing culturally universal norms for human sexual conduct, but Stoller does not attempt to do this. Instead, he deliberately restricts himself to Western society and begins by defining sexual deviation as "a preferred, habitual, compelling method of achieving sexual gratification other than by willing genital intercourse between human male and female." Under this rubric, he discusses such well-known phenomena as fetishism, bestiality and necrophilia; but, subsequently, he is forced to modify the implied definition of nondeviant behavior by specifying that "normal" heterosexuality involves "a relationship between people who recognize each other as *persons*," and not simply as "a male or female body." This permits him to include as deviations various forms of depersonalized heterosexual relations such as satyriasis, nymphomania, pedophilia and the like.

Stoller's descriptions and analyses of unusual sexual practices are informative, perceptive, and, of course, intrinsically interesting; but they could easily create an impression that "sexual deviation" is a catchall term loosely applied to so many diverse kinds of behavior that it has little meaning and less explanatory value. An important question is whether this apparent hodgepodge of behavior categories can be reduced to some sort of order that will facilitate logical analysis.

I believe that Stoller has indicated a possible solution to this problem and that it may be profitable to explore the possibilities laid open by this implicit suggestion. Two major subheadings in this chapter which point the way to some clarification are "Preference for Unusual Objects," and "Deviations Focusing on Special Kinds of Acts." In a different conceptual framework, these same headings identify two separate aspects of sexual interaction in which deviations from an arbitrary norm can be recognized. The first pertains to the types of external stimuli which lead to sexual arousal, and the second to forms of appetitive and/or consummatory behavior which result in sexual gratification or satisfaction.

If an appropriate schema could be developed, it might permit us to compare deviations cross-culturally and, what is more important, to integrate the evidence presented by Stoller into a broader framework represented by other chapters in this book. One potentially unifying approach would be to view the primary heterosexual relationship as one involving three successive, but overlapping and interacting, stages within each of which quantitative and qualitative deviations are possible. The arbitrarily defined stages are those of (1) initial arousal, (2) appetitive behavior with further arousal, and (3) consummatory behavior with final release or gratification through sexual climax.

Examination of Stoller's inventory suggests that, except for such rarities as necrophilia and preferential bestiality, practically all so-called deviations involve atypical sources of arousal or unusual patterns of appetitive behavior, whereas the final consummatory pattern is relatively invariant, consisting of either coital or masturbatory activity leading to the reflexive responses of ejaculation in the male and orgasm in both sexes.

Deviations focused primarily on external sources of sexual arousal include fetishism, pedophilia and masochism, to take but three examples. These are considered remarkable merely because we implicitly assume that the only "normal" stimuli for arousal of an adult male are certain characteristics of an adult female. Arousal engendered by exposure to a woman's shoe, to a young child or to severely painful stimulation is a consequence of stimulus substitution.

"Normal" appetitive behavior varies among societies but always centers upon noninjurious physical contact plus symbolic interaction in the form of language. One function of appetitive activity is to initiate or increase sexual arousal in the partner; but a second, and equally important, consequence is a positive feedback effect which intensifies erotic excitement in the performing individual. Deviant patterns characterized by unusual appetitive activity are exhibitionism, voyeurism, and sadism (and possibly a few less common examples mentioned by Stoller such as kleptomania and pyromania). These forms of behavior are noteworthy for two reasons: (1) Most of them involve no positive interaction with a partner, and sadism demands a *negative* response from the partner. In point of fact, all deviations in this general category are marked by the exclusion of a positive response from a second person; (2) the feedback effects are, nevertheless, sexually stimulating to the performer. Here, again, we seem to be dealing with examples of stimulus substitution.

Now, if we accept the hypothesis suggested in Chapter 1 to the effect that species-specific stimulus-response patterns responsible for heterosexual intercourse have evolved in the service of reproduction, it is reasonable to conclude that alternative or counterreproductive S-R patterns are, *from a strictly evolutionary point of view,* maladaptive deviations. With respect to the individual's psychosexual development, they must represent products of conditioning or other forms of learning.

This formulation does not imply that the behavior is maladaptive with respect to a given individual's psychological integrity or total life pattern. It may or may not be. Whether it is classifiable as socially deviant depends upon the sexual norms of the particular society within which the individual lives.

A biological or functional approach to the definition of normality is only one of several alternative possibilities, and quite possibly not the best that can be devised. It does have the virtue of demanding more precise identification of the "locus" of each deviation vis-à-vis the "reproductively normal" heterosexual pattern, and points to the possibility of theoretical analysis in terms of learned stimulus substitution.

INTRODUCTION

Sexual deviation has been defined in many ways, but for the first part of this discussion we shall define it as a preferred, habitual, compelling method of achieving sexual gratification other than by willing genital intercourse between human male and female. It is important to recognize that occasional sexual behavior of other types, which may be motivated by curiosity, boredom, or desire for variety, is not defined as a sexual deviation. The key words in the definition are, "preferred, habitual, compelling," for they indicate that the deviant behavior is not casual and is necessary. One must understand that, in the context of this chapter, the term "sexual deviation" implies neither health nor illness, goodness nor badness, usefulness nor uselessness; each condition will be described, not evaluated.

One more caveat is necessary. This discussion on sexual deviation is based exclusively on Western society; no effort is made to take a stance of cultural relativity or to inform the reader of findings from societies markedly different from those of Western countries.

This chapter will concentrate on sexual deviations that involve no known biological abnormalities, genetic, hormonal, anatomical, or neurophysiological, as specific causes for the conditions (except in intersexuality). Bypassing the issue of possible special biological contributions to the cause or maintenance of sexual deviations results in omitting reference to a vast literature that has examined these issues by means of animal research, by statistical attempts to show familial tendencies and, especially, by speculations, particularly those using analogies with either sexual behavior of free-ranging animals or, more often, behavior seen only when reproduced by the laboratory experimentalist. On the other hand, efforts by behaviorists and psychoanalysts who attempt to show that human sexual deviations are due to psychosocial forces are also incomplete. Therefore, the interested reader is referred to selected works in the bibliography rather than given a summary here.

The author will, however, express his opinion, for which there is evidence in some deviations. Sexual deviations in humans often result from the frustration of development of heterosexual interests in children by forces in the family, usually applied by parents who subtly or grossly let the growing child know that aspects of its budding sexuality are bad. If he is a boy, masculinity (as his society sees it), especially its attributes of aggressivenes and of associated pleasure in possessing females, is treated as morally bad or physically and psychologically dangerous. The reverse is done to girls and their developing femininity. The child victimized in this manner must develop compromises to preserve his or her sense of identity and capacity for sexual gratification, and at the same time comply with these parental demands. These compromises may involve new, habitual styles of behaving, and daydreams that will undo the painful, inhibiting pressures within that family. According to this theory, the specific deviation chosen is the result of the specific traumatic attitudes inflicted by the family on the developing child. The test of the theory comes only when one examines in fine detail each family member's exact modes of reacting and communicating to which the child is exposed.

There are many reasons why our understanding of the sexual deviations is fragmentary. For one, there are no adequate statistics regarding prevalence. Because the deviations are powerfully and publicly condemned, one can hardly discover who is doing what to whom sexually. (How many people in the U.S. prefer intercourse with animals—20; 200,000? How many in other parts of the world?) In addition, the same secrecy makes it difficult to determine whether a sexual act is performed out of necessity or only to add to one's repertory of skills and pleasures. However, two generalizations about prevalence are possible. First, many of these deviations exist only in males. Second, none is found exclusively in females. It seems, then, that sexually deviant behavior is practiced more by men than women.

Another problem in determining the prevalence of sexual deviations is that, because of fear or guilt, some people never actually perform their desired deviant act, but restrict themselves exclusively to fantasy. They may have the capacity to disguise their need while copulating with a partner, but their excitement and gratification secretly requires the deviant fantasy. Other individuals cannot, under any circumstances, simulate an efficient sexual performance and, not wishing to practice their deviant act, are reduced to masturbation using the obligatory fantasy or pornography that depicts their fantasy.

The manner in which we are going to describe the separate deviations could give the impression that each is a distinct entity. In some instances that may be true, but most common indeed is the presence of several deviations in one person, such as a man who becomes excited when dressed as a woman, bound in chains, and penetrated anally by another man.

Not only may deviations be multiple, but, in addition, sexual deviations often coexist with other types of emotional dysfunctions. They may be present in people suffering any psychiatric disorder. In fact, the more bizarre the sexual deviation, the more likely is the observer to find severe, additional psychiatric disorders such as the schizophrenias, organic brain disease, and mental retardation. On the other hand, many people with sexual deviations live creative lives with no more emotional disturbance than those without deviations.

Along with, and in part because of, inadequate information concerning the sexual deviations, methods of treatment are uncertain. Unfortunately, one general finding appears true. Except perhaps for some forms of homosexuality, up to the present most sexual deviations as defined here have not been eliminated by any kind of treatment. The reason for this may be that the deviant sex act is so necessary for emotional stability that, even in the face of the potential dangers that accompany its practice, the deviant cannot renounce his deviation. Alternatively, sexual deviations may contain a hidden need to run great risks, with the real possibility of being caught. It is commonly reported that in addition to genital excitement, there is paradoxically sought in performance of the deviant act a quite different excitement—anticipation of great danger.

The guarded prognosis in the treatment of most sexual deviations compares with that in the treatment of drug addiction and alcoholism, where the needs for the pleasure and risk-running outweight any logical consideration of the damages that accrue. This overpowering need probably explains why psychoanalysis and related treatments that succeed by discovering causes and dynamics of behavior have not done well in removing sexual deviations except, as noted earlier, perhaps some forms of homosexuality.

As yet no pharmacological, hormonal, surgical, or other, organic form of treatment has proven effective, although preliminary research hints that more successful approaches may be forthcoming in the next decade. At present, the greatest hope for treatment lies in current studies which suggest that behavioral techniques, such as aversion or deconditioning, can succeed in removing the need for some deviant states, such as fetishism, especially when the condition is uncomplicated by other deviant desires. This work is too new to be certain that the beneficial results are permanent, but the methods seem promising.

Finally, it is appropriate to add a few words about morality and its reflection in the law. Changes in Western society have modified the attitudes of many people concerning what is moral behavior for themselves and for others. Lawmakers now recognize that large numbers of citizens disagree with laws written to control sexual behavior, and these new opinions are being felt and at times reacted to. The major concept that is becoming evident, and is even incorporated into the law in some countries, is that sexual acts done in private between consenting adults are the concern of the individuals and not of the state. This makes sexual morality a private affair. Even with this change, legislation continues to recognize the unlawfulness of the sexual act if one partner is considered incapable of consenting in an informed way, as in sexual acts between an adult and a child, or sexual acts with a mentally defective person or a person rendered incompetent by psychosis. Acts without consent, such as rape, severe sadism, or necrophilia are still illegal. The philosophic position is that where there has been no victim, there is no crime —with the new understanding that with respect to the individual sexual act, society is no longer considered to be the victim.

PREFERENCE FOR UNUSUAL SEX OBJECTS

Fetishism

Fetishism is that condition in which genital sexual excitement is aroused by an inanimate object (e.g., rain coat) or body part (e.g., hair or foot) that is not a primary (e.g., penis) or secondary (e.g., breasts) sex characteristic.[1] (But we must pause a moment to recognize that the term "fetishism" has frequently been used with much broader meaning to imply, on the one hand, intense interest in an inanimate object without the occurrence of sexual excitement, and on the other hand, sexual excitement aroused by animate objects that are body parts, such as breasts or penises, in which the whole person is ignored. Whatever the relationship of these states may be to that which we are defining, we shall here restrict the meaning of fetishism to that just indicated.) Since we shall later define transvestism on the basis of the presence of accom-

---

[1]The term "genital sexual excitement" rather than simply "sexual excitement" will be used on occasion in this chapter to avoid confusion. First, it distinguishes locus of excitement and separates it from other body areas such as breasts, anus or skin from which people may report erotic sensations. Second, it distinguishes the described experience from other events for which people may also use the term "sexual excitement" but which do not include a sensation of arousal in the genitals. (For example, sexual excitement is sometimes said to accompany a sense of triumph without genital arousal in humiliating one's partner.) Third, the literature includes descriptions of experiences that are not sensed by the subject as erotic but for which the term "sexual" is used by the writer who believes there is an "unconscious" link between the felt experience and its "real," that is "unconscious," meaning.

panying fetishism, our discussion now is concerned with fetishism that does not involve garments of the opposite sex.

What seems important is that while the fetish may formerly have belonged to a person (for instance hair or shoes), it is clearly sensed as separate from that person. It is not simply an object that substitutes for a person, with the implication that the original owner of the fetish object would be preferred if he or she were present. On the contrary, the fetish is *preferred* to the owner. It is safe, silent, cooperative, tranquil, and can be harmed or destroyed without consequence. Nonetheless, the inanimate object and its former possessor are associated, and fetishists often prefer a used object or objects with distinctive smells, because these qualities serve as reminders that one specific person formerly possessed the object. Some of the fetishist's excitement derives subtly from that ownership that is implied in the smell or the worn appearance.

Fetishism is very rare in females. When found, it is most commonly linked to the smells and textures of materials. A special form of feminine fetishism is kleptomania. Kleptomania (stealing unneeded goods in large amounts, usually from stores) is present in both sexes but is much more prevalent in women than in men. It occasionally occurs because a woman has discovered that the act of laying hands on a particular class of object (usually cloth) with intent to steal suddenly and invariably provokes an orgasm.

CASE EXAMPLES

(1)

An unmarried man in his 20s has never had sexual relations with a male or female. He has, however, become acquainted with several prostitutes who cater to his one method (in addition to masturbation) of being able to have an orgasm. They undress him, lay him out on a bed, and put a pair of diapers on him. As the process progresses, he becomes increasingly excited, and, shortly before orgasm, he instructs them put a pair of rubber pants over the diapers. At the moment this is done, he ejaculates.

(2)

Less bizarre, more typical. An unmarried man in his 20s begins to be sexually excited whenever he looks at women's feet with shoes on. He becomes more so if he sees the feet naked, and is brought to orgasm if a woman steps on his penis with her naked foot, or if in masturbation he fantasies this action. He can only be aroused by feet.

Bestiality

In bestiality, animals are the preferred sexual objects. This deviation is probably rarer in reality than in the public's imagination. Very few cases have been reported in which animals are the preferred sex object. Much more commonly an animal is used, not by preference, but for lack of an available human partner as, for instance, by teenage boys on farms. Sometimes women are hired to pose with animals for pornographic photographs to be sold to men. A child may use a pet for masturbation without the animal itself precipitating the excitement but rather functioning to give a special quality of sensation to the genitals. Nonetheless, fantasies of sexual behavior between animals and humans commonly occur in mythology, folklore, and in pornography, where it is not the pictured bestiality per se that excites but rather the demonstration of a woman being degraded.

When true bestiality (preference for animals) is practiced by males, it frequently is accompanied by sadism, in which case the most intense excitement is produced not simply by the presence of the animal but by the animal being physically tortured and often killed.

CASE EXAMPLES

(1)

A number of household pets, acquired one after the other, disappeared from the family of a teenage boy over several months. He was then discovered by chance in the act of disemboweling a new pet and was, at the moment of discovery, alternately masturbating and further mutilating the animal. During psychiatric examination, he revealed that he had done similarly with the other pets, always doing this for sexual gratification. The activity would begin with his playing with the animals, but the playing became rougher until he was manifestly excited, at which time he would bind the animals, take out the knives to be used and then proceed to torture the animals first with cutting and then finally with disembowelment. He gave a history back into earliest childhood of having tormented animals and of slowly ripping apart insects, though in those days without accompanying erection.

(2)

Less bizarre, more typical. A single man, a farm laborer in his late 20s, has been having intercourse with animals since puberty. Being very shy, he has never gone with a woman. Although in his late teens he would have liked to, he now has no conscious desire for women. Two attempts with prostitutes found him impotent; these were his only heterosexual experiences. He has had no homosexual relations.

Necrophilia

Necrophilia is the act of sexual intercourse upon a corpse, with or without mutilation of the corpse ("necrosadism"). It is different from sexual murder in that the necrophiliac has not killed anyone. His excitement comes from the dead body, not, as in extreme sadism, from killing a living person. The only reported cases, and these are of the greatest rarity, are males. The act is probably only performed by individuals suffering from other signs of severe mental illness.

For the necrophiliac, a living woman may be desired in fantasy, but normal potency is impossible because he so hates and fears women. For him, the ideal woman is an unresisting one, one who is rendered absolutely safe by the guarantees emanating from her condition as a corpse.

CASE EXAMPLE (I am personally unfamiliar with any such case. The following is quoted from Krafft-Ebing.)

"Brierre De Boismont relates the history of a corpse-violator who, after bribing the watchman, had gained entrance to the corpse of a girl of sixteen belonging to a family of high social position. At night a noise was heard in the death-chamber, as if a piece of furniture had fallen over. The mother of the dead girl effected an entrance and saw a man dressed in his night-shirt springing from the bed where the body lay. It was at first thought that the man was a thief, but the real explanation was soon discovered. It afterwards transpired that the culprit, a man of good family, had often violated the corpses of young women. He was sentenced to imprisonment for life."

PREFERENCE FOR DEGRADED OR UNUSUAL HUMAN HETEROSEXUAL OBJECTS

Now it becomes necessary to modify our original definition of sexual deviation in which genital heterosexual relations was the standard against which deviation is measured. The fact is that heterosexual relations can, under certain circumstances, involve elements of deviance. True heterosexuality is better defined as a relationship between people who recognize each other as *persons*, than by the criterion that demands only that one's partner is recognized as a male or female *body*. Frequently, the ideal is not reached, and the following discussion deals with deviations related to this difference. The category used here measures how far one may deviate from the paradigm and still disguise from oneself the fact that the preferred act is not to be between people with their own identities, and thus not have fully to recognize one's deviance.

Satyriasis

The need by a man sexually to use an infinite number of women is called satyriasis (Don Juanism). In this state, the man cannot, and in fact must not, develop a lasting relationship with a woman whom he senses as a real person. Instead, he must move from one woman to the next as soon as one has granted him the right to seduce her. In fact, only the granting is necessary. Many such men prefer to avoid going through the actual act of intercourse once the woman has expressed her willingness. What seems to be an act of sex on such a man's part is, in fact, only an act of degradation and conquest. Many of these men, even those famous for their prowess, are impotent or suffer the partial impotency of premature ejaculation when forced to the test. Their technical brilliance lies in foreplay. Others are potent and skilled in the sexual athletics of coitus but cannot remain potent if forced to cohabit with the same woman for more than a few days.

Satyriasis involves degradation because the man does not value the woman for herself and as an individual. She is only a statistic in his endless amassing of numbers of subdued creatures belonging to the category: human female.

CASE EXAMPLE

The patient is a married man publicly renowned as a virile and promiscuous lover. His reputation guarantees a steady supply of women for his use, and his profession permits him to travel extensively; in fact he rarely needs to be present in his home. His wife has learned that her status, so precarious anyway, depends on her being gently considerate of her famous husband. Each night when he is away, and almost daily even when technically at home, he meets a new woman; almost always, this is someone who has heard of him. He learned years ago not to ask their names, for he discovered he became uneasy if he knew their first and last names, much less anything else that would force him to recognize that this female body that he was to reduce to sexual cravings incorporated a human identity within. Being experienced, he had no difficulty with the arrangements for his affairs, though interestingly, he would often make little logistical "errors," which, while permitting seduction, made the seemingly sure final act of intercourse impossible. However, on those occasions when he found himself in bed with the woman and obliged to perform, he usually had to seek recourse in fellatio in order to have a competent erection and only a few times a year did he actually vaginally penetrate any of the women. When he did so, he suffered premature ejaculation. He makes every effort never to see any of these women again.

Nymphomania

The equivalent activity in women is the unending changing of male sexual partners, never remaining with one or establishing a human relationship with him. As in the case of men with satyriasis, the act of intercourse is important to nymphomaniacal women, not for the gratification of lust, but for the gratification of revenge (via degradation of one's partner). Like the man with satyriasis, the nymphomaniac's capacity to seduce unlimited numbers of the opposite sex is used as proof that the members of the opposite sex are all beasts.

CASE EXAMPLE

One night, this stylish and sexually provocative woman in her 20s, learning that the famous man just described (satyriasis) was to be in her town, met him "by chance" in the bar of his hotel. She did so because he is famous in his profession and is known to have made love to innumerable women; she was consciously aware only that she would be honored if he were to do like-wise with her. Using sexual skills learned in her own innumerable en-counters with men, she seduced him into taking her to his room (ignoring her own observations that first he did not need to be seduced into seducing her and second that it was strangely difficult to actually get him into bed). She was excited contemplating his virility, by which she meant the mixing of his apparently intense yet gracefully expressed lust for her with a brutal coldness in all his remarks about women. However, her excitement was within her chest and abdomen but not genitals; this was a tension, an ex-pectation rather than a genital need. And so, she was curiously relieved when he indicated he wished to have oral intercourse rather than penetrate her vaginally. She performed as required till, with effort, he could ejaculate but expressed gently and repetitively her surprise and disappointment in his flawed manliness. Something about her challenge provoked a second at-tempt from him, a restitution he learned many years ago to avoid, since one of his secrets is that he is not really a great sexual athlete. His second performance was even more inept, and it now being her turn to be sat-isfied, she did so by means of a barrage of sarcasm which he interrupted by beating her. Now sexually excited, she was to be frustrated, because he precipitously dressed and left. A half an hour later, she was in another room with another man. Once—only once—in her teens, she had sexual relations with her (female) college roommate. While this was the only gratifying genital sexual experience she has ever had, she is still frightened by the memory.

USE OF PROSTITUTES

Some men need prostitutes not because of the unavailability of other women but because the prostitute's degraded status in society is a source of sexual excitement. Under these conditions, use of a prostitute con-stitutes a sexual deviation. Some prostitutes cater to such men by dress-ing and applying makeup so as to appear extravagantly immoral, de-graded, corrupt, and evil. The man requiring this sort of woman uses her as an inanimate fetish, instead of responding to her as another per-son. In his excitement, he will require her to perform acts that he per-sonally ranks as despicable. He will also smear upon her the language that in his youth he considered "dirty." This may lead to quaint per-formances, though the prostitute must not show her amusement at the old-fashioned behavior but rather is expected to perform as if duly degraded. At other times, the woman may be genuinely degraded, by society's grim standards (mentally defective, psychotic, old, ugly, poor).

A variety of the same deviation is represented by the man who literally dirties the woman by defecating or urinating upon her. While this need not be restricted to the use of prostitutes, one cannot always find a mate so well matched that she cooperates without charge.

This married man in his 30s greatly respected his wife when he was courting her because she had the admirable and necessary qualities of being cool, without apparent sexual feeling, of good family, and of meticulous appearance. However, the first time he had intercourse with her immediately after they were married he found himself inexplicably impotent. With practice and with fantasies in subsequent months he was able to manage enough of an erection that he could get her pregnant, but their sexual relations were joyless. They now have intercouse only a half dozen times a year.

However, despite intense guilt he is compelled to wander from his middle-class neighborhood about once a week in order to search out prostitutes. They must impress him as physically dirty, dressing and wearing makeup in a blatantly "whorish" manner; and they are expected to perform sexually in what he considers a "filthy animal" manner. Before intercourse he first curses them, deriding them in the most obscenely degrading language he can find. When finished with intercourse, he is filled with loathing, but his mood repairs itself in a few days so that about a week later he must seek out another such woman.

He describes his wife as a saint.

Pedophilia

Pedophilia is the need for sexual relations with pre-adolescent children. It is found only in males and appears in homosexual and heterosexual form, the latter being more frequent. While it usually consists only of looking at a nude child or caressing the child's body and genitals, pedophilia may in rare instances be accompanied by the greatest brutality, including mutilation and murder of the child. At times the child is invited to masturbate the man, perform fellatio, or submit to anal intercourse, but contact with his penis is by no means invariable.

The child may be a stranger, a friend of the family or an incestuous object, i.e., one's own child or other close relation. Many heterosexual pedophiles are married, experiencing great dissatisfaction in the marriage and suffering from a fear and distaste of adult women and their adult female bodies.

CASE EXAMPLE

The subject is a married man in his 30s. His wife was the first adult woman with whom he had sexual relations, and from the beginning to the present, these have been joyless, with little erotic pleasure, and marred by his difficulty in getting an erection and by premature ejaculation. His wife's body never appealed to him because it is an adult female's; he avoids seeing her because to do so provokes feelings ranging from uneasiness to disgust. An extramarital experiment with another adult woman produced the same effects.

Several times a year, he has found himself suddenly, unexpectedly, intensely excited and preoccupied with wanting a prepubertal girl to fondle. He has never experienced such excitement with, or thinking about, an adult woman. When he can get close to such a little girl, he seeks only to massage her body and fondle her genitals; he has never attempted penetration. On a few occasions, he has had a cooperative child touch his penis but, because of fear, has never permitted this to advance to ejaculation. When he leaves the child, he masturbates.

When trapped into needing an erection with his wife, he fantasies fondling a little girl.

DEVIATIONS FOCUSING ON SPECIAL KINDS OF ACTS

Exhibitionism

Exhibitionism is that condition in which sexual excitement is produced in the genitals by exhibiting them to others. The same term often is used to refer to behavior that is not deviant, but in this discussion it refers exclusively to display of the genitals when that act itself creates excitement in the exhibitionist. We do not include the exhibition of other parts of the body (e.g., breasts), the exhibition of prowess, or even genital exhibition which is used to arouse one's partner. In the sense of a genital sexual deviation, exhibitionism, as we define it, is found only in males.

The uninformed person may think the man who exhibits his genitals to women does so as a form of invitation to sexual intercourse. That is not so. First, he exhibits himself only to strangers or to women he scarcely knows, and never to a willing woman like his wife. Second, in those rare instances when the women show interest rather than concern or anger, the exhibitionist promptly flees. His motives do not spring from the unbridled excitement of a sexually aggressive man but rather the reverse. Exhibitionists are shy, passive individuals who express great concern about their feelings of inadequacy as males and their impotence in heterosexual relations. Thus, the act of exhibiting is not *in anticipation* of heterosexual relations but is *in itself* the man's sexual act. Actually, exhibition is only the first half of the act; the second half is masturbation.

The exhibitionist is more likely than any other sexual deviant to be caught by the authorities, so much so that the need to be caught may be part of the deviation itself (a necessary part of the excitement). Unfortunately, despite arrest and punishment, the likelihood that the exhibitionist will repeat his behavior and be caught again is extremely high, for the deviation does not achieve its object unless the sufferer believes he has caused a furor. It is as if, in exhibiting his penis, he must upset the observing woman and later the civil authorities; only then has he forced society to attend to the fact that he unquestionably is male, is masculine, and has a penis. Then he can be certain, temporarily, about his status as a man.

CASE EXAMPLE

This married man in his 40s has always been shy with women, and after 15 years of marriage still is passive around his wife. During their infrequent intercourse (every 6 weeks to 2 months) he has difficulty getting or maintaining an erection. While his wife constantly bullies him, he does not complain, believing that she is right to do so. In the last five years, he has succumbed to the urge to exhibit his penis to passing girls or women. This occurs on the street, in the daytime, under circumstances when he realistically runs great risk of arrest. In fact, he does this in the neighborhood where he lives, not even going to strange areas or cities.

He will stand to the side of a street and show his exposed penis to women passing in cars or to women walking on the other side of the street. He has an erection at these times. If he believes he was not noticed, he will shift his position or otherwise attempt to get their attention and when he has done so, he will not flee when he senses they are upset and might call for help.

On one occasion, he exposed himself to two teenage girls, who began chuckling and advanced toward him as if interested; this is the only time he has precipitously left the scene.

He has been arrested six times and has already spent time in prison. His reputation is ruined, his family is humiliated, and his professional status is in terrible disrepair. Nonetheless, he says he will probably repeat the act.

Voyeurism

In the practice of voyeurism, sexual excitement is produced by the act of clandestine "sexual" looking. Excitement occurs only when the act is performed in secret and when the voyeur believes that the one at whom he is looking neither knows, nor would approve, of the peeping. This deviation is found only in males looking at females.

As with the exhibitionist, the voyeur is uneasy with women and uncertain that he can get along competently with them. Also, as in cases of exhibitionism, the person toward whom the deviant act is directed is a woman, a heterosexual object. However, the act itself reveals a deficiency found so often in sexual deviations, namely that the man does not trust his heterosexual ability. Unlike exhibitionism, voyeurism involves no drive to be apprehended.

CASE EXAMPLE

This single man, in his early 20s, drives to a different residential neighborhood each night and surveys homes to find rooms where he can observe women undressing, while he is safely hidden in the bushes outside the window. When he finds a room in which a young woman is undressing, he becomes excited and masturbates. Although he can exhaust himself sexually after a couple of such experiences a night, he never satisfies his desire to peep, which is an insatiable hunger.

He also goes out on dates and occasionally has intercourse without problems of potency. He enjoys this intercourse but less than the masturbating while peeping. He is not especially aroused watching a girlfriend undress. No matter how closely her nude body conforms to his ideal, looking at her under these permissive circumstances is fairly casual. He says, however, that if he were to watch her undressing when she did not know he was looking, her nudity would then arouse him as much as does any unknown woman's.

Sadism

A sadistic individual becomes sexually excited when inflicting physical pain on another living creature. In the manner of definition used throughout this discussion, the meaning must be restricted exclusively to those pain-inflicting acts that sexually excite the aggressor. The pain inflicted may be as varied as any torture ever invented by any society. The object may be human or animal, of the opposite or same sex. In mild forms of sadism, the pain inflicted can be almost symbolic (e.g., beating someone with a soft object, fashioned to resemble a hard club). In such a case, the person attacked need only pretend to be in agony. At the other extreme, however, sexual excitement can only be aroused if the victim is brutally attacked, with the most dreadful case being the sadist who is satisfied only during the act of murdering his victim. In this situation, it is not the dead body that excites, but the dying, suffering, possessor of the body.

A common variant of sadism is rape.

Although there are innumerable reports of women who act sadistically towards boys and men and get nongenital pleasure (triumph) from it, much rarer is the woman who becomes sexually excited by doing so, and rarest of all is the woman who becomes sexually excited by inflicting physical pain on others. In the case of women, the excitement is usually nongenital. In males, however, the excitement is often directly genital.

CASE EXAMPLE

This married man in his 20s requested psychiatric help because he feared he would soon commit murder. Since adolescence, he has been excited by fantasies and pornography depicting women bound and tortured. During courtship of his wife, he introduced mild versions of his fantasy into their sex play, and in this manner only was able to proceed on to intercourse. Now, after 8 years of marriage, they invariably have intercourse by his first binding her tightly with ropes and then, with her still bound, having intercourse. She has noticed that gradually the binding has been less and less symbolic and more and more painful. On two occasions in the last year, binding around her neck choked her into unconsciousness.

It is the nature of his work to enter households of strangers to do repairs. He frequently meets housewives there, and the temptation to bind and torture them is becoming unbearable. So far, he has avoided doing so by going out to his repair truck and masturbating while looking at photographs of bound and tortured women. His fear of killing a strange woman stems not from a belief that such an act would be sexually exciting but rather that, having bound and tortured her, he would have to kill her to remove the witness.

Masochism

In masochism, genital sexual excitement is aroused when one is suffering physical pain under specific circumstances. The victim may prefer being whipped, cut, pricked, bound or spanked; but he does not seek or respond sexually to just any sort of physical pain. The areas of the body assaulted, the intensity and duration of the sadistic attack, and the person who is to inflict it are all circumscribed. The ritual must be carried out precisely or the pain will not develop its sexual character.

Variants are dangerous experiences not specifically painful, such as semi-strangulation or rendering oneself unconscious by anesthetics.

Masochism is considered the mirror-image of sadism, and yet one rarely hears of a true sadist teaming up with a true masochist, for the sadist needs a victim who suffers, not a sexually excited "victim." On the other hand, the masochist needs his assailant to act out of brutality, not sexual need.

In our society, masochistic fantisies and expectations are ubiquitous in the sexual lives of women, and yet in connection with their overt sexual behavior women rarely report sexual excitement specifically provoked by physical pain. Furthermore, when it *is* reported, careful questioning often reveals that the true source of excitement was the concentration of feeling and attention directed upon them by the person inflicting the pain, rather than the pain itself. In genuine masochism, it is the consciously experienced pain itself that excites.

CASE EXAMPLE

The wife of the man described above, under "Sadism," found, during her courtship, that their first intercourse, under cramped conditions in a car, where her husband fixed her arms and legs so that they could not move, was at first uncomfortable but soon aroused in her a feeling of "interest." In time, this progressed to mild excitement, and now, several years later, she is appalled to find herself greatly excited by being bound. She is frightened by her excitement, and she is frightened by her experiences of unconsciousness while being bound. She believes that her husband is dangerous, and at the same time she feels deeply that he loves her.

Minor Deviations

There are a number of conditions that need to be mentioned only briefly, either because they are quite rare, or are related to unremarkable variants in normative sexual behavior. Many of these do not qualify as sexual deviations unless the act is the preferred or necessary means by which the person achieves sexual gratification. If it is indulged in out of curiosity, desire for variety, or in the absence of a desired object, the behavior is not properly considered a deviation. Behavior that sometimes occurs, but does not meet our definition of deviation includes cunnilingus (mouth to vagina), fellatio (mouth to penis), anal intercourse, coprolalia (using obsecene language to excite oneself or one's partner), use of pornography, and masturbation. However, if an individual consistently prefers to use any of these in the presence of other opportunities, he may be considered sexually deviant.

Farther removed from normal behavior are: frottage (rubbing against strangers in crowds for sexual excitement), pyromania (fire setting for sexual excitement), and various acts involving specialized sex objects (such as crippled women, women smoking cigarettes, or people with special odors).

DEVIATION IN THE EXPRESSION OF MASCULINITY AND FEMININITY

Transsexualism

A transsexual is a biologically normal male or female who believes himself or herself to be a member of the opposite sex. Transsexuals are not simply dissatisfied with their assigned sex and eager to try being members of the opposite sex; they believe they are the result of a biological mistake and that they are a man (or woman) trapped, so to speak, in the physiological body of the opposite sex. For this reason, a transsexual may seek to change his or her body so that its appearance is consonant with the felt sense of sex. The condition may originate in childhood. It sometimes is detectable as early as the first two years of life. Throughout childhood, the transsexual boy or girl shows little or no behavior appropriate to the sex to which he or she biologically belongs, but instead reflects the interests and fantasies appropriate for the opposite sex. This includes kinds of clothes worn, games played, ways of walking and moving, and preference to be with and to be accepted by members of the "adopted sex" instead of being regarded as a member of the anatomically appropriate sex. The transsexual child's behavior may not be thwarted by the parents and may in fact be actively encouraged by the same-sexed parent, if not both of them, or any parental resistance to the behavior may be minimal and without effect.

In such circumstances, the condition proceeds unimpeded throughout later childhood, despite disparaging remarks by the child's schoolmates or by adults outside the family, and by the end of childhood clear-cut wishes to be transformed into the opposite sex are proclaimed. By the time they reach late adolescence many transsexuals, because of publicity currently given to the condition and the possibilities of artificially-induced body changes, are actively seeking such changes from physicians. By this same age, these individuals have learned the role skills necessary to pass undetected in society as a member of the opposite sex. The transsexual has no difficulty behaving like a member of the opposite sex, having felt like one and played at it for so long. Therefore, on deciding to "pass," he or she performs this potentially dangerous act very rapidly and successfully in the school or job environment or in other social situations.

In spite of such successes, the transsexual is intensely uncomfortable in what is felt to be an abnormal body, and therefore powerful efforts are made to achieve the appropriate body changes. For the male who wishes to be transformed into a female these changes consist of removal of facial and body hair by electrolysis; permanent use of female hormones to stimulate growth of breasts, increase size of buttocks, and otherwise create a softer, more rounded appearance; and most important, removal of the penis and testes, and the construction of an artificial vagina. Other physical transformations, such as voice pitch and timbre, or length of hair are accomplished without medical assistance. The female transsexual seeks removal of her breasts and internal reproductive organs (ovaries, fallopian tubes, and uterus) and administration of androgens to induce growth of facial and body hair and lowering of voice. At present, plastic surgery is an unreliable method of creating a normal-looking penis and is entirely unable to produce a sexually functioning organ. Without a penis, there is usually no great drive to obliterate the vagina.

When these anatomical changes have been accomplished, the transsexual often wants to marry, and in fact frequently does so. Legal complications due to one's birth certificate being in opposition to one's appearance generally are overcome, though rarely can one get the birth certificate changed. Although marriages are not legal, they are, nonetheless, entered into. Passports may be granted; driver's licenses are rather easily procured and, especially when one has the driver's license, one can easily "pass" without question in most social situations.

Up to the present time, unknown hundreds of transsexuals have had their bodies "transformed." When subjects are carefully chosen for these hormonal and surgical procedures, the end results seem favorable, in that formerly distraught and hopeless people now find they can live creatively and with greater tranquility. As yet, the long-term psychological results are not known.

Because they feel they are members of the sex opposite to the one their body reveals, transsexuals consider themselves psychologically heterosexual. As a result, the transsexual tries to choose sexual partners who are physically and psychologically normal members of the transsexual's own biological sex. Transsexuals clearly differentiate themselves from homosexuals and are not attracted to homosexuals. Male transsexuals, believing themselves truly female, choose as their partners men whom they consider masculine and heterosexual. Female transsexuals choose women who are feminine, may have been married and have had children of their own, and who have never had homosexual relations.

Surgically untreated transsexuals avoid using their genitals with members of the opposite biological sex. Until surgical transformation, they either do not receive, or try to avoid the complications of, sexual excitement in their genitals. They never become sexually excited by the clothes of the opposite sex.

CASE EXAMPLE

The patient is a biologically normal male in his 20s. He has been dressing in female clothes since age two.

At first, he would put on his sister's dresses and shoes, but soon expanded this to dressing completely so that he might appear and feel like a girl for as many hours a day as he was permitted, talking and acting as one and playing with girls in girls' games in which he was accepted as one of the girls. By age 4, he was saying that he was going to grow up to be a woman and that he wanted his penis and testes removed. His mother found his femininity delightful, while his father, who was almost never home during the boy's waking hours in childhood, played no significant role in the household; he did not stop his son's feminine behavior.

The male secondary sex changes of adolescence made the child frantic—sad, irritable, and seclusive. While formerly a good student, he now did marginal work. Then, after many months of terrible attendance in high school, he dropped out, and, hearing of the possibility of sex-transformation procedures, by age 18 he was trying to negotiate the necessary treatment on his own. Being a minor, this was not possible; however, he did leave home, now dressing all the time as a woman, and, with money earned by working, had facial hair removed. Shortly thereafter "she" convinced a physician to start "her" on female hormones so that "she" then developed breasts. At age 21, no longer needing parental consent, and having saved money, "she" found a surgeon willing to "transform" the genitals and to create an artificial vagina. "She" now works as a saleswoman in a fashionable store, is married to a man with whom "she" has regular vaginal intercourse, and hopes to adopt a child.

"She" has never been sexually excited by the women's garments. "She" continues overjoyed at having a female body and is content in her role as a woman.

Transvestism (Fetishistic Cross-Dressing)

Transvestism is a condition in which a man becomes genitally sexually excited by wearing feminine garments. While the term "transvestism" literally means cross-dressing, it is used here only for that condition in which wearing women's clothes causes genital excitement, and not for quite different situations in which cross-dressing also occurs, such as transsexualism or effeminate homosexuality. As a true sexual deviation, transvestism is found only in males. There are two groups. There are some men who, throughout life from the time the condition first manifests itself, find only one type of garment exciting (e.g., women's shoes or underwear). A second type of transvestite starts with a single garment fetish, but gradually the condition spreads so that the man occasionally wishes to dress completely as a woman. It is important to stress the fact that, in contrast to the transsexual, the transvestite regards himself as a man, does not wish his body transformed, and especially enjoys the fact that the insignia of his maleness, his penis, not only is intact but is the source of intense pleasure.

Transvestism usually becomes most obvious at or near the time of puberty or adolescence. The intense pleasure derived from women's garments often manifests itself the first time the boy masturbates. There are, however, cases in which transvestism does not become obvious until later in adolescence, and in rare instances even later in adult life. Not infrequently, there are precursors reaching back into childhood as early as 5 or 6 years of age, at which time the little boy discovers an intense excitement (though not usually localized in the genitals) when he puts on women's clothes.

In contrast to the transsexual boy who spontaneously puts on girls' clothes as soon as he can and as often as he can in order to feel like a girl, the transvestite frequently first experiences cross-dressing when others dress him in feminine apparel. This may take place when some female wants to reduce the boy's masculinity and humiliate him, but on subsequent occasions, when he dresses himself the result is the reverse. Then he does not feel humiliated but becomes genitally sexually excited, feels potent, and masterful in his potency.

Transvestism does not start as early as transsexualism. It appears only after a boy has clearly developed masculinity and after an unquestioned awareness of being a male has permanently stamped itself upon his identity. As boy, adolescent, and man the transvestite is almost always masculine, except at the times when he cross-dresses. He never considers himself a female and does not wish to become one, with the anatomical changes that implies. Transvestites are found in the masculine professions. They are almost always overtly heterosexual and may marry and have children.

This biologically normal man in his 20s is married, with children. He is a construction foreman.

Until he was three years old he lived with his mother and father, but his mother died, and then responsibility for his care fell upon his stepmother.

When he was four years old, she dressed him in girl's clothes to punish him for getting dirty. He had not cross-dressed spontaneously. She did this several times subsequently, and within two years he had arranged with a neighbor girl to dress him up regularly during their after-school play. The dressing-up died away for several years, but at age 12, he did it once again, almost casually. On starting to put his stepmother's panties on, he suddenly became intensely sexually excited and masturbated for the first time. For several years thereafter, he would only put on his stepmother's underwear and either masturbate or spontaneously ejaculate. Then, in mid-teens, he began taking underwear from the homes of friends' sisters, and in a year or so increased this activity to stealing women's underwear wherever he could find it. Aside from the moments when he put on these garments, he was unremarkably masculine in appearance, in athletic interests, and in daydreams of what he would wish to be in the future. He was attracted to girls and went out on dates, but, being shy, he had less sexual experience than some of his friends.

He proposed to the first girl with whom he had a serious affair, confessed his fetishistic cross-dressing to her, and was surprised and relieved when she not only was not upset but assisted him by offering her underwear and by purchasing new pairs for him as he wished. Starting within a year after marriage, he found it more exciting to put on more of his wife's clothes than just her underwear, and now he prefers dressing completely in her clothes and having her assist him in putting on makeup and fixing his wig.

He feels completely male and is accepted by all who know him as a masculine man. He does not desire sex transformation. He has never had homosexual relations and is sexually attracted only by women's bodies.

Homosexuality with Gender Identity Aberrations

Homosexuality is discussed at length in a separate chapter of this book and will be considered here only in the context of gender disorders, i.e., effeminate homosexuality in males, and masculine (butch) homosexuality in females. These can be contrasted to transsexualism and transvestism in that the homosexual individual almost always knows himself or herself to be a homosexual. As a consequence, the homosexual considers himself or herself to be unquestionably a member of the sex to which he or she was assigned at birth, and the sex indicated by his or her secondary sex characters. Nonetheless, these individuals prefer sexual relations with a person of their own sex and know themselves as members of the same sex. Therefore, they are not transsexual. Since he accepts the reality of his biological sex, the typical homosexual does not seek anatomical sex transformation, although some occasionally fantasize the possibility, without acting on it. Homosexual men and women do not wish to pass in society as a member of the opposite sex, or to be permanently accepted in the role. Those homosexual males who completely cross-dress do so as mimicry, with all the world knowing and applauding the success of the farce. No "passing" is involved—only caricaturing, with hostility toward the opposite sex being obvious. Homosexuals very rarely become sexually excited by the clothes of the opposite sex. They do not prefer women's bodies and do not marry females because of a sexual need to live with a woman.

CASE EXAMPLES

(1)

Effeminate male. This biologically normal man, in his 20s, is a women's hairdresser. He has never married, and although he has occasionally slept with his customers, he does so for practical rather than sexual or romantic reasons. His only gratifying sexual experiences are with men, and he is driven to having a new partner daily. He prefers anal intercourse but only when he is penetrated. If his partner requests that the patient be the penetrator, he loses his erection.

He has been effeminate since age 5 or 6 and has been teased for this throughout his life. While embarrassed and humiliated by the teasing, he has a compulsion to provoke more and more of it. Since boyhood, he has occasionally dressed up in women's clothes, especially at Halloween, but when doing so he has never become sexually excited. He has never wanted to be a female, does not wish "sex transformation," and has never attempted to pass as a woman. However, after years of practice, he can dress as a woman and at parties mimic a pretty one so successfully that he wins everyone's applause for his brilliant performance. Everyone knows it is a performance and that is what is most pleasurable for him.

(2)

"Butch" female. This biologically normal woman in her 20s, with a boyish nickname, is unmarried but has been living with the same woman for several years. From age 5, although never questioning that she was a female, she has wished she had been born a boy and tried whenever possible to look and act boyish. Skillful at sports, she was more or less accepted by the boys; however they constantly put her down, letting her know that they thought her inferior to them. By puberty, she had already had several crushes on women, and during midadolescence had her first sexual experience, with a woman teacher. Going on dates with boys a few times, she was so upset by their physical presence and by the demands on her to dress femininely that she quickly gave up the effort, and, guiltily admitting to herself her exclusively homosexual erotic needs, permitted herself several homosexual affairs before meeting the woman with whom she now lives.

At present, she dresses in a very masculine manner but her appearance raises no questions regarding her femaleness. Her sexual relations consist of mutual masturbation and mutual cunnilingus, both of which are invariably satisfying to her. She prefers girls more feminine than herself but has on a few occasions experimented with other "butches." This did not work well. At present, she works as an executive for an advertising agency, where her work is greatly valued.

Intersexuality

Since intersexuality is discussed in a different chapter, it is only necessary here to note that individuals with certain anatomical and/or physiological disorders of their reproductive or secondary sex anatomy may have a variety of sexual disorders. Hermaphroditic individuals (i.e., the genitals appear to be a mix of male and female), brought up from birth uncertain as to which sex they belong, may, in choosing sex objects, show varying degrees of bisexuality. In others, the hermaphroditism is hidden and the external genitals are those of the opposite sex. Because of the appearance of their genitals, these individuals often are assigned to the opposite sex. With clear-cut misassignment and without their parents knowing of the mistake, they develop an identity appropriate to that assignment, rather than to the one appropriate to their chromosomes, gonads, or other internal sexual organs (e.g., uterus, prostate). Thus, they will usually be psychologically heterosexual, regardless of the hidden biologic state.

There are, however, a few exceptions to this generalization. In males (not in females), constitutional hypogonadism (that is, a disturbance in the testes, probably associated with change in brain function from fetal life on) may be found in boys who desire to be female. Despite his apparently normal genital anatomy at birth (which results in assignment to the male sex), such an individual from earliest life on wishes to be a female, much as does the transsexual. These represent the rare cases in which there seems to be evidence of a biological factor overriding all effects of society and of family, pressing the child to wish to be a member of the opposite sex.

CASE EXAMPLES

(1)

Hermaphroditic identity. Because of excessive production of androgens by her adrenals during fetal life, this otherwise biologically normal woman in her 20s was born with masculinized genitals so that her clitoris was the size of a small penis. She also had a patent vagina, and so, at birth, her mother was told that although she was a hermaphrodite, "You might as well raise her as a girl." As a result, this mother was forever uncertain as to her daughter's sex. So now, as an adult, the young woman cannot feel herself to be either a male or female but has decided that she might as well live as a woman. As a result, she feels she is a freak, is chronically depressed, and considers herself doomed to a life without adequate sexual gratification or children (although she is fertile and, with minor surgical repair, biologically competent to have children). She is sexually attracted to men but feels that they would not want her.

(2)

Constitutional hypogonadism. This man is biologically abnormal, suffering from an additional sex chromosome (XXY). Although his body appeared unremarkably male at birth and he was so assigned, from early childhood he began acting as if he wished he were a girl and talked, as do transsexuals, of the possibility of growing up to be a female. He occasionally dressed in women's clothes (never with sexual excitement) and often dreamed of himself as a female. With puberty, he began to develop breasts and a body contour otherwise somewhat feminine. Sexual desire was minimal. Eventually, the proper diagnosis was made, and because of his by now very feminine behavior and desires, his normal-sized penis and atrophic testes were removed. Female hormones were prescribed to complete the "sexual transformation."

"She" now lives as a woman, is married, and is happy with life as a housewife. Sexual relations with the artificial vagina lead almost invariably to orgasm (although he never achieved orgasm with his male organs).

A note on another sort of biological disorder may be in place here. There are reports of aberrant feminine and/or fetishistic behavior, in males only, directly associated with temporal lobe disorder of the brain. When the brain condition is corrected, the deviant behavior disappears.

Deviations Related to Excretory Functions

Stimulation of Zones. There are men and women who develop undisguised sexual excitement in response to stimulation of the anus or urethra or by means of extreme filling of the rectum or bladder. Their sexual excitement is felt also in the genitals. Such people may masturbate to orgasm by rubbing the anus or urethral meatus without need of genital friction. Additionally, whether male or female, they may desire penetration of these orifices because of primary pleasure from the zone itself. Occasionally, a person will gradually work at enlarging the urethral meatus so that it can accept penetration of a penis or penis-sized object. In the most bizarre cases, one finds reports of remarkable foreign bodies emplaced in the rectum or bladder: electric light bulbs, door knobs, ping-pong balls and the like in the rectum, and nails, needles, and even snakes in the bladder.

Excretory functions. Some men and women become sexually excited when urinating or defecating on a homosexual or heterosexual partner. There are other people whose excitement is produced, not by excreting, but by being excreted upon.

Excitement from excretory products. Still other men and women, who do not belong to the above two categories, become excited when they smell or handle urine and feces.

Derivatives. There are individuals of both sexes who, without indulging in any of these three kinds of behavior are, nonetheless, excited by the use of what they consider "dirty," that is, excretory, language. In mild form this may simply enhance their otherwise unremarkable heterosexual relations, but in more severe cases it may be the preferred and necessary mode of behavior. For instance, there are obscene telephone callers who masturbate while engaging in dirty talking to a strange woman on the phone.

Fetishes often are stimulating only if they smell, and often that requirement is met only if the odor is specifically fecal or urinary.

SUGGESTED READING

Allen, C. 1969. *A Textbook of Psychosexual Disorders*. 2d ed. London: Oxford University Press.

Bieber, I.; Dain, H. J.; Dince, P. R.; Drellich, M. R.; Grand, H. G.; Gundlach, R. H.; Kremer, M. W.; Rifkin, A. H.; Wilbur, C. B.; and Bieber, T. B. 1962. *Homosexuality*. New York: Basic Books.

Ellis, H. 1936. *Studies in the Psychology of Sex*. New York: Random House.

Ford, C. S., and Beach, F. A. 1951. *Patterns of Sexual Behavior*. New York: Harper & Row.

Freud, S. 1905. Three essays on the theory of sexuality. In *Standard Edition of the Complete Psychological Works of Sigmund Freud*, vol. VII. London: Hogarth Press, 1953.

Kinsey, A. C.; Pomeroy, W. B.; and Martin, C. E. 1948. *Sexual Behavior in the Human Male*. Philadelphia: Saunders.

Kinsey, A. C.; Pomeroy, W. B.; Martin, C. E.; and Gebhard, P. H. 1953. *Sexual Behavior in the Human Female*. Philadelphia: Saunders.

Krafft-Ebing, R. *Psychopathia Sexualis*. New York: Physicians and Surgeons Book Co., 1932.

Marmor, J.,ed. 1965. *Sexual Inversion*. New York: Basic Books.

Money, J., and Ehrhardt, A. A. 1972. *Man and Woman, Boy and Girl*. Baltimore: Johns Hopkins University Press.

Stoller, R. J. 1968. *Sex and Gender, Vol. I*. New York: Science House.

8

BRAIN MECHANISMS CONTROLLING
SEXUAL BEHAVIOR

Richard E. Whalen

EDITORIAL PREFACE

A physiological perspective on behavior is achieved by analyzing the ways in which separate parts of the organism, i.e., the nervous, muscular, endocrine and other systems, contribute to the integrated, adaptive responses of the individual to his physical and social environment.

This quotation from Chapter 1 will introduce Richard Whalen's chapter on brain mechanisms and sexual behavior, but Chapters 8, 9 and 10 should be read as a unit since all three deal with the physiological foundations of sexuality. Whalen's approach is also closely related to discussions by Milton Diamond and by John Money, for he deals with prenatal differentiation of brain mechanisms.

A conventional treatment of relations between the brain and sexual functions might well begin with a discussion of experiments and clinical observations on the sexual behavior of animals and human beings experimentally or accidentally deprived of different brain areas. This could be followed by an account of sexual behavior produced by electrical or chemical stimulation of the brain, and so on.

Although he eventually covers these topics, Whalen has chosen to approach his subject more obliquely but with unexpected effectiveness. The first half of the chapter deals primarily with endocrine glands and brain functions rather than organismic behavior, which is taken up in the second half. There are several virtues to this topical sequence. In Figure 8.1, the reader is shown that the brain affects sexuality in two ways, namely by mediating overt behavior, and by controlling endocrine functions which in turn influence behavior. At the same time, he is led to understand the reciprocal nature of those neural and endocrine interactions that are responsible for the coordinated control of behavior patterns.

In discussing hormonal effects on prenatal sex differentiation in the brain, Whalen deals primarily with differences in the hypothalamic control of pituitary function in adulthood. These differences tend to be qualitative rather than quantitative and are, therefore, easier to assess than differences in behavior. For these reasons, it is worth noting his warning against incautious use of evidence of differentiation in lower mammals "as a model for the sexual differentiation assumed to occur in man," a caveat also mentioned by Money and Martin Hoffman.

After studying the evidence on neuroendocrine systems, a reader cannot help but be disappointed by the status of knowledge concerning brain mechanisms and sexual behavior. In his section on neurobehavioral systems, Whalen provides a reasonable synopsis of methods used and facts established, but no unifying principles emerge and no general theories are proposed. Just why this should be so is not immediately apparent. I am tempted to place most of the blame upon the failure of experimentalists adequately to conceptualize and then to measure the relevant behavioral variables, and part upon the apparent reluctance of many theorists to relinquish their search for a localized "sex center" in the brain.

Such evidence as is available shows that some parts of the brain, notably specific hypothalamic regions, exert indirect effects on sexual behavior by virtue of their control over hormone secretions, whereas other brain areas are more immediately involved in the reception and integration of sexually-relevant stimuli and the organization and execution of sexual responses. It is also established that sexual behavior is subject to both stimulatory and inhibitory control, with the result that animals and humans may respond to one type of brain injury or stimulation with a loss of sexual responses and to another type with apparent increase in sexual excitability.

Instead of depending on one or more "centers," sexual responsiveness and performance are served by a net of neural subsystems including components from the cerebral cortex down to the sacral cord. Different subsystems act in concert, but tend to mediate different units or elements in the normally integrated patterns. Whalen's description of the technical and methodological armamentarium now available for research on basic problems gives reason to hope that progress to their fuller explication may be due soon.

INTRODUCTION

During the late 1930s, experimental evidence began to accumulate which indicated that the brain plays a major role in the regulation of sexual function, and that it does so in two major ways. First, the brain controls the functional activity of the gonads by acting through the adenohypophysis or anterior pituitary gland (AP). Second, the brain mediates sexual excitability or libido and modulates sexual reflexes by responding to gonadal hormones and to sensory stimuli. A schematic illustration of relationships between the brain, the gonads and sexual behavior is presented in Figure 8.1.

Several features of Figure 8.1 are to be noted. The right-hand side of the diagram depicts the "closed circuit" relationships between the brain, hypophysis and gonads. The primary pathway involves the stimulation of the hypophysis by the brain and the subsequent stimulation of the go-

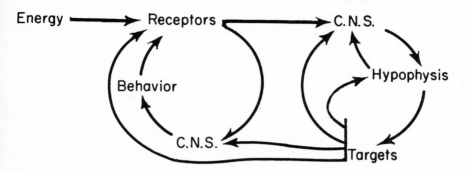

Fig. 8.1. *Relationships between the brain, the gonads, and sexual behavior.* From Whalen, *Hormones and Behavior* (New York: Van Nostrand, 1967).

nads by gonadotropic hormones which are secreted by the AP in response to the brain stimulation. The hypophysis exerts feedback effects upon the brain, and hormones secreted by the gonads exert feedback influences upon both hypophysis and brain.

The nonhormonal control system for sexual responses is shown on the left side of the diagram. This system is concerned with the integration of neural and sensory systems with behavioral output. The endocrine and nonendocrine systems are anatomically autonomous, although they are linked functionally. This chapter is devoted to describing the nature and function of these neural and endocrine systems which mediate sexual behavior.

We will consider first, relationships between the endocrine glands, especially the pituitary, and the nervous system, and second, the relationships between both nervous and hormonal systems and behavior of the individual.

NEUROENDOCRINE SYSTEMS

Anatomy and Secretory Characteristics of the Hypophysis

The pituitary gland, or hypophysis, is a complex structure containing two components of different embryological origin, and the differences in origin have important functional implications. One component, the adenohypophysis, or anterior pituitary, consists of epithelial tissue originating in Rathke's pouch in the buccal ectoderm. A second component is the neurohypophysis, or posterior pituitary, which consists of neural tissue extending from the floor of the third ventricle. The system which we shall use to describe different regions of the hypophysis is illustrated in Figure 8.2.

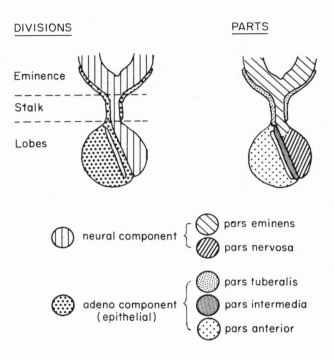

Fig. 8.2. *Diagrams representing sagittal sections of a conventionalized mammalian hypophysis showing the divisions, components, and parts.* The adenoeminence and adenostalk together form the pars tuberalis. The abenolobe is almost completely divided by the hypophyseal cleft into an anterior lobe and an intermediate lobe. In many mammals the anterior lobe is entirely composed of pars anterior tissue and the intermediate is entirely composed of pars intermedia tissue as shown here. For further details refer to the text. From H. D. Purves, Morphology of the hypophysis related to its function, in *Sex and Internal Secretions*, edited by W. C. Young (Baltimore: Williams & Wilkins, 1961).

On the left of the figure the neural and epithelial components of the hypophysis are distinguished. On the right, the parts ("pars") are presented.

The critical feature of the hypophysis is the secretory characteristic. It secretes ten different hormones. The *adenohypophysis* (pars anterior) produces two gonadatropic hormones: FSH, follicle stimulating hormone, which induces the maturation of the ovarian follicles and stimulates spermatogenesis in the testes, and LH, luteinizing hormone, which induces ovulation in the female and stimulates secretion of androgen by the testes in the male. In addition to these two gonadotropins, the adenohypophysis secretes other hormones, including prolactin which facilitates milk production by the mammary gland, ACTH, adrenocorticotropic hormone, which acts on the adrenal cortex, TSH, thyroid stimulating hormone, and GH, growth hormone. The *intermediate lobe* (pars intermedia) secretes two melanocyte stimulating hormones (α and ß MSH). The *neurohypophysis* (pars nervosa) produces oxytocin which influences the contraction of the uterus and plays a role in milk letdown, and vasopressin which has antidiuretic effects as well as vasopressor effects (producing a rise in blood pressure).

Control by the Nervous System

It has been clear for some decades that hypophyseal function, as reflected in the selective secretion of hormones, is controlled by the nervous system, but we have only recently begun to understand the mechanisms of such control. The problem has been most severe as it applies to the adenophypophysis because there are very few, if any, nerve connections between the brain and this lobe of the gland.

In contrast, neural connectivity with respect to the neurohypophysis is obvious since this part of the pituitary is little more than an evaginated segment of neural tissues (Fig. 8.2). A series of experiments reported in the 1920s included the curious observation that extracts from the hypothalamus possessed oxytocic, vasopressor and antidiuretic properties similar to those found with extracts from the neural lobe of the pituitary. This discovery made little sense until the 1950s, when it became clear that the hypothalamo-hypophyseal neuronal system was in fact an integrated *neurosecretory* system. The cell bodies of this system reside in discrete brain regions, e.g., the supraoptic and paraventricular nuclei of the hypothalamus; and the axons of these cells course caudally and enter the pars eminens. Some fibers terminate at the upper levels of the neurohypophysis while others terminate deep within the pars nervosa (Fig. 8.3).

It is now generally believed that the neurohypophyseal hormones, oxytocin and vasopressin, are synthesized in the cell bodies of the relevant neurons lying in the brain. Since the hypothalamo-neurohypophyseal system comprises two hormones (oxytocin and vasopressin) and two nuclei (the supraoptic and paraventricular), the question has naturally arisen as to whether each hormone is produced by a separate nuclear group. The answer seems to be "predominantly." In a variety of mammalian species, vasopressin is the principal hormone associated with the supra-optic nucleus, whereas oxytocin is chiefly related to the paraventricular nucleus. Although oxytocin and vasopressin may not be associated exclusively with separate nuclear groups, it is clear that both neurohypophyseal hormones are synthesized by neurons whose cell bodies lie in the supraoptic and paraventricular nuclei. These hormones are transported to the pars nervosa of the neurohypophysis where they are stored until released into the general circulation in response to a variety of external stimuli such as those derived from coitus and suckling.

Unlike the neurohypophysis, the pars anterior of the adenohypophysis (Fig. 8.2) appears to have no major neuronal input, yet this portion of the pituitary certainly is under the control of the brain. Over the past 20 years, a concept of "neurohumoral" control of adenohypophyseal function has developed. This concept holds that special types of neurons in the hypothalamus secrete "releasing factors" or "releasing hormones" which they discharge into the vascular or circulatory system supplying blood to the adenohypophysis. These factors, or hormones, in turn stimulate or inhibit the pituitary to release into the systemic circulation still other hormones which are synthesized in the pars anterior. Considerable evidence favors the validity of this hypothesis.

Although the pars anterior may not have direct neural connection with the brain, it is richly supplied by the vascular connections of the pituitary portal system. This system, illustrated in Figure 8.3, could serve to transport hypothalamic secretory products to the pars anterior. In most mammals, including man, the long and short portal vessels provide the only source of blood to the pars anterior. It is interesting to note that the long and short portal vessels appear to supply anatomically different areas of the adenohypophysis, and that the various long portal vessels supply discrete cell groups. The potential exists, therefore, for particular hypothalamic neurons to secrete their products into selected portal vessels so that releasing hormones produced by those neurons are carried to specific cells in the adenohypophyseal synthetic apparatus.

The foregoing argument assumes that hypothalamic neurons contact the vascular loop system of the stalk, and that the direction of blood flow is from the hypothalamus to the pars distalis. There are several reasons to believe that both assumptions are valid. In the first place, some nerve fibers from the hypothalamo-hypophyseal tracts, particularly those from the paraventricular nucleus, can be seen to terminate on the capillary system in the hypophyseal stalk, (i.e., the structure connecting the pituitary and the brain). In the second place, the tuberohypophyseal neurons provide a major input to the stalk. This tract, made of fine fibers, courses from the arcuate (infundibular) nucleus of the hypothalamus to terminate in the region of the capillary loops.

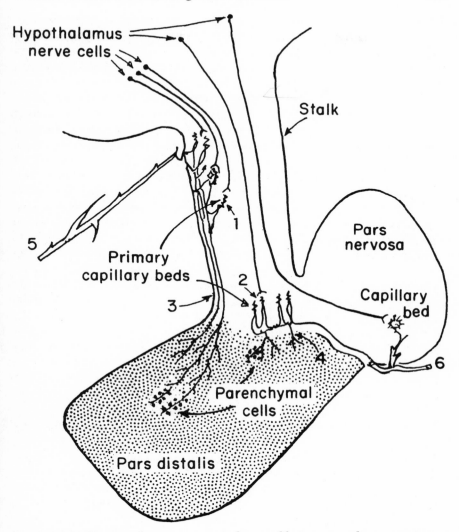

Fig. 8.3. *Diagram showing some of the possible neurovascular connections between hypothalamic nuclei and the pituitary gland.* Pathways are shown between nerve cells in the hypothalamus and parenchymal cells around sinusoids in the pars distalis. The axons of these nerve cells terminate on convoluted vessels of the primary capillary bed in the neural tissue of the stalk (1) or in the lower infundibular stem (2). Here the postulated neurohormones are believed to be transferred into the bloodstream and are then carried to specific groups of anterior lobe cells by long (3) or short (4) portal vessels. Another pathway is shown between a hypothalamic nerve cell and the capillary bed of the pars nervosa; (5) superior hypophyseal artery; (6) inferior hypophyseal artery. From J. H. Adams, P. M. Daniel, and M. M. L. Prichard, Distribution of hypophyseal portal blood in the anterior lobe of the pituitary gland, *Endocrinol.* 75(1964):120.

Current evidence thus suggests the existence of an appropriate morphological basis for the hypothesis that the adenohypophysis is under neural control, mediated by neurosecretory products carried to the adenohypophysis from the hypothalamus via the pituitary portal vessel system.

Chemical Nature of the Neurohypophyseal Secretions

The hypothalamo-hypophyseal chemotransmitter hypothesis states that chemical substances secreted by nerve cells in the hypothalamus are carried by a vascular link (i.e., via the circulatory system) to the adenohypophysis, where they stimulate the release of tropic hormones that have been synthesized by glandular cells in the adenohypophysis. This hypothesis demands the existence of discrete chemical substances localized within those brain regions which have access to the pituitary portal vessel system. Beginning in the mid-1950s, reports began to appear which seemed to demonstrate the existence of such chemicals. When extracts from the pars eminens and pars nervosa (Fig. 8.2) were administered to test animals, the pituitary-gonadal system showed signs of stimulation.

For example, McCann reported in 1962 that an extract from the pars eminens produced a depletion of ascorbic acid from the ovary. Furthermore, the degree of depletion was positively related to the amount of extract administered. The significance of these findings lies in the fact that ovarian ascorbic acid depletion is systematically related to the degree of secretion of luteinizing hormone by adenohypophysis. In the case of McCann's experiment, the extract presumably contained a substance which activated the release of LH from the adenohypophysis, and the LH in turn stimulated the ovaries, thus depleting ascorbic acid.

As research on this problem progressed, it became clearer and clearer that it was possible to extract from brain tissue a variety of chemical substances capable of stimulating different endocrine response systems. Some of these substances were termed "releasing factors" (e.g., CRF= adrenocorticotropic hormone releasing factor). Others were called "inhibiting factors," as in the case of an extract which decreased activity in the prolactin system and was named PIF. Today, these substances, which are now coming to be chemically identified, are termed hormones, since they fit the classical definition of a hormone, i.e., a chemical agent synthesized in one tissue, secreted into the vascular system and carried to a distant site of action. There is strong presumptive evidence for the existence of releasing hormones localized in brain tissue and related to each of the adenohypophyseal hormones.

It should be noted that, although great advances have been made during the past decade in isolating and identifying neural hormones which presumably control adenohypophyseal function, many problems still remain. For example, no one has yet been able to demonstrate the presence of a releasing hormone within the adenohypophysis itself. In addition, information on how extracts of the releasing hormone influence the cells of the adenohypophysis is extremely limited. Finally, a great deal of controversy still exists about the chemical nature of most of the releasing hormones and their localization within brain tissue. Of particular interest to our concern with the gonadal system, is the current uncertainty as to whether FSH-releasing factor and LH-releasing factor are the same chemical substance or whether they are distinct entities.

Physiological Interactions within the System

As indicated in Figure 8.1, adenohypophyseal hormones stimulate target tissues. When the target is a gland, as in the case of ovaries and testes, one response of the target organ is the secretion of its own hormones. Thus, FSH from the pituitary stimulates not only follicular growth in the ovary and spermatogenesis in the testis, but also stimulates the secretion of estrogens from the ovary. The pituitary hormone LH induces ovulation in the female, and in the male it stimulates the secretion of testosterone by the testis. The gonadal hormones, in turn, stimulate their own respective target tissues (e.g., ovarian hormones stimulate the uterus, and testicular hormones stimulate the prostate, seminal vesicles and penis).

It is now clear that one of the targets of the gonadal hormones is the hypothalamo-hypophyseal complex responsible for their secretion in the first place, and this represents a concept central to the understanding of neuroendocrine function, namely that of "feedback effects." Several forms of the underlying phenomenon have been analyzed.

Inhibitory feedback. Inhibitory feedback control is revealed by the effects of gland removal upon circulating hormone levels. Removal of one or both ovaries or testes results in a dramatic rise in circulating gonadotropic hormones secreted by the anterior pituitary. This rise can be prevented after operation by injection of the hormone normally supplied by the missing glands. Similarly, gonadotropins can be reduced to precastration levels by steroid treatment begun at any time after operation. Estrogens, progestins and androgens are potent in producing pituitary inhibition, although to different degrees. Furthermore, these steroids appear to be effective in both sexes.

The existence of inhibitory feedback has also been revealed by studies of the phenomenon known as "compensatory hypertrophy," in which removal of one of the paired gonads leads to the hypertrophy of the remaining gonad. In the rat, removal of one ovary may lead to a 50 percent increase in the weight of the other ovary within a 2-week period. This hypertrophy appears to reflect an increase in the release of FSH which, in turn, leads to abnormal follicular growth and ovulation. The administration of exogenous gonadal steroids (e.g., estrogens) prevents such hypertrophy. Compensatory hypertrophy also occurs after removal of one testis in the male.

Thus, it would appear that the synthesis and/or release of gonadotropin is normally under "tonic inhibition," i.e., constant or steady inhibition exerted by the gonadal steroids. The question naturally arises as to where the steroids exert their inhibitory effects. Theoretically, at least, they could act at the level of the brain to inhibit the secretion of gonadotropin releasing hormones. Alternatively, they could act at the level of the adenohypophysis to inhibit directly gonadotropin secretion. Finally, they could act at both levels simultaneously. Unfortunately it is difficult to distinguish between these possibilities. The most popular technique has been to implant minute amounts of a steroid directly into neural or hypophyseal tissues in a search for direct inhibitory action. Effects on ovarian weights of implanting estradiol benzoate in various brain regions in the rat, are illustrated in Figure 8.4. As can be seen, implants in the posterior hypothalamus, but not in the anterior hypothalamus, depressed ovarian weight, and this points to the conclusion that estradiol exerts its inhibition of gonadotropin secretion by inhibiting the secretion of neural releasing hormones. As noted above, removal of the testes also results in enhanced gonadotropin secretion, and it is clear that when testosterone is implanted in the pars eminens this hypersecretion does not occur.

Stimulatory feedback. In addition to inhibitory feedback, there is evidence that certain hormones exert stimulatory control of gonadotropin secretion. This conclusion is supported by a number of experiments which have shown that exogenous estrogen or progesterone can advance the time of ovulation during normal ovarian cycles in a variety of species, including man. Similarly, it has been demonstrated that hypothalamic implants of estradiol can induce precocious onset of puberty.

It may seem curious that hormonal stimulation is capable of both stimulatory and inhibitory effects. It has been suggested that these different effects are caused by different dose levels, or that the same steroid may have one or another effect depending upon the time of stimulation, that is, depending upon the nature and duration of previous hormonal stimulation. It is also possible that different neural subsystems are involved. Sufficient information is lacking for us to make a choice at this time.

Most of the research pertaining to feedback control of gonadotropin secretion has been carried out in animals, but the principles appear to apply to man. According to Franchimont (1971), who studied patients with Kleinfelter's syndrome (XXY chromosome pattern and testicular hypoplasia), there is an inverse relationship between the levels of LH and plasma testosterone in blood serum. Thus, high endogenous levels

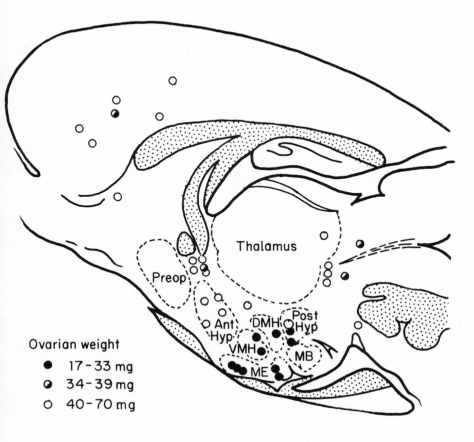

Fig. 8.4. *Sagittal diagram of rat brain showing location of chronic near-mid-line implants of estradiol benzoate (26 and 30 gauge tubing), with effects on ovarian weight.* Effects of the two types of implant were similar, but note normal ovarian weights from implants in the anterior hypothalamus-preoptic area. Data of Smith and Davidson, *Frontiers of Neuroendocrinology.*

of testosterone are associated with low LH levels, as one would expect if an inhibitory feedback system were operative. Franchimont also has shown that the administration of testosterone to healthy men is followed by a striking reduction in serum LH. In women, low doses of estrogen seem to depress FSH levels, but to exert only a modest effect on LH levels. High doses of estrogen depress both FSH and LH.

Short feedback. Classic feedback phenomena described above were long considered to comprise "the" feedback system. In recent years, a second feedback process termed the "'short feedback system" has been described. Short feedback represents an influence of adenohpophyseal hormones upon their own regulation. This control apparently is exerted by the action of the pituitary hormones upon brain mechanisms and not directly upon the adenohypophysis.

The first indication that pituitary hormones might influence the brain came from repeated discovery of tropic hormones in hypothalamic tissue. These observations were followed by a variety of studies indicating that gonadotropins could influence the electrical activity of the brain function, the release of FSH and LH, and the synthesis and release of gonadotropic releasing hormones.

A number of studies involving the direct application of gonadotropins to basal brain structures have revealed that this treatment is followed by lowering of pituitary and plasma FSH and LH levels. Other experiments showed that brain implants of gonadotropins reduce hypothalamic stores of releasing hormone.

Finally, there is some indication that removal of the pituitary, following removal of the gonads, leads to an elevated blood level of the gonadotropic releasing hormones produced in the hypothalamus. These three lines of evidence are consistent with the hypothesis that the gonadotropic hormones, much as the gonadal hormones, can exert inhibitory control of pituitary function. Whether the tropic hormones and gonadal hormones do this by influencing the same neural elements is not yet established. Nor is it known whether the tropic hormones reach the median eminence region directly through hypophyseal-hypothalamic vessels, or whether they reach the relevant neural sites through the systemic circulation.

Evidence is also beginning to emerge which indicates the existence of ultrashort feedback systems, that is, feedback control of neural releasing hormone secretion by the releasing hormones themselves.

Recapitulation

We have reviewed some of the evidence underlying the theoretical model of neuroendocrine interactions, presented in Figure 8.1. Several points are especially significant: (1) Gonadal hormone secretion, as well as gametogenesis, is controlled by the secretion of the pituitary gonadotropins, FSH and LH; (2) Gonadotropin secretion is directly controlled by releasing hormones which are synthesized in basal brain and released into the portal vessel system; (3) In some complex fashion, which is not completely understood, the synthesis and discharge of the releasing hormones are controlled by, (a) gonadal hormones, (b) gonadotropins, and (c) endogenous levels of the releasing hormones themselves. Both stimulatory and inhibitory feedback systems exist, although their interactions under physiological conditions are not known. Thus, the brain, pituitary, and gonads are continuously linked in their function. Alteration in one system leads to compensatory alterations in the others. If this system were isolated from the rest of the brain, and if all the interactions consisted of inhibitory feedback, a null point would be reached and stable levels· of hormone secretion would be found at all times. This, of course, is not the case. Stimulatory as well as inhibitory systems exist, and the neuroendocrine control system is itself controlled by stimuli from the external and internal worlds.

Patterns of Hormone Secretion

Sex differences. There are dramatic sex differences in patterns of hormone secretion in all polyestrous species of mammals. Males secrete their gonadotropic and gonadal hormones in a tonic, or more or less continuous fashion, although some fluctuations do occur. For example, there are significant diurnal variations in plasma testosterone level. Concentrations are highest at 8 A.M. and decline as much as 34 percent by 8 P.M. Other fluctuations occur in connection with changes in social stimulation. For example, men under stress, such as soldiers preparing for combat, show markedly depressed androgen levels. Notwithstanding occasional variation, the hormone secretion pattern in males is basically tonic.

The basic pattern of the polyestrous female, in contrast, is cyclic. The estrous, or menstrual cycle is characterized by, and in fact depends upon, pronounced fluctuations in the secretion of FSH and LH, and of estrogen and progesterone. In lower mammals, the typical cyclic changes in sexual receptivity or "heat" are closely tied to the pattern of hormone secretion. The rat, for example, has a 4-day estrous cycle. The first two days are classified as *diestrus,* the third as *proestrus* and the fourth as *estrus.* Originally this classification was based on the types of cells present in the vaginal epithelium, as determined by vaginal lavage: FSH secretion, which occurs during diestrus, promotes follicular growth and the secretion of estrogen. Estrogen brings on the proestrus state of vaginal and uterine development and ultimately the estrus stage. LH release, which occurs in the estrogen-stimulated animal, facilitates progesterone secretion and brings about ovulation. In the rat, sexual receptivity is induced by the sequential action of estrogen and progesterone, with maximal receptivity occurring approximately 6 hours after the onset of progesterone secretion and 6 hours before ovulation. These relationships are illustrated in Figure 8.5.

Clearly, pituitary and gonadal hormone secretion patterns are closely linked in time with changes in sexual behavior, in the vaginal smear pattern, and in uterine weight.

In rhesus monkeys and man, the occurrence of sexual behavior is less closely tied to endocrine events than it is in lower mammals. Females of both species engage in sexual intercourse throughout the menstrual cycle.

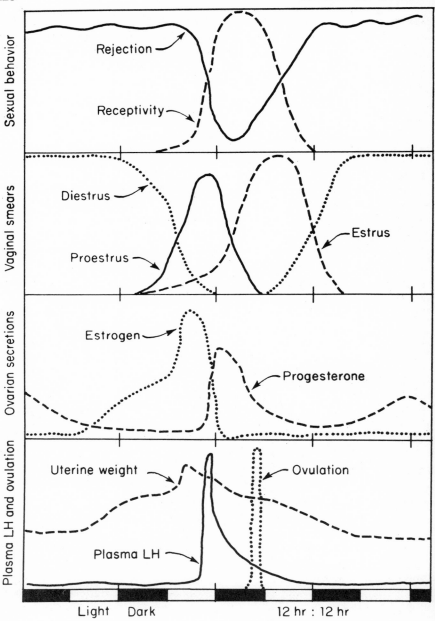

Fig. 8.5. *Temporal relationships between female sexual behavior and vaginal smears, ovarian secretions, uterine weight, plasma LH, and ovulation.* Adapted from Hardy (1969), Hori et al. (1968), Kobayashi et al. (1968), and Uchida et al. (1969).

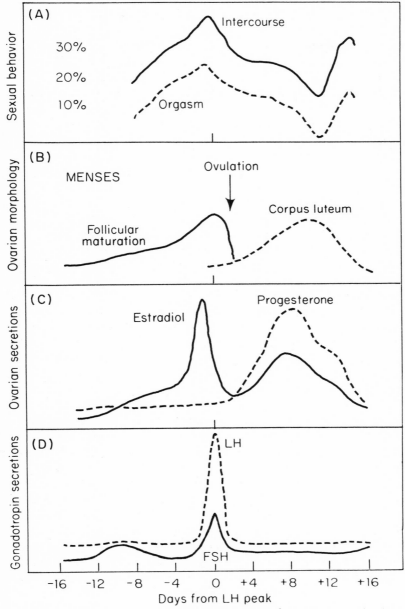

Fig. 8.6. *Scheme representing the temporal interrelationships of sexual be-havior, ovarian morphology, ovulation, and plasma estradiol, progesterone, LH, and FSH* during the human menstrual cycle. Adapted from numerous sources (see W. G. Luttge, 1971).

Nonetheless, there is evidence to suggest that sexual behavior and hormone secretion are not completely independent. One example is illustrated in Figure 8.6. These data of Udry and Morris (1968), based upon daily reporting by subjects, indicate that in women intercourse and orgasm are more likely to occur at the time when estradiol secretion is at its maximum.

In the human female, as in lower mammals, FSH secretion is followed by a rise in estradiol secretion. When follicular maturation is complete, a surge of LH secretion occurs, which is followed by ovulation and a rise in plasma progesterone.

Control of conception. In recent years, great interest has been generated in the nature of hormone secretion patterns, due to attempts to modify those patterns for the purposes of conception control, which embraces both contraception to prevent pregnancy and the stimulation of ovulation to allow pregnancy in previously infertile women.

With respect to the induction of ovulation, two basic techniques are in use. The first involves the administration of gonadotropins, human pituitary gonadotropin (HPG), human menopausal gonadotropin (HMG), and human chorionic gonadotropin (HCG) from pregnant women. The first two possess both FSH and LH activity, while the third possesses LH activity almost exclusively. Administration of HPG or HMG induces follicular development. When administration of either is followed by HCG treatment, ovulation occurs. Such treatment has proven to be effective, but of course only in patients whose ovaries are capable of follicular maturation. These gonadotropin treatments appear to work by direct activation of ovarian tissue.

A more recent development in ovulation control involves the administration of clomiphene citrate. Clomiphene is an antiestrogenic compound, initially developed for possible use as an oral contraceptive. However, in the human it was found to induce ovulation. Clomiphene causes heightened secretion of estrogen, indicating either that it stimulates the ovary directly or acts via stimulation of pituitary gonadotropin secretion.[1]

Modern developments in contraception also involve the modification of endocrine events. The orally active contraceptive pills developed in the 1950s were designed to disrupt the normal ovulatory process. It seems clear now that these agents do prevent conception by blocking ovulation. Presently, two types of treatment regimen are in use. The combinational pills which are taken daily throughout most of the month contain an estrogen and a progestin. The sequential regimen, in contrast, involves

---

[1]Since clomiphene is antiestrogenic, it is entirely possible that it competes for sites of action of estrogen at feedback centers in the hypothalamus or pituitary. Feedback centers would then not "see" circulating estrogen and would stimulate gonadotropin secretion, thereby causing estrogen secretion.

the administration of estrogen during the first part of the cycle, followed by estrogen plus progestin through the remainder of the cycle. The primary synthetic estrogens used are ethynylestradiol and mestranol. The progestins include medroxyprogesterone acetate, chlormadinone acetate, norethindrone, and norethynodrel.

Since the primary effect of hormone treatment is the inhibition of ovulation, the steroids could exert their effects on the ovary directly, on the pituitary, or on the brain. They could alter either FSH and/or LH secretion. Current evidence suggests that the progestin component is effective in eliminating the mid-cycle LH peak. The estrogen component seems to reduce FSH output. While the exact site of action of these agents is not yet known, the evidence indicates that these treatments do alter the fundamental neurohormonal feedback processes which control normal reproductive function.

Sexual differentiation. As indicated earlier, the neuroendocrine system which controls gonadotropin secretion differs in the two sexes. The pattern of hormone secretion in the female is cyclic while in the male it is tonic. Animal research of the past two decades suggests that this difference in pattern of secretion reflects differentiation in the brain which takes place early in development and is under hormonal control. Several lines of evidence combine to indicate that neural factors are involved. First, although an ovary transplanted to a male secretes estrogen, it does so at a steady rate or "tonically," and this suggests that the hormone secretion pattern is not determined by the ovary itself. Second, a female pituitary transplanted to a male will show tonic secretion of gonadotropins, while a male pituitary transplanted to a female will show cyclic secretion, indicating that the pattern is not determined by the hypophysis. Since neither gonad nor hypophysis is sexually differentiated, it is likely that males and females differ due to differences in the brain. This conclusion has been supported by experiments in which the hormonal state of the developing organism was manipulated. Administration of testosterone propionate to the female guinea pig before birth, or to the female rat within the first few days after birth, leads to the development of the tonic, or masculine, pattern of gonadotropic hormone secretion. In the case of males, removal of the testes, or treatment of the developing individual with an anti-androgenic agent such as cyproterone acetate, leads to development of the cyclic, or feminine pattern of hormone secretion. It is now well established that the changes brought about in the patterns of hormone secretion by "androgenization" of the female and "deandrogenization" of the male reflect changes in neural functioning. It is also clear that this process of hormonally-controlled differentiation is limited to a "sensitive period" of development which occurs prenatally in the long-gestation guinea pig and neonatally in the short-gestation rat. What is not yet clear is just where these changes occur or what they reflect in terms of precise modification of neuron physiology.

Differentiation of male and female patterns of pituitary and gonadal hormone secretion has many parallels with the morphological differentiation of the genital tracts in the two sexes. Experimental treatments which lead to tonic hormone secretion often are accompanied by a virilization of the female genitalia; and treatments which lead to cyclic secretion may be associated with vaginal development in the male. This correlation, however, is not complete, since tissues involved in neural and peripheral differentiation appear to have slightly different sensitive periods.

The neural differentiation process which occurs in lower mammals has been taken by some authorities as a model for the sexual differentiation assumed to occur in man because the process of genital differentiation in rats and men appears to be quite similar. Generalizing from one species to another should be done with great caution. Differences are numerous. For example, extensive androgen treatment of the pregnant rhesus monkey produces genital pseudohermaphroditism in female offspring, much as it does in the guinea pig and rat and in man. However, this treatment does not appear to produce in monkeys the tonic pattern of gonadotropin secretion and concomitant anovulatory sterility which it reliably induces in rats and guinea pigs. To take another example, women suffering congenital adrenal hyperplasia do not necessarily show permanent anovulatory sterility, although they possess masculinized genitalia.

In such cases, the enlarged adrenal secretes increased levels of adrenal androgens and these induce masculine differentiation of the external genitalia. Therapeutic treatment involves the chronic administration of cortisol to reduce ACTH secretion in an inhibitory feedback fashion. The adrenals regress and androgen levels return to normal. In addition to virilizing genital tissue, the high androgen levels inhibit gonadotropin secretion, and as long as these conditions obtain the woman is anovulatory. However, when the adrenal is controlled by cortisol treatment gonodotropin secretion returns and ovulation may occur. In these patients androgenization during development does not seem to have altered neural function permanently as it does in lower animals. In light of these considerations, the similarity between monkeys or humans and lower mammals in the differentiation of the neural control of gonadotropin secretion must be considered only presumptive. Elucidation of these similarities and differences is important if completely rational therapies are to be devised for the treatment of the endocrine component of human hermaphroditism.

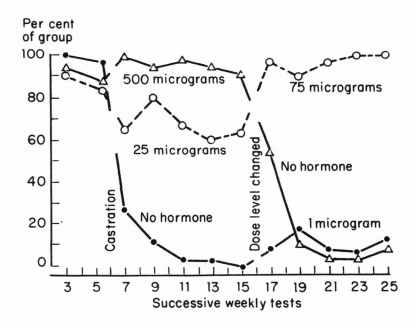

Fig. 8.7. *Proportions of three experimental groups ejaculating at least once during the test.* From Beach and Holz-Tucker (1949).

NEUROBEHAVIORAL SYSTEMS

The neuroendocrine systems which control the pituitary and gonads are obviously important in the development and function of human sexuality and reproduction. However, these systems do not comprise the complete set of neural and neuroendocrine systems involved in sexuality. Hormones influence other neural centers which are independent of those involved in control of the pituitary and gonads, and in addition there are still other neural systems which are involved in sexuality but are more or less independent of hormonal control.

Relations between Hormones and Behavior

It has been known for centuries that the gonads of animals play an important role in their reproductive behavior. Aristotle described the effects of castration in birds, and was familiar with some of the effects of castration in man, such as changes in the secondary sexual characteristics. In the mid-1800s, it was discovered that castrated cockerels exhibit a regression of the accessory sex tissues and a cessation of mating, and that castrates given testicular grafts would exhibit comb growth and a resumption of mating behavior. These were interesting beginnings, but it was not until the present century that man fully realized that the gonads exerted such effects because of their chemical secretions; and it was not until the 1930s that estrogen, progesterone and testosterone were chemically identified.

The isolation, identification and synthesis of the gonadal hormones led to a rapid proliferation, in the United States in the 1940s, of studies of the effects of gonadectomy and hormone replacement. The results of one such study are illustrated in Figure 8.7, which shows the frequency of ejaculation responses in gonadectomized male rats untreated or injected with different amounts of testosterone propionate dissolved in oil. Clearly the intensity of the behavior was directly related to hormone dose up to an asymptotic level, beyond which an increase in dose had no effect.

In these, and most, studies of the endocrine control of mating behavior, male behavior has been activated by testosterone and female by estradiol and progesterone. Some work has demonstrated that it is possible to induce lordosis behavior in female rats by injecting testosterone, suggesting that the systems which are activated are not entirely specific to specific hormones. However, it should be noted that the administration of a given hormone does not insure stimulation by that hormone because it may be metabolized in the body and take a different form, which then exerts specific effects. The differential activation of target tissues by different hormonal metabolites has become an important research issue in recent years. In 1968, it was shown that following the administration of testosterone, the cells of the prostate, an androgen target tissue, contain predominantly not testosterone but dihydrotestosterone which is a different chemical compound. Furthermore, it has been shown that dihydrotestosterone is more potent than testosterone in inducing growth of cells in the prostate. Because of these observations, investigators have come to believe that different hormone-sensitive tissues are selectively sensitive to different hormone metabolites.

With this in mind, one must ask whether the induction or maintenance of masculine behavioral responses in gonadectomized males is due to action of the administered testosterone or to one of its metabolites. Some evidence shows that in rats testosterone and androstenedione, but not dihydrotestosterone can maintain mating, although as already noted, dihydrotestosterone effectively maintains seminal vesicle and prostate weight. Thus, the maintenance of mating and the maintenance of some peripheral reproductive tissues are under differential hormone control.

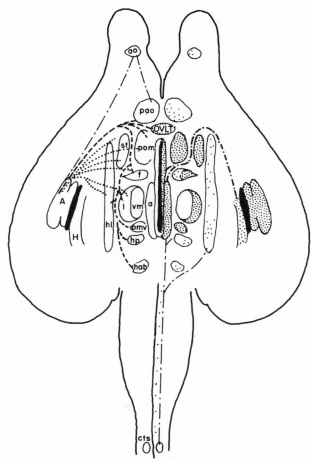

Fig. 8.8. *Estrogen-neuron systems in the rat brain.* Schematic drawing of a
hypothetical horizontal plane of the rat brain showing the distribution of
estrogen-neurons and probably related nerve fiber tracts. Estrogen-neurons,
which exist in selective areas of the periventricular brain, are indicated by
stipples (right portion of the picture). The intensity of the stipples reflects
the frequency of the occurrence of estradiol-concentrating neurons in the
different areas. Few estrogen-neurons exist frontally in the n. olfactorius
anterior and caudally in the ventrolateral portions of the substantia grisea
centralis throughout the brain-stem. Few estrogen-neurons exist also in the n.
commissuralis tractus solitarii.
Pathway:——stria terminalis; . . . . ventral amygdalofugal pathway; -.-. portion
of the fornix, probably medial corticohypothalamic tract; ——.——. left: tractus
olfactorius, right: tractus longitudinalis periependymalis.
ABBREVIATIONS: A, amygdala; a, n. arcuatus; ao, n. olfactorius anterior; cts,
n. commissuralis tractus solitarii; f, n. paraventricularis; H, hippocampus; hab,
n. habenulae lateralis; hl, lateral hypothalamus; hp, n. posterior hypothalami;
1 vm, n. ventromedialis hypothalami, pars lateralis; OVLT, organum vas-
culosum laminae terminalis (representing also the organon subfornicale and
n. triangularis septi); poa, parolfactory region; pom, n. preopticus medialis;
pmv, n. premamillaris ventralis; st, n. interstitialis striae terminalis. (Black areas
indicate the ventricular system.) From Green, Luttge, and Whalen (1970).

Although mating can be stimulated by either testosterone or androstenedione, the fact that the male secretes more of the former than of the latter would suggest that normally testosterone is the behavior-activating hormone.

With respect to the female, current evidence suggests that in the rat lordosis can be induced by either estradiol or estrone, but not by estriol, and that the experimental induction of lordosis by testosterone depends upon metabolic conversion of testosterone to estradiol.

A very important question concerns the locus at which these steroids act to modulate behavior. Several approaches have been taken to this problem. One useful technique has been the administration of radiolabeled steroids followed by steroid localization using autoradiographic or liquid scintillation techniques. This technique has revealed that systemically administered androgen and estrogen tend to localize in similar limbic system structures, including the septum, hypothalamus and amygdala. The estradiol-sensitive systems in the female rat, as determined by Stumpf (1970), are illustrated in Figure 8.8, and the testosterone uptake pattern is similar.

As determined by liquid scintillation counting in our laboratory, the uptake pattern for progesterone is somewhat different than that for estradiol or testosterone. We have found that following injection of ^{3}H-progesterone, radioactivity concentrates to a greater degree in mesencephalic than in diencephalic structures (Whalen and Luttge, 1971).

Localization studies involving the application of radiolabeled hormones are of distinct value in generating a qualitative "picture" of those cells which bind a given steroid, and in providing a basis for quantitative statements about the relative concentration of radioactivity in one structure or another, but such studies cannot determine the chemical nature of the hormone which is localized, nor can they determine functional significance. For example, although radioactivity concentrates in both anterior and posterior hypothalamus following estradiol administration, the radioactive material is not estradiol alone. After estradiol is administered and the tissue steroids are extracted and chromatographically separated, estrone as well as estradiol can be found in the hypothalamus, particularly the posterior hypothalamus. Furthermore, as far as function is concerned, the mere localization of a gonadal hormone in a particular region of brain tissue cannot tell us if that site is one where the hormone acts to control behavior, or where it acts to stimulate or inhibit gonadotropin secretion.

Other experimental approaches must be taken to determine whether a particular site of hormone stimulation is behaviorally meaningful. Historically, the most important technique has been the placement of selected brain lesions. The lesion method, however, has limitations similar to the radioactive tracer method. If mating behavior is eliminated or disturbed following lesion placement, the result could be due (1) to a disruption of those neurons which control gonadotropin secretion, (2) to a disruption of those neurons which respond to hormones and mediate behavior, or (3) to a disruption of nonhormone sensitive neurons which are involved in the control of behavior. For example, it has been demonstrated that lesions in both anterior and posterior portions of the hypothalamus eliminate mating in male rats. Posterior but not anterior lesions are accompanied by gonadal atrophy. Presumably, posterior lesions eliminate mating behavior indirectly by producing a functional castration. The fact that posterior hypothalamic lesions involving the pars eminens lead to gonadal regression has been demonstrated in rats, cats, dogs and rabbits of both sexes. Animals with such lesions mate normally if administered exogenous hormones, and this supports the conclusion that the altered behavior is due to withdrawal of gonadal hormones.

Why do male rats with lesions in the anterior hypothalamic-preoptic region cease to mate? In this case, mating cannot be reinstated with massive testosterone injections. It is possible that the anterior lesion destroys hormone responsive tissue, but one cannot be sure. It is equally plausible that this lesion destroys a hormone-insensitive part of the brain which, nevertheless, is critical for mating to occur.

At present, the most promising technique for locating those neurons which control behavior as a result of their hormone sensitivity involves the direct application of hormone to neural tissue. Studies using this technique were initiated by Harris and Michael in 1958. They implanted needles coated with the synthetic estrogen, stilbestrol, into various regions of the brain of ovariectomized cats. In their first study, these investigators found that implants in the mammillary region of the hypothalamus induced mating behavior in the spayed female. Subsequent work by Michael (1965) revealed that a single locus was not involved. Implants were effective from the mammillary region in the posterior hypothalamus, anterior almost to the region of the diagonal band.

These results are important, because they show that hormone-sensitive neurons controlling behavior are organized as an extensive circuit involving several neural nuclei rather than as an anatomically distinct "sex center." The outmoded and untenable concept of a "sex center" in the brain was based on lesion studies which were interpreted as showing that a single area was critical for mating to occur. Such limited areas may be necessary and at the same time not sufficient for behavior control. They may comprise only one of several stages or units in the total neural system which underlie sexual activity.

In 1962, Lisk reported that he had induced lordosis behavior in female rats by implanting estradiol in the diencephalon. Lisk found that the most sensitive region was located ventral to the preoptic area. At the same time, implants in the preoptic area, in the suprachiasmatic nucleus and in the anterior hypothalamic area, were effective although less so than implants below the preoptic area. In our laboratory, we have found that sexual behavior can be stimulated in female rats with estradiol implants located as far anterior as the bed nucleus of the diagonal band, and as far posterior as the ventromedial nucleus. Similar findings have been reported by others. Thus, the female rats, like the female cat, appear to have an extensive organized system of neurons located throughout basal diencephalic structures which respond to estrogen and participate in the control of mating responses. Not all species are the same. The rabbit, for instance, possesses a more regionally localized estrogen-sensitive system in the posterior hypothalamus.

Less work has been done to identify neural sites which respond to androgen and which control male mating responses. Davidson (1966) found that by implanting testosterone propionate in certain brain areas he could restore mating responses in castrated male rats. The medial preoptic region was the most sensitive area, although a few implants as far posterior as the mammillary region did lead to mating. Lisk (1967) also found active sites in the anterior hypothalamus, but not in the posterior hypothalamus of the male rat. Much more research is needed on this problem and as yet we cannot formulate any firm conclusions about the neurohormonal circuitry which underlies masculine behavior.

Finally, almost no work has been done on the locus of action of progesterone. As explained earlier, progesterone acts synergistically with estrogen to induce sexual receptivity in the rat. The possibility exists that progesterone acts on the same neurons which respond to estrogen. Preliminary observations by Lisk (1966) suggest that this is true. On the other hand, a more recent study of this problem by Ross and his colleagues (1971) indicated that in the estrogen-primed rat lordosis is induced by progesterone implants in the mesencephalic reticular formation. This finding is quite interesting in light of the finding of a high concentration of radioactivity in the mesencephalon following the administration of tritiated progesterone (Whalen and Luttge, 1971). If these observations can be confirmed, they would suggest that estrogen and progesterone exert their interactive stimulatory effects on mating by acting on different neural elements.

The data from the hormone implant studies thus indicate that organized systems in the brain respond to hormones and mediate mating responses. The systems appear to be anatomically extensive and to be similar, but not identical, across species. It should be noted, however, that even the estradiol-sensitive system, which is the one studied most extensively, is not yet known in its complete form.

Brain Lesions and Behavior

Since we now know that exogenous hormones tend to be accumulated and retained in specific neural systems, and that direct application of hormones to parts of those systems can activate behavior, we can now more profitably examine the effects of various brain lesions upon sexual behavior. As we have pointed out, it is difficult to evaluate the nature of a brain lesion effect upon behavior. If a lesion in the preoptic area of the diencephalon results in the cessation of mating, we do not know whether our lesion has eliminated hormone sensitive elements or hormone insensitive elements underlying mating. However, since we now know that the preoptic area accumulates androgen, and that direct application of androgen to the preoptic area will lead to mating behavior in castrated animals, we have some reason to presume that our preoptic lesion has eliminated hormone-sensitive elements. Similarly, lesions which disrupt mating, but which destroy brain areas that neither accumulate hormones nor respond to hormone implants, probably involve elements which are independent of the hormone control system. With this in mind, we can now examine studies in which lesions have been reported to alter sexual behavior.

The rat has been the most thoroughly examined species, having been the subject in dozens of studies. Nevertheless, precise generalizations have not emerged. The weight of the evidence favors the notion that the diencephalic lesions which reduce or eliminate male mating responses tend to be medial rather than lateral, and tend to be located in the preoptic region, in the anterior hypothalamus and in the region surrounding the suprachiasmatic nucleus. In most, but not all, cases with such lesions massive doses of testosterone failed to restore mating responses. A similar pattern emerges for the control of female behavior. Lesions in the anterior hypothalamus tend to eliminate mating without the possibility of restoration by exogenous hormones.

Results of work with other species are similar to those obtained with the rat. Male mating responses are reduced or eliminated in the guinea pig by lesions in the anterior hypothalamus or in the ventromedial nucleus. In the female guinea pig, lesions of the anterior median eminence and anterior arcuate nucleus eliminate mating. In the female cat, anterior hypothalamic lesions interfere with mating, while in the female rabbit sexual responses are eradicated by posterior lesions in the region of the mammillary body.

In many of these experiments, some of the brain operated animals continued to mate in a normal fashion even though their lesions appeared similar to those found in animals which ceased to mate following operation. In one study of male rats, substantial lesions of the preoptic region had no influence on sexual performance. In spite of these dramatic inconsistencies in the literature, the brain lesion technique has recently been applied to man. Patients with long histories of pedophilic homosexuality have been subjected to unilateral lesions of the medial hypothalamus. Success has been claimed, with an amelioration of the intense sexual drive of these individuals, but this is difficult to understand since unilateral lesions have never been found to reduce sexual activity in animals.

It is fair to conclude that studies of basal brain lesions which disrupt mating have contributed suprisingly little to our understanding. Localization has been imprecise, and we still have little knowledge as to the exact nature of the deficit produced by the lesion. More interesting than experiments reporting behavioral deficit, are the few studies which have demonstrated an increase in sexual activity following lesioning. In the female guinea pig, lesions of the anterior hypothalamus, and in the female rat lesions in the premammillary region, have been found to result in acceptance of the male when the female was in a diestrous condition or was castrated and given no hormone treatment. In the male rat, lesions at the junction of the diencephalon and mesencephalon increased ejaculation frequency and reduced the duration of the non-mating refractory period which follows ejaculation in this species. These preliminary studies, although in need of confirmation, suggest that there are neural inhibitory systems which participate in the control of mating responses.

Some of the most interesting data indicating neural inhibitory systems controlling mating, have come from studies of the effects of lesions of the temporal lobe. In 1939, Kluver and Bucy reported that removal of the temporal lobes in rhesus monkeys resulted in a variety of dramatic symptoms, including "hypersexuality." Since this initial demonstration, hypersexuality has been reported to occur following temporal lobe lesions in males in a variety of species. The symptoms include autoeroticism, the mounting of unusual objects such as members of other species and even toys, and the display of mating responses in novel environments where mating usually does not occur. Hypersexuality has also been attributed to one man who received bilateral temporal lobe lesions to control seizures. This man reportedly became exhibitionistic following surgery, although there was no evidence that he engaged in coital activities more frequently than before surgery.

It is notable that the hypersexuality which has been described in animals may reflect changes in perceptual systems rather than in sexual motivational systems. The affected individuals seem to mate at inappropriate times, and in inappropriate places, with inappropriate objects, rather than to mate more frequently or with greater intensity with the normal sexual object. While there has been remarkedly little study of this interesting phenomenon, some evidence indicates that the pyriform cortex is the critical temporal lobe tissue mediating the aberrant sexual performance.

Finally, there have been numerous studies concerned with effects of neocortical lesions upon mating performance. Here, as in the case of other types of lesions, controversy exists, although it does seem clear that both sex and species can influence the effects of cortical injury on sexual behavior. Research in the 1940s led to the conclusion that in the male rat the size of the cortical lesion, rather than its locus, determined the degree of disruption of mating. Reexamination of this problem in the 1960s, however, suggested that lesion location rather than size was critical. Small dorsolateral or frontal cortical lesions inhibited mating, whereas large posterior lesions seemed to have little or no effect. The effects of cortical lesions have been attributed to changes in the sexual arousability of the operated animals.

In male cats, cortical lesions seem not to influence sexual excitability. Instead, they disrupt mating by altering sensory and motor functions. While complete decortication eliminates mating in male cats, smaller lesions do not. Cats with frontal cortex lesions have difficulty performing the motor acts of mating, while cats with occipital lesions have difficulty in finding a mate, presumably because of visual deficits associated with injury to this brain area.

Unlike the case of male animals, in female rats, cats, guinea pigs and rabbits neocortical lesions, even complete removal of the cortex, may have no obvious effects upon the animal's ability or willingness to display the lordosis posture. In fact, in one study the lordosis posture of rats was found to be exaggerated and held for a longer duration than usual following neocortical removal. Thus, specific neocortical lesions can disrupt and eliminate the mating patterns of males of some species while having no major influence upon the mating pattern of the female. It seems reasonable to speculate that these sex differences in cortical control relate to the relative simplicity of the postural adjustments required of the female for mating relative to those in the male.

What should be clear from the many studies utilizing brain lesions to define the neural control of sexual function, is that neural subsystems exist which lie outside of the brain regions that accumulate and respond to sex hormones. In addition, these subsystems seem to function by controlling sexual arousal or motivation, by mediating the sensory and perceptual control of sexuality, and by participating in the motoric execution of sexual responses. Thus, the concept of sex-related systems rather than a sex center begins to emerge.

Electrical Stimulation Studies

The predominant effects of such brain lesions upon mating as have been demonstrated, have been inhibition or disruption of performance. It is particularly difficult to evaluate changes of this nature. A different approach to the central problem is represented by attempts to elicit sexual responses by electrical stimulation of the brain. In 1962, Vaughn and Fisher reported success in one such endeavor. Male rats with electrodes permanently implanted in the anterior hypothalamus were stimulated during alternate 5-minute periods. Their sexual activity while the stimulation was turned on was impressive. During 220 minutes of stimulation, one rat achieved 174 mounts without intromission, 81 intromission responses and 45 ejaculations! Normally, a male rat will ejaculate no more than 7 or 8 times in a 4-hour period. Other investigators have produced similar effects in male rats and oppossums, although not without difficulty, and inhibitory loci as well as excitatory loci have been found.

Electrical stimulation of deep structures of the brain in man is a relatively recent development. Nonetheless, introspective reports by patients electrically stimulated in the region of the septum or temporal lobe, indicate that the stimulation has "erotic" overtones. Sexual pleasure and even orgasm-like experiences have been described by patients, and the occurrence of flirtatious behavior has been observed by the therapists. Careful study of such patients should provide a wealth of new data and increased understanding of the neurology of human sexuality.

As yet, there have been relatively few reports describing the activation of the complete mating pattern by electrical stimulation of the brain. This is not surprising. On the contrary, it is surprising that the electrical stimulation of a single point in the brain could, under any circumstances, activate an organized pattern which has so many individual components. It is, in fact, a great deal easier to evoke individual components of the sexual response system. For example, in a detailed series of studies, MacLean and his coworkers (1973) have described the neural circuitry controlling erection in the male squirrel monkey. The system is composed of several parts which involve the septum, the mammillary bodies, the mammillothalamic tract, the anterior thalamic nuclei and the anterior cingulate gyrus. The medial part of the medial dorsal nucleus and the medial septo-preoptic region are nodal points for evocation of erection, according to MacLean, and the medial forebrain bundle seems to be the descending pathway from these nodal points. The discharge of semen may also be brought about by central stimulation. In the squirrel monkey, the spinothalamic tract and points within the thalamus are effective in this regard. In the rhesus monkey, stimulation of the preoptic region has elicited erection, accompanied by pelvic thrusting, and followed by the explosive discharge of semen containing motile sperm. The discharge of semen following electrical stimulation has also been reported to occur in rats, but with this species the evidence suggests that what was involved was emission, the relatively passive movement of semen through the urethra, rather than ejaculation, the forceful expulsion of semen.

To understand the neural basis of genital reflexes, it is important to distinguish between emission and ejaculation, since they appear to be under different neural control. In a classic paper, Semans and Langworthy (1938) showed, by stimulating the nerves which innervate the penis of the cat, that stimulation of the parasympathetic sacral roots produces a strong erection, and that stimulation of the sympathetic innervation produces emission of semen into the urethra, but not the expulsion of that semen from the penis. Stimulation of the internal pudendal nerves is needed to produce ejaculation. Stimulation of the sympathetic innervation leads to detumescence of the penis. Thus, in the cat, sympathetic and parasympathetic systems appear to control emission and ejaculation respectively.

It is likely that the spinal cord systems which mediate genital reflexes are normally under the control of the higher brain systems. Nonetheless, they can function independently, as shown by descriptions of individuals following spinal transection. Spinal transection itself, as with men executed by hanging, or with surgical transection in animals, may even produce priapism and ejaculation. Following surgical transection of the cord in the male rat, Hart (1967) has demonstrated that one can elicit erections and what he has termed "quick-flips" and "long-flips," i.e., movements of the phallus which seem to parallel intromission and ejaculation movements in the intact animal. In the spinal male dog, one can elicit several reflexes. These include erection, shallow thrusting of the type which usually precedes intromission, rapid thrusting and hind-leg movement which accompany insertion in the intact animal, ejaculation, and the prolonged erection which is associated with "locking" in this species. Similarly, the male cat with spinal transection retains elements which appear the same as the animal's normal genital reflexes.

It has long been known that genital reflexes may be retained following spinal cord injury in human males. Examinations of hundreds of patients have led Comarr (1970) to the conclusion that over 90 percent of patients with upper motor neuron lesions will have erections, while less than 25 percent will have erections if there are lower motor neuron lesions. Surprisingly, however, the reverse is true for ejaculation, which occurs more frequently in individuals with lower lesions. Orgasm, the "psychic" component which usually accompanies ejaculation, is typically lost following spinal cord injury.

Females of a variety of species appear to retain at least rudimentary sexual reflexes following spinal cord transection. Hart (1969) has demonstrated partial lordotic responses in the rat, and in the dog the lateral curvature of the hind quarters which follows stimulation by the male in intact bitches. In the spinal female cat, it is possible to elicit forelimb flexion, lateral deviation of the tail and hind limb treading responses, all of which are components of the receptive posture in normal cats.

Unfortunately, nothing appears to be known about the sexual reflexes in women who have sustained spinal injury. Even though Masters and Johnson have provided a wealth of detail about the nature of the physiological responses which accompany sexual stimulation in women, their procedures apparently have not been applied to patients with cord injury. Such an analysis is needed.

Taken together, the evidence makes it appear that the spinal cord of both males and females contains neural subsystems which are involved in the expression of sexual behavior. While it is customary to think of these systems simply in terms of their neural elements, there is evidence that these reflex systems are hormone-sensitive in some cases. There is clear evidence that testosterone regulates the intensity of all genital reflex components in the male rat, and of some components in the male dog. In the case of females, estrogen clearly facilitates the sexual reflexes in dogs, may do so in cats, but apparently does not do so in rats. No evidence is available for the hormonal modulation of sexual reflexes in women or in men.

SUMMARY

The neurology of sexual behavior is a complex affair, involving subsystems at all levels of the neural axis from the spinal cord to the cerebral cortex. Both hormone-sensitive and hormone-insensitive elements participate. Some of these neural systems control or modulate sexual excitability, that is, the propensity of the organism to react to sexual stimuli from outside the organism, and to hormonal and non-hormonal stimuli from within the organism. Some of these systems are sensory and perceptual mechanisms which allow the organism to detect and orient towards appropriate sexual partners; others are involved in the organization of genital reflexes; still others directly control the motor movements involved in the participation of coitus. The complex sequences of activities which constitute mating do not depend upon any single system. All of the systems mentioned participate at one or more stages of the sexual act. Thus, as we have emphasized before, there is no sex center; there are, rather, interacting neuronal subsystems that mediate different facets of the sexual process which brings two individuals together for pleasure and progeny.

REFERENCES

Adams, J. H.; Daniel, P. M.; and Prichard, M. M. L. 1964. Distribution of hypophyseal portal blood in the anterior lobe of the pituitary gland. *Endocrinology* 75:120.

Beach, F. A., and Holz-Tucker, A. M. 1949. Effects of different concentrations of androgen upon sexual behavior in castrated male rats. *J. Comp. Physiol. Psychol.* 42:433.

Comarr, A. E. 1970. Sexual function among patients with spinal cord injury. *Urol. Int.* 25:134.

Davidson, J. M. 1966. Activation of the male rat's sexual behavior by intracerebral implantation of androgen. *Endocrinology,* 79:783.

――――. 1969. Feedback control of gonadtropin secretion. In *Frontiers of Neuroendocrinology 1969.* Edited by W. F. Ganong and L. Martini. London: Oxford Univ. Press.

Franchimont, P. 1971. The regulation of follicle stimulating hormone and luteinizing hormone secretion in humans. In *Frontiers of Neuroendocrinology 1971,* edited by L. Martini and W. F. Ganong. London: Oxford Univ. Press.

Green, R.; Luttge, W. G.; and Whalen, R. E. 1970. Induction of receptivity in ovariectomized female rats by a single intravenous injection of estradiol-17ß. *Physiol. Behav.* 5:137.

Hardy, D. F. 1969. The estrous cycle of the female rat. Unpublished Ph.D. dissertation. University of California, Irvine.

Harris, G. W., and Michael, R. P. 1964. The activation of sexual behaviour by hypothalamic implants of estrogen. *J. Physiol.* 171:275.

Hart, B. L. 1967. Testosterone regulation of sexual reflexes in spinal male rats. *Science* 155:1283.

――――. 1969. Gonadal hormones and sexual reflexes in the female rat. *Horm. Behav.* 1:65.

Hori, T.; Ide, M.; and Miyake, T. 1968. Ovarian estrogen secretion during the estrous cycle and under the influence of exogenous gonadotropins in rats. *Endocr. Jap.* 15:215.

Kobayashi, F.; Hara, K.; and Miyake, T. 1968. Luteinizing hormone concentrations in pituitary and blood plasma during the estrous cycle of the rat. *Endocr. Jap.* 15:313.

Kluver, H., and Bucy, P. 1939. Preliminary analysis of functions of the temporal lobes of monkeys. *Arch. Neurol. Psychiat.* 42:979.

Lisk, R. D. 1962. Diencephalic placement of estradiol and sexual receptivity in the female rat. *Amer. J. Physiol.* 203:493.

――――. 1966. Sexual behavior: Hormonal control. In Neuroendocrinology, edited by L. Martini and W. F. Ganong. New York: Academic Press.

――――. 1967. Neural localization for androgen activation of copulatory behavior in the male rat. *Endocrinology* 80: 754.

Luttge, W. G. 1971. The role of gonadal hormones in the sexual behavior of the rhesus monkey and human: A literature survey. *Arch. Sex. Behav.* 1:61.

MacLean, P. D. 1973. New findings on brain function and sociosexual behavior. In *Contemporary Sexual Behavior: Critical Issues in the 1970s.*

Edited by J. Zubin and J. Money. Baltimore: Johns Hopkins University Press.

McCann, S. M. 1962. A hypothalamic luteinizing-hormone-releasing factor. *Amer. J. Physiol.* 202:395.

Michael, R. P. 1965. Oestrogens in the central nervous system. *Brit. Med. Bull.* 21:87.

Purves, H. D. 1961. Morphology of the hypophysis related to its function. In *Sex and Internal Secretions.* Edited by W. C. Young. Baltimore: Williams & Wilkins.

Ross, J.; Claybaugh, C.; Clemens, L.G.; and Gorski, R. A. 1971. Short latency induction of estrous behavior by intracerebral gonadal hormones in ovariectomized rats. *Endocrinology* 89:32.

Semans, J. H., and Langworthy, O. R. 1938. Observations on the neurophysiology of sexual function in the male cat. *J. Urol.* 40:836.

Stumpf, W. E. 1970. Estrogen-neurons and estrogen-neuron systems in periventricular brain. *Amer. J. Anat.* 129:207.

Uchida, K.; Kadowaki, M.; and Miyake, T. 1969. Ovarian secretion of progesterone and 20α-hydroxypregn-4-en-3-one during rat estrous cycle in chronological relation to pituitary release of luteinizing hormone. *Endocr. Jap.* 16:227.

Udry, J. R., and Morris, N. M. 1968. Distribution of coitus in the menstrual cycle. *Nature* 220:593.

Vaughn, E., and Fisher, A. E. 1962. Male sexual behavior induced by intracranial electrical stimulation. *Science* 137:758.

Whalen, R. E. 1967. *Hormones and Behavior.* New York: Van Nostrand.

Whalen, R. E., and Luttge, W. G. 1971. Differential localization of progesterone uptake in brain. Role of sex, estrogen pretreatment and adrenalectomy. *Brain Res.* 33:147.

9

HORMONAL CONTROL OF SEX-RELATED BEHAVIOR

Frank A. Beach

EDITORIAL PREFACE

This chapter should be read as a unit with Chapters 8 and 10, for together they present a physiological perspective on sexuality as described in Chapter 1. In addition, the present chapter deals with some concepts already developed in Chapters 2 and 3, by Milton Diamond and John Money, respectively.

The first major issue stressed in this chapter is the difference between developmental and concurrent effects of sex hormones. Although developmental effects have been discussed extensively in Chapters 2 and 3, the treatment to follow emphasizes several new points. (1) It explains the basic differences between effects of a hormone acting during development and the same hormone acting in adulthood. (2) It points out that exposure of a female fetus to androgen can have two independent types of effects on behavior, namely masculinization and defeminization and, conversely, that depriving a male fetus of androgen may induce behavioral demasculinization, feminization or both. (3) It marshalls evidence to show that certain types of prenatal effects of hormones on the brain will be manifest in adult behavior only if sex hormones are present at the time of testing in adulthood, whereas, in other types of behavior, the effects may appear at the time of puberty without the necessity of further hormonal stimulation. These observations are believed to be theoretically relevant to psychological changes accompanying puberty in human development.

A second section of the chapter deals with concurrent effects of sex hormones in animals and human beings. Major differences between developmental and concurrent effects include the fact that the latter are temporary, reversible and repeatable. Comparisons of concurrent effects in females of different mammalian species reveal that ovarian hormones generally increase sexual attractivity, receptivity and proceptivity, as these characteristics are defined in Chapter 11. At the same time, important species differences in receptivity exist, with the result that most female rodents will mate with any male when stimulated by ovarian hormones; female dogs and cats will mate only when hormonally stimulated but may be "selectively receptive," refusing some males while receiving others; and female monkeys or apes will sometimes allow copulation even when no ovarian hormone is present.

Male animals of all species depend to varying degrees upon testicular hormone for sexual responsiveness and potency. Behavioral effects of increase or decrease in sex hormones are less abrupt in males than females, and individual differences are marked, but in the long run complete withdrawal of testosterone markedly depresses or totally eliminates potency in all species. Despite this finding, it is important to observe that some males of several species including dogs, monkeys and man retain the ability to copulate for years after castration.

Of great importance is the fact that for many animal species nonhormonal factors tend to modulate the concurrent effects of hormones upon sexual responses. A female dog's or monkey's tendency to solicit copulation by males is increased by estrogen, but her choice of mates is not indiscriminate, and invitations to copulate may be directed exclusively to certain males and never to others. Males of the same species also display mating preferences which do not depend on their hormonal status.

The proposed theoretical interpretation of hormonal effects on sex-related behavior is that they modify S-R contingencies by selectively altering responsiveness to particular forms of stimulation. In keeping with an evolutionary approach to human sexuality as set forth in Chapter 1, it is hypothesized that the kinds of S-R mechanisms most likely to be influenced by gonadal or pituitary hormones are those involved in the mediation of behavior related to reproducing, e.g., mating and care of young.

For nonprimate mammals, both components of the essential S-R mechanisms are determined primarily by epigenetic forces, whereas learning and practice contribute to their formation in nonhuman primates and are their principal determinants in human beings. Those sexually differentiated behavior patterns which are closely related to reproduction are affected by hormones in our own species, but their influence is often obscured, partly because appropriate behavioral endpoints have not yet been studied, and, partly because differences in experience produce differences in details of the S-R bonds on which the hormones operate.

It is suggested that, despite individual and cultural differences, appropriate investigational methods will reveal that interaction of hormonal and nonhormonal determinants underlies the sex-related and reproductively significant behavior of human males and females.

INTRODUCTION

The term "sex-related behavior," as used in this chapter, includes not only intercourse and other genitally oriented activities, but also many other responses generally thought of as more characteristic of males than of females or vice versa, e.g., aggressiveness in the male and nurturance in the female. Although many glands influence behavior directly or indirectly, this discussion is confined to the so-called "sex hormones," namely androgens, estrogens and progestins, which are secreted by the testes, ovaries, adrenal cortex and, in pregnant females, the placenta.

Effects of sex hormones upon human behavior, as well as that of other species, are mentioned briefly or described in detail in several other chapters, but here I shall attempt to organize different types or bodies of evidence in a broad overview in order to achieve two objectives. One aim is to integrate existing knowledge concerning our own and other species with a view to highlighting important differences and similarities between man and other animals. The other is to extract from these inter-specific comparisons any general principles or theories that may increase our understanding of human sexuality.

One extremely important generalization which applies to humans and animals alike is that the effects of sex hormones on behavior can be sep-arated into two broad classes. The first includes what I shall call "de-velopmental" effects, and the second comprises "concurrent" effects. The difference is clearly illustrated by an example based on anatomy and phys-iology rather than behavior.

During development of male embryos, differentiation of a prostate gland will occur only if male hormone is present to act upon the cells which will form the new organ. Once the gland has been fully formed, its basic structure remains unaltered, even if there is no further andro-genic stimulation. This exemplifies a *developmental effect* of testis hor-mone. However, in the absence of stimulation by male hormone, a com-pletely differentiated prostate gland will not function physiologically. When an adult man or male rat is castrated, his prostate becomes much smaller and stops secreting prostatic fluid. If the castrated individual now receives a series of testosterone injections, his prostate enlarges and re-sumes its secretory activity which will continue only as long as the nec-essary male hormone is supplied. This is an example of *concurrent ef-fects* of testis hormone.

Developmental Effects

Although the term "developmental" has not been used by other authors, many examples of this class of hormonal effects are extensively discussed in three other chapters. Whalen explains that the type of control the brain is going to exert over the pituitary gland, and thus over the ovaries, throughout adult life is irrevocably determined before birth by the hor-mones present at that time. Diamond and Money summarize a large number of animal experiments and clinical studies of human patients to demonstrate that abnormal hormonal conditions before birth may result in a baby girl's being born with a penis or a baby boy's being born with a vagina. In fact, the presence or absence of male hormone during pre-natal life may influence sex-related behavior in childhood or even later.

Distinguishing Characteristics

There are four ways in which developmental and concurrent effects are distinguishable. (1) The former normally occur only during a limited phase of development and are difficult or impossible to induce before or after this specific period. (2) Once they have occurred, developmental effects tend to be permanent and irreversible, although some of them may subsequently be overidden by nonhormonal influences. (3) Some developmental effects are grossly undetectable at the time of their occurrence and only become manifest later in the individual's lifetime. (4) The delayed appearance of certain developmental effects depends upon additional stimulation by sex hormones which must be present at the time of expression.

Experiments on Animals

Whalen, Diamond and Money have summarized the evidence which shows that the presence of testis hormone during embryonic and fetal development is essential for normal differentiation of masculine reproductive organs including the penis, and that genetic females may develop masculine rather than feminine internal and external genitalia if they are exposed to androgenic stimulation before birth. The same authors state that brain development is also affected and that this in turn can modify sex-related behavior shown after birth. It is this aspect of developmental effects which concerns us here.

Behavior of females. When pregnant guinea pigs, mice, rats, dogs or monkeys are injected with testosterone, the sexual development of their female offspring is modified in several ways. For all species, affected females are born without an external vagina and often possess a penis. Rodents and dogs exhibit few mating responses in adulthood unless they are treated with sex hormones at that time. Injections of male hormone cause experimental females to exhibit masculine copulatory reactions, more frequent and complete than any which can be evoked from normal females, though qualitatively inferior to those of a normal male. On the other hand, when the same animals are treated with ovarian hormones, they fail to exhibit the normal feminine mating patterns which appear in unmasculinized females in response to the same hormones. When androgen-treated female dogs become mature, they often adopt the male posture for urination, fully elevating one hind leg and directing the urine at some conspicuous target. This masculine behavior appears at the normal age of puberty, even though no androgen is administered after birth.

The adult mating patterns of prenatally treated female monkeys have not yet been studied, but their social interaction with other infants is clearly modified in a masculine direction. They show more rough-and-tumble play, more threat responses and more play mounting than normal females, though less than normal males. These differences appear without any postnatal hormone administration and are, therefore, in a different category from the copulatory reactions of rodents and dogs, but similar to the urinary behavior of the latter.

One interpretation of these various findings is that if female animals are artificially exposed to male hormone during prenatal development, the results include two distinct changes in their adult behavior. One class of changes involves behavioral *masculinization* and the other comprises *defeminization*. These are independent concepts and, in fact, with appropriate androgen treatment, female dogs can be almost totally defeminized without at the same time being masculinized. The distinction is of theoretical importance for several reasons. It fits nicely with the hypothesis, proposed in Chapters 2 and 11, that male and female behavior are mediated by separate "mechanisms" in the central nervous system, and that both types of mechanism are present in genetic females as well as genetic males. It further allows for the possibility that increases or decreases in masculinity need not inevitably and automatically imply complementary changes in femininity. According to this hypothesis, for example, a girl or woman might easily possess various masculine traits without any impairment of her simultaneous or complementary femininity.

The possibility that natural prenatal "masculinization" of females may occur without any experimental treatment, is suggested by observations on normal female rats which have developed in a uterine position directly between 2 male fetuses. When such females are compared with others having different types of uterine placement (i.e., between two other females or between a male and a female), the former prove to be slightly but significantly modified in a masculine direction both anatomically and behaviorally, even though they remain biologically female and capable of all normal reproductive functions. The tentative explanation for this particular case is that androgen secreted by the adjacent male fetuses was absorbed by the affected females and induced a very mild degree of masculinization, but these findings suggest a more powerful hypothesis.

It is worth considering the possibility that in many species, including our own, there are certain physical and behavioral traits which depend upon some degree of prenatal androgenic stimulation for their normal expression in postnatal life. In the case of females, the essential androgen might come from the maternal adrenal. One implication of this notion is that some individual characteristics, presently classified as masculine or feminine, might prove merely to be more or less dependent upon prenatal androgenic stimulation and therefore be normally present in both sexes, though perhaps more strongly developed in genetic males.

Behavior of males. Theoretically, it should be possible experimentally to prevent normal sexual differentiation in male animals by depriving them of secretions of their own gonads, but this has not yet been achieved. Castration with survival to adulthood cannot be performed early enough to exclude effects of the embryonic testis upon the embryonic brain. Nevertheless, it is feasible to inject the mother with "antiandrogens" and partially block the fetal testis hormone from influencing its target tissue. Furthermore, for some species sexual differentiation is incomplete at the time of birth, and in such cases castration of newborn males prevents the full developmental effect of male hormone. The expected effects should include both feminization and demasculinization.

Male rats castrated at 1 to 4 days after birth (but no later) are clearly feminized in that they exhibit female mating responses when injected with ovarian hormones during adulthood. At the same time, their male copulatory behavior following injections of testosterone is deficient, and this has been interpreted as proof of partial demasculinization, although some experts believe the deficiency reflects smallness of the penis rather than incomplete masculinization of the brain.

Clearer evidence for behavioral demasculinization is seen in the decreased fighting behavior of male rats which have been castrated at birth and given testosterone in adulthood. Male dogs castrated as neonates do not mate normally as adults, but their failure could be due to inadequate penile development. The same animals show the adult male urinary posture only part of the time and often revert to the juvenile posture which indicates not feminization but incomplete masculinization of brain mechanisms.

Observations on Human Beings

There is no question that sex hormones exert powerful developmental effects on multiple aspects of human sexuality, although many such effects are indirect and others are obscured by their interaction with various nonhormonal determinants, to be discussed later in this chapter.

A very obvious example of hormonal effects derives from their control of the external genitalia. Whether a baby is born with a penis or an external vagina is determined by the occurrence or nonoccurrence of androgenic stimulation before birth. Babies without a penis are classified as girls, are raised as girls and develop a feminine gender identity. This also occurs in biological males born with undescended, abdominal testes but suffering an inherited inability to utilize the male hormone which may be secreted by their own sex glands. Such individuals often grow up to be perfect "psychological females." Babies born with penises are assigned as boys, reared as boys and develop masculine gender identities. Thus it is that the developmental effects of the presence or absence of androgen have an indirect but exceedingly important influence upon every individual's sexual behavior, thoughts and feelings.

The question is whether this is the only kind of developmental effect that occurs, or whether some differences between males and females are traceable to the influence of hormones on brain development before birth. Kagan's chapter lists a number of psychological differences between infant boys and girls, and in many cultures around the world little boys tend to be physically aggressive, competitive and venturesome, whereas girls are more likely to be sedentary, nurturant and less combative than boys. Many authorities see all such sex differences as products of parental attitude and social training and reject any alternative explanation. A less extreme view is suggested by Money's description of the "tomboyism" that characterizes girls who have been prenatally exposed to abnormal degrees of androgenic stimulation but assigned as females at birth and reared in the feminine mode. Money believes that such evidence may "establish a relationship between a prenatal masculinizing influence and subsequent behavioral traits." Elsewhere in the same chapter he adds the following significant observation:

> No one knows how many genetic females born with normal female genitalia may, in fact, have been subject to prenatal androgen excess too weak to influence the external anatomy, though perhaps sufficient to influence the brain.

An alternative hypothesis, suggested above, is that both males and females are normally subject to prenatal androgenic stimulation, though to different degrees; and that for both boys and girls the probability that certain types of behavior will develop is positively or negatively related to the extent of androgen influence before birth. Within normal limits, the issue is not one of masculinization of females or feminization of males but, instead, involves the degree of prenatal androgenization and individual differences in sensitivity to androgenic hormone.

Diamond's position on the problem of sex differences in brain organization, and their eventual effects upon behavior, is that such differences not only exist and are affected by androgen but that they have the power to affect such complex attributes as gender identity and sexual object choice in adulthood. In its most extreme form, this view could lead to the conclusion that exclusive male homosexuality, lesbianism and transsexualism are manifestations of atypical brain organization. This is extreme indeed, and yet conservative theorists like Stoller and Money occasionally express views with a similar ring, as witness the following statement in Money's discussion of the "unresolved dualism of transsexualism."

> There may well be an as yet undiscovered fetal metabolic or hormonal component which induces a predisposition to ambiguity or incongruity of postnatal gender identity differentiation. There may be a special disposition in

the organization of the brain toward the acquisition of roles and their dissociation in the manner of multiple personality or fugue states.

Money goes on to state that such prenatal dispositions, if they exist, need to be augmented by postnatal experience; but Stoller is impressed by intersexual individuals whose powerful conviction of gender identity from very early childhood runs counter to the sex in which they have been reared. In particular, he views some boys with constitutional hypogonadism and feminine gender identity as exemplars of a . . . "biological factor overriding all effects of society and of family, pressing the child to wish to be a member of the opposite sex."

CONCURRENT EFFECTS

Definitions and Functions

Concurrent effects of hormones upon behavior differ from developmental effects in being reversible, repeatable and not limited to a brief phase in the individual's lifespan. They are so named because the occurrence of the behavior tends to be temporally linked to and dependent upon the presence of the hormones.

Two functions of the reproductive glands are production of eggs or sperm and secretion of hormones; and the dual processes generally go hand in hand, with the result that hormones which facilitate sexual behavior are produced in maximal concentrations at those times when both sexes are fertile, and mating has the highest probability of resulting in reproduction of the species. Among species which breed during only one period in each year, the time that males are potent and attracted to females is also the time that they possess an ample supply of sperm, and the correlation is due to the fact that the sperm-producing testis is also secreting testosterone, which is responsible for the male's sexual behavior. In some species, the same hormone is responsible for increased combativeness which males show during the breeding period.

As far as females are concerned, the production of ripe eggs in the ovary coincides with its secretion of estrogenic hormone which (1) makes the female attractive to males, (2) causes her to be attracted to males, and (3) induces her to receive males in copulation. When copulation results in pregnancy and eventually in parturition, the female undergoes a series of endocrine changes, and various hormones are essential to behavior involved in preparation for birth of the young, as well as cleaning, nursing, and protecting them throughout the lactation period.

Effects in Females

As explained in Chapter 8, the occurrence of ovulation in many mammals is preceded by several hormonal changes, including a marked rise in secretion of estrogen plus a much smaller increase in progesterone. Progesterone then increases sharply following ovulation.

Sexual "attractivity" for males. For a number of mammals, the immediate preovulatory period is one in which females show increased activity, more exploratory behavior and decreased timidity or fearfulness. It is also the time that females are sexually attractive to males; and experiments on rodents, dogs, monkeys and apes show that a female's stimulus value for the male is increased when she is treated with estrogen and decreased when the hormone is withdrawn. The estrogen-induced sexual attractivity of female primates is depressed by progesterone. One study of a small group of married women revealed that husbands were less likely to initiate sexual relations during the period immediately after the wife had ovulated and was therefore beginning to secrete increasing amounts of progesterone.

The mechanisms through which estrogen influences sexual attractivity vary from species to species, but odor and taste of the female's secretions and excretions often are involved. Estrogen changes the chemical composition of perspiration, urine and vaginal secretions; and males are sexually stimulated by smelling and tasting these products of the female body. For some primate species, estrogen changes the appearance of the genital region, and the swollen "sex skin" serves as a visual stimulus to males.

Attraction to males. Part of a female's value as a sexual stimulus for males derives from the fact that ovarian hormones cause her to be attracted to males and to exhibit various kinds of behavior which engage the male's attention and arouse him sexually. As defined in Chapter 11, a female's sexually "proceptive" behavior ranges all the way from merely approaching, investigating and remaining near the male, to her display of explicit invitations or solicitations of copulation.

The pattern varies according to species, but in all cases investigated estrogen has proven to be a hormone capable of inducing or greatly increasing the female's attraction to males. Solicitation in the form of increased "sexual presentation" is stimulated in female monkeys by treatment with testosterone as well as estrogen, and this is one reason for Money's conclusion, in Chapter 3, that androgen is "the libido hormone" in both sexes. The fact is that estrogen probably is more effective than androgen and, furthermore, androgen has no effect upon the female's attractivity and probably none upon her readiness to accept the male in copulation.

Sexual receptivity. The readiness of a female to accept and cooperate with the male in the act of copulation is the only valid measure of her sexual receptivity; and in all nonhuman mammals receptivity is either totally dependent upon or significantly increased by ovarian hormones.

For most species, estrogen alone is the key factor, but in some cases estrogen priming must be followed by progesterone to achieve the full effect.

There are marked species differences in the degree to which hormones affect a female's willingness to copulate. Control is most nearly complete for animals such as guinea pigs, rats, mice and hamsters in which stimulation by ovarian secretions is the *sine qua non* of sexual receptivity. If the hormones are present, the female will mate; if they are absent, she will not. For more complex species, such as the dog, estrogen is a necessary but not a sufficient cause; and although a bitch is never receptive without estrogen, when stimulated she may receive some males and reject others.

The basis for receptivity in man's nearest relatives, the various nonhuman primates, is even more complicated and diversified. Female gorillas will mate only during their period of fertility and maximal estrogen secretion, but monkeys and chimpanzees may allow copulation at any stage of the menstrual cycle. Highest degrees of sexual readiness still are associated with high levels of estrogenic stimulation but the correlation is far from perfect.

The role of sex hormones in the sex life of women is unclear, partly because nonhormonal determinants exert effects tending to obscure relationships between body chemistry and behavior, and partly because psychological and behavioral measures used to date are inadequate for the task. Evidence summarized in Chapter 10 shows that increase or decrease in estrogen or progesterone affects emotional responses in many human females; and in Chapter 3 it is indicated that psychosexual changes accompanying puberty include hormonally induced increase in sex drive. However, before more precise descriptions of hormonal effects on sexual attractivity, proceptivity and receptivity can be achieved, it will be necessary to formulate better operational definitions and devise more objective measures of psychological variables involved in sexual responsiveness of our own species.

Maternal behavior. The young of some mammals are so well developed at birth that dependence upon the mother is limited to a relatively brief period of nursing, but in many species maternal responsibilities begin before parturition and continue at least until weaning. We know that placental hormones are intimately involved in preparatory behavior such as the pregnant rabbit's and rat's nest building which begins several days before parturition. When blood from a nursing mother rat is introduced into the circulatory system of a virgin female, the latter begins to show maternal responses within a few hours, retrieving foster young, building a nest around them and crouching over them in the nursing posture. Similar behavioral changes can be induced in nulliparous females by appropriately timed injections of estrogen, progesterone and prolactin.

The maternal behavior of primates is influenced by a multiplicity of variables, and the contribution of hormones has not been specifically investigated, but it is clear that they are involved in the reactions of human mothers to their babies. For example, "letdown," or reflexive injection of milk into the ducts leading to the nipple, is caused in part by the pituitary hormone oxytocin; and release of oxytocin into the mother's bloodstream can be stimulated by the sound of the baby's cry, by seeing the baby or by the immediate sensation of suckling. Stimulation derived from nursing also contributes to secretion of prolactin which is essential to milk production; and as long as lactation continues, regular ovarian and menstrual cycles are not resumed.

Behavior of Males

Contra-male aggression. For most mammals, sex differences in behavior include a stronger tendency on the part of males to engage in aggressive activity, particularly against other males; and it is known that male-male fighting is markedly increased by testosterone. Male farm animals may be prevented from becoming excessively pugnacious by prepubertal castration, and the same operation markedly reduces fighting in male mice and rats. Males of some seasonally breeding species, such as deer and antelopes, may engage in general combat or fighting for specific territories when androgen levels rise at the beginning of the mating period. Castrates rarely fight but will do so if treated with testosterone.

Sexual attractiveness. A male's capacity to attract females which are ready to mate can be affected by his hormonal condition. Female rhesus monkeys, allowed to choose between normal and castrated male partners, usually prefer the former even when actual mating is prevented. Female dogs in heat prefer the odor of urine from intact males to that from castrates. When a female hamster in heat is confronted with two males confined in wire cages, she responds by ignoring a castrated male and standing next to the normal male's cage in the posture assumed during copulation.

Attraction to females in heat. It is generally believed that although sexual interest is not truly "latent" during human childhood, as Freud suggested, there is a definite increase in sexual drive at the time of puberty, when the secretion of gonadal hormones increases dramatically. This change is particularly obvious in adolescent boys, and a similar surge of heterosexual attraction is evident in males of other species. Among some animals, like sea lions and baboons, young adult males are socially subordinate and are prevented from copulating with females in heat. Nevertheless, they behave differently from immature males and clearly show their sexual attraction to females. Normal male rats will cross electrified grids or overcome other obstacles to reach an estrous female, and after castration the strength of this approach tendency decreases to a very low level but then rises again if the castrate is given androgen treatment. Although castrated dogs and monkeys do not totally lose their attraction to females, in the absence of testis hormone sexual arousal is less intense and prolonged.

Potency. The ability to achieve penile erection, to maintain it for normal durations, and to display ejaculatory reflexes of normal strength is clearly influenced by testosterone in both animals and men. Following castration in adulthood, male rodents may continue to pursue females and attempt copulation for many weeks, but the ability to achieve penetration usually is lost by one month after operation and ejaculation disappears even earlier. Testosterone injections reverse these changes and restore full potency, although the castrated male is permanently sterile.

In some larger mammals, including dogs and farm animals such as cattle and horses, males castrated after attaining adulthood retain some copulatory ability for years, but their potency is drastically reduced so that erection is delayed and transitory, and ejaculatory reflexes are weak and foreshortened.

Very similar symptoms have been described for human males. Congenital failure to secrete normal amounts of testis hormone is usually associated not only with impotence but also with diminished heterosexual interest. Removal of the testes after adolescence ordinarily is followed, after intervals of several months to several years, by partial or complete loss of potency. Initial changes may involve primarily interference with ejaculatory mechanisms and thus with orgasmic responses. Subsequently, or sometimes simultaneously, there is deterioration in the ability to achieve and maintain erection. In some cases, replacement therapy by testosterone injection or implantation restores normal sexual function, but more evidence is needed to establish the generality of these findings.

EXPLANATIONS OF CONCURRENT HORMONAL EFFECTS

Changes in Drive or Motivation

In discussing the effects of androgen treatment of homosexual men, Hoffman says the hormone tends to increase sexual drive, but in the homosexual direction. Money's interpretation of the increase in sex hormones at puberty is that they "have the power to regulate the strength of the libido, but not the stimulus to which the libido responds." Concepts represented by such terms as drive, libido and motivation have a certain descriptive value and are useful at one level of discourse, but they are not sufficiently precise to serve any explanatory function.

If it has any meaning at all, the statement that prolactin increases maternal drive in female rats means that under the influence of this hormone the female will exhibit certain kinds of behavior toward very young animals of her species. To say that testosterone affects the aggressive drive in a male animal means that the frequency of particular patterns of behavior directed toward other individuals, e.g., attack, or threat of attack, is increased or decreased by increases or decreases in the concentration of the hormone. In other words, concepts of drive, motivation, and the like eventually must be reducible to statements concerning the frequencies, intensity, etcetera with which specified types of behavior are observed to occur.

Changes in S-R Probabilities

Every behavioral event constitutes a response to some form of stimulation, regardless of whether the response is performed overtly or merely occurs in fantasy. One approach to analysis of the effects of hormones upon behavior is to examine the manner in which they affect relations between certain types of stimulation and particular patterns of response. For example, we have already noted that administration of estrogen to female animals changes the responses they are likely to make to stimuli provided by the male when he attempts to mate. Using verbal shorthand we say the hormone renders the female sexually receptive, but in data language we are referring to the probability that specific types of stimulation will elicit an equally specific pattern of behavioral responses.

Changes in behavior can reflect changes in effectors such as muscles or other structures used in the performance of particular responses. In some seasonally breeding rodents, the vaginal aperture is sealed most of the year but opens when stimulated by estrogen and, in this manner, the hormone facilitates successful mating. Male deer utilize their antlers when fighting other stags and success in combat leads to greater opportunities for mating with females. Normal growth of the antlers before mating season depends on testosterone, and thus the hormone indirectly affects sexual behavior through its control of these specialized effector structures.

A second way in which hormones might alter stimulus-response probabilities would be to increase or decrease the individual's sensitivity to particular types of stimulation, and there is a good deal of evidence indicating that sex hormones do exert such effects. For example, normal male rats distinguish between the odors of estrous and nonestrous females, but castrated males fail to make such distinctions. If the castrated individual is injected with testosterone, he shows selective responses equal to those of a normal male. Female hamsters that are not in heat do not discriminate between a normal male and one that has been castrated; but, under the influence of estrogen, a female clearly prefers the intact male and will stand beside his cage for long periods of time while totally ignoring the castrate. Female dogs investigate urine deposited by either males or females of their species and ordinarily find male urine less stimulating; but when she is in heat, a bitch is much more strongly attracted to male than to female urine and, in addition, distinguishes between urine from castrated and from normal males, showing a distinct preference for the latter.

All of the foregoing examples deal with the senses of smell and taste, but there are many cases in which hormones are known to affect responsiveness to other types of stimulation, including those involving touch and hearing. In hypogonadal men, sensitivity of the glans penis to light tactile stimulation increases under androgen therapy, and sensitivity of the female breasts, especially the nipple, is heightened by estrogen. When female rats are injected with estrogen this causes an increase in sensitivity to touch in the skin adjacent to the external vagina. Female mice with a nursing litter are more responsive than nonlactating females to the ultrasonic cries emitted by baby mice.

Although effects of hormones on receptor and effector mechanisms undoubtedly exist and influence sex-related behavior to some degree, most theories concerning concurrent hormonal effects concentrate on the central nervous system, and the rest of this discussion deals with one approach to this alternative.

Theoretical Interpretation

The following suggestions are presented as a working hypothesis rather than a definitive theory. They do not incorporate or attempt to account for all known facts, but may serve as a temporarily useful heuristic model for organization of much that is known, and for indicating profitable lines of future investigation.

We begin with the assumption that the most important way in which hormones produce concurrent effects upon behavior is to induce temporary changes in brain function. Furthermore, the salient changes take place in as yet unlocalized but theoretically specifiable functional systems concerned with the mediation of different patterns of sex-related behavior. In agreement with Diamond and numerous other writers, we suggest that there are physiological and probably anatomical distinctions between the neural circuits mediating certain types of female-related behavior and complementary patterns of male-related behavior.

The factors controlling original organization of the hypothetical sex-related brain mechanisms undoubtedly include prenatal effects of sex hormones, but this is only part of the story. Postnatal influences clearly are involved and particularly important for those species whose adult behavior is heavily dependent on learning through practice and/or tuition. Regardless of how they are laid down it is postulated that the basic mechanisms for female-related and for male-related behavior are present in all normal individuals of each sex. A basic bisexuality of the brain is an old notion mentioned by Diamond and alluded to by several other contributors to this book, but it is one which needs several qualifications.

One qualification is that in genetic males the male-related system is more completely organized or more easily activated than the female-related system, while a converse relationship exists in genetic females. A second qualification is that in both sexes feminine response mechanisms are rendered more sensitive to stimulation by estrogen, whereas, again in both sexes, masculine response systems are selectively sensitized by androgen. Finally, the male-related system in genetic males is more responsive to androgen than is the male-related system in genetic females; and the female-related system in genetic females responds more strongly to estrogen than does the female-related system in genetic males.

This theoretical formulation indicates many predictions concerning concurrent effects of different hormones on sex-related behavior. It would be expected, for example, that male-related S-R patterns would be facilitated by androgen in both sexes, but more so in genetic males than females. For some species, at least, this is true. Mounting behavior increases in castrated male and female rats injected with testosterone but responses of males are more frequent and vigorous than those of females. In a species whose adult males are notably aggressive, the hypothesis predicts that androgen will increase fighting by both males and females but will have a stronger effect in males; and confirmatory results have been obtained in experiments on inbred mice castrated before puberty.

We would anticipate that ovarian hormones might elicit feminine mating responses in males as well as females but that males would be less responsive than females, and it has been found that although male rats will exhibit the female response of lordosis after treatment with estrogen, prolonged administration is necessary and the behavior is qualitatively inferior to that shown by spayed females given much less hormone.

Sex differences in behaviors that are not normally dependent upon concurrent hormonal stimulation should, according to the hypothesis, be unaffected by any increase or decrease in sex hormones during maturity, and this prediction is borne out by studies of urination behavior in dogs. Adult males elevate one rear leg for 98 percent of their urinary acts whereas females adopt a squatting posture 92 percent of the time. Males castrated in adulthood do not change their urinary posture after operation, indicating that the behavior is not under concurrent control by testis hormones. The expectation would therefore be that urinary posture of adult females would be unaffected by testosterone administration, and experimental results show this to be the case.

The last example illustrates an important caveat. It should not be assumed a priori that every sex difference in behavior is caused or influenced by sex hormones acting concurrently. For example, simplistic theories which explain the display of male-linked behavior on the part of genetic females by postulating a surplus of androgen are pointless unless it is established that androgen is responsible for the same behavior in genetic males.

MULTIPLE DETERMINANTS OF SEX-RELATED BEHAVIOR

According to our working hypothesis, hormones exert their concurrent effects by increasing or decreasing responsiveness to particular patterns of stimulation, thereby modifying certain S-R contingencies. In psychological terms, androgen, estrogen, prolactin or some other hormone may be said to affect the perception, interpretation or behavioral significance of certain types of stimuli. For instance, when a female rat is in the hormonal state that normally accompanies lactation, a newborn rat is for her an object to be protected, cleaned and nursed; but when the same female is in a different hormonal state, the rat infant may be an object to be ignored or even eaten.

If the S-R connections upon which hormones operate were fixed and immutable, hormonal effects on behavior would be equally invariant and predictable, but such is not the case, for all complex behavior is under multiple controls. A hormone, or combination of hormones, can increase the probability that a particular pattern of response will occur, but hormones cannot make behavior happen. The stimuli which eventually evoke a hormone-sensitive reaction are determined in part by preformed connections in the brain, but programming of the connections themselves is determined by a combination of genetic and experiential influences whose relative importance varies from species to species and to some extent from individual to individual.

Nonhormonal determinants in animals. It is sometimes argued that although hormonal factors clearly influence sex-related behavior in animals, they are of little or no importance in our own species because human sexuality is so powerfully controlled by social conditions and individual learning that it is immune to modification by physiological agents such as glandular secretions. The facts are that hormones can and do affect learned behavior in both animals and men.

Convincing examples in the case of animals are provided by changes that accompany the pubertal increase in sex hormones. Male and female monkeys and chimpanzees engage in various forms of "sex play" or incomplete coital interaction from late infancy to puberty, but at the onset of adolescence heterosexual copulation becomes a more complete, integrated and truly "consummatory" pattern of social behavior. Males and females reared in total isolation from members of their species may display signs of increased erotic arousability when they reach puberty but newly-joined heterosexual pairs are totally incapable of successful copulation. Execution of the coordinated motor patterns essential to genital union apparently depends on learning, which normally occurs over a period of years before hormonal levels increase at puberty. When the pubertal rise in gonadal hormones brings increased sensitivity to sexual stimulation, there is normally interaction with brain mechanisms, organized by experience and capable of mediating successful copulation. If the mechanisms have not been organized through learning, the hormone merely raises excitability which can easily lead to biologically inappropriate forms of interaction.

All animals normally are sexually attracted by members of their own species, but this specificity may depend on experience. In experiments on "sexual imprinting," eggs of one bird species were given to adults of a different species, which incubated them and raised the young. When males reared under such conditions reached sexual maturity they engaged in courtship and employed the same copulatory patterns as normal males but showed a strong preference for mating with females of the foster parents' species instead of females of their own kind. Testis hormone induced a normal tendency to show sexual responses, but abnormal social conditioning in early life resulted in atypical "object choice," i.e., in response to biologically inappropriate sexual partners.

There are several species of mammals, ranging from elk and wild sheep to sea lions, in which lactating females, although they are strongly maternal, are responsive exclusively to their own young and will not tolerate nursing or even close approach by another female's offspring. Hormonal factors associated with lactation are essential to maternality, but the specific stimulus pattern capable of eliciting maternal responses is dependent upon learning which may occur in a brief period after parturition. Ewes will reject their own lambs if the latter are removed immediately after birth and returned a few hours later.

The adult male hamadryas baboon with 1 to 3 permanent female consorts does not attempt to mate with females in another male's "harem" even though he is fully potent and quite capable of perceiving their sexually receptive condition. When his own females are in estrus, he copulates with them repeatedly, which suggests that although testosterone secretion is quite adequate for normal sexual responsiveness the activation of primary sexual behavior is subject to nonhormonal social control.

Some sexually experienced male dogs, castrated in adulthood, become almost totally impotent within a few months, whereas others can still achieve erection and exhibit ejaculatory reflexes 5 years after the operation. A complete explanation of the differences is not available, but an important factor probably is that potency seems to survive longest in males whose daily social contacts are limited and whose principal opportunity for interaction is in periodic exposure to a female in heat.

We already have noted that, even when they are in estrus and therefore strongly stimulated by estrogen, many female dogs and monkeys exhibit clear-cut preference for certain males while showing reluctance or downright refusal to mate with others. Males of the same species also may display choice behavior, being much more prompt and persistent in their attempts to mate with some females than with others. Two-way preference patterns of this sort allow us to apply the concept of "sexual compatibility" to mating relationships in nonhuman species. Absence or unilaterality of sexual attraction leads to infrequent or conflictual coital relations, whereas mutuality in sexual preference, or absence of selectivity on both sides, promotes repeated mating with a minimum of rejection or disinterest.

Nonhormonal determinants in human beings. The most important difference between behavioral effects of hormones on animals and on people is not that our own species has become insensitive to hormonal influences, but that nonhormonal determinants play a much greater role in structuring all aspects of human behavior, including those which are directly affected by hormones in most animals. The fact is that certain aspects of our sex-related behavior may be more influenced by hormones than present investigational methods are capable of revealing.

Hormonal effects on animal behavior are relatively obvious because we deliberately define and measure them in terms of objective, directly observable and quantifiable overt responses such as the speed with which mating is initiated, frequency of mounting, duration of intromission, number of lordosis responses, or, time spent building a nest, amount of paper used for the nest, speed with which scattered young are retrieved, and so on. In contrast, effects of the same hormones in women and men traditionally have been inferred from answers to questionnaires and interviews or even from analyses of dream content; results have been expressed in terms of covert changes in emotional feelings, in "libido," or in responsiveness to nonbiological or secondary stimuli such as erotic literature or pictures.

If we wish to compare hormonal effects in different species, we must use indices with cross-species validity which, in the case of men and women, might include speed and magnitude of penile erection or vaginal lubrication, duration and intensity of physical stimulation sufficient to produce orgasm, number and strength of muscular contractions involved in sexual climax, duration of post-orgasmic refractory period, et cetera. It would also be meaningful to measure frequency of intercourse and/or masturbation under reasonably constant conditions of opportunity. Some of these variables have been examined, but rarely in combination with differences in hormone levels.

The foregoing examples consist of consummatory response measures, but it has been postulated that concurrent effects of hormones primarily involve S-R relationships, and this raises the very difficult problem of identifying the stimuli conductive to the initiation of sex-related behavior in human beings. The problem is particularly complicated in human beings because the range and nature of the effective stimuli are much more variable in *Homo sapiens* than in any other species. This diversity in turn is due to the fact that both direct and vicarious personal experience play a major role in shaping each individual's concept of which stimuli are and which are not sexually arousing. As long as the stimuli remain undefined, it is impossible to measure, or even detect, any putative hormonal effects; but when we can specify both the responses and the stimuli we are enabled to determine whether particular S-R contingencies are modulated by changes in the concentration of hormone.

IMPLICATIONS FOR HUMAN PSYCHOSEXUALITY

It is apparent that present knowledge of concurrent effects of hormones in human life is disappointingly limited; therefore, this chapter concludes with a consideration of what future research may reveal.

The search for hormonal correlates of sex-related behavior in humans should be based upon the following generalizations. (1) Sexually differentiated behavior patterns known to be hormone-dependent in other species involve responses essential to reproduction. (2) Sexually differentiated behavior in human beings extends over a wider range and includes many patterns with no reproductive significance. (3) For the human species, both reproductive and nonreproductive sex-related behaviors develop in the individual under the directive influence of personal experience and social learning.

These three statements suggest the probability that for our species some sex differences in behavior are much more likely than others to be affected by hormones. The most promising candidates are those response patterns directly and immediately related to reproduction of the species, e.g., genitally oriented sexual activities, nurturant responses to infants, and so on. Even within these arbitrarily chosen limits, the magnitude, specificity and direction of hormonal control must be strongly influenced by previous experience of the individual.

Sexual responsiveness to certain forms of direct physical stimulation probably is independent of learning, but, with this exception, experience plays a major role in determining the kinds and combinations of stimuli that are sexually arousing for the individual. The final, consummatory responses of sexual climax are essentially reflexive and need no experiential preparation (which is not to say they are immune to learned modification), but various forms of preparatory or appetitive behavior are acquired through learning and elaborated by experience.

The working hypothesis that hormones affect behavior by modulating S-R contingencies presupposes the prior existence of S-R connections upon which the hormone can operate. In the case of nonprimate species, the necessary bonds are preformed as part of the epigenetic process of sexual differentiation. In nonhuman primates, they are laid down partly under epigenetic control and partly under the influence of early learning. In human beings, the major resposibility for establishment of the essential S-R mechanisms rests upon learning, and until the mechanisms are organized no hormonal change can produce discrete behavioral effects. To describe psychosexual development metaphorically, we can say that biological and social forces combine to organize the brain in a manner which maximizes the probability that certain S-R connections and not others will be formed. With respect to those sexually differentiated responses having potential reproductive relevance, we can expect that gonadal hormones will influence the occurrence of R when S occurs. This will hold true, even though the exact nature of S differs for different cultures and for different individuals within the same culture. It will even be the case when S does not represent the reproductively appropriate partner but is, instead, associated with a second person of the same sex.

According to this point of view, an increase in sex hormones should not occasion an increase in sex-related behavior until the brain mechanisms for mediation of such behavior have been organized as a consequence of social learning; and Money explains in Chapter 3 that precocious hormonal puberty is not accompanied by equally premature psychosexual development. On the other hand, experience by itself should not suffice to guarantee normal sexual development, and clinical accounts of hypogonadal males reveal that they do not acquire normal responsiveness to sexual stimuli unless testosterone replacement occurs.

In Chapter 5, Davenport documents the extreme variety of sexual rules and practices characterizing different societies around the world, and in their respective chapters, Kagan and Money emphasize that within one and the same society there are marked individual differences in experiental history. In view of the acknowledged importance of learning and experience for the shaping of adult behavior, how can we account for the prevalence of those S-R mechanisms which are essential to survival of the human species?

The answer is that Nature and Nurture are in collusion. As stated by Diamond in Chapter 2, male and female infants come into the world with a set of constitutional, behavioral biases, some of which are sex-linked. Included in the inventory are sex differences in the propensity for acquiring, practicing and perfecting different patterns of behavior. Congenital sex differences in behavior potential can be extended and exaggerated, obliterated or even reversed by social conditioning, and different societies have managed to achieve all of these modifications to greater or lesser degree. The only behavioral difference which are never contravened by any society are those essential to its own survival, namely those necesary for reproduction.

Procreation and childrearing may be hedged about by restrictions, taboos and prohibitions, but every society eventually expects and reinforces reproduction. Even those cultures with the most repressive attitudes toward sexual expression covertly prepare their members for the establishment of families and production of offspring. In extreme cases, opportunities for sexual learning may be delayed until maturity, but eventually they are provided.

The basis for hormonal influence upon sex-related behavior is therefore conceived as a joint product of physiological determinants predisposing males and females to form different S-R patterns, directly or indirectly related to reproductive behavior, and social determinants which differentially reinforce behavior tendencies adapted to the culturally defined male and female roles necessary for production and rearing of offspring. The basic S-R patterns to which the two types of determinants are oriented are the same, and it is upon these patterns, or S-R bonds, that sex hormones exert their effects.

REFERENCES AND RECOMMENDED READINGS

Beach, F. A. 1970. Hormonal effects on socio-sexual behavior in dogs. In *Mammalian Reproduction. Edited* by M. Gibian and E. J. Plotz. Berlin:
———. 1975. Behavioral endocrinology: An emerging discipline. *Amer. Scientist,* 63: 178-87.
———. 1975. Hormonal modification of sexually dimorphic behavior. *Psychoneuroendocrinology,* 1: 3-23.
Davidson, J. M. 1972. Hormones and reproductive behavior. In *Hormones and Behavior.* Edited by S. Levine. New York: Academic Press.
Michael, R. ed. 1968. *Endocrinology and Human Behavior.* London: Oxford University Press.
Money, J. and Ehrhardt, A. A. 1972. *Man and Woman, Boy and Girl: Differentiation and Dimorphism of Gender Identity from Conception to Maturity.* Baltimore: Johns Hopkins University Press.
Terkel, J., and Rosenblatt, J. S. 1968. Maternal behavior induced by maternal blood plasma injected into virgin rats. *J. Comp. Physiol. Psychol.* 65: 479-82.
Whalen, R. E. 1967. *Hormones and Behavior.* New York: Van Nostrand.

10

PSYCHOLOGICAL EFFECTS OF
HORMONAL CHANGES IN WOMEN

Frederick T. Melges and

David A. Hamburg

EDITORIAL PREFACE

This chapter, by two psychiatrists, summarizes a large number of clinical studies which show that normal changes in hormone levels often are associated with concurrent changes in a woman's feelings and behavior. This is not the same as saying the hormones are a direct cause of the psychological changes because, as the authors carefully point out, nonhormonal factors are always involved. Nevertheless, their material is relevant to a physiological perspective on human sexuality, and in this connection it should be compared with Chapters 8 and 9, which depend primarily upon animal experiments rather than clinical material.

Frederick Melges' and David Hamburg's data and interpretations can also be seen as extensions of topics covered in Chapters 2 and 3. Whereas the chapters by Milton Diamond and by John Money depart from effects of hormones in prenatal life and utilize endocrine pathology as a source of much of their theorizing, Melges and Hamburg concentrate upon "concurrent" hormonal effects, as defined in Chapter 9, and deal with their manifestation from puberty through menopause.

It would be unreasonable to expect that effects of ovarian hormones on the psychology of women would be as simple and direct as those which the same hormones produce in the behavior of guinea pigs, dogs or monkeys, and, in fact, no such clear-cut correlations have been discovered. Nevertheless, it is illuminating to analyze relations that do exist between endocrine changes and concomitant alterations in feminine psychology.

The theoretical importance, as well as the complexity, of such correlations are nicely illustrated by the authors' account of changes occurring just prior to adolescence. Menstrual periods usually begin at 12 to 13 years of age, but secretion of ovarian estrogen starts to increase at about 8 to 9 years and is markedly accelerated at approximately age 11. During the 18 months prior to the first menstrual period, the breasts and other secondary sex characteristics begin to develop, and a bodily growth spurt starts just when the girl begins to secrete estrogen in a monthly rhythm, but before she has her first period. For 12 to 18 months after the first period, menstrual cycles tend to be irregular and unpredictable, but thereafter they usually settle into a more or less regular rhythm.

It is essential to recognize that the hormones which induce bodily growth, breast development and menstruation are, at the same time, exerting their influence upon the brain, and thereby upon the girl's emotional and intellectual reactions. It is also important to recall that reactions of the brain to hormonal stimulation are affected by the residual effects of previous experience which leaves a lasting imprint on neural organization.

On the basis of these postulates, one might anticipate that similar hormonal events could produce dissimilar consequences in different individuals, and such is the case with respect to psychological reactions to menarche. Melges and Hamburg note that instead of proving a major trauma, the onset of menses can serve "as a focal point in a girl's acceptance of her feminine sexual role," but this will, to a large extent, depend upon "the anticipatory guidance and emotional cues [she] receives from her mother and other significant females [which] deeply influence her own integration and acceptance of this critical period in her life." Girls with appropriate preparatory experience are likely to react to the hormonal consequences of puberty "by integrating the menstrual cycle into their developing concept of themselves as women." In other words, if the necessary experiential foundation has been laid, hormonal changes in early adolescence can contribute to normal development of an adult feminine gender identity.

During adulthood, hormonal changes occurring in the course of the menstrual cycle appear to be associated with a progression of emotional changes, so that relatively high levels of estrogen during the preovulatory phase tend to correlate with self-ratings of pleasantness, activation and sexual arousal. These feelings are apt to decrease as progesterone levels rise following ovulation; and for the last few days before menstruation, about one woman in five experiences moderate to severe feelings of irritability, tension, and sudden shifts of mood.

Melges and Hamburg point to the similarity between these psychological changes and symptoms commonly associated with withdrawal of sedative drugs. The comparison is based partly on the fact that ovarian hormone levels decline rapidly in preparation for menstruation and thus deprive the brain of chemical stimulation to which it has been exposed for several weeks. Another instance of precipitous drop in endocrine stimulation occurs at the end of pregnancy, and the immediate postpartum period typically is one of extreme emotional lability. It is not suggested that emotional changes during the puerperium are due exclusively or directly to withdrawal of the pregnancy hormones, but that hormonal changes produce modifications in responsiveness to particular types of stimulation. As indicated in Chapter 9, this is precisely the role that sex hormones play in other species, as for example estrous females become sexually proceptive and receptive in response to the male, or when castration decreases aggressive behavior in males.

In general, it can be said that for animals and humans alike hormones play a permissive role. They may make certain types of behavior possible, but they cannot make behavior happen. By altering the reactiveness tendencies of women, ovarian hormones modify the stimulus-response contingencies affecting behavior and thus alter the relative probabilities for the occurrence of one type of behavior in contrast to another.

One final observation relates this chapter to the evolution of human sexuality as described in Chapter 1. It is likely that during the hunting-and-gathering period which occupied 99 percent of man's evolutionary history, postmenarchal females were either pregnant or lactating for most of their lives. Very few lived to the age of menopause, and therefore the reproductive period probably lasted less than two decades. In many present-day societies, women have a reproductive life of more than 30 years, in the course of which only one or two pregnancies may occur, and even these may not be followed by a prolonged lactational period with consequent suppression of ovarian cycles. One result is that the brain and the rest of the body are subjected to repeated surges of hormonal stimulation and withdrawal, much more numerous and closely spaced than the target tissues and organs were evolved to withstand.

If 33 years were to intervene between menarche and menopause, and if there were no interruptions due to pregnancy or lactation, a woman could expect to experience no fewer than 400 menstrual cycles in her lifetime. If she bore 3 children and nursed each one for 6 months, the woman would still experience over 300 menstrual cycles. In contrast, a woman of prehistoric times possibly had no more than 15 years of reproductive life and nursed her surviving young for at least 2 years, which would allow time for no more than 10 periods of menstruation in a lifetime. Even if these hypothetical figures are extreme (and they are, of course, simply guesses), the implied contrast is of theoretical importance.

Few would deny that spaced pregnancies are highly desirable from the viewpoint of society as well as that of the individual woman, and in this country it is widely accepted that no woman should bear children unless she so desires. However these considerations do not gainsay the biological fact that civilization has given women a physiologically abnormal status which may have important implications for the interpretation of psychological responses to periodic fluctuations in the secretion of ovarian hormones.

INTRODUCTION

For centuries, physicians have recognized behavioral syndromes that occur in association with changes in the sexual and reproductive functions of women. These syndromes include psychological changes related to menarche, premenstrual tension, postpartum psychosis, and involutional melancholia. Milder variants, such as "postpartum blues" and menopausal irritability, also are known. Prior to World War II, attempts to explain these various syndromes consisted primarily of psychoanalytic speculations derived from intensive clinical work. Emphasis was placed on the relationship between bodily changes and a woman's concept of her feminine role. Recently, studies have been conducted in an attempt to determine relationships between the hormonal psychological changes involved in these syndromes. This chapter summarizes much of the current thinking about these "womanly" conditions.

MENARCHE

The menarche is defined as the occurrence of the first menstrual period in young girls. Over the past 100 years, the average age of menarche in Western society has dropped from 16 to 17 years in 1860, to 12 to 13 in 1960. The reasons for this earlier onset have not been investigated. Speculations referring to changes in nutrition and social factors affecting hormonal changes have not been followed up with systematic studies. In light of the common clinical observation that the onset of menses is stressful for many girls, it is even more surprising that psychological studies, including psychoendocrine investigations, are generally lacking with regard to this more youthful aspect of adolescence. It is clear that the menarche and puberty have been much neglected in investigation of adolescence.

Physiology

The onset of puberty in the human female involves an interaction between ovarian hormones and certain cells of the brain, particularly in neurons in the hypothalamus. It has recently become apparent that the beginning of puberty is triggered by hypothalamic cells rather than by an autonomous system of endocrine glands, such as the ovaries and adrenals. It appears that the hypothalamus controls the output of gonadotropins from the anterior pituitary gland. The gonadotropins are the follicle-stimulating hormone (FSH) and the luteinizing hormone (LH). The gonadotropins promote the development and the secretion of hormones by the ovaries, and thus eventually regulate the menstrual cycle, which is discussed later in this chapter. The ovaries of women, and those of females of other mammalian species, secrete various hormones, including estrogen and progesterone, which in turn exert a "feedback effect" upon the hypothalamus and thus regulate the output of FSH and LH by the pituitary.

Gonadotropins are not secreted in detectable quantities in young girls, but they become detectable in small amounts a few years prior to menarche. Concentrations of these hormones increase rapidly during adolescence, and in adulthood they reach a plateau which is constant except for slight fluctuations of FSH and LH during the menstrual cycle. The rate of estrogen excretion in the urine increases at about 8 or 9 years of age and becomes particularly accelerated at about age 11. However, excretion of estrogen does not become cyclic until about eighteen months prior to menarche. During the eighteen months prior to the first menstrual period, secondary sex characteristics begin to develop, and a spurt in bodily growth starts at about the same time that estrogen secretion becomes cyclic. It is worth repeating, for emphasis, the fact that in young girls the changes in internal secretions begin prior to the onset of menarche, i.e., prior to any overt manifestation of their changing internal state.

Menarche is followed by a variable period lasting approximately 12 to 18 months during which the menstrual cycles of many girls are irregular and unpredictable. It is impossible to predict the year of menarche for any particular girl, and this adds to the anticipatory anxiety of parents and children alike with respect to the forthcoming event. For some girls, puberty—as indicated by the onset of the menses—may be precocious (onset before 10 years), while for others it may be delayed (onset after 15 years).

Psychology

When a boy matures early sexually and physically, this usually entails greater peer-group prestige, but the same is not true for girls. In fact, in one study, girls who matured early were rated by observers as more submissive or socially indifferent than were late-maturing girls. The former also scored lower on peer-group ratings of popularity and prestige.

According to the psychoanalytic view, the menarche has long been considered one of the traumata of a woman's life, and its positive aspects as a focal point in a girl's acceptance of her feminine and sexual role have received little emphasis. The anticipatory guidance and emotional cues a girl receives from her mother and other significant females deeply influence her own integration and acceptance of this critical period in her life. Kestenberg (1961) observed that most young girls who accepted the menarche and did not view it as a trauma shared a number of characteristics: (1) They were not left to their own devices to gain information, but were advised to a considerable degree by their mothers and friends as well as by their physician. (2) They accepted menstruation as a necessary nuisance in maintaining their group identity as girls who would become women and mothers at a later date. (3) The experience of menstrual cramps served to localize many diffuse and poorly defined internal changes prior to the onset of menarche. This had a stabilizing effect, in that young women could now point to a definite physical phenomenon to explain their previously ill-defined symptoms, which may have been partially related to the increases in ovarian hormones and accompanying changes in secondary sex characteristics that antedate the onset of menarche. (4) After menarche, once the menstrual cycle became regular, the uncertainty associated with not knowing when bleeding would occur was reduced, and consequently anxiety was also diminished. Furthermore, the regularity of the cycle became an organizing reference point for many of the girls who integrated the menstrual cycle into their developing concept of themselves as women.

BEHAVIORAL CHANGES DURING THE MENSTRUAL CYCLE

Fluctuations of mood frequently occur in relation to changes in estrogen and progesterone secretion that take place in successive stages of the menstrual cycle. Mood changes are most marked in the 4 to 5 days prior to menstruation; and the so-called "premenstrual syndrome" is perhaps the commonest endocrine-induced behavioral disorder. Approximately 30 to 50 percent of normal, young, married women are bothered to some extent by premenstrual cramps, backaches, headaches, general irritability, mood swings, tension or depression. However, only about 10 percent of the affected experience these symptoms to such a severe degree that their everyday activities have to be interrupted. The usual mildness of the premenstrual syndrome should not detract from the importance of its influence on the psychological adjustment of many women, particularly those who frequently experience severe distress.

Epidemiological studies have shown that the 4 days prior to menstruation, combined with the days of menstrual bleeding, are marked by a definite increase in the proportion of women who commit suicide, engage in criminal acts of violence, and who, as pilots, have serious or fatal airplane accidents. The premenstrual and menstrual stages combined include approximately 8 days of the total 28-day average cycle for women. Dalton (1964) found that during the premenstrual and menstrual phases 45 percent of industrial employees called in as sick; 46 percent of acute psychiatric admissions and 49 percent of acute medical and surgical admissions took place during this period. During the same stages of the cycle, 49 percent of female prisoners had committed their crimes, and 52 percent of emergency accident admissions occurred. In addition, 54 percent of all children attending clinics because of minor coughs and colds were brought in when their mothers were in the premenstrual and menstrual phase. Thus, the psychological changes that occur during this phase of the menstrual cycle can have serious consequences for a susceptible woman and also for society at large and should not be looked upon as a minor nuisance.

Psychophysiology

Results of clinical and laboratory studies suggests that the psychological changes which occur during different stages of the menstrual cycle may be related to fluctuations in hormonal conditions and particularly to cyclic changes in estrogens and progesterone. In the normal menstrual cycle, there are two peaks of estrogen secretion. (1) An "ovulation peak" occurs about mid-cycle near the end of the follicular phase; and (2) a "luteal peak" occurs about day 21 of a normal 28-day cycle. Secretion of progesterone begins about mid-cycle and reaches a peak concentration approximately on days 21 to 24, after which it falls off rapidly. Since estrogen is secreted throughout the cycle, it predominates in the first half of the cycle, whereas progesterone is secreted along with estrogen in the second half of the cycle.

Estrogen and progesterone have been shown to produce different behavioral effects in laboratory animals and in human beings. For example, in rats and humans estrogens lower seizure thresholds and progesterone has the opposite effect. The threshold for induction of electroconvulsive seizures in spayed rats is raised by administration of progesterone. Epileptic female patients have a high incidence of seizures in the premenstrual period, and progesterone therapy lowers the incidence of such seizures. Large doses of progesterone will produce general anesthesia and moderate doses will produce sedation.

The sedative action of progesterone is important, because it suggests the possibility that the normal rise and fall of progesterone during the menstrual cycle produces a syndrome akin to sedation followed by the withdrawal phenomena commonly associated with sedative drugs. Preovulatory plasma levels are about 1 microgram percent, and in the second half of the cycle they rise to about 2–3 micrograms percent. This 2- to 3-fold increase in blood levels is accompanied by a 7-fold increase of progesterone secretion during the second half of the cycle. Several days before the onset of the next menstruation there is a rapid decrease in progesterone secretion, and by the first day of menstruation no detectable amounts are present. Kopell, Lunde, Clayton, and Moos (1969) found that, during the premenstrual phase, women report impaired concentration and show alterations in time judgments and visual perception. The authors postulate that a mild confusional state occurs during the premenstrual phase when progesterone levels are declining.

The changes in progesterone concentrations are accompanied by alterations in the production of other hormones, and specific hormonal-behavioral interactions need further study. Changes in aldosterone, for example, and their effect on water retention may be important in the case of patients complaining of premenstrual bloating and edema. Reichlin (1968) believes that estrogen withdrawal may be the primary factor responsible for premenstrual mental symptoms. Other investigators have proposed that the ratio between progesterone and estrogen is important in inducing the mood changes which occur during the menstrual cycle. Vogel, Broverman, and Klaiber (1971) posit that estrogen exerts a central adrenergic effect (perhaps by inhibiting brain monoamine oxidase), and that progesterone tends to counteract this adrenergic effect. It is relevant to note that administration of exogenous progesterone blocks the confusional states induced by lysergic acid diethylamide (LSD). These are promising leads, but the precise relationships between changes in progesterone, estrogen and other hormones, and behavioral alterations during the menstrual cycle remain to be determined.

Cyclic Psychological Changes during the Menstrual Period

Results obtained in recent studies at Stanford are generally consistent with the classic study of Benedek and Rubinstein (1939) in showing that the estrogenic phase or first half of the menstrual cycle is characterized by a sense of wellbeing and alertness, as indicated by self-ratings of pleasantness, activation, and sexual arousal. In the second half of the cycle, concomitant with the gradual rise of progesterone production in the post-ovulation phase, there is a decrease in feelings of pleasantness, activation, and sexual arousal. Then, during the few days prior to the period of menstrual bleeding, when both estrogen and progesterone are declining, there occurs the onset of typical premenstrual symptoms, such as irritability and anxiety coupled with water retention and pain.

These findings were derived from studying 15 women throughout two consecutive menstrual cycles. The data showed that each woman was fairly consistent from one cycle to another with respect to the types and severity of symptoms she showed during the menstrual, intermenstrual, and premenstrual phases. Another approach showed that women differ in their patterns of cyclic change. This was revealed by replies to the Menstrual Distress Questionnaire constructed by Moos (1969). This questionnaire was given to 839 wives of graduate students at a large American university. Over 20 percent of these women complained of moderate, strong, or severe symptoms of irritability, mood swings and/or tension in the premenstrual phase of their most recent menstrual cycle. Individual patterns were also found in this larger sample, suggesting that the so-called premenstrual syndrome might be better termed the premenstrual syndromes, to indicate the existence of subgroups characterized by different patterns of distress. Some women experienced primarily dysmenorrhea (pelvic cramps) during menstruation, but no unpleasant moods in the premenstrual phase. Other women complained primarily of unpleasant moods (mainly irritability and emotional lability) in the premenstrual phase, but no pain or cramps at the time of menstruation.

Differences in individual patterns have important theoretical and practical implications, and it might be advisable for the 20 percent of women, who regularly experience moderate to severe cyclic changes in moods and symptoms, to use the Menstrual Distress Questionnaire for several successive months in order to plot the patterns of their changes. By doing this, they may prepare themselves psychologically for days of emotional instability secondary to changes in hormonal state. This could provide a means by which a woman could anticipate and cope with these periods of increased emotional vulnerability. This sort of psychological preparation could be valuable and important. Many individuals with severe premenstrual mood changes never recognize the connection between their emotional changes and the premenstrual period except by hindsight— that is, only after their period begins. Before the onset of menstrual bleeding, these women often ascribe their emotional upsets to minor difficulties with their husband or children, difficulties which, at other stages of the cycle, would have been easily overcome. Unfortunately, the emotional conflict and injury that occur with loved ones during an unexpected period of premenstrual vulnerability may linger as scars in vital family relationships, scars which are hard to dismiss by the uninformed who do not take into account a particular woman's cyclic emotional vulnerabilities. For this reason, not only should a woman know her own pattern, but, in addition, other people with whom she has significant relationships should be apprised of the facts so that they can be more supportive at critical periods in her cycle.

Neuroticism and Menstrual Symptoms

Physicians, mostly men, often discount a woman's premenstrual or menstrual complaints as being all "in her head" and therefore not worthy of medical attention. This is an error, which stems partly from difficulties that a male physician has in empathising with a woman and partly from Western cultural factors of the masculine self-image which derogates emotional displays as evidence of weakness. It is true that some types of women may tend to exaggerate their complaints, but this does not mean that these individuals are not suffering. Dysmenorrhea does not appear to be correlated with neurotic tendencies. In contrast, various psychological symptoms, such as irritability, depression, and tension which may occur in the premenstruum, often take a severe form in women who score high on neuroticism. To state the case another way, women who are irritable and emotionally unstable in their intermenstrual phase tend to experience premenstrual unpleasant moods of greater than average severity. This does not mean, of course, that all women who complain of premenstrual tension are neurotic. Furthermore, if some of them are neurotic, this does not mean that they are not suffering. In fact, such women may require more medical attention than normal women to help them adjust to their increased emotional instability at various phases of the menstrual cycle.

Coppen and Kessel (1963) employed the Maudsley Personality Inventory and found that neuroticism was higher in women whose periods were irregular than in women having regular cycles. This association has been observed by other investigators, but as yet there is no clear-cut interpretation. It is possible that psychic distress may cause menstrual irregularity through neuroendocrine influences. On the other hand, the unpredictability of irregular periods may produce uncertainty and anxiety in some women who, since they cannot predict when they will bleed from the vagina, fear social embarrassment. This suggestion is consonant with Kestenberg's finding (1961) that the year or so of irregularity which follows the menarche in young girls adds to adolescent unpredictability and anxiety. Once the menstrual periods become regular, the cyclic changes become nodal punctuation points around which the developing woman begins to organize and pattern her life. The cyclic changes in mood, and clearly demarcated menstrual periods, become integral to a woman's feminine self-concept. If these cyclic changes are irregular, a woman may be less likely to use them as predictable points for organizing her monthly activities.

Sexual Activity and the Menstrual Cycle

Benedek and Rubinstein (1939) conducted an intensive study of 15 women under psychoanalytic therapy. They kept records of the subject's free associations and dreams in relationship to hormone levels, the latter being inferred from vaginal smears. Results showed that active heterosexual striving increased with estrogen production in the first half of the menstrual cycle; whereas, during the second half of the cycle, a passive-receptive sexuality with a narcissistic self-centered state appeared to be associated with progesterone. At mid-cycle, which is the time of ovulation, there was the "highest integration of sexual drive." These findings were derived from women in therapy, but they have been replicated in more recent studies of cyclic changes in the sexual interest of normal women.

Udry and Morris (1968) focused on the distribution of overt sexual behavior in the menstrual cycle. The highest rates of intercourse and orgasm occurred about mid-cycle, which is the time when ovulation usually takes place. From the beginning of the cycle, there was a gradual increase in the rate of intercourse and orgasm, until the peak occurred around the time of ovulation. In the latter half of the cycle, there was a decline, with a brief increase before the end of the cycle, just before menstruation. The authors point out that different samples of women may have slightly different patterns, depending on age and socio-economic factors. The importance of these findings is that women may be definitely more sexually responsive at some times of the menstrual cycle than at others. The greater likelihood of orgasm at mid-cycle and just before menstruation should be taken into account in sexual counseling.

Effects of Oral Contraceptives

In a recent study at Stanford, Moos (1968) examined the characteristics of the menstrual cycle in women taking steroid contraceptives. Four hundred twenty women on various oral contraceptives were compared with a control sample of 298 women, not taking steroids, but using other means of contraception. Women using oral contraceptives reported a slightly shorter than average cycle length, a slightly shorter than average length of menstrual flow, and in general a much more regular menstrual cycle. Women not using oral contraceptives complained of greater severity of symptoms of pain, difficulties in concentration, negative affect (restlessness, tension, depression, irritability) and behavioral change (decreased work performance and efficiency). These conditions appeared in both the premenstrual and menstrual phases. Thirty-six percent of the non-oral group complained of moderate disabling irritability in the premenstrual phase, whereas only 24 percent of the oral group reported similar complaints. There was no difference between the two groups in the intermenstrual phase.

Among women taking oral preparations, there was a difference as to the type of oral contraceptive used. A comparison was made between women using combined medications (estrogenic and progestogen agents in each pill) and women taking sequential preparations in which an estrogenic agent is given for the first 15 days and then a combination of estrogen and progesterone agents is administered for the last 5 days in an attempt to duplicate the normal hormonal cycle. The results showed that the women on sequential steroids had significantly more complaints of water retention symptoms and negative affect. In general, it appeared that premenstrual distress tended to be greater in women taking the sequential pills.

Since the estrogen-progesterone combination pills are associated with less premenstrual distress, this raises the possibility of utilizing these medications for the regulation and amelioration of premenstrual symptoms in the 20 percent of women who experience severe recurrent cyclic distress within their natural menstrual cycle. Norethynodrel with mestranol (Enovid) given in doses of 5 or 10 mg twice daily for 10 days, beginning about the thirteenth day before the expected period, has been reported as being effective in preventing severe premenstrual distress. In certain women, where no estrogenic agent is indicated, medroxyprogesterone (Provera), 10 mg per day starting about the tenth day before the expected period, has been effective in relieving severe premenstrual symptoms.

POSTPARTUM

There is a 4- to 5-fold increase of risk of mental illness (especially psychosis) during the first 3 months after a woman has given birth. The period shortly after parturition is one of the most vulnerable times for a woman to develop a nervous breakdown. Besides those individuals who experience severe postpartum psychiatric reactions, about two-thirds of normal women develop a brief period of increased emotional lability in the first 10 days postpartum. This is termed the *postpartum blues*. These emotional reactions in the puerperium are ironic since, for most women and their families, the birth of a child is expected to be a happy occasion. When crying, depression, or bewilderment follow childbirth, it appears inexplicable to the new mothers as well as to their families and, in some cases, to their physicians.

The risk for women being hospitalized for a psychiatric illness is relatively lower during pregnancy than at other times. Thus, although many women complain of various disturbances during pregnancy, most of the evidence indicates that they are less vulnerable to severe psychological disturbances at this time. Therefore, the changes that occur from immediately before to shortly after delivery are particularly important for understanding the increased emotional vulnerability postpartum.

Physiology of the Puerperium

Knowledge of factors which trigger the onset of labor in humans is fragmentary, and very few investigations of the metabolic changes that follow delivery extend beyond the usual 3-day lying-in period. Nevertheless, the available studies are of interest to the behavioral scientist because they indicate that the most massive changes in hormones and fluid balance occur within the first 10 days postpartum. It is in this period that most women experience the postpartum blues; and the onset of 64 percent of acute postpartum psychiatric syndromes takes place within these first 10 days.

During the 9 months of pregnancy, there are gradual increases of chorionic gonadotropin, estrogens, progestins, adrenocortical hormones, androgens, 17-ketosteroids, and levels of circulating thyroid hormone. Concentrations of most of these hormones decrease precipitously within 3 days postpartum. Chorionic gonadotropin, which is secreted in large amounts during pregnancy, falls to undetectable levels within 12 hours after delivery. At the onset of labor, urinary levels of estrone and estradiol are approximately 100 times higher, and the estriol level 1,000 times higher than those seen during the luteal phase of the menstrual cycle. After delivery, estrone and estradiol reach the normal non-pregnancy level within the first 7 days; but estriol does not return to normal until about 14 to 21 days postpartum. During the last trimester of pregnancy, progesterone secretion is about 10-fold greater than it is during the luteal phase of the menstrual cycle and about 65-fold greater than progesterone production during the follicular phase.

Urinary excretion of the metabolites of progesterone, such as pregnanediol, is slightly reduced or unchanged in the course of labor, and within 6 to 8 days after parturition the levels fall rapidly to non-pregnant normal values. Within 7 days postpartum the urinary excretion per 24 hours of 11-oxycorticoids diminishes from third trimester levels of 1.5 mg per 24 hours to normal levels of approximately 1.2 mg per 24 hours. The chief regulating hormone for sodium and potassium, aldosterone, is secreted in increasing amounts during pregnancy, so that at term the levels average 25 mg percent; but after parturition the aldosterone level drops precipitously to 5 mg percent. Changes in secretion of this hormone and other related mineralocorticoids produce concomitant changes in fluid and water balance. These may be psychologically important, because changes in fluid balance and ionic concentrations have been implicated in some depressive illnesses.

Alterations in thyroid hormone secretion have also been associated with behavioral changes. The psychoses (usually paranoid) and the depressions of hypothyroidism are well known. During gestation there is an increase in thyroid function, as evidenced by measures such as the protein-bound iodine, the butanol-extractable iodine, and I^{131} uptake. Some of the increase in the protein-bound iodine may be related to the capacity of estrogen to increase the amount of bound thyroxin in the serum, but this does not explain changes in the other measures. Within about 10 days after delivery, serum iodine titers of the protein-bound iodine and butanol-extractable iodine return to normal levels. In some patients, transient readings within the hypothyroid range occur around 14 days postpartum. The postpartum emaciation and cachexia which characterize Sheehan's syndrome of pituitary infarction may be due to hypothyroidism secondary to anterior hypophyseal insufficiency. Behavioral changes, even psychosis, have been noted to occur in Sheehan's syndrome.

In summary, during pregnancy, the mother's brain is exposed to increasing levels of many different hormones and then, following delivery, there is a precipitous drop of many of these endocrine agents. This again raises the possibility that withdrawal from hormones may produce a syndrome which mimics states of confusion and irritability that follow withdrawal of psychoactive drugs such as barbiturates and opiates. Also, it is known that alterations in mood occur in patients whose doses of corticosteroids are abruptly withdrawn. More specific investigations of these possibilities are in order. Also, one must not neglect concomitant changes, such as alterations in fluid and electrolyte metabolism, and the secretion of prolactin (the milk-producing hormone), which rises sharply about 3 days postpartum.

Finally, in addition to this multitude of metabolic changes, numerous psychosocial changes occur shortly after delivery, and these may be important contributors to postpartum emotional vulnerability. The psychosocial changes include obvious changes in the body (diminution of girth and increase in breast size), which may alter a woman's perception of her body, an integral aspect of her self-image. Also there is the necessary adaptation to caring for a demanding infant, who is unable verbally to specify his needs.

Postpartum Blues Syndrome

The postpartum blues syndrome differs from the more severe psychiatric reactions in that it is a period of mild emotional lability which rarely lasts beyond 10 days after parturition. Results of a prenatal and postpartum study of 39 normal women in an obstetrical clinic led Yalom, Lunde, Moos and Hamburg (1968) to describe the postpartum blues as consisting of episodic crying spells, rapid swings of mood, and a heightened sensitivity to interactions with other persons, including the infant. The women appeared particularly sensitive to supposed rejection by others. Two thirds of these women experienced episodes of crying lasting at least 5 minutes, and 13 percent cried continuously for 2 hours, but rarely longer than 3 hours. Crying spells occurred throughout the first 10 days postpartum. There was no peak of crying or depressive bouts at 3 days postpartum, a finding which challenges the notion of "third day blues."

It is paradoxical that depression scores revealed by subjective inventories and interview ratings were correlated with crying spells during the first two days after delivery, and thereafter only a low correlation was obtained (+0.34). This suggests that postpartum crying episodes do not necessarily reflect sadness. Some women cried out of happiness, but most could not explain why they were crying. In fact, the women were often puzzled by their own emotionality and commented that their crying behavior was uncharacteristic of them. Study of 10-day periods before parturition and in the eighth month postpartum showed that only about 20 percent of the women had cried within these 10-day prepartum control periods. Moreover, in contrast to their postpartum crying, the crying spells of these same women during the control periods were briefer and usually could be attributed to an identifiable stress.

Yalom, et al. (1968) examined the predisposing factors to the postpartum crying spells and depression ratings. There were significant correlations between tendencies toward crying and depression and the following seven factors: lower parity, greater distress during previous pregnancy, increased length of time from last pregnancy, previous postpartum depression, greater menstrual difficulties, younger age at menarche, and shorter length of menstrual flow. Women who had the most acute postpartum depressive episodes also had a longer first stage of labor. Women who had the severest crying spells had a more fatiguing and unpleasant labor as well as a history of postpartum blues.

None of the 39 women was grossly confused or disoriented in the postpartum period, and memory and attention were normal. The lack of subjective confusion and absence of general personality disorganization are aids to distinguishing the postpartum blues from more severe psychiatric reactions.

The etiology of postpartum blues, better termed "postpartum emotional lability," has not been established. The most reasonable assumption is that the increased emotional vulnerability of postpartum women stems from an interaction of postpartum hormonal changes and increased environmental stresses associated with maternal responsibilities. Treadway, Kane, Jarrahi-Zadeh, and Lipton (1969) studied catecholamine and corticosteroid factors in association with psychological changes from 6 weeks prepartum to 1 and 2 days postpartum. The womens' subjective reports indicated that in the immediate postpartum period they experienced increased feelings of deactivation, social affection, and pleasantness, along with a decreased interest in social contacts.

Pre- to postpartum changes in the biochemical factors measured were not striking, and, most importantly, there were no significant correlations between the psychological and biochemical variables. It is possible, however, that the pleasantly drowsy state reported by these women might be related to hormones which the investigators did not study, namely, prolactin or progesterone. Prolactin and progesterone have been shown to influence maternal behavior in animals, and progesterone is known to be a central nervous system depressant. Rapid changes in these hormonal factors, as well as changes in fluid balance, may account for some of the emotional lability of the postpartum period, but the problem needs more specific research.

Postpartum Psychiatric Reactions

In women with specific predispositions to mental illness, postpartum emotional lability may increase the susceptibility to becoming psychotic or seriously depressed during the immediate postpartum period. Melges (1968) studied 100 women who required psychiatric care within 3 months postpartum and found that the onset of a postpartum mental illness occurred within the first 10 days postpartum in 64 percent of the cases. Thereafter, the time of onset declined gradually through the 3-month period.

The most telltale symptoms of postpartum mental illness include severe confusion, changes in the sense of duration along with confusion of past-present-future, depersonalization (i.e., feeling strange and unreal), irritability, rapid changes in mood (fluctuating from tears to gaiety in a matter of minutes), severe insomnia, and inexplicable, uncontrollable crying spells lasting beyond 2 to 3 hours. The most pervasive emotions are those of shame, helplessness, and depression, sometimes to the point of hopelessness. Feelings of being inadequate mothers and rejection of the infant are common complaints. Although confusion is a distinctive characteristic, women who suffer a postpartum psychiatric reaction are not usually disoriented (i.e., unlike patients with acute organic brain syndromes, these women can accurately report their names, where they are, and the calendar date).

It can be seen that symptoms characteristic of diverse psychiatric syndromes, including schizophrenia, depression, and mania, can occur during early puerperium of these patients. The fluctuation of the symptoms has made it difficult for psychiatrists to consider a postpartum psychiatric illness as a separate entity, or to describe it as a typical reaction that can be classified within the standard psychiatric nomenclature. The prognosis of postpartum psychiatric reactions, whatever the diagnosis, generally is considered to be better than that of nonpuerperal mental illness.

The incidence of a postpartum psychiatric reaction is 1 or 2 per 1,000 live births. If a woman has had a previous postpartum psychiatric reaction, the risk of her having another one is increased to about 1 out of 5 subsequent births. This risk was found to be even higher in Melges' sample of 100 women requiring postpartum psychiatric hospitalization. Considering 81 multigravidous women, it was found that 44 percent of their previous pregnancies had necessitated postpartum psychiatric care. Thus, women who have had at least 1 postpartum psychiatric illness tend to have recurrence of psychiatric difficulties in periods following subsequent pregnancies.

The history of a previous psychiatric disorder of any kind also increases the risk of a postpartum mental illness. Reich and Winokur (1970) have shown that this risk is especially increased for women who have had previous episodes of manic depressive illness of the bipolar type (that is, manic illness cycling with depressive episodes.) For this type of patient, postpartum psychiatric reactions follow about 30 percent of their births.

Although changes in endocrine and fluid balance undoubtedly play a role in the precipitation of postpartum illness, psychological conflict connected with assumption of the mothering role appears to be a paramount factor in maintaining the illness. Ambivalence with respect to mothering occurs in about 90 percent of women who require postpartum psychiatric care. The relative non-communicativeness of the infant is important in this conflict. The baby either cries or is quiescent. It does not specify guidelines for its care. Mothers who became mentally ill often interpret the infant's crying as raging rejection of themselves as well as desperate need for them. As a result, they feel trapped in a situation which they often do not know how to handle. Inability to cope with the demands of the infant frequently prompts them to turn to their own mothers, or to images of their mothers, for guidelines as to how to care for the infant. However, adopting their own mothers' ways of mothering may only augment the conflict, since women who develop postpartum psychiatric reactions often have had mothers who rejected them. Therefore, in taking their own mothers as models for caretaking, the new mothers often begin to reject the infant, just as they felt rejected as children.

Rejection of the infant transfixes the mother with guilt, for she consciously does not want to be like her own dominating and rejecting mother. Therefore, in this situation, the identities of the new mothers vacillate; they feel helpless without the images of their mothers, yet ashamed when they behave like their own mothers. Indecision, perplexity, and a loss of personal efficacy mounts. Uncertain in their role as mother, and yet without a positive maternal model, these women feel lost and confused.

In the older literature, this confusion was attributed to a delirium. This may have been true, in view of some of the toxic infectious states that occurred before the availability of antibiotics. In recent studies, however, there is no evidence in these women for a classical delirium which would be reflected in impaired intellectual tests and slowing of the EEG.

Relationships between hormonal changes and the fluctuating symptoms of postpartum mental illness have not been explicitly studied. Research on this problem is needed, since some postpartum psychiatric reactions resemble the protean symptoms of a "steroid" psychosis. Endocrine changes may render some women particularly vulnerable to postpartum mental illness, but since there are 12 reported cases of women requiring psychiatric care shortly after the adoption of an infant, physiological changes alone cannot be presumed to be the entire explanation for all postpartum reactions. Motherless monkeys (female macaques raised without a mother) are known forcefully to reject their own infants, which may indicate that some learning and modeling factors are important for normal maternal responses in nonhuman primates.

The most likely hypothesis is that a combination of physiological and psychological factors make the puerperium a period of increased emotional vulnerability and stress. For women suffering severe postpartum reactions, conflict over mothering a relatively noncommunicative infant prevails in maintaining the emotional turmoil.

Menopausal Distress

Four terms are commonly used to refer to certain symptoms described by women in their late forties. These are the menopause, the climacterium, the involutional period, and the "change of life." These diverse terms reflect, in part, the different interpretations given to complaints of middle-aged women. Strictly speaking, the menopause refers to the cessation of the menses; the climacterium refers to involution of the ovaries and associated processes; the involutional period refers primarily to advancing age; and the "change of life" refers to an altered life style. Despite these different definitions, the four terms are often used interchangeably.

To simplify our discussion, the words *menopause* and *menopausal* will be used as general terms to refer to changes that occur in association with the natural cessation of the menses, which takes place gradually in most women over a two- to five-year period. The term *involutional* will be used to refer to those symptoms that may reflect a woman's adjustment to advancing age and to changes in her role as a mother, housewife, and sexual partner. We will attempt to make a distinction between the usual symptoms of the menopause in normal women, and those rare psychiatric syndromes which are termed *involutional melancholia* and *involutional paranoid state*. Symptoms of the normal menopause, such as "hot flashes" and increased irritability, may have some relationship to changes in ovarian and gonadotropic hormones, but the relationship between endocrine changes and the severe involutional psychiatric disorders remains obscure.

Psychophysiology

In American women, the menopause, or cessation of menstruation, usually takes place between ages 45 and 49, with an average of 48 years. This is later than the 42 to 45 age period mentioned in textbooks written a half-century ago, and the delay in the age of onset of the menopause has been attributed to better nutrition and general improvement of health.

In the course of about 33 years, which is the average menstrual life span, there is a progressive decrease in the number of oocytes (immature egg cells) remaining in the ovary after each ovulatory cycle. Advancing age brings a gradual decline of ovarian secretory activity which extends over 2 to 5 years. As ovarian senility advances, ovulation becomes less regular and menstruation irregular. The ovary becomes less sensitive to gonadotropin stimulation and less and less estrogen is secreted. Menses cease when there is not enough estrogen to stimulate growth of the uterine endometrium. Eventually, estrogen levels fall so low that they fail to inhibit the pituitary, and, as a consequence, large quantities of pituitary gonadotropins, primarily FSH, are secreted. As a consequence, the urinary gonadotropin level rises and remains high during and after the menopause.

It was formerly thought that the increase in gonadotropin levels was responsible for one common accompaniment of the menopause, the so-called hot flashes (flushing of the skin, feelings of warmth, and marked bouts of sweating, chiefly around the head, neck and upper thorax). This interpretation seems unlikely, in view of reports that hot flashes occasionally occur in cases of hypopituitarism, and are absent in girls who have congenital ovarian failure accompanied by high gonadotropin secretion. Furthermore, hot flashes usually are relieved by estrogen treatment. Reichlin (1968) postulates that hot flashes and associated mental symptoms probably represent an estrogen-withdrawal syndrome analogous to effects of withdrawing sedative drugs such as barbiturates and morphine.

There usually is a decline in a woman's sexual activity around the age of 60, although it is well established that some women remain sexually active and orgastic well beyond the menopause. Research has shown that the common decline in a woman's sexual activity often is related to the husband's declining sexual interest, which tends to begin when he is approximately 60. On the other hand, many estrogen-deficient women experience a loss of sexual interest which can be reversed by estrogen replacement therapy. In such cases, the loss of sexual interest may be due to regressive changes in the female genitalia, induced by estrogen deficiency. These atrophic changes consist of thinning and friability of the epithelium of the vulva and vagina as well as a decrease in vaginal secretions. Such changes obviously can result in discomfort during sexual intercourse, and therefore may be more important in influencing sexual behavior than levels of ovarian hormones per se.

With advancing age, depressive reactions increase in frequency in both women and men; but they are about three times more frequent in women. Robinson, Davis, Nies, Ravaris, and Sylwester (1971) found that in both sexes, after about age 45, the enzymatic activity of monoamine oxidase (determined by autopsied hindbrains as well as plasma and platelet assays in living subjects) declines progressively. Monoamine oxidase is an enzyme which catalyzes one of the major pathways for degrading biogenic amines, 5-hydroxytryptamine (serotonin) and the catecholamines (epinephrine and nor-epinephrine). Monoamine oxidase inhibitors are effective drugs in treating some depressed patients. The inhibition of monoamine oxidase is thought to increase biogenic amines in the brain, thereby producing a stimulatory effect which reverses depression. Robinson, et al. (1971) found that from about age 45 plasma and platelet monoamine oxidase activity is significantly higher in women than in men. This suggests that, starting at the time of the menopause, women begin to have less biogenic amines than men. Whether these changes in monoamine oxidase activity are related to decrease in the secretion of ovarian hormones, and whether they are implicated in the relatively greater frequency of depressive episodes in women with advancing age, are exciting possibilities for further research.

Menopausal Symptoms

There are many controversies in the psychiatric literature as to whether so-called menopausal or involutional symptoms can be attributed to an altered hormonal balance or to the woman's increasing fear that she will no longer be sexually attractive and reproductively functional. Although about 90 percent of all women experience some increased irritability during their late forties, only about 25 percent bring their troubles to the attention of a physician. It has been estimated by gynecologists that no more than about 10 percent of the female population has severe menopausal symptoms as a result of endocrine dysfunction.

When the physician is faced with complaints by a woman in her late forties, the obvious problem is to differentiate those symptoms based on endocrine dysfunction and those based on her apprehension about the "change of life," i.e., a change in her role in society. One attempt has been made to differentiate between those symptoms which may be due to psychosocial changes and those presumably based on endocrine-menopausal factors. Neugarten and Kraines (1965), using the Blatt Menopausal Index and other measures, compared two groups of women 45 to 54 years of age. Members of one group of 40 subjects evaluated themselves as menopausal, largely on the basis of recent cessation or irregularity of their menses. The other group consisted of 60 subjects who reported themselves as being either pre- or postmenopausal, and as not experiencing recent irregularity or cessation of menses. The significant differences (P<.05) in the percentages of women reporting various symptoms, according to their self-reported menopausal status, are listed in Table 10.1.

This investigation is obviously limited by the fact that the two groups were differentiated primarily on the basis of each woman's judgment that she was or was not menopausal, according to her menstrual history. Some circularity may have been introduced, since a woman who believed herself to be menopausal may have reported more so-called menopausal symptoms. Nevertheless, the study represents the first systematic attempt to differentiate age-dependent symptoms from symptoms related to the

TABLE 10.1

Percentages of Women Reporting Symptoms within the Age Period of 45-54 Years
According to Self-Reported Menopausal Status.
(From Neugarten and Kraines, 1965).

Symptoms	*Menopausal Women*	*Pre- or Post-Menopausal Women*
Somatic		
Hot flashes	68	28
Cold sweats	32	16
Weight gain	61	41
Heavy menstrual "flooding"	51	24
Breast pains	37	10
Skin crawls	15	3
Headaches	71	47
Psychologic		
Irritable and nervous	92	71
Feel blue and depressed	78	56
Feelings of suffocation	29	2

cessation of menses. Some symptoms commonly regarded as part of the menopause, such as tired feelings, gastrointestinal upsets, numbness and tingling, rheumatic pains, and insomnia were not significantly different between the two groups. The telltale symptom of hot flashes, commonly used as a defining characteristic of the menopause, was present in more of the menopausal women. This difference could not be explained completely as a product of aging or the psychosocial changes in the late forties and early fifties. Hot flashes consist of warmth and sweating around the upper portion of the body and neck and they usually occur 10 to 12 times per day, with each episode lasting from one-half to 3 minutes. There have been no studies to determine whether other so-called menopausal symptoms, such as cold sweats, breast pains, irritability, and depression are temporally correlated with the appearance of hot flashes. A longitudinal study of changes in symptoms in association with one another might provide a more complete picture of the menopausal syndrome. There have as yet been no studies which attempt to isolate sub-syndromes of menopausal changes.

The natural menopause appears to involve a more complex and prolonged constellation of symptoms than does surgical menopause. In the latter case, the symptoms frequently last only 3 to 4 months. Data from a National Health Survey show that from 25 percent to 30 percent of American women now aged 50 to 64 have had a surgical menopause, most commonly as a result of a hysterectomy. In such women, prolongation of an emotional reaction beyond 6 months is likely to be due to psychological causes, such as the fear of cancer or the loss of reproductive function.

In treating hot flashes, also termed vasomotor instability, gynecologists have been placing increasing reliance upon estrogen therapy, which seems to be quite effective. The dose administered is usually quite small, consisting of 0.5 mg of diethylstilbestrol or 0.625 mg of conjugated estrogens daily, in 20-day courses, repeated after a 1-week interval. In response to this regimen, many women report an increased sense of well-being and an increase in sexual activity. The latter change may be due to the restoration of normal vaginal epithelium and secretions.

Some of the mental symptoms that accompany hot flashes may dissipate as a result of estrogen therapy. This is particularly true of anxiety and irritability. However, depression may not be relieved by exogenous estrogen. In such cases, the woman is experiencing the involutional period as a true change of life, and may be suffering from the "empty nest syndrome" in which she feels useless now that her children have grown up and she is left alone without her former duties and responsibilities. The threat of death, plus the loss of friends and of the spouse through illnesses associated with advancing age, are additional factors which loom within this era. The psychotherapeutic task here is to find some way of motivating the patient to become engaged in new activities that extend beyond her former duties as a mother, housewife, and sexual partner. Positive aspects of the years past fifty must be pointed out so that the patient anticipates her coming years with hope for rewards.

Involutional Psychiatric Syndromes

The Diagnostic and Statistical Manual of Mental Disorders (DSM-II), published by the American Psychiatric Association in 1968, describes two syndromes that arise in some women during the late forties and early fifties. These are involutional melancholia and involutional paranoid state.

Involutional melancholia is classically described as a depressive episode of major proportions occurring for the first time in the involutional period, without a prior history of manic-depressive illness. The involutional period generally refers to ages 45 to 55 for women and 50 to 65 for men. Women receive the diagnosis of involutional melancholia about 3 times more often than men. The symptoms of worry, anxiety, severe insomnia, feelings of guilt, and preoccupations with the body (hypochondriasis and somatic delusions) occur, but they do not distinguish this entity from other types of depressive illness. DSM-II asserts that involutional melancholia differs from a psychotic depressive reaction in that the former is not due to some life experience. This assertion may be in error, since most clinicians find some evidence of the empty nest syndrome in women who have severe depressions for the first time within this age period.

One feature which distinguishes involutional melancholia from other depressive reactions is the great amount of psychomotor agitation and pacing seen in patients with this medical problem. Such behavior is in contrast to the marked slowing of reactions usually seen in depressive illness. Many authors have stressed a premorbid personality of extreme compulsiveness and conscientiousness in individuals who develop involutional melancholia, but such a type of personality is often seen in individuals who develop depressions of any type.

In present-day psychiatric practice, the diagnosis of involutional melancholia is used rarely, being applied to only 7.2 patients per 100,000 psychiatric hospital admissions. The diagnosis is used more frequently for women from lower social classes and those with relatively little education. The diagnosis is applied more frequently to widowed and divorced individuals than to women living with their husbands.

The etiology of involutional melancholia is unknown. Gershon, Dunner, and Goodwin (1971) emphasize the importance of genetic factors in depressions of all types, including involutional melancholia. It is possible that genetic forces may influence various hormonal changes, which in turn are involved in some subsyndromes of depression.

Whether endocrine changes are implicated in involutional melancholia is a problem that calls for intensive and extensive research. Many times the fullblown syndrome of a distraught, hand-wringing, hypochondriacal, meticulous woman does not appear until 3 to 7 years after the menopause. It is still possible that earlier endocrine changes may have contributed to the woman's emotional instability, which later becomes a fixed depressive reaction. Ripley, Shorr and Papanicolaou (1940) attempted to treat involutional melancholia with estrogenic hormones. Grading the response to estrogen in terms of changes in vaginal smears, they found no effect on this severe disorder. However, as Rosenthal (1968) points out, estrogen therapy may have been initiated too late, and different results might have been obtained if estrogen had been administered before the patients' disorders became chronic. At present, the most common regimen for treating this disorder is the administration of tricyclic antidepressant drugs and, if there is no response to this medication, to begin a course of electroconvulsive therapy. Approximately 80 percent of involutional melancholics respond well to electroconvulsive therapy, and the remission is usually maintained for at least three years. It is generally felt that these patients are inaccessible to depth (insight-oriented) psychotherapy, and therefore supportive reassurance and assistance in coping with environmental stresses are recommended.

Closely related to involutional melancholia is the involutional paranoid state. The latter is distinguished from schizophrenia in the absence of the typical schizophrenic thought disorder, that is, of loosening of associations. Most cases of so-called involutional paranoid state are characterized by manifestations of heightened suspiciousness grafted on a basically depressive illness. As with involutional melancholia, this diagnosis should be used rarely. A diagnosis which depends mainly on the age of the patient suffering from various symptoms probably reflects the age-dependent psychosocial adjustments that must be made during a critical life phase. For women and men alike, major adaptations must be made to the massive changes which take place during this stage of life, often viewed as a twilight zone that follows the peak of productivity between ages 25 to 50. Recent studies indicate that the anticipation of loss of function in sexual activity and in work after 50 years of age is based on old wives' tales. Both men and women remain capable sexually and vocationally long after 50, so that the dreadful myth of physiological dysfunction should be dispelled. A woman with pride in her physical attractiveness and her achievements may view advancing age as a threat to her self-image, and may view more youthful members of her circle as usurping a valued role which she has carried out for years. In today's society, with its emphasis on youth and vitality, such suspicions are sometimes understandable. If a woman has wittingly or unwittingly subscribed to the cultural emphasis on youth and sex, when she reaches 40 or 50 years of age, she may believe that she is no longer attractive, is washed out, and over the hill. All too often, such a woman, in a desperate attempt to recapture her youth, may resort to the use of excessive make-up, plastic surgery, and clothes which are more appropriate for her daughter. According to Erik Erikson (1959), such behavior comprises symptoms of isolation, stagnation, and despair, indicating that the woman has not solved the crises of the mature years by finding ways to become intimate and productive beyond those of reproduction and sex.

In 1945, the psychoanalyst Helene Deutsch, heavily influenced by the Freudian emphasis on sex, described the involutional period as one involving a momentous struggle for a woman in which "resignation without compensation is often the only solution." Twenty-three years later, in 1968, Marya Mannes pointed out that, although hormone therapy may allow modern woman to remain "biologically female" longer than in years past, this does not mean that older women will perforce be sexually attractive to men. The "change of life" from her positive view must become a transmutation from sex to social affection and commitment, from "specific passion to general compassion."

CONCLUSION

A prominent researcher once remarked that he had spent most of his life attempting to confirm what his wife already knew. But there's the rub:

men often do not know "psychofemininendocrinology," to coin a word that reflects the mysteries which often perplex men as physicians, husbands, and fathers. Recent advances in neuroendocrinology and biobehavioral approaches to the menstrual, postpartum and menopausal periods are steps toward understanding psychological changes and specific vulnerabilities that women experience.

REFERENCES

American Psychiatric Association. 1968. *Diagnostic and Statistical Manual of Mental Disorders.* 2d ed., DSM-11. Washington, D.C.; American Psychiatric Association.

Benedek, T., and Rubinstein, B. 1939. The correlations between ovarian activity and psychodynamic processes. I. The ovulative phase. *Psychosom. Med.* 1:245-70. II. The menstrual phase. *Psychosom.* Med. 1:461-85.

Coppen, A., and Kessel, N. 1963. Menstruation and personality. *Brit. J. Psychiat.* 109:711-21.

Dalton, K. 1964. *The Premenstrual Syndrome.* Springfield, 111: Charles C. Thomas.

Deutsch, H. 1945. The climaterium. In *Psychology of Women,* Vol. II. New York: Grune and Stratton.

Dunlop, E. 1968. Emotional imbalance in the premenopausal woman. *Psychosom.* 9:44-47. July-August supplement.

Erikson, E. H. 1959. Identity and the life cycle. In *Psychological Issues* 1: 1-70. New York: International Universities Press.

Gershon, E. S.; Dunner, D. L.; and Goodwin, F. K. 1971. Toward a biology of affective disorders. *Arch. Gen. Psychiat.* 25:1-15.

Kestenberg, J. S. 1961. Menarche. In *Adolescents: Psychoanalytic Approach to Problems and Therapy.* Edited by Sandor L. Lorand and Henry I. Schneer. New York: Hoeber.

Kopell, B. S.; Lunde, D. T.; Clayton, R. B.; and Moos, R. H. 1969. The variations in some measures of arousal during the menstrual cycle. *J. Nerv. Ment. Dis.* 148:180-87.

Mannes, M. 1968. Of time and woman. *Psychosom.* 9:8-11. July-August issue.

Melges, F. T. 1968. Postpartum psychiatric syndromes. *Psychosom. Med.* 30: 95-107.

Moos, R. H. 1969. Menstrual distress questionnaire: Preliminary Manual. Obtainable from the Department of Psychiatry, Stanford University School of Medicine, Stanford, California, 94305.

———. 1968. Psychological aspects of oral contraceptives. *Arch. Gen. Psychiat.* 19:87-94.

———. 1969. A typology of menstrual cycle symptoms. *Amer. J. Obstet. Gynec.* 103:390-402.

Moos, R. H.; Kopell, B. S.; Melges, F. T.; Yalom, I. D.; Lunde, D. T.; Clayton, R. B.; and Hamburg, D. A. 1969. Fluctuations in symptoms and moods during the menstrual cycle. *J. Psychosom. Res.* 13:37-44.

Neugarten, B. L., and Kraines, R. J. 1965 "Menopausal symptoms" in women of various ages. *Psychosom. Med.* 28:266-73.

Reich, T., and Winokur, G. 1970. Postpartum psychoses in patients with manic depressive disease. *J. Nerv. Ment. Dis.* 151:60-68.

Reichlin, S. Neuroendocrinology. 1968. In *Textbook of Endrocrinology*, 4th ed., Edited by Robert H. Williams. Philadelphia: Saunders. Pp. 967-1016.

Ripley, H. S.; Shorr, E.; and Papanicolaou, G. N. 1940. Effective treatment of menopause depression with estrogenic hormone. *Amer. J. Psychiat.* 96:905-14.

Robinson, D.S.; Davis, J. M.; Nies, A.; Ravaris, C. L.; and Sylwester, D. 1971. Relation of sex and aging in monoamine oxidase activity of human brain, plasma, and platelets. *Arch. Gen. Psychiat.* 24:536-39.

Rosenthal, S. H. 1968. The involutional depressive syndrome. *Amer. J. Psychiat.* 124:21-35. May supplement.

Treadway, C. R.; Kane, F. J.; Jarrahi-Zadeh, A.; and Lipton, M. A. 1969. A psychoendocrine study of pregnancy and puerperium. *Amer. J. Psychiat.* 125:1380-86.

Udry, J. R., and Morris, N. M. 1968. Distribution of coitus in the menstrual cycle. *Nature* 220:593-96.

————. 1970. Effect of contraceptive pills on the distribution of sexual activity in the menstrual cycle. *Nature* 227:502-3.

Vogel, W.; Broverman, D. M.; and Klaiber, E. L. 1971. EEG responses in regularly menstruating women and in amenorrheic women treated with ovarian hormones. *Science* 172:388-91.

Yalom, I. D.; Lunde, D. T.; Moos, R. H.; and Hamburg, D. A. 1968. The "postpartum blues" syndrome. Description and related variables. *Arch. Gen. Psychiat.* 18: 16-27.

SUGGESTED READINGS

Benson, R. C. 1963. Endocrinology of the puerperium. *Clin. Obstet. Gynec.*, 5, 639-654.

Hamburg, D. A. 1966. Effects of progesterone on behavior. In *Endocrines and the Central Nervous System*. Edited by R. L. Levine. Association for Research in Nervous and Mental Disease., 43:251-63. Baltimore: Williams and Wilkins.

Hamburg, D. A.; Moos, R. H.; and Yalom, I. D. 1968. Studies of distress in the menstrual cycle and the postpartum period. In *Endocrinology and Human Behavior*. Edited by R. P. Michael. London: Oxford University Press. Pp. 2-24.

Kales, A.; Allen, C.; Scharf, M. B.; and Kales, J. D. 1970. Hypnotic drugs and their effectiveness. *Arch. Gen. Psychiat.* 23:226-32.

Zarrow, M. X.; Brody, P. N.; and Denenberg, B. H. 1968. The role of proges-
terone behavior. In *Perspectives in reproduction and sexual behavior.*
Edited by M. Diamond. Bloomington, Indiana: Indiana University Press.
Pp. 363-89.

11

CROSS-SPECIES COMPARISONS AND
THE HUMAN HERITAGE

Frank A. Beach

EDITORIAL PREFACE

As admitted in the introductory section of this chapter, an inventory of animal mating habits would scarcely be relevant to the major purposes of our book, but, on the other hand, authors of other chapters have made so many references to sexual functions in animals that some more formal analysis of the animal evidence with a rationale for comparisons with human sexuality is necessary.

One objective of Chapter 11 is to explore some of the ways in which the facts about sexual behavior of any given species can be integrated into a theoretical framework that includes other aspects of the total species repertoire. The suggested concept of a "sociosexual matrix" represents an extension of William Davenport's demonstration that human sexual conduct is best understood when viewed in a perspective provided by the "internal logic and consistency" of a total culture.

Another major purpose of this chapter is to consider different levels of interspecific comparison and their significance. There are good reasons to be wary of egregious extrapolations in which surface or formal similarities between species are uncritically put forward as evidence for commonality in causal origins or identity of mediating mechanisms. A case point is the occurrence of homosexual interactions in various species and their relevance or irrelevance to our understanding of human homosexuality. The general problem of using animal models in human psychology is a thorny one, but certain basic rules of choice should be agreed upon.

Finally, some tentative suggestions are made concerning ways in which the study of human sexuality might be strengthened and enriched by adoption and modification of certain practical and theoretical approaches that have proved fruitful in investigation of other species.

RATIONALE AND PURPOSE

At first thought, it may seem strange that a book about human sexuality should include a chapter dealing with sexual behavior in animals, but the rationale is simple. Every chapter of this book, except Stoller's discussion of sexual deviations, makes some reference to behavior of non-human species, and without results of animal experiments Chapters 2, 3, 8 and 9 could not have been written in their present form. It is, therefore, logical to examine more directly those aspects of sex in animals which students of human behavior deem relevant to their subject.

A second reason for dealing with this topic is the foundation it provides for an evolutionary perspective on human sexuality as set forth in Chapter 1. Man is no more a naked ape than chimpanzees are hairy people, but he is a mammal and a primate, and as such shares certain physical and behavioral characteristics with other members of his class and order. In Chapter 5, Davenport seeks "cultural universals" in human sexuality by comparing different societies. Here, we compare different species to determine which, if any, of man's sexual traits can be traced to his primate ancestry or to his even more remote mammalian origins.

The cross-sectional approach described in Chapter 1 will be used to compare and contrast sexual behavior of different species, but the aim is not to compile an encyclopedic zoological inventory of mating habits across the animal kingdom. The goal is to emphasize those comparisons between men and animals which can provide insights into human behavior—comparisons that may forever elude us if we concentrate exclusively upon man himself. Some, but not all, similarities between related species are products of their common ancestry. Resemblances are important, but differences often are equally significant, and we shall therefore place equal emphasis on both aspects of comparisons between *Homo sapiens* and other mammals.

Levels of Comparison and Constraints on Inference

Descriptive Level

The comparative approach begins with descriptions of formal similarities in the sexual behavior of different species, and these are both numerous and readily discernible to the most casual and uninformed observer. However, the identification of response patterns common to several species is only a first step, and the mere existence of close resemblances is unilluminating.

It is a fact that some men and all male mink inflict physical injury upon their sexual partners, but, taken in isolation, one of these facts does not help us to understand the other. It is a fact that mouth-genital contact is a regular precursor to coitus in many mammals, but establishment of this fact has no direct explanatory value with respect to human fellatio and cunnilingus.

Surface similitude by itself does not justify theoretical inference. This observation is so trite that it would be trivial were it not for the fact that the implied caveat is so often ignored in practice. For example, the fact that some animals engage in homosexual behavior has often been mentioned in discussions of human sexuality, with the implication that the mere existence of the similarity proves something or other about homosexuality in man, e.g., that homosexuality is "biologically normal." The conclusion may or may not be correct but the comparative evidence is irrelevant and neither supports nor denies the deduction.

Analytical Level

Careful description and measurement of behavior patterns is, of course, essential to interspecific comparison, but the results of this process constitute raw material for analysis at a more meaningful level. The similarities and differences having primary importance are those pertaining to causal mechanisms and adaptive functions. We are ultimately concerned not with the outward form of behavior but with the factors that cause it and the needs it serves.

This generalization has important bearing on procedures to be followed in the comparative approach. It emphasizes the necessity for intraspecific analysis as an indispensable basis for interspecific comparison. Knowledge of the causes and functions of behavior within a species is an essential precursor to the interpretation of resemblances or differences between species.

BASIC FEATURES OF MAMMALIAN MATING BEHAVIOR

Evolutionary Considerations

Patterns of heterosexual mating vary in detail from one type of animal to the next, but for every species, including our own, the basic pattern is an end-product of evolutionary development. As emphasized in Chapter 1, coitus fulfills the essential function of perpetuating the species and if it did not meet this need it would not have evolved, or would not survive as a species characteristic. In evolutionary perspective, copulation, intercourse or mating patterns exist because they are essential for species survival.

To say that animals and people engage in sexual intercourse because if they did not do so their species would die out does not mean that animals copulate with conscious intent to reproduce, any more than it means that men and women have intercourse for the sole purpose of having babies. What such a statement does mean, at least as far as animals are concerned, is that the physiological bases (or S-R contingencies discussed in Chapter 9) guaranteeing the occurrence of fertile mating are "built into" the hereditary potential of every species. Over millions of years, the genotype of the species has been constantly screened by natural selection to preserve its reproductive success. Widespread genetic or nongenetic deviations seriously reducing the occurrence or effectiveness of heterosexual mating could never have survived.

We cannot estimate the contribution of the species genotype to human hetrosexual intercourse. Although many features of human sexuality obviously are controlled, if not created, by social conditioning, the possibility remains that behavior essential for reproduction is built up through experience from a core of unlearned S-R patterns mediated by genetically controlled mechanisms. One aspect of the sex act that does not depend on experience is the positive affect or reinforcing effect of sexual climax, and this phenomenon has interspecific generality.

Since no animal mates in order to reproduce, but animals must mate in the service of species survival, we are faced with the problem of identifying the source of reward or positive reinforcement which impels individuals to copulate. The problem has scarcely been recognized as far as sexual activity is concerned, although many experiments have attacked similar questions relating to survival of the individual. Neither animals nor people eat in order to avoid death by starvation, but we have a good deal of information concerning the mechanisms that increase or decrease food intake. In contrast, we know relatively little about the mechanisms responsible for survival of the species.

Temporal Distribution of Sexual Activity

The vast majority of animals engage in no sexual behavior at all during most of the year, and for all nonhuman species copulatory activity is periodic rather than continuous. This is because mating is closely tied to reproduction, generally occurring only when a male and female are fertile and copulation can lead to pregnancy. At those times when they normally are infertile, adult males and females are unresponsive to sexual stimulation. As explained in Chapters 8 and 9, timing of sexual receptivity in females, and potency in males, is determined by ovarian and testicular hormones, secretion of which is controlled by the same pituitary hormones that govern production of eggs and sperm.

Perhaps 90 percent of all mammals are seasonal breeders, but some tropical species normally reproduce throughout the year and still others do so under domestication. In these cases, males are more or less constantly fertile and potent whereas the female's periods of sexual receptivity and attractiveness are synchronized with the cyclic maturation of egg cells in her ovaries, and mating therefore occurs only when copulation can result in impregnation.

The relevance of these facts to a comparative analysis rests on the

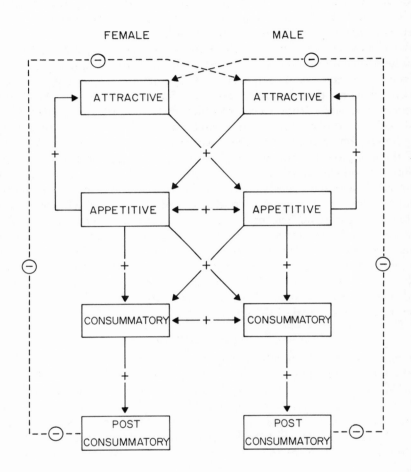

Fig. 11.1 *Successive phases and reciprocal interrelations in heterosexual mating.*
(1) Partner's attractivity stimulates appetitive behavior which has 4 effects.
Display of appetitive behavior enhances the general attractiveness of the performer, elicits complementary appetitive responses by the partner, evokes consummatory behavior by the partner, and produces feedback stimuli leading to
initiation of consummatory behavior by the performer. (2) Execution of consummatory behavior has 2 effects. It stimulates the occurrence of consummatory responses by the partner and produces feedback effects leading to the
post-consummatory phase or state in the performer. (3) The post-consummatory phase is associated with temporary loss or reduction in the performer
of responsiveness to the stimuli which initially contributed to sexual attractiveness of the partner. From Beach (1976).

marked independence of human sexual activity from comparable degrees of hormonal control. Production of sperm and eggs and secretion of sex hormones are determined by pituitary hormones, just as in other mammals; but effects of testosterone, estrogen and progesterone on the brain, and thus on psychological functions, are much less obvious and obligatory. As a result, human sexual behavior is not physiologically confined to reproduction and has come to serve many nonreproductive functions.

Some nonhuman primates appear to belong somewhere between man and nonprimate mammals. Although gorillas mate only when the female is in estrus, this is not true of chimpanzees or monkeys. At least, when they are maintained in captivity these animals will sometimes copulate when the female is not in estrus and therefore is infertile. It is not certain why some primates, and especially man, are less affected than "lower" mammals by hormones, but one theory relates relative degrees of relaxation from endocrine control to the more advanced development of higher brain regions. In particular, the cerebral cortex reaches its greatest elaboration in man and, to a lesser degree, in other primates; and although this cannot be the only factor involved, the hypothesis is that cerebral control tends to modulate and reduce the direct effect of hormones on the sexual activity of man and some of his nearest relatives.

Four Phases in the Mating Sequence

Figure 11.1 is a schematic representation of 4 successive stages that can be identified in the mating pattern of many mammals (Beach, 1976). The scheme is oversimplified but heuristically useful for it emphasizes two basic generalizations. (1) Sexual activity is fundamentally a relational process, demanding interaction between two individuals. (2) Successful completion of the pattern necessitates stimulus input and behavioral output on the part of both partners.

Sexual attraction. We are accustomed to thinking of sexual attractivity primarily in terms of the female as the "attractor" and the male as the "attractee," whereas, in fact, the phenomenon is mutual and reciprocal, and in both sexes of nonhuman species is hormone-dependent.

Male rats prefer the odor of urine from females that have been stimulated by estrogen to that from females without estrogen; but if a male is castrated, he no longer shows the preference, even though he is capable of discriminating between the two odors. Male dogs are strongly attracted to vaginal secretions from a bitch in heat, and the strength of the attraction can be decreased either by bringing the female out of estrus or by castrating the male. Male monkeys and apes are stimulated by the sight of an estrous female's estrogen-stimulated sex skin, as well as by the smell and taste of her vaginal secretions.

When she is in estrus, the female hamster will promptly approach a caged male and stand outside his cage in the position she normally assumes for copulation. She is attracted partly by the male's odor and partly by the ultrasonic calls he emits. Castrated males are much less attractive, and even normal males are ignored when the female hamster is not in estrus. Female dogs in heat prefer the odor of urine from normal males to that from castrates, but when the females go out of estrus the preference disappears. Female monkeys are more sexually attracted to normal than to castrated males and are more likely to show attraction when they themselves are in estrus.

The basis for sexual attraction in human beings is complex and, to some extent, variable among societies, as noted in Chapter 5. There have been suggestions that simple cues, such as body odor, are involved, but reliable evidence is lacking and the most important determinants almost certainly are cognitive templates (or schema in Kagan's terminology) built up through experience.

Appetitive behavior. Sexual attractiveness is an abstraction, a quality inferred from observations of behavior of males or females in response to particular stimuli or individuals. For example, when a male pursues and attempts repeatedly to mate with an estrous female we infer that she is sexually attractive to him. Pursuit and attempts to copulate are two types of male appetitive behavior which often takes more elaborate forms termed "courtship" even though courtship is not a masculine prerogative. As indicated in Figure 11.1 appetitive responses to males are a normal element in the female's sexual repertoire. A great deal has been written about sexual receptivity of females, but of equal importance, is the sexual *proceptivity* which estrous females exhibit when they take the initiative in approaching, investigating and sexually soliciting the male (Beach, 1976).

Appetitive behavior is just as much a female as a male function and is heavily dependent upon ovarian hormones in most species of mammals. For the ewe, proceptivity is expressed simply in the form of "ram-seeking" as the estrous female searches out, investigates and stands beside the male. More complex appetitive patterns are exemplified by the "teasing" behavior of a bitch in heat when she alternately approaches and then runs from the male, sometimes nipping or striking his body and often positioning her vulva directly in front of his muzzle. The sexual "presentation" responses of female apes and monkeys are obviously proceptive and consist of adopting the copulatory position directly in front of the male while exposing the vaginal area.

Masculine appetitive activities include various forms of bodily contact with the female, the most universal of which involve touching, manipulating and licking the external vagina. This serves a dual function, common to all forms of appetitive activity in both sexes, namely sexually to stimulate the individual performing the behavior and simultaneously to stimulate the partner. Appetitive behavior serves to increase sexual attractiveness, to raise levels of sexual excitement, and to synchronize the actions of the pair, thus facilitating mutual readiness for transition to the consummatory phase of the mating pattern.

A final characteristic of appetitive interaction is its selective or "screening" function with respect to potential incompatibility between members of a heterosexual pair. As noted in Chapter 9, some female dogs in heat are very receptive to certain males but unwilling to mate with others. Nonpreferred partners are rejected when they exhibit appetitive behavior, i.e., before they can mount, whereas a sexual favorite is the object of proceptive approaches and invitations by the estrous bitch. Female monkeys also display selective proceptivity by soliciting and presenting to some males while ignoring others.

Male sexual preferences are manifest in the unequal distribution of appetitive responses to different females. This is true of species as widely different as the rat, dog and chimpanzee, but for many mammals males appear less selective than females if the latter are able to control the mating relationship.

In Chapter 5, Davenport's discussion of the erotic code analyzes various forms of human appetitive behavior much of which is symbolic, socially structured and totally dependent on learning. However, his treatment of sexual intercourse includes behavior strictly analogous to appetitive behavior of nonhuman species; and from Kinsey, as well as other sources, we know that precoital activities frequently involve stimulation of the genitalia and other body areas much as they do in other mammals.

Consummatory behavior. Consummatory responses comprise the species-specific copulatory pattern which for most mammals is relatively stereotyped and unremarkable. The principal male acts are mounting, thrusting, inserting the erect penis and ejaculating. The essential female acts are assumption of the mating posture which facilitates the male's achievement of intromission, plus maintenance of this position until intravaginal ejaculation has occurred. After the male has mounted, the female may adjust the position of the vulva so as to compensate for any misdirection of his preinsertion thrusting movements. In most species, these simple activities comprise all of the female's receptive behavior.

For nearly all terrestrial quadrupeds, including monkeys, coitus invariably occurs a posteriori and this is the normal position for apes as well, but several variants do occur. Ventral, or face-to-face, copulation is sometimes achieved by chimpanzees, and some female gorillas solicit coitus by lying supine and rhythmically raising and lowering the pelvis, after which they may draw the male down upon them and complete the act in this position.

As explained in Chapter 5, human intercourse occurs in a variety of positions in all societies but the most widely preferred posture is some variant of the face-to-face relationship. The female-superior position is well known and widely used but apparently less common than its reverse.

Postconsummatory behavior. In all mammals that have been carefully studied, males become temporarily impotent following ejaculation and show no appetitive responses to females for an additional period of time after the physical ability to copulate has been regained. Duration of these "absolute" and "relative" refractory phases vary according to species, age and individual, and especially according to the number of preceding ejaculations during the same mating episode. Males of some species, such as the mink, maintain a single insertion for several hours, during which multiple ejaculations appear to be followed by subsequent periods of inactivity. Male primates, including man, are capable of ejaculating within a few seconds or minutes after insertion and then become temporarily refractory to sexual stimulation. Young adults may mate several times in succession, but older individuals are less likely to do so.

Female mammals, in general, are sexually receptive as long as they are physiologically in estrus, and during this period are capable of many more matings than the male of their species. Nevertheless, there is evidence suggesting that female animals which have just finished copulating with a potent male experience a temporary period of reduced proceptivity. Whether or not climax occurs is unknown, although some observers believe it takes place in female monkeys. If this is the case, the nonhuman primate resembles the human female in her capacity for multiple orgasms far in excess of the male's ability to achieve multiple ejaculations.

The Sociosexual Matrix

In his cross-cultural analysis of human sexuality, Davenport stresses the impossibility of understanding sexual behavior in isolation from the total social fabric of which it is a part. The same statement applies to interpretation of sexual activities of animals which live in socially structured groups. Laboratory studies of mating behavior of dogs and monkeys have proven immensely valuable because they permit simplification and control of many variables normally operating in the natural environment. It is, however, essential to supplement such investigations with field observations of the animals in their normal physical and social milieu.

Except for solitary species, male and female animals rarely mate in a social vacuum but usually do so in a social environment composed of other individuals whose relationships to both members of the pair can directly or indirectly affect their sexual interaction. For example, the dominant bitch in a dog pack may interfere when males attempt to mate with another female; and subordinate talapoin monkeys never approach an estrous female if the dominant male is nearby, but copulate with her promptly if he is removed.

In species without a complex social structure, such as the guinea pig or rat, males copulate and beget offspring as soon as their testes produce mature sperm, but the Anubis baboon has very few opportunities to inseminate adult females until several years after he becomes fertile. He not only must attain his full growth, but must also achieve a social position high enough to include access to receptive females. In other primate species, mating privileges are reserved for a few dominant males and these are the same individuals who control excessive ingroup aggression or act in concert to repel predators against the group.

Large troops comprised of hundreds of Hamadryas baboons are divisible into small "family" groups consisting of one adult male with 1 to 3 adult females and their young. Males copulate exclusively with their own females and intermale competition over females never occurs, for females are adopted or kidnapped while still immature and kept by the same male until they are old enough to mate. The one-male group structure has no compelling reproductive advantages but is economically adaptive. Successful foraging for food depends on daily fractionation of the troop into the small groups that can more effectively exploit the widely scattered food sources. Reconvening of the large troop before nightfall is a protective device against predators, and the absence of conflict over any female who may be in estrus allows for close association until the next day's dispersal.

Examination of the complete spectrum of mammalian sexual patterns reveals differences which range from apparently indiscriminate copulation in some species to longterm monogamous mateships in others. It is obvious that no species could survive if its sexual behavior incorporated elements inimical to reproduction of the group. For instance, if sexual contests between adult males frequently resulted in death of both individuals, such behavior would not persist from generation to generation. However, it does not suffice that mating behavior be devoid of counter-adaptive elements. Close inspection reveals that the sexual habits of many animals bear a functional relationship to other behavior patterns which also are essential to the effectiveness or biologic success of the species. For example, pair bonding, which may involve a high degree of monogamy or sexual exclusivity, is often found in species in which the male participates in care and rearing of the young. If the parental role is solely the female's responsibility and "fatherhood" does not exist, mating between males and females does not necessitate protracted precopulatory courtship or formation of a close and enduring heterosexual relationship.

Davenport opines that the structuring of sexual relationships in every human society is affected by and congruent with the "internal logic and consistency" of that particular society. It appears that a comparable principle applies to the sexual behavior of some nonhuman species. If the total complex of social behavior possesses discernible structure affecting a variety of kinds of interindividual behavior, patterns of sexual activity will be congruent and consonant with nonsexual social patterns, which is to say the internal consistency of the overall social structure will be maintained. An important implication of this concept is that fully to comprehend the causes or consequences of sexual behavior, it is necessary to understand the relationships between sexual and nonsexual social behavior.

HOMOSEXUAL BEHAVIOR

A characteristic feature of human sexual behavior is the fact that it serves many functions in addition to reproduction, as for example in the diversion of heterosexual intercourse from procreational to other social goals. We have seen that, to a limited extent, this is true of heterosexual interaction in some nonhuman species, but men and women engage in sexual activities even less related to perpetuation of the species, e.g., homosexual behavior. The animal counterpart of human homosexuality will be discussed at length, partly to counteract widespread misinterpretations in the psychiatric and popular literature, but chiefly to illustrate the analytical approach to interspecific comparisons.

Homosexual activities are fairly common in various nonhuman mammals, but to understand the comparative or evolutionary significance of such behavior we must be able to answer three questions. (1) Precisely what kinds of sexual interaction occur between individuals of the same sex? (2) How is this behavior in each separate species controlled, and how does it develop? (3) What significant relationships, if any, are there between homosexual behavior in nonhuman species and homosexuality in our own?

Basic Definitions

Homosexual behavior in animals can be analyzed in terms of three independent variables. (1) First comes the genetic sex of the two individuals, i.e., XX or XY. (2) The second variable is the "sex" of the behavior pattern displayed by each participant, and it must be emphasized that in the case of animals the reference is always and exclusively to mating behavior, e.g., mounting and pelvic thrusting are elements in the male pattern, whereas female patterns involve specific proceptive and receptive reactions.

A male genotype is not associated exclusively with the masculine mating pattern, nor does the female genotype produce only feminine coital responses. On the contrary, biologic males occasionally show feminine mating behavior and, even more frequently, genetic females mount other individuals in masculine fashion. When the genetic sex and behavior pattern are congruent, e.g., when XY individuals display the masculine pattern, the behavior is *homologous*. When genetic sex and the mating pattern are incongruent, e.g., when biologic females show mounting and thrusting, the behavior is *heterologous*.

(3) The final variable is the "sex" of the stimulus pattern to which the individual is reacting. To a large degree this stimulus consists of the appetitive and consummatory behavior displayed by the partner (the masculine or feminine pattern), but often there are additional elements, e.g., special odors emanating from the estrous female, or special vocalizations uttered by the sexually aroused male.

When the sexual behavior of animals is analyzed in terms of these three variables, one important generalization which emerges is the *principle of S-R complementarity*. There is a high probability that occurrence of the feminine stimulus pattern will be correlated with the execution of masculine rather than feminine coital responses. Conversely, the masculine stimulus pattern has a strong tendency to elicit the feminine and not the masculine pattern of sexual behavior. The relevance of such correlations to homosexual behavior rests upon the fact that the principle of S-R complementarity is independent of the genetic sex of the interacting individuals. In other words, the feminine stimulus pattern is likely to elicit masculine responses in both males and females, and feminine copulatory reactions are most commonly evoked by the masculine stimulus pattern, regardless of the biological sex of the responding individual.

If S-R complementarity were the only determinant of sexual interactions, the result would be a condition of completely balanced behavioral bisexuality, but this never occurs. There always is an imbalance due to *sex-linked prepotency* in motor patterns and stimulus sensitivity. In both sexes, homologous behavior is more easily elicited than the heterologous reactions, and both males and females are more responsive to heterologous than to homologous patterns of stimulation.

Homosexual Interactions in Males

When they are sexually aroused, male animals of some species will mount inanimate objects, and semen for artificial insemination is collected while bulls or stallions are mounted on wooden dummies which do not remotely resemble a cow or mare. It is, therefore, unremarkable that male-male mounting is fairly common in a number of mammals including some rodents, carnivores and primates. Superficially this would seem to violate the principle of S-R complementarity, but there are two reasons for rejecting this conclusion. First, males are much more likely to mount others when the latter display female behavior, and second, male-male mounting does not always belong in the category of sexual behavior.

S-R complementarity and "spontaneous" bisexuality. Display of female proceptive and receptive responses is rare in most nonprimate males unless they have been experimentally feminized in infancy, as explained in Chapter 9, and then given ovarian hormones as adults. However, when this is done the experimental males behave like estrous females and are readily mounted by other males of their species. As would be predicted from the complementarity principle, males displaying female behavior are much more stimulating and are more frequently mounted than nonfeminized males.

There are a very small number of male rats that spontaneously exhibit the entire proceptive and receptive repertoire of an estrous female and are at the same time fully capable of perfectly normal masculine sexual performance. They are in no sense demasculinized, but instead are completely bisexual as far as behavior is concerned. When such an animal is approached and investigated by another male, he exhibits female proceptive responses, is therefore mounted, and then reacts with the receptive response of lordosis. If the second male is replaced by an estrous female, the bisexual individual immediately shifts to the male response pattern, pursuing the female, mounting her repeatedly and eventually ejaculating. In these rare animals, we can see the principle of S-R complementarity operating in one and the same individual.

Nonsexual social relations. Unlike most nonprimates, virtually all male monkeys and chimpanzees display certain species-specific responses very similar to those shown by an estrous female when she solicits copulation. This is the "present" response; when one male presents to another, the second animal often responds by mounting. From a purely descriptive viewpoint, this behavior is undeniably homosexual, but to understand its causes and functions it must be related to other aspects of the social matrix in which it is embedded.

In some cases, presentation is an expression of social inferiority or submission, and characteristically is displayed by low ranking individuals of either sex toward more dominant male or female members of the social group. In other species or other circumstances, one male may present to another as a gesture of appeasement after some disagreement. When two young males are closely associated for some period of time they may occasionally present to and briefly mount one another without thrusting, erection or other signs of emotional arousal, and such behavior has been interpreted as an expression of social affect or friendship rather than a sexual response.

Homosexual Interactions in Females

Female-female mounting is common, having been described for 13 species, representing 5 different orders of mammals (Beach, 1968). Under certain conditions, females of several species will also mount males and even inanimate objects. Nevertheless, mounting by females is most readily evoked when the stimulus object is another female who is in estrus, in other words, when S-R complementarity exists. In one experiment, female rats tested with other females which were receptive or nonreceptive mounted the former an average of 11 times and the latter only 4 times per test. It should be noted that the complete male mating pattern rarely occurs; the final behavioral accompaniments of the male's intromission and ejaculation usually are lacking but have been observed in some females even though they lack a penis.

Cross-species comparisons of rodents, bovidae and carnivores indicate that a female is most likely to exhibit mounting behavior when she herself is in estrus and therefore sexually proceptive and receptive. Under this condition, the female exhibits the entire repertoire of feminine mating reactions as long as she is with a potent male; but when he is replaced by an estrous female, the original female immediately shifts to the masculine role as she pursues and mounts her new partner. Once again, the evidence reveals a potential for bisexual behavior displayed in accordance with the principle of S-R complementarity.

Theoretical Interpretation

We cannot generalize to all mammals, but for those species referred to above, the occurrence of homosexual behavior is influenced by three types of determinants, namely the external stimulus pattern, the organization of brain mechanisms and the type of hormones present. We already have considered the controlling effects of heterologous versus homologous stimulus patterns but little has been said about hormones and especially about the brain.

Bisexuality of brain organization. In several other chapters, it is explained that early in development every individual has the potential for developing either male or female reproductive organs, but not both. The central nervous system also is potentially bisexual, and Diamond and Whalen stress that the brain is a special case, since differentiation of mechanisms for mediation of male behavior does not necessitate suppression of those controlling female behavior and vice versa. The same individual cannot develop both a penis and a vagina, but the same brain can contain mechanisms for both male and female behavior.

This concept has far-reaching implications touching the general problem of sex differences in all species. The basic hypothesis of neural bisexuality posits the existence of separate systems in the brain for male and for female behavior, and postulates further that the two systems exist in normal females and males. If this view is correct, the sexual behavior of an individual cannot be described in terms of one unidimensional scale extending from female or feminine at one end to male or masculine at the other. This outmoded concept of a single masculine-to-feminine continuum must be discarded and replaced by a new one, based on the coexistence of male and female systems in the brain. Translated into psychological terms, this formulation encourages us to think in terms of varying degrees of masculinity and femininity *within the same individual,* which is to say that bisexual organization of the brain potentially permits the individual to be behaviorally or psychologically both masculine and feminine, instead of merely one or the other. In terms of more physiological concepts, bisexuality of central nervous system mechanisms implies that brains of both genetic males and genetic females include neural circuits capable of transducing and translating heterologous input into homologous output as well as mediating heterologous responses to homologous stimuli.

If the male and female systems were equally responsive in both sexes, homosexual and heterosexual behaviors should occur with equal frequency, but this does not occur for two reasons which are, the *sex-linked prepotency* of integrative brain mechanisms, plus sex differences in secretion of and sensitivity to gonadal hormones.

Despite S-R complementarity, in both sexes evocation of homologous responses by heterologous stimuli normally takes precedence over elicitation of heterologous reactions by homologous stimulus patterns. In other words, masculine responses to feminine stimuli are prepotent in males while the obverse S-R relationship is prepotent in females. Sex-linked prepotencies may be partly determined by genetic factors and are probably related to prenatal effects of hormones on sexual differentiation of the brain.

Effects of sex hormones. In all nonhuman species, the heterosexual responsiveness and potency of males are profoundly affected by androgen, just as proceptivity and receptivity of females are influenced by ovarian hormones. These correlations have sometimes encouraged simplistic explanations of homosexual behavior as an expression of endocrine pathology in adulthood, and to the prediction that females could be made homosexual by testosterone treatment, while the same result would occur if males were given estrogen.

An important fact ignored in these predictions is that male and female systems are not equally responsive to male and female hormones. Males react more strongly than females to androgen, whereas estrogen and progesterone have more marked effects in females than in males. It is true that in some species (but not in others), females show increases in mounting frequency after administration of testosterone; and repeated injections of estrogen induce males to exhibit lordosis. However, in both instances the behavior generally is quantitatively and qualitatively inferior to normal mating responses of the opposite sex, and the amounts of hormone needed to produce the substandard behavior are far greater than dosages that elicit completely normal mating in the opposite sex.

This is to say that although masculine mechanisms in both males and females react to androgen, they are much more sensitive in males than in females; and, conversely, the responsiveness of feminine mechanisms to estrogen is much greater in females than in males. Another relevant observation is that normal females show maximal frequencies of mounting behavior while they are under stimulation by ovarian hormones; and spontaneous bisexual behavior in males depends upon testicular secretions, for when a bisexual male is castrated both masculine and feminine patterns disappear.

The evidence clearly indicates the following conclusions. (1) The homosexual behavior which occurs normally in some nonhuman mammals is not associated with any excess of heterologous, or deficiency of homologous, gonadal hormones. (2) It is facilitated in both sexes by the presence of normal amounts of homologous hormones. (3) Although in some species it may be increased by exogenous heterologous hormones, supraphysiological doses are needed to produce behavioral responses which tend to be incomplete and difficult to elicit.

Comparisons with Human Homosexuality

Earlier in this chapter we learned that formal similarities in the sexual behavior of different species may or may not lead to the discovery of principles or valid generalizations applicable to all mammals or all primates, but that such inferences are not allowable prior to separate analysis of causal mechanisms responsible for the behavior in each species. Such an analysis clearly reveals basic differences between human homosexuality and the homosexual activities of nonhuman mammals.

Potential bisexuality of brain organization certainly persists in man, but in homosexuality the principle of S-R complementarity is completely abrogated. The stereotype cherished by an uninformed heterosexual public includes S-R complementarity as an essential tenet with the result that homosexual men are expected to be effeminate and lesbians are envisaged as extremely masculine individuals. The facts are quite the opposite for, as Hoffman notes in Chapter 6, most homosexual men are attracted to masculine rather than effeminate partners, and other authors stress the fact that lesbians are attracted to each other on the basis of mutual femininity. The essence of homosexuality lies in its homophilic foundation and not in the overt behavior through which the homosexual attraction or love is expressed. Nongenital sex-related behavior is irrelevant; for example, as Stoller states in Chapter 7, male transvestites rarely are homosexual, and, as Hoffman observes, effeminate mannerisms in men or masculine characteristics in women are unrelated to sex object choice.

What we observe in nonhuman animals is temporary inversion of mating roles, which is theoretically explainable in terms of biologically programmed S-R relationships that are to some extent influenced by both developmental and concurrent effects of sex hormones, as defined in Chapter 9. This differs from human homosexuality in terms of both causal mechanisms and functional outcomes.

MASTURBATORY BEHAVIOR

Stimulation of one's own genitals is one form of sexual behavior that does not demand a partner, that can be practiced in private, and that can produce the consummatory response of orgasm. It is, therefore, unsurprising that self-masturbation is extremely common behavior, particularly in repressive societies or under conditions in which alternate sources of sexual outlet are unavailable. Estimates of the incidence of habitual masturbation in American and European societies run as high as 85 to 95 percent for males but much lower for females. In Chapter 5, Davenport describes masturbatory behavior of males and females in different societies, noting its cross-cultural ubiquity even in the presence of severe proscription, and its apparently more frequent occurrence in males than females for most, if not all, cultures.

Male Animals

All male mammals nose, lick, mouth or otherwise manipulate their own genitalia under various conditions, and particularly just after or between episodes of mating behavior. These responses constitute autogenital grooming and do not qualify as self-masturbation. Males of many species also nose, sniff or lick the penis of another individual, but this investigative behavior is not accompanied by any indication of sexual excitement on the part of either animal and should not be classified as masturbation.

In contrast, it is appropriate to refer to masturbation when a male animal repeatedly achieves erection and ejaculation by stimulating the penis or some other erogenous zone. For example, one male cat living in a laboratory cage developed a technique of mounting his food dish and making copulatory movements that led to penile erection and ejaculation. This behavior usually occurred when the male could see other cats copulating on the floor below his cage. Rubbing the erect penis against the substrate is frequently practiced by male porcupines and porpoises, and one captive monkey habitually employed this form of stimulation to achieve ejaculation. A unique type of masturbation is displayed by red deer stags during the rutting season, when they repetitively draw the tips of their antlers through low-growing vegetation and thus induce both erection and ejaculation. This behavior, which involves no direct stimulation of the penis, is common during the mating season and is not affected by the availability of sexually receptive hinds.

Captive monkeys and chimpanzees masturbate manually and orally, often inducing ejaculation in the process. This activity has sometimes been interpreted as a completely abnormal form of sexual outlet produced by heterosexual deprivation and other artificial conditions incident to a captive existence. Any such explanation is contraindicated by the fact that masturbatory behavior is shown in the natural habitat by adult males of some species, even though they have unrestricted access to receptive females. This is true, for example, of socially dominant male monkeys who copulate with an estrous female upon one occasion and masturbate to ejaculation a short time later, even though the female is still available. Under these conditions, self-stimulation can scarcely be classified as a substitutive activity, or as a response to deprivation and sexual frustration.

This is not to say that animals never engage in substitutive masturbation. For example, although self-stimulation to the point of ejaculation appears to be rare or nonexistent in feral chimpanzee males, it is, as already noted, common in captivity. It is possible that the difference is due in part to the lack of freedom and variety (i.e., the "boredom") which characterizes a confined existence. This explanation seems preferable to one based exclusively on deprivation of heterosexual contacts. Mating opportunities in the wild are far from frequent, but still adult masturbation is very rarely seen; and captive males masturbate even when permanently caged with females. Therefore, although masturbation is in no sense abnormal, its frequency may be affected by a male's living conditions.

It should be added that under very special conditions "sexual frustration" may lead to masturbation. In one experiment, male rhesus monkeys were confronted with spayed females which had been rendered sexually attractive but not sexually receptive. When exposed to such females some males masturbated to ejaculation.

Female Animals

In view of the cross-cultural consistency with which observers report a male-female difference in both incidence and frequency of autogenital stimulation, there may be some evolutionary significance to the fact that masturbation is reported to be much less frequent in female than in male animals. It is possible that when females mount other animals, as described earlier in this chapter, the mounting animal may achieve some genital stimulation, and there is one description of female stump-tail macaque monkeys exhibiting signs of sexual climax while thrusting on the back of a second female.

Captive monkeys and apes occasionally insert foreign objects in their vaginas and move them rhythmically to and fro; and female farm animals in heat sometimes rub the congested vulva against projections in the inanimate environment. These responses may or may not represent masturbatory activity but, in primates at least, they differ from male masturbation in their notable infrequency and in the absence of any accompanying signs of sexual arousal.

Comparisons with Human Masturbation

The self-stimulatory activities of male monkeys and apes are so similar to autogenital behavior in human males that we are justified in provisionally defining male masturbation as a basic primate trait. As far as females are concerned, the evidence is less convincing, but sex differences in frequency seem common to humans and other primates and planned observation of nonhuman species is needed before any conclusion is justified.

In human males, the socialization of sex referred to in Chapter 1 includes group and mutual masturbation in boys and adolescents. Masturbation of one individual by another, and especially of a male by a female is not seen in animals although it is ubiquitous in our own species. Finally, human masturbation usually is evoked and/or accompanied by fantasy which relates it psychologically to sexual interaction with a partner.

Despite these, and possibly other, species differences, masturbatory behavior of men and other primates probably is traceable to their shared mammalian origin. The primary stimuli for genital excitation are similar and the outcome, namely ejaculation and climax, is similarly reinforcing.

CONCLUSION

Cross-species comparison of sexual behavior in nonhuman mammals reveals widely distributed similarities some of which clearly extend to

Homo sapiens as well. The theoretical significance or explanatory value of shared patterns of response cannot be assessed until the causal mechanisms have been analyzed for each species. When this is accomplished, some shared patterns prove to arise from different origins and to subserve different functions. Nevertheless, there are others which reflect man's evolutionary heritage and his genetic relationship to all mammals, and especially to other primates.

REFERENCES

Beach, F. A., ed. 1965. *Sex and Behavior.* New York: Wiley. 1974. 2d. ed. New York: Robert E. Krieger.

―――. 1968. Factors involved in the control of mounting behavior by female mammals. In *Perspectives of Reproduction and Sexual Behavior: A Memorial to William C. Young.* Edited by M. Diamond. Bloomington: Indiana University Press. Pp. 83-131.

―――. 1976. Sexual attractivity, proceptivity, and receptivity in female mammals. *Horm. Behav.* 7:105-38.

Ford, C. S., and Beach, F. A. 1951. *Patterns of Sexual Behavior.* New York: Harper & Hoeber. (Also available in paperback.)

Manning, A. 1972. *An Introduction to Animal Behavior.* 2d ed. Reading, Mass.: Addison-Wesley. (Paperback.)

SUGGESTED READINGS

Beach, F. A. 1945. Bisexual mating behavior in the male rat: Effects of castration and hormone administration. *Physiol. Zool.* 18: 390-402.

―――. 1964. Biological bases for reproductive behavior. In *Social Behavior and Organization among the Vertebrates.* Edited by W. Etkin. Chicago: University of Chicago Press.

―――. 1970. Hormonal effects on socio-sexual behavior in dogs. In *Mammalian Reproduction.* Edited by M. Gibian and E. J. Plotz. Berlin: Springer-Verlag.

Carpenter, C. R. 1942. Sexual behavior of free-ranging rhesus monkeys. II. Periodicity of estrus, homosexual, autoerotic and non-conformist behavior. *J. Comp. Psychol.* 33: 143-162.

Chevalier-Skolnikoff, S. 1974. Male-female, female-female, male-male sexual behavior in the stumptail monkey, with special attention to the female orgasm. *Arch. Sex. Behav.* 3: 95-116.

Hafez, E. S. 1969. Edit. *The Behavior of Domestic Animals.* 2nd edit. Baltimore: Williams and Wilkins.

Herbert, J. 1970. Hormones and reproductive behavior in rhesus and talapoin monkeys. *J. Reprod. Fertil. Suppl.* 11: 119-140.

Hess, J. P. 1973. Some observations on the sexual behavior of captive lowland gorillas. (Gorilla G. gorrilla). In Comparative Ecoolgy and Behavior of Primates. Edited by R. P. Michael and J. H. Crook. New York: Academic Press.

Kummer, H. 1971. Primate Societies: Group Techniques of Ecological Adaptation. New York: Aldine.

Masters, W. H. and Johnson, V. E. 1966. Human Sexual Response. Boston: Little-Brown.

McGinnis, P. R. 1973. Patterns of sexual behavior in a community of free-living chimpanzees. Doctoral dissertation. Stanford University.

Meyerson, B. J. and Lindstrom, L. H. 1973. Sexual motivation in the female rat. A methoodligical study applied to the investigation of the effects of estradiol benzoate. Acta Physiol. Scand. Suppl. 389: 1-80.

Michael, R. P. 1968. Gonadal hormones and the control of primate behavior. In Endocrinology and Human Behavior. Edited by R. P. Michael. London: Oxford University Press.

Nadler, R. D. 1975. Cyclicity in tumescence of the perineal labia of female lowland gorillas. Anat. Rec. 18: 791-797.

Rowell, T. 1972. Social Behavior of Monkeys. Penguin. London.

Saayman, G. S. 1970. The menstrual cycle and sexual behavior in a troop of free-ranging chacma baboons. (Papio ursinus). Folia Primat. 17: 297-303.

Schaller, G. B. 1964. The Year of the Gorilla. Chicago: University of Chicago Press.

Young, W. C. 1961. The hormones and mating behavior. In Sex and Internal Secretions. 3rd ed. Edited by W. C. Young. Baltimore: Williams & Wilkins.

Young, W. C. and Orbison, W. D. 1944. Changes in selected features of behavior in oppositely-sexed chimpanzees during the sexual cycle and after ovariectomy. J. Comp. Physiol. Psychol. 37: 107-143.

Zubin, J. and Money, J., Eds. 1973. Contemporary Sexual Behavior: Critical Issues in the 1970s. Baltimore: Johns Hopkins University Press.

CONTRIBUTORS

Frank A. Beach, Ph.D., Sc.D., Professor of Psychology, University of California

William H. Davenport, Ph.D., Professor of Anthropology, University of Pennsylvania

Milton Diamond, Ph.D., Professor of Anatomy and Reproductive Biology, University of Hawaii, School of Medicine

David A. Hamburg, M.D., President, Institute of Medicine, National Academy of Sciences, Washington, D.C.

Martin Hoffman, M.D., Senior Psychiatrist, Center for Special Problems, San Francisco Department of Public Health and Assistant Clinical Professor of Psychiatry, University of California

Jerome Kagan, Ph.D., Professor of Human Development, Department of Psychology and Social Relations, Harvard University

Frederick T. Melges, M.D., Director of Psychiatric Education and Research, Stanford Program at Santa Clara Community Mental Health Services, Stanford University School of Medicine

John Money, Ph.D., Professor of Psychology and Associate Professor of Pediatrics, Johns Hopkins University

Robert J. Stoller, M.D., Professor of Psychiatry, University of California

Richard E. Whalen, Ph.D., Professor of Psychobiology, University of California

INDEX OF SUBJECTS

Inhibition, 94, 96, 104, 240
Initiation, sexual, 10, 125, 158
Innate neural differences, 51. *See also*
   Nervous system
Insertion. *See* Intromission
Insomnia, 284, 290
Intellectual development, 97
Intellectual traits, 18
Intercourse, sexual
   adulterous, 119, 125, 140, 144, 148
   anal, 11, 155, 201, 211
   animal, 153
   extramarital, 121, 124ff., 143
   general, 1, 50, 125, 148–51, 220, 230,
     278, 304
   marital, 134–35, 290
   postpartum, 123
   premarital, 9, 11, 116, 121, 124ff., 143,
     145–46
Intersexuality, 64, 212–13
Intromission, 242–43, 303, 309
Inversion of mating roles, animals, 312
Involutional psychological states, 290–92.
   See also Menopause
Iodine, 281
IQ, Intelligence tests, intelligence, 69, 91,
   107–8, 181
Irritability, 108, 276, 288, 290

Jealousy, 20
Jokes. *See* Humor
Jural system. *See* Law

Kiss, 129
Kleptomania, 191, 196
Klinefelter's syndrome, 55, 64, 76, 224

Labia. *See* Sexual organs
Lactation, 14, 38, 73, 257, 263, 271
Language, 75, 84, 88, 106–7
Latency, 81, 122
Law, 8, 117, 137, 195
Leadership, 48, 69
Learning, conditioning, and practice, 5,
   13–14, 16, 18, 50, 63, 121, 145, 192,
   260, 262–63, 266, 299
Legitimacy, 10
Lesbian. *See* Homosexuality
Let-down reflex, 257
Levirate, 142
Libido, 33, 56, 81, 216, 258, 264
Libido hormone, 82, 255
Limbic system. *See* Nervous system
Lime, 8
Linguistic skills, 51
Loneliness, 94, 98
Longevity, 118

Lordosis, 77, 234ff., 242, 243, 261
Love, 63, 75, 81, 124, 130, 171
Love affair, 81
Lover, 73
LSD, 276
Luteinizing hormone (LH). *See*
   Hormones

Magic, 130–31, 137, 151
MAPS (Make-a-Picture-Story test), 181
Marriage
   common law, 144
   general, 53, 69, 116–17, 121, 123–24,
     138–39
   homosexual, 183
   polyandry, 116, 141
   polygamy, 116, 125, 141–42, 143
   ritual, 157
Masculinization, 23, 36, 66ff., 75, 83, 249,
   251
Masculinity, 73, 99
Masochism, 154, 191, 205–6
Masturbation, 1, 79, 124, 149, 152–53,
   155, 159, 170, 193, 197, 201–2, 206,
   209, 212, 265, 312ff.
Maternal behavior, 69, 108, 256–57, 263,
   283
Mating behavior, animal
   female, 234, 238, 250, 252, 303
   general, 298–99
   male, 234, 238, 250, 303
Menarche. *See* Puberty
Menopause
   general, 118, 269
   physiology, 286ff.
   psychological effects, 288–292
   surgical, 289
Menstrual Distress Questionnaire, 276
Menstruation, menstrual cycle
   attitudes toward, 124
   beliefs concerning, 131–37, 160
   nonhuman primates, 256
   physiology, endocrine control, 40, 118,
    227, 274–76
   psychological effects, 14, 276ff.
   sexual activity, 278–79
   See also Puberty, Menopause
Mental illness, 11, 164, 167, 182, 194, 197,
   274, 280, 283, 291
Mental retardation, 194
Milk let-down, 219, 257
Mind-body dichotomy, 13
Minority group, homosexual, 182–86
Missionaries, 119
Model, modeling, 56, 232, 285
Modesty, 81, 123, 127–28
Modulation, 34

INDEX OF AUTHORS

INDEX OF PEOPLES, BY TRIBE, CULTURES, COUNTRY OR NATIONALITY

INDEX OF ANIMAL SPECIES